TRANSLOCAS

TRIANGULATIONS
Lesbian/Gay/Queer ▲ Theater/Drama/Performance

Series Editors
Jill Dolan, Princeton University
David Román, University of Southern California

Associate Editors
Ramón H. Rivera-Servera, University of Texas Austin
Sara Warner, Cornell University

TRANSLOCAS

The Politics of Puerto Rican Drag and Trans Performance

Lawrence La Fountain-Stokes

UNIVERSITY OF MICHIGAN PRESS

Ann Arbor

Published in the United States of America by
the University of Michigan Press
Manufactured in the United States of America
Printed on acid-free paper

First published April 2021

Names: La Fountain-Stokes, Lawrence Martin, 1968– author.
Title: Translocas : the politics of Puerto Rican drag and trans performance / Lawrence La Fountain-Stokes.
Description: Ann Arbor : University of Michigan Press, 2021. |
    Series: Triangulations: lesbian/gay/queer/theater/drama/performance |
    Includes bibliographical references and index.
Identifiers: LCCN 2020053142 (print) | LCCN 2020053143 (ebook) |
    ISBN 9780472074273 (hardcover) | ISBN 9780472054275 (paperback) |
    ISBN 9780472126071 (ebook)
Subjects: LCSH: Cross-dressers—Puerto Rico. | Female impersonators—Puerto Rico. | Transgender people—Puerto Rico. | Hispanic Americans—Social conditions. | Gender expression—Puerto Rico.
Classification: LCC HQ77.2.U6 L3 2021 (print) | LCC HQ77.2.U6 (ebook) |
    DDC 306.76/8097295—dc23
LC record available at https://lccn.loc.gov/2020053142
LC ebook record available at https://lccn.loc.gov/2020053143

Pero sí contra vosotros, maricas de las ciudades,
de carne tumefacta y pensamiento inmundo,
madres de lodo, arpías, enemigos sin sueño
del Amor que reparte coronas de alegría.

Contra vosotros siempre, que dais a los muchachos
gotas de sucia muerte con amargo veneno.
Contra vosotros siempre,
Faeries de Norteamérica,
Pájaros de La Habana,
Jotos de México,
Sarasas de Cádiz,
Apios de Sevilla,
Cancos de Madrid,
Floras de Alicante,
Adelaidas de Portugal.

¡Maricas de todo el mundo, asesinos de palomas!
Esclavos de la mujer, perras de sus tocadores,
abiertos en las plazas con fiebre de abanico
o emboscados en yertos paisajes de cicuta.

Federico García Lorca,
"Oda a Walt Whitman" (1930)
Poeta en Nueva York

Contents

Digital materials related to this title can be found on the Fulcrum platform via
the following citable URL: https://doi.org/10.3998/mpub.11314788

Acknowledgments

There are many people and institutions to thank for the completion of this project. I first got my feet wet in what was for me the new field of performance studies thanks to Diana Taylor and to the participants of the Hemispheric Institute of Performance and Politics' *Encuentro* held at UNIRIO, the Federal University of the State of Rio de Janeiro, Brazil, in 2000. I went on to use the word *translocas* and to write a paper about Puerto Rican drag performance during my fellowship year in the seminar on performance led by Carolyn Williams and Elin Diamond at the Center for the Critical Analysis of Contemporary Culture (CCACC), now known as the Center for Cultural Analysis at Rutgers, the State University of New Jersey, New Brunswick, in 2002. I wish to thank my former Rutgers colleagues Ben. Sifuentes-Jáuregui, Yolanda Martínez-San Miguel, Camilla Stevens, and César Braga-Pinto for their unwavering support. I also benefited from the intellectual stimulation and collegiality of the Global Ethnic Literatures Seminar led by Tobin Siebers at the University of Michigan in 2004 and from a 2006 Woodrow Wilson Career Enhancement Fellowship.

My first scholarly publication from this project appeared in Spanish in 2005. I thank Alberto Sandoval-Sánchez and Frances R. Aparicio for the encouragement to write about Jorge B. Merced for their special issue of *Revista Iberoamericana* on Latinx literature and culture, and for their support over the years. I also wish to thank Susan Stryker, Paisley Currah, and Lisa Jean Moore for publishing an English-language version of my essay in their special issue of *WSQ: Women's Studies Quarterly* on "Trans-" in 2008. Subsequently, Jill Lane had me submit my article "Translocas: Migration, Homosexuality, and Transvestism in Recent Puerto Rican Performance" to the peer-reviewed, multilingual electronic journal *emisférica,* where it appeared in 2011 in English, Spanish, and Portuguese with the translation assistance of Pablo Assumpção Barros Costa, while Marcial Godoy encouraged me to submit a preliminary version of my work on Freddie Mercado for *emisférica*'s special issue on Caribbean rasanblaj, edited by Gina Athena Ulysse in 2015. ¡Gracias Jill! ¡Gracias Marcial!

Before realizing this would be a book, and before I was even using the word "transloca," I started publishing performance and theater reviews about some of the artists featured in *Translocas* in the Puerto Rican weekly newspaper *Claridad* in 1996, and have never stopped. I reprinted many of these early pieces in my more recent volume *Escenas transcaribeñas: Ensayos sobre teatro, performance y cultura* (2018), published by Isla Negra Editores in Puerto Rico, notwithstanding the challenges of Hurricanes Irma and María. I wish to thank Rafah Acevedo, Lowell Fiet, Alida Millán Ferrer, and Carlos Roberto Gómez Beras for their support. I also thank all of the readers in Puerto Rico and the diaspora who have encouraged me to write about our national culture. The Center for Puerto Rican Studies at Hunter College, CUNY, has also been crucial in this respect; special thanks to Xavier Totti, editor of *CENTRO Journal*, for more than ten years of collaborations. Additional research for this book was conducted at the University of Michigan Library (Special Collections Research Center).

At the University of Michigan Press, I am particularly thankful to LeAnn Fields for her friendship, professional encouragement, and support, and to Anna Pohlod and Melissa Scholke for their editorial assistance.

I have presented numerous versions of these chapters at colleges, universities, and international professional conferences. I particularly wish to thank Marisa Belausteguigoitia, Lucía Melgar, Stephany Slaughter, and Hortensia Moreno for the positive reception I received at the Programa Universitario de Estudios de Género at the Universidad Nacional Autónoma de México and for publishing my work in the unfortunately short-lived, no longer available electronic journal *Revista Re-d: Arte, cultura visual y género* and in the anthology *Representación y fronteras: El performance en los límites del género*, both in 2009. I also wish to thank Diego Falconí Trávez, Santiago Castellanos, and María Amelia Viteri, who published "Epistemología de la loca: Localizando a la transloca en la trans-diáspora" in their anthology *Resentir lo queer en América Latina: Diálogos desde/con el Sur*, which appeared with Editorial Egales in Spain in 2014, and for their warm reception during my trips to Ecuador and Catalonia. More recently, I benefited from the welcome of Grace Dávila at Pomona College, where I spoke about Kevin Fret, and of Mabel Cuesta (University of Houston) and of Jorge L. Chinea and the staff of the Center for Latino/a and Latin American Studies at Wayne State University, who invited me to speak about Javier Cardona. These are but some of the many generous interlocutors and invitations I have had for this project over the last seventeen years, which have also included Erika Almenara and Rachel ten Haaf (University of Arkansas); Arlene Dávila and María Josefina Saldaña Portillo (New York University); Theresa Delgadillo (while at the Ohio State University); Walfrido Dorta (Susquehanna University); Lowell Fiet and Rosa Luisa Márquez (Universidad de Puerto Rico, Río Piedras); Claire F. Fox and Darrel Wanzer-Serrano (while at the University of Iowa); Paola S. Hernández (University of Wisconsin); Guillermo Irizarry and Jacqueline Loss (University of Connecticut); Anne Lambright (while at Trinity College); Greggor Mattson (Oberlin College); Maylei Blackwell and Uri McMillan (UCLA); Danny Méndez and Sheila Contreras (Michigan State University); Mabel Moraña and Ignacio M. Sánchez Prado (Washington University in St. Louis); John Nieto-Phillips (Indiana University, Bloomington); Donald E. Pease and Israel Reyes (Dartmouth College); Ramón H. Rivera-Servera (while at Northwestern University); Radost Rangelova (Gettysburg College); Lissette Rolón Collazo and Beatriz Llenín Figueroa (Universidad de Puerto Rico, Mayagüez); Sandra Ruiz and Dara E. Goldman (University of Illinois, Urbana Champaign); and Lillian Manzor and Gema Pérez Sánchez (University of Miami), among many others. I also appreciate the support and friendship of Francheska Alers-Rojas, Jossianna Arroyo, Manuel Avilés-Santiago, Ruth Behar, William Calvo-Quirós, Luis Carle, David Caron, Iván Chaar-López, María Eugenia Cotera, Clare Croft, Arnaldo Cruz-Malavé, Beth Currans, Dama Estrada, Marc Felion, Fausto Fernós, Licia Fiol-Matta, Francisco J. Galarte, Juan G. Gelpí, Anita González, Laura G. Gutiérrez, Jarrod Hayes, Jesse Hoffnung-Garskof, Holly Hughes, E. Patrick Johnson, Betina Kaplan, Petra Kuppers, Sophie Large, Javier E. Laureano, Lourdes Martínez-Echazábal, Nancy Raquel Mirabal, Jonathan Montalvo, Anthony P. Mora, Esther Newton, Urayoán Noel, Marcia Ochoa, Ricardo L. Ortíz, Andrea Parra, Mario Pecheny, Silvia Pedraza, Antonio Prieto Stambaugh, Joseph M. Pierce, José Quiroga, Yeidy M. Rivero, Víctor Hugo Robles, Juana María Rodríguez, Rafael Rosario, Rubén Ríos Ávila, Margarita Saona, Horacio Sívori, Deborah R. Vargas, Charlie Vázquez, Salvador Vidal-Ortiz, and Magdalena Zaborowska. Muchas gracias a todes ustedes and my profuse apologies to all the persons I have neglected to mention by name.

I have enormous debts of gratitude to my colleagues and to the graduate and undergraduate students and staff at the University of Michigan, Ann Arbor, in the Departments of American Culture, Romance Languages and

Literatures, and Women's and Gender Studies and in the Latina/o Studies Program, and to all of the institutions and additional individuals and friends who have contributed to this research, whom I look forward to thanking individually. I especially want to thank the College of Literature, Science, and the Arts at the University of Michigan for granting me Associate Professor Support Funds and a Michigan Humanities Award, as well as the National Center for Institutional Diversity for a Think-Act Tank Grant for our Queer/Cuir Américas Work Group. Thank you to Kerry White for reading this manuscript during the COVID-19 quarantine, and to Gregory E. Dowd, Enrique García Santo-Tomás, Alejandro Herrero-Olaizola, Cristina Moreiras-Menor, and Alexandra Minna Stern for reading earlier drafts. Perhaps my biggest debt is to the drag, trans, and otherwise queer or *cuir* Puerto Rican artists, filmmakers, activists, and writers who so generously have helped me in many occasions, and who have given all of us the gift of their work. Thank you.

Introduction

Translocas piss people off, but sometimes they also make us laugh and even cry. They (or should I be saying we, us Puerto Rican and Caribbean translocas) are upsetting and exhilarating but also dreadful, redundant, and passé. Hilarious but simultaneously boring. Gorgeous except when absolutely hideous or simply plain. Political except when we are not. Alive except when we are dead: assassinated, like the homeless trans woman Alexa Neulisa Luciano Ruiz in 2020 or the young Puerto Rican trap singer Kevin Fret in 2019, or burned and dismembered like the adolescent Jorge Steven López Mercado in 2009, or lost to AIDS like Lady Catiria in 1999, or swept up by the winds of a hurricane and left to die by the side of the road. Stuck in the past with fake Lee Press-On Nails and clichéd jokes, boomeranging audiences into the future, snapping the present out of its complacency, challenging its teleological insistence on narratives of progress, modernity, and integration. Puerto Rican, Latinx, and Caribbean translocas (whether gay or straight, transgender or cisgender, dead or alive, male or female or simply fabulous) shatter molds in different colonial languages and geographies, but especially in the multiple transatlantic and trans-Caribbean crossings between English and Spanish, dragging our bilingual cultural legacies like bright flowers or exotic birds in the tropics or as carcasses at the slaughterhouse, highlighting and subverting the negative connotations of the term "travesty" (a false, absurd, or distorted representation) embedded at the heart of the word "transvestism," at least in its Spanish variant of *travestismo*.[1]

Disreputable, cross-dressing, effeminate, and transgender translocas transubstantiate, vomit, and sometimes even clean ourselves up, engaging with abjection as much as glamour.[2] We are dirty and messy, undesirable and offensive, except when we are bright and shiny like jewels or so nondescript or dainty that we make others and ourselves fall asleep. Translocas, whether insane women, effeminate homosexuals, drag performers, or transgender subjects, are way too many things in an ever-expanding transgeographic rhizomatic map that inhabits and pushes out from the tropics and engulfs other spaces and locales. We are central and unacknowledged parts of the Caribbean and its diaspora, as the Puerto Rican writer Mayra Santos-Febres (2005, 2013) has noted, in a context in which transvestism can be a strategy of survival.[3] We are also nothing, like queers, like Puerto Rico, like dead or dismembered bodies, like wilted flowers, like me.

For effeminate *locas*, like "sissies," "nellies," "fairies," "faggots," "pansies," "queens," and "queers" in English and *bichas* (or *bixas*) and *veados* and *travestis* in Brazilian Portuguese and *folles* in French and *massisi* in Haitian Kreyòl and *batty bwoys* and *battymen* and *buller men* in Jamaican Patois and West Indian English and *maricas* and *maricones* and *mariquitas* and *mariposas* and *muxes* and *patos* and *pájaros* and *putos* and *vestidas* in a variety of dialects of Spanish, seem to wreak havoc just by existing, but other times simply irritate, upset, and bore.[4] We are like the *maricas*, *faeries*, *pájaros*, *jotos*, *sarasas*, *apios*, *cancos*, *floras*, and *adelaidas* that the murdered Spanish poet Federico García Lorca invoked and condemned in his renowned "Oda a Walt Whitman" ("Ode to Walt Whitman") of 1930, where Lorca hyperbolically accused those of our kind of having "pensamiento inmundo" (filthy thoughts) and of being "murderers of doves! / Slaves of women, bitches of their dressing tables," contrasted to the masculine camaraderie and rugged bearded persona embodied by the canonical nineteenth-century American poet Walt Whitman: a more palatable, gender-conforming, homosexual role model.[5]

Transloca disruption, geographically specific but also diasporically promiscuous, happens particularly when we don a wig, makeup, breast forms, hip and buttock pads, feminine clothes, jewelry, and high heels, or when we transform our bodies and have gender reassignment surgeries or other cosmetic procedures that change our appearance and bring forth new identities, especially when we throw ourselves onto the street, on a stage, on a movie screen or television or computer or typewritten page or into cyberspace. But it can also happen as part of casual, everyday life, simply by feigning a limp wrist, applying some lip gloss, sparkling a cheek with glitter, or speaking and singing in falsetto or in an affected way. *Translocas: The Politics of Puerto Rican Drag and Trans Performance* is precisely about this discomfort, about the shock we create or the banal acceptance we receive: the politics of transformation, whether as an art form, a cultural representation, an embodied personal experience, or a social movement for the recognition of our basic human rights.

In spite of being the object of frequent hatred and antipathy, translocas survive and carry on; we perform our lives and enjoy the performances and company of others. At times a career, an arts practice, a survival strategy, or part of the expression of a gay, queer/*cuir*, nonbinary, or transgender identity, the Puerto Rican *loca*, drag, and trans theatrical, film, literary, activist, and cabaret/nightclub performances that I am invoking with the neologism "transloca" do myriad things. *Transloca performances* are quite similar to but also unlike the effeminate embodiments and drag and trans performances of other groups, ethnicities, and nationalities across the globe: some absolutely shocking, other times surprisingly nondescript, as scholars such as Esther Newton ([1972] 1979), Marjorie Garber (1992), and Laurence Selenick (2000) have discussed, but here refracted through a Caribbean or "Caribglobal" lens, to use the term Rosamond S. King (2014, 1–7) has proposed in her book *Island Bodies: Transgressive Sexualities in the Caribbean Imagination*, highlighting local specificities in a global context. Translocas echo the stigma and anxiety clearly expressed by Lorca and maintain the potentially dangerous edge of the word *loca* in Spanish, what the Argentine poet and scholar Néstor Perlongher called "*loca* sex" (2019, 19–25), identified by the Chilean activists and performers Pedro Lemebel and Víctor Hugo Robles as the *loca*'s rupture, questioning, and destabilization of dominant norms: the oblique look that challenges hegemonic conventions (Robles 2015, 274); a practice that at times violates the law and social and religious orthodoxies and that has been met with violence and even death. Translocas also partake of what the queer Brazilian artist Hélio Oiticica called "tropicamp," a term inspired by the Puerto Rican drag performer Mario Montez's Caribbean-inflected (tropical, Latin American) camp performance: a culturally specific, decidedly not Anglo-American queer sensibility and practice that invokes a different universe of significations marked by glamour, humor, and Latin American referents.[6] Translocas are also "signifying queens," as the Cuban American scholar Oscar Montero (1998) has called Latinx queer subjects who wreak havoc and turn things upside down. This paradoxical tension between irrelevance and danger leads to simultaneous dismissal and overinvestment: swept aside because of our supposed frivolity yet simultaneously demonized as horrendous threats.

Contradictions, or rather paradoxes, rule this book. While transloca

performances (principally, acts of *transformismo*) are typically understood as lighthearted, inconsequential, and humorous performative gender practices, frequently those of effeminate cisgendered gay or queer/
cuir men who at times dress or perform as women or in a feminine way,
referred to in Puerto Rico as *transformistas, travestis,* and *dragas,* appearing
on mainstream television and theatrical stages practically every day, these
embodiments can also be those of transgender or gender-nonconforming
individuals and of cisgendered women dressing in theatrical hyperfem-
inine attire (what Laura G. Gutiérrez [2010, 118] refers to as "same-sex
masquerade and gender parody"), or who dress in a masculine way, and
are occasionally seen as highly charged, biased, or controversial representations (threatening, misogynistic, illegal, immoral, confusing, debased).[7]

At the simplest level, transloca performance frequently challenges
hetero-, homo-, and transnormative gender narratives, particularly when
we question expectations and social conventions about masculinity and
femininity, although we are simultaneously at risk of reinscribing hegemonic models of gender and sexuality and of assimilating into neoliberal
models of consumption and commercialization (Berlant 1997; Duggan
2003; Lopes 2002, 102–3; Puar 2007; Snorton and Haritaworn 2013; Vaid
1995), for example through the uncritical participation in or reception of
cultural products such as the television reality competition *RuPaul's Drag
Race,* a major space for Puerto Rican drag and trans representation.[8] At
the same time, as Latin American, Caribbean, and diasporic, colonial,
queer- and trans-of-color subjects, Puerto Rican translocas also negotiate
local, regional, national, and transnational specificities, marked by particular histories and contexts similar to the ones explored in the rich Latin
American scholarship on this topic, for example in Jean Franco's (1999)
and Nelly Richard's articulation of a politics of difference in the performances of Francisco Casas and Pedro Lemebel, also known as the Yeguas
del Apocalipsis (Mares of the Apocalypse) in Chile, or in Denilson Lopes's
(2002), Ben. Sifuentes-Jáuregui's (2002), Héctor Domínguez Ruvalcaba's
(2007), Laura G. Gutiérrez's (2010), Vek Lewis's (2010), Giuseppe Campuzano's (2008, 2013), Miguel A. López and Fernanda Nogueira's (2013),
and Antonio Prieto Stambaugh's (2000, 2014, 2019) nuanced discussions
of the cultural representation of Latin American transvestism over many
decades, but also highlighting questions of race, particularly of Blackness
and of African descent.[9]

In its specificity and particularity, transloca performance partakes of
the *ser marica* (being or becoming faggot) and of the *inflexión marica*

(faggot inflection) that Paco Vidarte ([2007] 2010) and Diego Falconí Trávez (2018) propose as a radical challenge to the imperialist reach of the Anglo-American category of "gay," similar to how Marlene Wayar (2019) and others posit *travesti* (and not *transgénero,* or transgender) as a vernacular Latin American category and critical framework, or as Wayar proposes, following D. W. Winnicott, "una teoría lo suficientemente buena" (a good-enough theory).[10] In this sense, translocas are more *cuir* than queer, if we understand *cuir* as a variant spelling of "queer" in Spanish that emerged as a way to mark a distance from the English language and from global North activist and theoretical frameworks; similarly, translocas are more *travesti* than transgender, following the usage of the term *travesti* in Latin America.[11]

Drag and trans performance matters to the nation and to our conceptions of Puerto Ricanness and Latinidad. In his landmark book *Performance in America: Contemporary U.S. Culture and the Performing Arts* (2005), the queer Latino scholar David Román highlights the centrality of drag and of other types of performance in US national debates and conceptualizations. Through varied examples, Román demonstrates the multiple ways the performing arts grapple with complex social issues that affect Americans and allow for myriad subject positions and community stances. Similarly, in his book *Performing Queer Latinidad*, the queer Puerto Rican scholar Ramón H. Rivera-Servera illustrates how "performance played a critical role in the development of Latina/o public culture in the United States at the dusk of the twentieth and the dawn of the twenty-first centuries" (2012, 6), a gesture that builds on, expands, and dialogues with José Esteban Muñoz's (1999, 2009, 2020) and Juana María Rodríguez's (2003, 2014) key insights on queer- and trans-of-color performance and identity. Muñoz in particular was interested in drag performance as a space for the contestation of racism and nationalism, as in the work of the Chicana / African American artist Vaginal Davis (1999, 93–115), and for challenging ethnic and sexist chauvinism, as in the Cuban American Carmelita Tropicana's (Alina Troyano's) drag king impersonation of the suave bus driver and ladies' man Pingalito Betancourt (1999, 128–35). Meanwhile, Rodríguez highlights the ways individuals are obliged to perform in certain ways for the state (for example, during asylum proceedings) or online (2003), and how artists such as the Chicana Xandra Ibarra (La Chica Boom) radically challenge conventions through their performance (2014, 148–51).

Following these scholars' leads, I argue that Puerto Rican transloca practices and drag and transgender performances and representations, whether on the page, stage, street, or screen, are key to understanding translocal Puerto Rican, American, Latin American, and Caribbean national imaginaries and social processes, for example, by serving as a mechanism for historical memory and for intergenerational transmission of knowledge, as when a transloca or drag performer embodies a historical figure from the past, what David Román refers to as "archival drag" (2005, 137–78).[12] Yet, as I suggested earlier through my inclusion of violent, perhaps unsettling and abject, references, the translocas I focus on also move complexly between the acknowledgment of, critical engagement with, or experience of violence, bodily decay, death, and lack of futurity (the lack of a positive envisioning of the future to come, a critical position that I do not necessarily subscribe to), counterpoised by a more utopian bent, mediated through camp humor, a political engagement with abjection as a strategy of empowerment, and an explicit acknowledgment of Puerto Rican coloniality through a queer- and trans-of-color and queer and trans diasporic lens.[13] Similarly, if we take the queer (or Latin American variant *cuir*) and trans disruptions of *marica* and *travesti* seriously, transloca performance must be understood as a political practice that challenges the status quo.

Translocas: The Politics of Puerto Rican Drag and Trans Performance is an effort to apprehend this multiplicity through the exploration of very specific artistic practices (some better known, others less) in the context of translocal Puerto Rican culture, understood as one marked by colonial politics, geographical displacements, and translation. This book entails the documentation and analysis of the lives and work of a select group of cisgender and transgender artists and activists to show the very different uses they make of drag or trans performance and cultural or activist representation in Puerto Rico and in the United States. It is also about the reception of this work and its multiple meanings for diverse audiences, as well as the *crónica*, *testimonio*, or auto-ethnographic reflection of a self-identified Puerto Rican transloca (a queer man, myself) who is a fan of transloca performance and who has performed in drag for over a decade.

As it happens, while I was conducting this research, I was invited by the Puerto Rican drag performer, performance artist, and podcaster Fausto Fernós to appear with him and his husband Marc Felion in *Cooking with Drag Queens*, a user-generated drag queen cooking show filmed in Chicago and circulated on YouTube.[14] While I had painted my fingernails black and blue as an undergraduate and even worn a plaid skirt on occasion, I had never really dressed in drag before, except perhaps (rather unremarkably) for a Halloween drag ball at Harvard College. The fact that I ended up performing as Lola von Miramar (my drag persona) as I wrote about drag as a recently tenured professor at the University of Michigan is not that unusual: numerous researchers, including Esther Newton (1972), Jack Halberstam (1998, 231–66), and Leila Rupp and Verta Taylor (2003) also describe being integrated into the drag performances they were writing about, a reflection of the highly participatory nature of this art form and of its embrace of amateur practitioners; the diasporic South Asian scholar Kareem Khubchandani (2015), also known as LaWhore Vagistan, is an example of a drag queen whose performance practice is directly tied to their research and pedagogy on diasporic queer nightlife. Other scholars such as the Peruvian Giancarlo Cornejo (2019) describe a rather different case: being invited to dress in feminine clothes and accompany a female trans sex worker, or *travesti*, to a site of street prostitution in Lima, where a near run-in with the police created enormous tension and put the young ethnographer's life at risk. My drag practice has entailed similar scares, as I describe below.

Practicing drag as an art form allows for a different, more nuanced appreciation, an embodied experience that can complement, expand, or transform perceptions and understandings, as I discuss in chapter 6 in relation to Jorge B. Merced. While it can make the research process more fun, it creates its own challenges, particularly given the stigma attached to drag performance in certain professional contexts, the potential transphobic violence one is exposed to, and the ways it can lead practitioners (or audiences) to question a subject's sexual and gender identity. I have experienced these advantages and disadvantages personally, which has made the experience of appearing as Lola von Miramar enjoyable but also at times challenging. It is precisely this tension, between joy and fear, elation and violence, that is at the heart of transloca performance and of transloca lives.

Translocations, Displacements, Disciplinary Fields

What do transloca performances, entailing *loca* subjectivities, drag and trans embodiments, and varied multimedia, theatrical, and literary representations, mean in Caribbean and diasporic Puerto Rican and Latinx contexts at a moment of profound social and economic crisis, increased

migration, transgender hypervisibility, quickly shifting public perceptions, intensified media coverage, and legal reforms?[15] How do Spanish-
language and Spanglish, Latin American, Hispanic Caribbean, and Latinx
vernacular categories such as *loca, draga, travesti, transformista,* and
vestida and neologisms such as *transloca, translatina,* and *cuir* relate to
broader conceptualizations of gay, queer, drag, and transgender practices
and identities in English, Spanish, and other languages such as Portuguese
and French? How are all of these terms *translated,* if this is even possible?[16]
What are the limits and potentialities of cultural and linguistic translation? And how do artists, activists, and scholars fail or succeed?[17] Furthermore, how do these transloca conceptualizations fit in, challenge, or
dialogue with the longer tradition of scholarship on nonnormative gender
identities and drag and trans performance by pioneering researchers in
LGBTQ, queer of color, queer migration, queer diaspora, and Latin American and Caribbean *cuir* studies and with new disciplinary knowledge in
the quickly expanding field of transgender studies, marked by anthologies
such as the two-volume *Transgender Studies Reader* published in 2006 and
2013 and by innovative peer-reviewed journals such as *TSQ: Transgender
Studies Quarterly,* established in 2014?[18] And how do Puerto Rican, Nuyorican, Diasporican, and AmeRícan artists, activists, artivists, and scholars
reenvision the meanings and uses of stigmatized categories such as *loca,*
the practices of drag, and the multiplicities of "trans" as a prefix and as a
noun, be it regarding the transgender, transsexual, transnational, translational, translocal, transglobal, or transglocal, a neologism that bridges the
transnational, the global, and the local?[19]

In this book, I focus on an idiosyncratic group of Puerto Rican artists, activists, and performers who have been active since the 1960s, particularly Sylvia Rivera, Nina Flowers, Freddie Mercado, Javier Cardona,
Jorge B. Merced, Erika Lopez, Holly Woodlawn, Monica Beverly Hillz,
Lady Catiria, and Barbra Herr. I engage their lives and work through the
lens of *transloca performance* in order to show how they destabilize or,
to the contrary, reify dominant notions of gender, sexuality, and race,
while also engaging issues of class, national identity, migratory displacement, and social justice. I also discuss a small number of transloca literary
representations, including a short story by Manuel Ramos Otero; documentary films such as *Paris Is Burning* (1990), *The Salt Mines* (1990), *La
aguja / The Needle* (2012), and *Mala Mala* (2014); and the murders of Jorge
Steven López Mercado in 2009 and of Kevin Fret in 2019. My scholarship is enriched and in dialogue with the valuable analysis of other key

Puerto Rican translocas such as the flamboyant astrologer and television personality Walter Mercado (Barradas 2016; Colón-Zayas 2012; Hedrick 2013; Taylor 2003), greatly celebrated for his style, baroque excess, and discourse of love and inclusion, who has been described as an "extravagant Puerto Rican astrologer, psychic, and gender nonconforming legend" and as a "gay Latinx icon" (Dry 2020), but also criticized for his conservative, pro-US statehood (pro-annexation) political views, for abusing his white privilege, and for his solidarity and friendship with right-wing anti-Castro Cubans in Miami and San Juan such as Julito Labatut, who has been linked to extreme acts of violence; the astrologer is the subject of a major Netflix documentary, *Mucho Mucho Amor: The Legend of Walter Mercado* (Costantini and Tabsch 2020), which points, precisely, to the complex negotiations required to succeed (and survive) as an effeminate Puerto Rican entertainer, and to the ways in which a transloca performer uses costume, makeup, hairstyle, jewelry, movement, voice, and persona to create an intense relationship with audiences, who feel utterly transformed by their embrace of the artist and strive to touch him in the flesh. I also refer to the leading cabaret and theatrical drag performer Antonio Pantojas, whose work has been discussed by scholars such as Félix Jiménez (2004), Javier E. Laureano (2007, 2016), and Carlos Manuel Rivera (2014) and who served as a mentor and inspiration to contemporary performers such as Barbra Herr.[20] Pantojas is a particularly interesting case as a committed leftist *travesti* who suffered homophobic exclusions from the pro-independence movement (Rodríguez Martinó 1990) and who eventually stopped performing in drag due to his frustration with his limited employment opportunities (Del Valle 1995).

This book is not a thorough or comprehensive history of Puerto Rican queer male effeminacy or of drag and trans performance, but rather a theorization based on historical events and on the works of very specific individuals who shed light on a broader phenomenon. These particular artists' and activists' lives and cultural productions allow me to reflect critically on the uses of nonhegemonic, antihomonormative, and antitransnormative queerness and of drag and trans performance for varied personal, communitarian, aesthetic, political, cultural, educational, pedagogical, and social purposes. My selection of artists, activists, and representations has to do with my own experiences meeting specific individuals and attending their performances or interacting with available documentation, be it recordings, films, works of literature, or television programs, an ephemeral and fragile archive (a "living archive of desire") of queer and trans Puerto Ricanness and Latinidad (Roque Ramírez 2005, 2008); the specificities of their work; and my interest in challenging universalizing discourses that see English-language terms such as "gay" and "queer" and even "trans" as generalizable symbols of progress and modernity, eclipsing local, vernacular conceptions.[21] It also has to do with my desire to present *loca* and "transloca" and other terms such as *marica, travesti,* and *cuir* as unstable and dangerous categories of meaning or as optics, epistemologies, or types of praxis that can challenge and hopefully not reinscribe myriad orthodoxies and essentialisms.

I bring together Puerto Rican drag and trans femininities and, on occasion, masculinities under the term "translocas" and, in some cases, *transmachos* and *transmachas,* extremely aware of how drag and trans performance are overlapping yet distinct cultural formations that should not be simply conflated. I am particularly interested in *loca,* drag, trans, and for that matter, *transformista* and *travesti* as temporally marked concepts that reflect particular historical moments. I am also interested in the terms' complex relationship and contiguity, for example, how a leading figure such as the New York Intralatina Puerto Rican / Venezuelan Stonewall pioneer and community activist Sylvia Rivera self-identified early in her life as a "drag queen," "street queen," and "street transvestite" (indexing her homelessness and poverty), particularly in the 1960s and early 1970s, and came to self-identify as a trans woman by the late 1990s and early 2000s, shortly before her death.[22] While not a traditional artist, Rivera's political performances as a highly visible trans activist of color fully inform this book; Rivera is a STAR (a street transvestite action revolutionary), as in the name of the organization that she coestablished in 1970 with her friend and coconspirator, the African American Marsha P. Johnson, a light in the firmament that has led my way.[23] Originally perceived as an alcohol- and drug-consuming, homeless rabble-rouser and firebrand, Rivera has come to be recognized as a national symbol in the United States, becoming the first transgender person featured at the Smithsonian National Portrait Gallery in Washington, DC, where she appears in a photo by the gay Puerto Rican photographer Luis Carle with two additional trans women: Rivera's partner Julia Murray and the Puerto Rican Stonewall veteran Cristina Hayworth, who originated the first LGBTQ march in San Juan in 1991 (see figure 1).[24]

Sylvia Rivera's movement between "drag queen," "street queen," "transvestite," and "trans" anticipates that of other performers I discuss, such as Holly Woodlawn and Barbra Herr. It also reflects how someone might

Fig. 1. Cristina Hayworth, Sylvia Rivera, and Julia Murray in New York City. Photo by Luis Carle, 2000.

have initially presented as a drag queen in *RuPaul's Drag Race*, such as the Puerto Rican Peruvian American Carmen Carrera in 2012, or as Monica Beverly Hillz did in 2013, only to eventually disclose a different self-identification as a trans woman.[25] The contiguities and confusions of drag and trans that I negotiate through the category of transloca performance are historically grounded, socially constructed, and theoretically productive and should not be simply dismissed; it is impossible to discuss drag performance without acknowledging the centrality of trans experience to this art form.[26] It is also important to acknowledge how some Puerto Rican cisgender or gender-nonconforming women, for example the San Francisco–based Erika Lopez and Marga Gomez (who is Cuban Puerto Rican), have occasionally embraced female drag, that is to say, the campy, exaggerated, theatrical representation of femininity, as a strategy of empowerment, not to mention the phenomenon of "drag kings," which I do not discuss at length in this book, making our conceptualization even more complex.[27]

Parsing Prefixes, Scrutinizing Words

There is a fundamental link between sexual and gender enactments, spatial location or geography, and queer migrations and diasporas.[28] In this context, the "trans-" in transgender, transvestite, *transformista*, and transsexual can be productively linked to the "trans-" in translocal, transglocal, and transnational, following Meg Wesling's (2002) provocation in relation to the drag queens portrayed in the Cuban documentary *Mariposas en el andamio* (*Butterflies on the Scaffold*), directed by Margaret Gilpin and Luis Felipe Bernaza (1996), an earnest, low-budget, yet very engaging film that proposes the revolutionary potential of openly gay, working-class drag performers in Havana—what we could call "Communist Caribbean *locas*"—showcasing their everyday integration into social and cultural practices of the Cuban Revolution.[29] This film led Wesling to ask, "Is the 'trans' in transsexual the same as the 'trans' in transnational?"—a question that she reformulated in her essay "Why Queer Diaspora?" (2008).[30] More recently, modernist scholar Jessica Berman (2017) has also explored this question in greater detail in her essay "Is the Trans in Transnational the Trans in Transgender?," focusing on Virginia Woolf's *Orlando*, on the case of the Danish transsexual Lili Elbe, on US passports, on feminist science fiction, and on diasporic Indian literature, among other examples, while the trans scholar C. Riley Snorton has demonstrated how "the 'trans-' in 'transatlantic' is not only about movements across space but also about movements across time and being, and concomitantly about movements across blackness," particularly "the degree to which the 'trans-' in transatlantic literature bears a resemblance to the 'trans-' that modifies conceptions of gender," as seen in his analysis of *Three Negro Classics* by Booker T. Washington, W. E. B. Du Bois, and James Weldon Johnson (2017, 107).[31]

Translocas: The Politics of Puerto Rican Drag and Trans Performance works through the spirit of these questions, at times directly, at others more obliquely, in the multiple and constantly shifting, variable iterations of trans vocabularies and displacements, particularly by joining the prefix "trans-" (across, beyond, through) to the vernacular Spanish-language sociolinguistic category of *loca* as a political gesture that marks multiplicity and complexity, a move that is similar to and in dialogue with the multiple (transnational, translational) examples highlighted by the scholars included in the 2016 special issue of *TSQ: Transgender Studies Quarterly* titled "Translating Transgender" and in the 2019 special issue "Trans Studies en las Américas," coedited by Claudia Sofía Garriga-López, Denilson Lopes, Cole Rizki, and Juana María Rodríguez.[32]

Historically, the prefix "trans-" has enabled multiple key Latin American, Caribbean, and Latinx theoretical terms that account for cultural fusion and negotiations, albeit not necessarily in relation to gender and sexuality. Some of these terms include Fernando Ortiz's ([1947] 1995) "transculturation," Juan Flores and George Yúdice's (1990) "transcreation," Enrique Dussel's (2012) "transmodernity," Laurietz Seda's (2009, 2018) "trans/actions" and "trans/acting," and Guillermo Gómez-Peña's "transculture" (1996, 10–12), a concept that Gómez-Peña is actually critical of, preferring to embrace the notion of the hybrid. In counterpoint, reflections on the prefix are also at the heart of contemporary analyses of gender and sexuality, a privileged site of transgender studies, for example, the thirteen keyword essays on terms beginning with "tran-" or "trans-" in the inaugural issue of *TSQ*, including my contribution on "Translatinas/os."[33]

While "trans-" indicates a type of movement or displacement, *loca*, the second term that structures the title of this book, stands in its most common etymological sense for "madwoman" in Spanish, but also means "effeminate man" or "queer," similar to English-language usages such as "pansy," "nelly," "fairy," "Mary," and "queen" and to other Spanish-language terms such as *marica*, *mariquita*, and *maricón*, which are diminutive and augmentative variations of the proper name *María*. *Loca* is a common, everyday word, used as an insult but also in some very specific contexts as a term of endearment; while potentially disparaging and at times offensive, it also used occasionally as an in-group marker of identity and recognition, and can also be a radical signifier of political consciousness.[34] It is also a Puerto Rican folkloric category, alluding not only to every neighborhood's or town's effeminate man (la loca del barrio or la loca del pueblo), but also to one of the four characters in one of the archipelago's most famous religious celebrations, las Fiestas de Santiago Apóstol (the Feast of St. James the Apostle) held annually in Loíza in late July, where the character of la Loca has traditionally been played by ostensibly masculine, heterosexual Afro–Puerto Rican men in blackface who cross-dress for the occasion and aggressively tease passersby, a practice that has expanded over the last several decades, to the chagrin of some, as effeminate gay men and trans women also enact the role.[35] The loca is also a character in other Puerto Rican festivities such as the Ponce carnival, held before Lent, as the important folklorist Teodoro Vidal has documented (1982, 2003). "Loca" is also the name of the protagonist of Manuel Ramos Otero's ([1980] 1992) short story "Loca la de la locura" and of the main character in Ángel Lozada's (2006) novel No quiero quedarme sola y vacía, a hallucinating narrative in which the protagonist has a relationship with another loca and constantly verges on the precipice of madness.[36] Loca is a very particular word, in a context where words matter. And, as the queer Filipino-American anthropologist Martin F. Manalansan IV (2003) incisively demonstrated in his discussions of the transnational, diasporic traveling of queer Tagalog and English-language terms such as bakla, beauty, and diva, words are not necessarily translatable; they acquire new and shifting meanings in their transoceanic crossings and carry a specific universe of queer significations.

With the neologism "transloca," I link the stigmatized category of male homosexuality and effeminate male behavior and, with greater care, female transgender performance, to that of women's madness or subversion, as well as to geography and space, especially to contemporary discussions of translocality.[37] I differ in some ways from the Cuban American scholar Sonia E. Alvarez (2014), who summarized the work of a group of researchers working in translation who also used the term "transloca" in their anthology Translocalities/Translocalidades to self-identify as transnational Latin American and US Latina feminists; as I explain in more detail in chapter 1, my effort is closer to that of the queer Chicano scholar Lionel Cantú Jr., who first proposed its use to the Transnational Feminist Politics of Translation research group with a queer camp feminist inflection.[38]

In my conceptualization, translocas and *translocura* (transmadness, transqueenness, transfaggotry) can be seen as new social formations and identity positions and as a radical (ludic) performance modality, but also as the site of violence, social marginalization, and death. I have used the word "transloca" since 2002 to make sense (or *nonsense*) and to organize (or *disorganize*) the rather different and multiplying iterations of Puerto Rican drag, transgender, and *loca* experience and performance, here and elsewhere, across boundaries and genres and historical timeframes. Numerous artists and activists have used drag and transgender performance to challenge, reconceptualize, and transcend gender roles and sexual identities in the Americas, to present new forms of masculinity and femininity, and to envision non-gender-binary identities and practices. Drag and trans performance has also served as a form of employment. Others have used drag and trans performance as a way to create a crisis of interpretation that confuses and destabilizes expected ideals, and leads to different realms, such as the nature of androgyny; the relationship of the large body and of excess to femininity; the blurring or hypervisibilization of racial distinction; the issue of racial and class prejudice; the role of art and audience participation; and the question of what is human, what is animal or nonanimal, and what is divine.

Transnational and Translocal Puerto Rican Contexts

The Puerto Rican "transnation," seen as a sociopolitical and cultural sphere, extends well beyond the geographic confines of the Caribbean—that is to say, beyond the Puerto Rican archipelago, including the island of Puerto Rico and the smaller inhabited island municipalities of Vieques and Culebra—to include the diaspora, where the bulk of the Puerto Rican population currently resides.[39] Currently, there are over eight million Puerto Ricans, including more than five million in the diaspora, constituting the second-largest Latinx group in the United States. Historically, Puerto Rican diasporic populations settled mostly in the US Northeast, extending from Boston to Philadelphia, particularly in the metropolitan areas of New York, New Jersey, and Connecticut, but also including sites in the Midwest such as northeastern Ohio and the Chicago region, as well as more distant locations such as California and Hawaii. More recently, this diaspora has centered primarily in Florida, especially in the Orlando and Tampa metropolitan regions, with continuing migration to historic sites as well as to Texas, the US Virgin Islands, and the Dominican Republic.[40] This scenario has only been amplified recently as a result of a profound and long-standing economic crisis and of natural catastrophes such as Hurricanes Irma and María in 2017; multiple devastating earthquakes in 2020; and the coronavirus pandemic (Rosa and Robles 2020).[41]

As Juan Flores, Jorge Duany, and other scholars have shown, the links of continuity between these multiple spaces are numerous, although it is also important to recognize the particularities and differences of each.[42] Inversely, as Duany (2002) and Yolanda Martínez-San Miguel (2003) have argued, migration to Puerto Rico from other countries, especially from Cuba and the Dominican Republic, but also from Latin America, the United States, and the French- and English-speaking Caribbean, and reverse or return migration of US Puerto Ricans back to the island have historically made the island itself a multiethnic and, to a limited extent, multilingual and multidialectal society. Thus, when one speaks of Puerto Rican as well as of global culture, it is necessary to account for this translocal condition, that is to say, the knowledge and experience of inhabiting different spaces and of being in intimate contact with diverse communities at multiple locations.[43]

Scholars such as Elizabeth M. Aranda, César J. Ayala, Rafael Bernabe, Jorge Duany, Ramón Grosfoguel, Agustín Lao-Montes, Frances Negrón-Muntaner, and Mayra Santos-Febres have highlighted the historical, political, and affective framework for contemporary Puerto Rican translocality.[44] Lao-Montes (1997, 176), for example, invokes Benedict Anderson's (1992) concept of "imagined communities" and Henri Lefebvre's (1991) notion of "social space" as a way "to imagine the Puerto Rican community as a translocal social space (a transnation)," recognizing the dense interconnections of Puerto Ricans who live dispersed across geographical locations due to colonial processes and the specific structures that anchor these connections. Expanding Lao-Montes's analysis, I contend that the drag and trans embodiments that I read under the optic of transloca performance create, challenge, and disorganize these translocal "imagined communities" (envisioned as cohesive groups based on shared affinities and experiences) and social spaces (that is to say, spaces constituted through social relations and conceptualizations).

Translocality can be defined as the interlinked experiences of persons in diverse geographic locations, whether in the country of origin or in the diaspora, who nevertheless are in complex and constant daily, weekly, monthly, or yearly contact, be it through travel, migration, communications, or other forms of exchange; who live in the intimacy of these interactions and of the knowledge they generate; who might not even be living in different sovereign nations, but rather in different locations marked by profound linguistic and cultural differences in the same nation-state, for example as diasporic metropolitan subjects vis-à-vis colonial, insular ones.[45] Translocality entails a multiplicity of knowledges, family and other personal connections, economic and cultural remittances (Flores 2009), and actual physical displacements. It is a more intimate form of connection than what we usually associate with the transnational, closer to what we could call transcolonial, perhaps similar to what Yolanda Martínez-San Miguel (2014) has termed, following Aníbal Quijano, "coloniality of diasporas," referring to the recurrent and complex exchanges between present and former colonies and their colonial metropoles, a situation that emulates Ramón Grosfoguel's (2003) analysis of Puerto Rico following a world-systems theory model.

Theater, performance, film, literature, music, and other arts have been profoundly affected by this translocal reality and have reflected this phenomenon extensively. Theater scholar Lowell Fiet (1997), for example, has referred to Puerto Rican dramatic arts as a "puente aéreo entre ambas orillas" (an air bridge between both shores).[46] The development of queer Puerto Rican sexualities has also been deeply marked by this experience, as Puerto Ricans have become part of a much broader wave of queer and trans diasporas, and Puerto Rican social formations have been caught up in processes of globalization, including gay or LGBTQ liberation, queer tourism, capitalist commodification, and rising transgender visibility.[47]

In *Translocas*, I link traditional and innovative conceptions of performance, place, gender, and sexuality and bring them together with migratory spatial analysis as a way to question and rethink the meanings of these concepts. In fact, the very terms "gay," "queer," and "transgender" already assume unstable positions and categories within the wide range of that which is understood as masculine, feminine, androgynous, nonbinary, indeterminate, or in between; of hetero-, homo-, bi-, and pansexual attractions; of perversions and the most commonly accepted stereotypes and assumptions within the sphere of the sexual. More importantly, we must consider the particularities of Boricua or Puerto Rican sexuality, with its ample repertoire of terms in English and Spanish entailing greater or lesser pejorative connotations, which include standard and nonstandard vernacular terms such as *pato* (literally a duck, but used figuratively to refer to a homosexual or effeminate man), *pata* (lesbian or masculine woman), *maricón, afeminado, ponca, loca, travesti, vestida, bugarrón, marimacho, marimacha, tortillera, bucha, papi chulo, banjee, butch queen, femme queen,* and *thug.*[48] The term "transloca" engages with and complicates this list.

What (or Who) Are Translocas?

Translocas are many things, contradictory ones, to be sure: performers, innovators, marginals, exiles, eccentrics, troublemakers, lovers, loners, and friends who live in a transnational/translocal context marked by cultural, racial, and linguistic mixtures and juxtapositions.[49] To be a transloca is to tread a dangerous ground, to make and break allegiances, and to redefine meanings and sensibilities. It is potentially to disidentify as an active practice of cultural and political contestation in the sense advanced by José Esteban Muñoz (1999), who argued that the disidentificatory practices of queer persons of color entail complex, strategic negotiations of power through the selective adscription and rejection of normative identities and practices. As Muñoz stated, "Disidentification is the third mode of dealing with dominant ideology, one that neither opts to assimilate within such a structure nor strictly opposes it; rather, disidentification is a strategy that works on and against dominant ideology" (1999, 11). Translocas also operate in the realm of "queer futurity," the spaces of possibility for envisioning a potential world to come or utopia: "Queerness is that thing that lets us feel that this world is not enough, that indeed something is missing" (Muñoz 2009, 1).[50] They also engage the "theories in practice" of home, hope, utopia, and friction that Ramón H. Rivera-Servera (2012) presents as part of the daily lives and strategies of resistance that queer Latinxs engage in as part of *convivencia diaria* (daily encounters and shared experiences), a term Rivera-Servera borrows from the ethnographers Milagros Ricourt and Ruby Danta (2002). Finally, translocas negotiate the "politics of representation, identity, location, and affinity" that Alberto Sandoval-Sánchez and Nancy Saporta Sternbach (2001, 4) identify as crucial to Latinx theater and performance, particularly when viewed through the lens of Latin American theories of transculturation.

What do the many performers, artists, and activists that I bring together in this book think of the label "transloca"? There is no doubt that these individuals could not be more different from one another and that, in fact, some are not thrilled by this neologism. For this reason, it might be more useful to think of transloca performance (a type of action) as a *cuir, marica,* or *travesti* modality, one that is not necessarily bound to specific (racially or nationally marked) bodies, more than to think of transloca as an identity; it is a praxis that can account for contradiction, hybridization, and resistance. Hopefully, "transloca" is a mutable and expansive or capacious concept that can account for variations and different national contexts; for example, the American scholar Jacqueline Loss (2013, 51–60) has found the term useful to discuss the work of the Cuban writer and drag performer Pedro Manuel González Reinoso, also known as Roxy and as La Rusa Roxana Rojo (the Russian Roxana the Red), and the American scholar Camilla Stevens (2019, 94) frames her analysis of the Dominican performer Waddys Jáquez's *P.A.R.G.O.: Los pecados permitidos* (2001) in relation to translocas, while the Brazilian photographer Evna Moura (2013) has used the word to title her series of photos about Brazilian drag queens and queer people at the "Festa da Chiquita," a LGBTQ event that forms part of the annual Círio de Nazaré religious procession in Belém do Pará.[51] At times, I have felt that my theorization might be more a critical-interpretive fantasy of mine, that of the transloca scholar and artist: Lola von Miramar's delusions. Nevertheless, I have found it useful to compare multiple artists and activists in relation to the historically important but also culturally and geographically specific concept of transculturation.

For the Cuban ethnographer Fernando Ortiz ([1947] 1995), cultures that come in contact do not necessarily erase or substitute each other, but rather find a dynamic balance—at times mediated through profound violence—in which elements of each persist but, more importantly, are transformed and coexist as a new formation; transculturation, seen as "the merging and converging of cultures," serves as an alternative or corrective to the American sociological term "assimilation" (Ramírez 2017, 16). While Ortiz was most interested in the particular situation of Cuba, specifically in the coming together of European and African influences that he symbolized through the metaphor of *ajiaco* (a rich stew with many diverse ingredients), I will focus on a translocal Puerto Rican context in which transnational Indigenous, African, Hispanic, and Anglo-American elements predominate, and where new notions of sexuality and space have radically transformed people's understandings of self.[52] And while the Cuban ethnographer clearly felt that European (and, need we say, heterosexual) culture was superior and would dominate the mix, I have the suspicion that in the Puerto Rican case, all bets are off.

I propose that we see the prefix "trans-" at the core of *transformation*—change, the power or ability to mold, reorganize, reconstruct, construct—

and *transgeographical*, as in the transcontinental, transatlantic, transhemi-spheric, and transarchipelagic, but also transversal, oblique, and not direct. This transgeneric transitoriness implies several challenges to dominant notions of Puerto Ricanness that do not accept migration—the migrant diasporic community and/or immigrants in Puerto Rico—or queer sexu-alities and alternative gender identities. It can also be associated with the transgression of mediums or artistic genres that Francisco José Ramos (1998) identified as part of the "poetics of experimentation" that marks the artistic production of a number of contemporary visual artists such as Freddie Mercado, a modality of experimentation that the art historian Haydee Venegas (1998) referred to as *travestismo* (transvestism). It also has to do, as previously mentioned, with the conceptual and terminologi-cal instability Meg Wesling (2002) has hinted at and with queer ethnog-rapher Marcia Ochoa's (2008) playful theorization of *loca*-lization as the confluence of queer sexuality, space, and place among Venezuelan drag queens and transgender women in Caracas.

Loca, in its own right, also suggests a form of hysterical identity, patholo-gized at the clinical level, scandalous at the popular one, constitutive of the individual lacking sanity, composure, or ascription to dominant norms: effeminate homosexuals, madwomen, rebels for any cause; marginalized categories that in an ironic and playful gesture I wish to resemanticize in the style of and in resistance to the Anglo-American term "queer": *loca*, as *maricón* (faggot) friends calls one another, as a sign of complicity and understanding, of being *entendidos* (those in the know, *in the life*), and not necessarily as a hostile insult, joke, or putdown, although perhaps that too, if one is to do justice to cruelty as an art or strategy for survival, or sim-ply, as an acknowledgment of self-hatred; *loca* as the felicitous yet critical, perhaps decolonial coming-together of Susan Sontag's "Notes on Camp" (1964), Esther Newton's *Mother Camp: Female Impersonators in America* (1972, 1979), and Denilson Lopes's "Terceiro manifesto camp" (2002, 89–120), with the good graces of Judith Butler (1990), Marjorie Garber (1992), Arnaldo Cruz-Malavé (1995), and Ben. Sifuentes-Jáuregui (2002), as a high-camp extravaganza, or as a homage to the drag house system por-trayed in the documentary *Paris Is Burning* (1990) as well as in the televi-sion reality competition *RuPaul's Drag Race* (2009–2021) and in the more recent TV series *Pose* (2018–2019), all with a *cuir* Latin American *loca* and *marica inflection* (Falconí Trávez 2018; Perlongher 2019).

The performative character of this transloca condition is reflected in the transvestic game, which occurs with greater ease in the sphere of social interaction but also extends into theory and literature, as the Cuban writer Severo Sarduy (1982) demonstrated in his essays on simulation and in his multiple experimental 1960s and 1970s novels, populated by drag queens as they were.[53] By *performative*, I am referring to verbal and bodily enactments brought forth through public repetitions in real life and on the stage or space of artistic representation, following Judith Butler's elaborations in *Gender Trouble: Feminism and the Subversion of Identity* (1990), where the feminist philosopher expanded J. L. Austin's theorizations of linguistic performative utterances, which is to say, of words that do things, to account for the social construction of gender via naturalized, reiterative everyday practices.[54] "Transvestic game," in turn, accounts for the knowledge of the artificiality, or more correctly, the arbitrary nature of the classification of signs, whether racial, ethnic, sexual, gender, class, or motile, and the possibility for their manipulations and reinventions or contestations, at least according to a writer such as Sarduy. The performers, artists, activists, and artivists in question, in different ways and at different moments, allude to or incarnate this sphere, as gendered and sexed bodies marked by race, ethnicity, class, age, and unorthodox desire, and located voluntarily or involuntarily in varied geographical contexts.

Becoming Lola: Self-Reflexivity and Drag

I too have now become a diasporic, translocal, and exaggeratedly bilingual Midwestern transloca, a writer and college professor who occasionally performs in drag on stage and online. While I have lived in Michigan since 2003, it is fair to say that I was already a *loca* long before I ever donned my first wig. My first appearance as Lola von Miramar at the behest of Fausto Fernós and Marc Felion of the *Feast of Fun* podcast in 2010, specifically for their *Cooking with Drag Queens* YouTube series, has led me to learn a lot more about the practice of drag than I ever envisioned, ranging from the intricacies of makeup, feminine clothing, and jewelry to the subtleties of girdles, padding, hosiery, and wigs, not to mention lip-synch, choreography, and onstage humor.[55] As I am not an ethnographer or professionally trained as a theater practitioner, I initially approached drag and transgender performance strictly as an audience member, reader, film viewer, and critic—a privileged white or light-skinned Latinx *loca* one, to be sure;

Fig. 2. Marc Felion, Lola von Miramar, and Fausto Fernós on the set of *Cooking with Drag Queens*, Chicago, 2015. Photo by Fausto Fernós.

one who was initially taught to conduct literary and cultural analysis, who later became immersed in performance studies and who appraised performances, trying to understand what went into them.

While it is certainly not necessary to practice an art form in order to understand it or to relate to it psychically and to internalize it as constitutive of one's subjectivity (Lopes 2002, 67–88), there are some advantages, and I hope that my explicitly and implicitly performative experiences enrich the discussions that I offer in the pages to come. In fact, as I mentioned earlier, there is a long tradition of having the researcher "drag it up," whether by dressing or performing in drag or assisting with the drag show, at least since the appearance of Esther Newton's pioneering *Mother Camp* in 1972. Similarly, in *Female Masculinity*, Jack Halberstam (1998) describes attending and being invited to compete in drag king contests in New York City, while lesbian feminist scholars Leila Rupp and Verta Taylor (2003) describe performing in drag as part of the research process for their ethnography of the 801 Cabaret in Key West, Florida. The sociologist Joshua Gamson (1998, 139–40), on the other hand, begins a chapter on transgender participation on television talk shows by discussing a personal experience in which his dressing in drag with seven friends in San Francisco created significant anxiety for those who encountered them in public. And in their master's thesis "'Estar perra es la onda': Arte, escena y miradas drag en la Ciudad de México," the Puerto Rican scholar Jaime Géliga Quiñones (2016) describes the process of becoming-drag (*devenir draga*) as one of going "De Jaime el investigador a Juanita Caminante la drag tropical" (From Jaime the researcher to Juanita the Wanderer, Tropical Drag Queen) (48–51), including photo documentation of their transformation.

A different example is that of African American gay or self-described "butch queen" ethnographer Marlon M. Bailey (2013), who made walking a category in a ball in search of a prize a central focus of his methodological approach to exploring the Black LGBTQ and drag ballroom scene, as described in his book *Butch Queens Up in Pumps: Gender, Performance, and Ballroom Culture in Detroit*. In this case, Bailey performed in professional masculine business attire and envisioned himself as an insider/outsider, highlighting his embrace of Dwight Conquergood's concept of "coperformative witness" (a dynamic relationship between researcher and the subjects traditionally identified as informants or ethnographic subjects), also identifying scholar and performer E. Patrick Johnson (2003) as a role model for engaged and participatory critical performance studies scholarship; Rivera-Servera (2012, 19) also embraces Conquergood's term. I too have become a coperformative witness of sorts, as well as an occasional "butch queen up in pumps" (a queer-of-color man in drag), at times more actively involved in actual performances, on other occasions as an audience member that shares his enthusiasm and joy, frequently through a notably loud, disruptive laugh.

The exhilaration of performance is addictive; the pleasures of audience interaction are extremely fulfilling. Performing in drag, perhaps all performance, entails becoming an/other, embodying a self-projection that is different from oneself, where the self is temporarily suspended or intensified, similar to donning a mask and truly transforming into the character, falling into a performative trance that displaces regular subjectivity with a heightened, alternative one. This book is a reflection on drag and transgender performance as an artistic practice, a form of entertainment, a catalyst for community growth, and a mechanism of self-expression; it is a reflection that surges from the experience of being a devout fan of drag and trans performance (one who adores the artists on the dance floor or stage or screen, and who performs the quite dramatic, over-the-top identity of a fan) as much as from the experience of becoming a bona fide performer. It is also a chronicle of the fear of violence and rejection, of the anguish produced by the possibility that one will be attacked for dressing in drag (Cornejo 2019) or for being a trans person or an effeminate man or a *loca*, and of paranoid anxiety regarding difficult or challenging personal and professional relations with femmephobic or transphobic individuals.

I have experienced these fears firsthand, for example in Buenos Aires in 2013, when anonymous individuals (apparently hotel employees) aggressively harassed me late at night on the phone inquiring about a *transcomunicador* (transcommunicator), perhaps believing I was a trans sex worker, after I returned from an event in full costume, which led me to barricade myself in my room and to relive in my mind anti-*loca* dictatorship-era-like scenes of violence of the type that Néstor Perlongher (2019) has described, and that I associated with the gay political thriller *Apartment Zero* (1988, dir. Martin Donovan). Ironically, I was staying at the Bauen Hotel, a site recuperated by workers after the Argentinean financial collapse of 2001, to attend the ninth biennial meeting of the International Association for the Study of Sexuality, Culture and Society (IASSCS), and had just performed at the conference's party held at the historic Club Español, an ornate art nouveau-inspired Catalan modernist-style building located on Bernardo de Irigoyen Street in the historic center region. It seems that having hundreds of hotel guests who researched topics related to sexuality was not advantageous for this Puerto Rican drag queen, who got clocked and intimidated when she got home. This anecdote is trivial compared to the physical aggression and lethal violence routinely experienced by effeminate men and trans women across the globe, but my fear was real and has marked my research process.

This and other experiences (for example, having a senior colleague in the profession, now deceased, feign surprise at seeing me dressed in masculine clothes, when he assumed I was now transgender; or having to explain to a gay, masculine-oriented potential sexual partner that I perform in drag; or shaving my facial hair off and seeing how it changes and demasculinizes my appearance, an awkward experience for someone who is attracted to bearded gay men referred to as "bears") have led me to embrace the Chicana lesbian writer Cherríe Moraga's conceptualization of "theory in the flesh," a critical practice grounded in personal experience and life history.[56] "Theory in the flesh" implies recognizing that knowledge is created from lived experience as much as from scholarly research and philosophical reflection. As Moraga indicates, "A theory in the flesh means one where the physical realities of our lives—our skin color, the land or concrete we grew up on, our sexual longings—all fuse to create a politic born out of necessity" (Moraga and Anzaldúa 1983, 23).[57] It suggests a very particular type of investment in knowledge that recognizes its everyday impacts and social and political ramifications. It signals a deep commitment that comes from phenomenological experience (knowledge filtered through the body and the senses) or from what the Chicana scholar Stephanie Fetta describes as a somatic transaction or corporeal process engaging the "soma—the perceptive and expressive body" (2018, 2) as much as from analytic thought.

My book is foremost an argument for Puerto Rican transloca performance or *translocura* as an epistemology, a way of seeing the world, and a cause for shifting the way we see: a potentially radical tool for expanding perception and understanding. It is also a discussion of an art form and practice that I have come to embody and better understand, and the nuanced appraisal of very specific individuals with very concrete artistic, political, and cultural experiences.

Book Structure

In the chapters that follow I trace the heterogeneity of Puerto Rican transloca performance. In chapter 1, I engage queer and feminist theoretical debates on the term *loca*, particularly in the social sciences and in creative literature, as a way to contextualize how the broader fields of Latin American, Latinx, LGBTQ, and women's, gender, and sexuality studies have focused on these issues, highlighting the profound disagreements about the term's usefulness, paying particular attention to complex recuperations of the word. Given the stresses of anti-Black racism, misogyny, ableism, xenophobia, femmephobia, transphobia, and homophobia, not everyone is excited to recuperate or engage the term *loca*.

In chapter 2, I go on to posit Puerto Rican transloca performance as an epistemology or critical and experiential method that oscillates between joy and death, highlighting three examples: the transnational success of the light-skinned drag performer Nina Flowers (Jorge Flores), who appeared on *RuPaul's Drag Race* in 2009; the brutal murder of the aspiring young fashion designer and makeup artist Jorge Steven López Mercado that same year; and the songs and videos of the assassinated trap singer Kevin Fret, who was known for his fearless celebration of *loca* alterity and was killed in 2019. Here, I contrast Nina Flowers's joyful recuperation of *loca* and her effusive transloca performance to the radical violence that marked the end of López Mercado's and Fret's lives, but also to López Mercado's and Fret's differential articulation of self.

Subsequently, in chapter 3, I document how drag and trans performance became a strategy for combating the violence of poverty and the stigma associated with the phrase "welfare queen" in the work of the Afro-Puerto Rican writer and performer Erika Lopez, the light-skinned actress and cabaret star Holly Woodlawn, and the Black trans performer Monica Beverly Hillz, juxtaposing their experiences to the life and activism of Stonewall veteran Sylvia Rivera. I posit the *transloca drag of poverty* as a tactic of resistance that embraces humor, anger, glamour, parody, and political discourse to overcome social marginalization and impoverishment, frequently marked by anti-Black bias.

Additional chapters home in on specific performers. In chapter 4, I analyze drag as a sociocultural and cognitive disruption and historical archive (the *ultrabaroque drag of rasanblaj*), focusing on the light-skinned performance artist Freddie Mercado through the framework of *rasanblaj* (reassembly) and the *ultrabaroque*. I highlight Mercado's visual arts practice (painting, sculpture, installation, and performance art) and his historical reenactments of the famous mayor of San Juan, doña Fela (Felisa Rincón de Gautier), and of the renowned singer, composer, and television host Myrta Silva, as well as his hybrid, comical, and at times grotesque, abject, or monstrous creations, emphasizing the centrality of collaboration, improvisation, and recycling in his work. I am particularly interested in Mercado's questioning and challenging of the borders of race, ethnicity, gender, sex, and the human in relation to nonhuman animals, monsters, and divinities, including his critical approach to matters of Afrodiasporic life and experience, and the artist's negotiations of poverty and bias.

In chapter 5, I propose the *transloca drag of race* as a framework to understand the dancer and actor Javier Cardona's political intervention denouncing anti-Black racism, reading his piece *You Don't Look Like . . .* (1996) as a rescripting of the Snow White fairy tale in which Cardona becomes the Evil Queen as a means to challenge the exclusions of Afro–Puerto Ricans from the media industry. I see Cardona engaging and questioning folkloric transloca traditions and using popular music, parodic blackface, mirrors, photographic images, performative objects, audience interaction, confessional storytelling, and choreography to make a crucial antiracist statement.

In chapter 6, I highlight transloca performance, drag embodiment, and music (particularly the genre of the bolero) as tools of identity building and community building in the diaspora. Here, I focus on the light-skinned actor and director Jorge B. Merced and the Pregones Theater of the Bronx's 1997 play *El bolero fue mi ruina* (*The Bolero Was My Downfall*), an adaptation of Manuel Ramos Otero's short story "Loca la de la locura" ("The Queen of Madness"). I contend that Merced's life experiences, particularly his processes of *transloca approximation* and *transloca incorporation* (a type of "theory in the flesh"), are crucial elements that determine the success of this theatrical production, in which storytelling and lip-synching boleros serves to affirm *cuir* and *travesti* diasporic Latinx identity and community.

Finally, in chapter 7, I take a slightly different approach, highlighting two light-skinned New York–based Puerto Rican transgender performers: Lady Catiria and Barbra Herr. I see the hormonally and surgically modified body of Lady Catiria and her 1990s weekly performances at La Escuelita nightclub in New York City as works of art, highlighting the artistic value of lip-synch and of burlesque performance and their potential for creating community. I also discuss Lady Catiria's 1996 embrace of AIDS activism, particularly as a participant in the Miss Continental Pageant in Chicago. I then focus on the language- and music-centered cabaret and theatrical enactments of Barbra Herr, particularly Herr's one-woman show *Trans-mission* (2017), highlighting her impassioned plea for social transformation and acceptance. In the epilogue, I reflect on this journey and offer additional thoughts on the current status of transloca representation and performance.

ONE

Theorizing *la Loca*
Feminist and Queer Debates

¿Qué le falta a lo queer para que se convierta en locura, al estilo
latinoamericano, estilo Perlongher, Lemebel o Arenas? Le hace
falta raza, clase, le falta realidad social y política, y, al parecer,
le falta amor.
—Paola Arboleda Ríos (2011)

Locas produce drama, disagreement, and anger, and suffer social exclusion and marginalization, even when they can also entertain audiences
and challenge authority.[1] While key queer Latin American writers such
as the Argentine Néstor Perlongher, the Chilean Pedro Lemebel, and the
Cuban Reinaldo Arenas provocatively recuperated and deployed the term
loca in their essays, fiction, and poetry as a term of radical alterity in the
late twentieth century, others have been more resistant, notwithstanding
the (at the time closeted) Puerto Rican singer Ricky Martin's 1999 exhortation for us to embrace "Livin' la Vida Loca."[2] Some rebellious gender-
nonconforming women have also claimed the term. For example, multiple
women graffiti writers in the Americas identified as "graffiti grrlz" by Jessica Nydia Pabón-Colón (2016, 2018) proudly call themselves *locas* at the
same time that they resist the label of "feminists" and engage in women-
centered praxis. In her essay "To(o) Queer the Writer—Loca, escritora
y chicana," the woman-of-color feminist Gloria Anzaldúa ([1991] 2009)
indicates how the word *loca* is closer to her experiences as a working-class,
South Texas Chicana than the term "lesbian," which is monopolized by
white women who are not attentive to the particularities of race, language,
and class. And in his *Locas* comics (part of the *Love and Rockets* series),
the Chicano artist Jaime Hernández (2004) carefully conveys the lives of
complex Chicana gender-nonconforming queer women.[3]

There are complex and wide-ranging tensions regarding the uses of *loca* or *la loca* in Latin American, Caribbean, and Latinx feminist and gender and sexuality studies, where scholars have expressed mixed feelings about its efficacy, and concerns about its disappearance, eclipsed by the global adoption of English-language terms such as "queer" and "gay." In this chapter, I work through these productive tensions, analyzing cases from diverse academic fields and from a range of countries and regions, as a way to situate and better understand the Puerto Rican artists and activists I discuss in the rest of the book.

Normative Spanish-language sources such as the *Diccionario de la lengua española* of the Real Academia Española (RAE) indicate the challenges and ambiguity of *loca*.[4] While the signifier clearly has a queer meaning—concretely, the current tenth entry as *hombre homosexual afeminado*, or "effeminate homosexual man," a 2018 revision to the former rather incomplete definition as *hombre homosexual*, or homosexual man (RAE 2001), which conflated the effeminate gender expression that characterizes the *loca* with same-sex sexual activity—Puerto Rican translocas undoubtedly contaminate ourselves with the term's additional significations: *que ha perdido la razón* (one who has lost the use of reason); *de poco juicio, disparatado e imprudente* (of little judgment, crazy and reckless); *que excede en mucho a lo ordinario o presumible* (that far exceeds the ordinary or presumed); *mujer informal y ligera en sus relaciones con los hombres* (a woman who is informal and light in her relationships with men); *prostituta* (prostitute)—that is to say, assuming that the queer or *cuir loca* has not evacuated her *locura* or lost her Spanish-language or Latin American specificity, whether because of migration or normativization.

Locas preoccupy, cause concern, and disconcert, similar to the way Anglo-American, Latinx, queer-of-color, and Canadian faggots do, as the writer and activist Mattilda Bernstein Sycamore (2012) brilliantly demonstrates in *Why Are Faggots So Afraid of Faggots?*, a volume in which a variety of contributors challenge mainstream, assimilationist LGBTQ conceptions. As the title page indicates, Sycamore's book poses "flaming challenges to masculinity, objectification, and the desire to conform." Sycamore describes their volume as "an emergency intervention" edited by "a genderqueer faggot and a queen with a certain amount of notoriety [who is] incredibly inspired by the politics and potentials of trans, genderqueer, and gender-defiant culture" (2012, 2). The recuperation of the term "faggots," also visible in Larry Mitchell's 1977 fable/manifesto *The Faggots and Their Friends between Revolutions* (but strongly resisted in

Larry Kramer's 1978 sex-negative novel *Faggots*), is linguistically specific, temporally marked, and meaningful in the United States (and Canada) in very particular contexts in the late 1970s and early 2000s but also in the 2017 "Faggot Manifesto" presented by the SPIT! (Sodomites, Perverts, Inverts Together!) collective formed by the artist Carlos Motta, the writer and curator John Arthur Peetz, and the artist Carlos María Romero, which seeks to reclaim the term, affirming: "A faggot is not a corporation. A faggot is not a polite citizen. A faggot is not a commodity to be traded. A faggot is not sanitary. A faggot is not just a rich white gay man" (SPIT! 2017, 6).

In France, it is *folles* (the French equivalent of *locas*, referring to madwomen and effeminate male homosexuals) as a term and an identity or practice, as in the celebrated play, musical, and film *La Cage aux Folles*, who disquiet and who have been recuperated as transgressive signifiers of queer political resistance, as Jean-Yves Le Talec (2008) explores in his very insightful and carefully researched *Folles de France: Repenser l'homosexualité masculine*. In his book, Le Talec highlights the French liberationist group Les Gazolines as well as the political and cultural interventions of the Sœurs de la Perpétuelle Indulgence, the French equivalent of the Sisters of Perpetual Indulgence, a street performance group that uses drag and religious attire as part of its social critique (Fitzsimons 2019).

Meanwhile, in some Spanish-speaking contexts, the term that has been mobilized as a sign of queer/*cuir* alterity and activism is *marica*. For example, in the introduction of his *Ética marica* (*Marica Ethics*), the Spanish *cuir* philosopher and activist Paco Vidarte expresses his desire that his book serve as "un interruptor. Un dispositivo que corta la corriente," that is to say, as a switch or device that cuts off electric power ([2007] 2010, 9); he understands the *marica* subject as one who rejects the fascist legacy of Franco's dictatorship and who questions and challenges assimilationist gay imperatives under democracy.[5] For Vidarte, the anarchic power of *marica* as a posture, which he invokes together with *bollos* (lesbians) and trans subjects, is to disrupt and serve as an anticapitalist, antibourgeois cog in the system, engaging in a type of "política perra" (bitch politics) that wanders, nomad-like, as if inspired by the radical theorists Gilles Deleuze and Félix Guattari (1986b), without a clear destination in mind. In his *Nación marica: Prácticas culturales y crítica activista* (*Marica Nation: Cultural Practices and Activist Critique*), the Chilean author Juan Pablo Sutherland references the American direct-action group Queer Nation and invokes Néstor Perlonguer's essay "Matan a un marica" ("They Kill a *Marica*");

reading the sign *marica* as a "lugar de castigo, privilegio de asesinato y genocidio permanente en una identidad bastarda" (a site of punishment, an entitlement to permanent murder and genocide in a bastard identity) (2009, 23). Fellow Chilean Pedro Lemebel, meanwhile, appealed to a *mariconaje guerrero* or warrior faggotry (quoted in Arboleda Ríos 2011, 114–16). Finally, in the anthology *Inflexión marica: Escrituras del descalabro gay en América Latina* (*Marica Inflection: Writings of Gay Breakdown in Latin America*), the Ecuadorian lawyer and literary scholar Diego Falconí Trávez identifies *loca*, *marica*, and *lo cuir* as some of the diverse fragmented and localized ways of signifying sex-gender difference in Latin America, indicating that they are "tres muestras de la imposibilidad (incluso el peligro) de pensar una América Latina uniforme desde la política sexual" (three samples of the impossibility—in fact, the danger—of thinking a uniform Latin America in relation to sexual politics) (2018, 10).

It is not only faggots, fairies, sissies, *folles*, *maricas*, and queers, or rather, homonormative, assimilationist gays and transnormative individuals who fear or distance themselves from *locura* (referring to madness or queerness); some feminists also reject this position, particularly when understood as a pathology or stigmatizing status that marks women. Divided or mixed assessments also appear within Latin American and Latinx queer studies, where *loca* has mostly received a positive valorization from scholars such as Marcia Ochoa, Horacio Federico Sívori, María Amelia Viteri, Susana Peña, and Salvador Vidal-Ortiz, but also been labeled as a problematic or undesirable term. Ultimately, Perlongher's, Lemebel's, and Arenas's commitment to *loca* and its use by countless others substantiate broader claims to the relevance and value of this word.

Latina Feminist Concerns and the Queer Feminist Origins of "Translocas"

There is an inherent tension in the way the Spanish-language term *loca* circulates among Latin American and Latinx women and among some feminists, and this tension affects queer deployments. In contrast to the partial recuperation of the literary character of the madwoman as a symbol of feminist resistance explored in the North American second-wave feminist classic *The Madwoman in the Attic* by Sandra M. Gilbert and Susan Gubar (1979), a widely influential scholarly volume named after a character in Charlotte Brontë's novel *Jane Eyre*, some Latina scholars have been more wary of engaging the radical potential of *locura* (madness), seeing it as linked to mental illness and not as a poetic trope or as a sign of radical revolt. One example is Marta Caminero-Santangelo's (1998) scholarly monograph *The Madwoman Can't Speak, or, Why Insanity Is Not Subversive*, where the critic rejects literary madness as liberatory; as she states, "My theoretical starting point is the suggestion that a search for the subversive madwoman in literature not only involves some violent repressions of its own . . . but also is fundamentally misguided, since the symbolic resolution of the madwoman as an alternative to patriarchy ultimately traps the woman in silence" (4).

Caminero-Santangelo's critical stance is echoed by Lyn Di Iorio Sandín (2004) in her *Killing Spanish: Literary Essays on Ambivalent U.S. Latino/a Identity*, where the Puerto Rican scholar points to the problems with the insistence on the madness of Latina women, particularly in the context of contemporary novels published in the United States in which the female protagonists consistently die. Other scholars such as Vilma Santiago-Ortiz (2001), Patricia Gherovici (2003), and Christopher Christian (2019) have also focused on Puerto Rican women and mental health issues in the diaspora through the lens of the medical and social sciences, including analyzing the *ataque de nervios*, also referenced as the "Puerto Rican syndrome."[6]

The threat of madness, of losing one's judgment and falling into the marginalized and excluded condition of she who does not have the use of reason, is anathema to many. For example, the Puerto Rican–Cape Verdean American feminist Caridad Souza (2001) rejects the term *loca* in her essay "Esta risa no es de loca" ("This Laughter Is Not That of a Madwoman"), included in the anthology *Telling to Live: Latina Feminist Testimonios*. The title of Souza's piece, as suggested by its epigraph, is a feminization of renowned Puerto Rican salsa singer Héctor Lavoe's verse "Esta risa no es de loco" (This laughter is not that of a madman) (Souza 2001, 114), the opening line of the song "Vamos a reír un poco" ("Let's Laugh a Little") from his 1976 album *De ti depende*.[7] In her *testimonio*, Souza discusses the all-too-present risks that she faces as the daughter of working-class immigrants, specifically as an Afro-descendant colonial subject in a context in which the unequal relations of power between the United States and Puerto Rico and the problems of poor women of color are not recognized.

For Souza, the silence that dominates gendered and racialized colonial relationships of exploitation (that of the unspeakable, what people prefer to downplay or not discuss in informal contexts) threatens to provoke madness, particularly given the effort to negotiate the cultural, social, and political contradictions of her life. In this context, the author affirms the power of laughter as an antidote, insisting that "laughter has always been a part of my survival mechanism" (2001, 122). Here Souza's performative laughter coincides with that of the French Algerian feminist Hélène Cixous as articulated in Cixous's classic essay "The Laugh of the Medusa" (1976), a laughter meant to empower women and resist phallogocentrism, racism, and colonialism through writing, but also through the physical and auditory gesture of a body that gives in to a powerful emotion and makes it tangible, visible, and audible; a somatic response to racialization (Fetta 2018). Souza's testimonial narrative, which also includes a black and white photo of her family dancing, posits writing as a tool of transformation and bridges Blackness and womanhood as sites of resistance, a key conceit of Cixous's essay.

For the Puerto Rican literary scholar Lisa Sánchez González (2001), the marginalization of Puerto Rican and Latina feminists in the United States affects everything.[8] In her book *Boricua Literature* the critic decries this situation in a bilingual and contestatory way, moving freely between English and Spanish, destabilizing dominant monolingualism and ideologies of linguistic purity. As Sánchez González writes, "Speaking from this contradictory space renders the Latina feminist quite painfully global, local, and ultimately, *loca en la boca*, transforming experience into an *escritura* both capable and incapable of 'competing with food' in our mouths (Deleuze and Guattari 1986)" (2001, 139).[9]

This condition of being *loca en la boca* (mad or crazy in the mouth), in which the affect of anger or the pathology of madness is gendered feminine, marked by the linguistic tensions between English and Spanish, creates the paradox of simultaneous intelligibility and confusion. In this way, the Puerto Rican feminist critic attempts to capture and transform Deleuze and Guattari's meditation on Franz Kafka's writing, that is to say, their conceit regarding the tension of a mouth that alternates between speaking and eating, which is mediated by the possibilities of writing; a mouth that is caught between basic instincts for nutrition and language's ability for symbolization, but particularly one negotiating the situation of the German language in Prague (initially as part of the Austro-Hungarian Empire, and then in Czechoslovakia) in contact with Czech and Yiddish, as was Kafka's case. The Puerto Rican critic argues that the challenges of this multilingual framework can also help us to understand the Latinx experience in the United States.

In her text, Sánchez González also affirms the need to speak of a feminism that is full of specificities, those of Latina feminism (Cotera 2017), a *loca*-lized feminism that challenges hegemonic feminism (that is to say, Anglo-American feminism written with an uppercase *F*) and that takes advantage of the pioneering decolonial Chicana feminist Emma Pérez's concept of "*un sitio y una lengua* (a space and language) that rejects colonial ideology" (Pérez 1991, 161), even when this project will be belittled. As Sánchez González writes, "*Loca*-lizing theory is often construed as a hysterical project, since speaking to and from a collective, radicalized, and unapologetically Latina-centric *lengua y sitio* (tongue and location) (Pérez 1991) means upsetting the Feminist establishment, only, in the end, to be dismissed, forgotten, or plagiarized" (2001, 139–40).[10] This sentiment echoes Pérez's own self-referential theoretical ruminations and the kinds of anecdotes she presents in her earlier piece.

Not all Latin American or Latinx self-identified feminists reject the utility of self-affirmation as *locas*; some advocate for the embrace of the term "translocas" as a sign of critical resistance. For example, the women who published the anthology *Translocalities/Translocalidades: Feminist Politics of Translation in the Latin/a Américas* (Alvarez et al. 2014) adopted the neologism "translocas," using the plural *locas* with the capitalized prefix "trans-," written with emphasis in the original. The Cuban American feminist scholar Sonia Alvarez has summarized this group's views, emphasizing "how feminist discourses and practices travel across a variety of sites and directionalities to become interpretive paradigms to read and write issues of class, gender, race, sexuality, migration, health, social movements, development, citizenship, politics and the circulation of identities and texts" (2014, 1).[11] As Alvarez points out,

> Because our transit across multiple boundaries disrupts the prevailing common sense in many of the localities through which we move in ways that sometimes make us seem outright mad (in a double sense), we early on adopted the nickname *Translocas* for the cross-disciplinary, cross-border research group of Latina and Latin American(ist) feminists who brought this edited collection into being. (2014, 3)

This double sense of mad (as angry and crazy) and of performing madness negotiates forces that can empower but also stigmatize. While "translocas" is not used in their case principally in relation to homosexuality or to the transgression of male gender, Alvarez does indicate that "we embrace the transgressive, queer, transgendered sense of the term as well" (2014, 4).

In an endnote, Alvarez credits the deceased Chicano gay scholar Lionel Cantú Jr., a specialist on Mexican gay male migration to the United States, for coining the term:

> Lionel Cantú was the first to call our group Translocas and was among the most enthusiastic and insightful founding members of our Transnational Feminist Politics of Translation research group, the "most *loca* of all," as he liked to say. This book is dedicated to his memory. His untimely death in the early stages of this project was an inestimable emotional and intellectual loss for Translocas and all those who knew and loved him. (Alvarez 2014, 18 n. 3)

Lionel Cantú Jr.'s participation in a transnational feminist Latinx/Latin American research group and his performative insistence that he was *la más loca de todas* (an affirmation that we can imagine accompanied by gestural and tonal signification, perhaps a high pitch and waving hands) signals a different model for collaboration that values humor or light-heartedness along with serious commitment, and that does not envision the two as a contradiction. Cantú's gesture sees the intrinsic interlocking dynamics of gender and sexuality and the benefits of collaborative research that is not based on essentialist notions of identity or on the perception that only women can be feminists.[12] Early publications stemming from the *Translocalities/Translocalidades* project, including a version of Alvarez's introduction published in Brazil in 2009, neglected to mention Cantú's role and the centrality of queerness.[13] I like to think of my own work, and this book in particular, as an extension of his insights, and as a modest homage.

The queerness and potential humor of *loca* is polysemic and multifarious. Like Sánchez González, the Colombian American feminist anthropologist Marcia Ochoa takes advantage of fragmented spellings of the word "localizing" in multiple languages by separating the verb *localizar* in Spanish and *localize* in English, using a hyphen after the root (in Spanish, the lexeme *loc* and its morpheme *a*, separated from the morphemes *-lizando* or, in English, *-lizing*) in her own bilingual research about the situation of transgender sex workers in Venezuela, as she discusses in her articles "Ciudadanía perversa: Divas, marginación y participación en la 'loca-lización'" (2004) and "Perverse Citizenship: Divas, Marginality, and Participation in 'Loca-lization'" (2008).[14] Here, Ochoa is interested primarily in locating herself as a queer Latinx ethnographer, or as she says, "a butch dyke baby of the Colombian brain drain, coming to consciousness

as a gender-nonconforming 'foreigner' in the United States of America"
(2008, 152) who is similar to but also markedly different from her Venezuelan interlocutors. She also wishes to flesh out the multiple performative
meanings of the term *loca*, particularly as a synonym for "diva," encom-
passing but also different from *transformista*, which is the preferred term
for transgender sex workers on Avenida Libertador in Caracas, the subject
of Ochoa's research.[15] As Ochoa writes:

> Those who are "fabulous" sometimes appear as divas or *locas*. Of
> course, I use *loca* in its most generous and honorific sense, as a cate-
> gory used in many places *de ambiente* to refer to its boldest and most
> scandalous actors. The word is used to refer to effeminate gay men
> and also to *transformistas* and transgender women. (2008, 151–52)

For Ochoa, *loca* is a useful signifier, whose multiplicity of meanings
facilitates critical feminist ethnographic work. Further in her essay, she
explains:

> I am drawn to *locas* because although I fit quite easily into a "good"
> citizenship, I too have experienced the process of marginalization,
> and I want to understand how power and marginalization work so
> that we can begin to imagine the possibilities of our collective sur-
> vival. I am drawn to *peluqueras* (hairdressers), *divas*, *locas*, and *putas*
> both because in my experience I have always been legible to them
> and because they often scandalize me. In my community, they have
> been those willing to take risks, *las atrevidas*. These trans women
> are important to me precisely because they complicate the political
> project; they are the ones who bring shame upon themselves, their
> families, the nation. And they are not afraid of this shame; rather,
> they embrace it, turn it around, use it as a weapon. (2008, 152)

Ochoa's highlighting of *loca* strategies of survival and shamelessness,
which she fleshes out in relation to Don Kulick and Charles Klein's (2009)
research on *travestis* in Brazil, is useful in relation to diasporic Puerto
Rican translocas such as the Stonewall pioneer Sylvia Rivera, the actress
Holly Woodlawn (whom Ochoa cites), and the drag performer Mario
Montez, who was similarly faced with situations of humiliation, as the
ample scholarship on Montez's treatment in Andy Warhol's reality-based,
somewhat improvised film *Screen Test #2* (1965) attests; in Montez's case,

I have argued elsewhere (La Fountain-Stokes 2011a) that *sinvergüencería* (shamelessness) becomes a deliberate strategy to maintain personal dignity and camp conceptions of beauty and glamour in a hostile environment, specifically while posing as an aspiring Hollywood film star that is being screamed at and interrogated by an irate off-camera director played by Ronald Tavel.[16] In Ochoa's work, *locas* have as much to do with abjection as they do with glamour, a tension that the Brazilian anthropologist Larissa Pelúcio (2009) also highlights when writing about Latin American trans sex workers in Europe. Unfortunately, Ochoa moves away from a sustained engagement with the term *loca* in her book-length exploration titled *Queen for a Day:* Transformistas, *Beauty Queens, and the Performance of Femininity in Venezuela* (2014).

The Unease of Loca: *Queer Latina/o American and Latinx Debates*

Ochoa's initial embrace of the multiple possibilities of *loca* to express her personal subject position and the experiences of her interlocutors is refreshing, particularly when we consider how stigmatized the term is. This is particularly evident when contrasted to the findings of Latina sociologist Marysol Asencio in her article "'Locas,' Respect, and Masculinity: Gender Conformity in Migrant Puerto Rican Gay Masculinities" (2011), which resonates with some but not all of the ethnographic findings of Rafael L. Ramírez (1993, 1999), Horacio Federico Sívori (2004), Carlos Ulises Decena (2011), Susana Peña (2013), and María Amelia Viteri (2014). Asencio's empirical research documents contradictory and highly charged feelings regarding the use of the pejorative or stigmatizing usage of *loca* among thirty-seven masculine-identified Puerto Rican gay men in the United States "who had been raised in Puerto Rico and migrated Stateside as adults" (2011, 335). The scholar identifies strong (what seems to be almost vitriolic, homophobic, or transphobic) resistance to the usage of the term:

> Most of these migrant men note the importance of masculinity in their development and interactions with others, particularly other men. They resist identification of themselves as effeminate and distance themselves from locas (effeminate gay men). They associate locas with overt homosexuality, disrespect, and marginality. (Asencio 2011, 335)

Here *loca* appears as absolutely undesirable, the synthesis and focus of all abjection and stigma. "If only we could get rid of *locas*, everything would be alright," her interviewees seem to suggest, as they centralize all of their problems with effeminateness in homosexual men (particularly its Puerto Rican variant), and rush toward the modernity of Anglo-American "straight-acting," masculine gayness, identified with the English language and with the "equal partners" model that envisions relationships between two masculine, gay-identified men that are perceived as "equal" in their social status and who are not stigmatized by the Latin American *activo/pasivo* dichotomy (Vidal-Ortiz et al. 2010).

Asencio builds on the earlier work of the Puerto Rican anthropologist Rafael L. Ramírez (1993, 1999), who agrees that effeminacy and homosexuality are stigmatized in Puerto Rican society, particularly linked to the term *maricón* (the augmentative of *marica*) but who is more generous in the multiple significations he sees for *loca*. Ramírez ascertains the highly gendered nature of Puerto Rican social relations and the correlation between masculinity and power, identifying this system as sexist, seeing "sexism" as a more accurate term that "machismo," which is culturally coded and discriminatory, as it suggests that Latino men, Hispanic culture, and the Spanish language are intrinsically more biased or patriarchal than American men, American culture, and the English language.[17] Ramírez also acknowledges the complexity of *el ambiente* (the gay social world or scene), which he identifies as very heterogeneous and constituted in opposition to "straights," who are unaware and do not interact with it. Within the *ambiente*, he proposes the categories of *entendido* (a person in the know), *ponca* (a weak male, or a man whose gender expression or self-presentation is perceived as gay because of feminine mannerisms but who does not claim a gay identity), *bugarrón* (a masculine-acting man who has sex with men and does not self-identify as queer), and *loca*, a term he contrasts to the more modern (and recent) "gay." Here, *loca* is seen as a vernacular category for homosexuality, marked by a wide range of effeminateness (from slight to dramatic) and perceptions of sexual passivity (being the receptor) that might or might not accurately respond to actual practices. As Ramírez indicates about *loca*:

> This category is the most diverse and most complex. It is made up of a very heterogeneous population that differs in at least six main characteristics: (1) the degree of acceptance of his sexuality; (2) the level of participation in *el ambiente*; (3) sexual preferences; (4) ges-

tures, bearing, dress, in addition to position and presentation in the continuum associated with the masculine-effeminate feminine; (5) color, class, education, and occupation; and (6) place of residence. (1999, 98)

In Ramírez's model, greatest scorn is reserved for *poncas*, given their ambiguous relationship to *el ambiente*, as well as for *locas vestidas* and *locas partidas*. The greater stigma of these last two categories, which are linked to effeminacy and cross-dressing, is class specific and linked to social prestige:

> The higher in the ranks of class, color, power, and occupation, the more we tend to find a tendency to present a manly bearing, at least in public. In those circles, *locas vestidas* (drag queens), who are men who dress like women, or *locas partidas*, who are men who look too effeminate, are not accepted. *Locas partidas* are seen more frequently in the lower strata of the social classes. (1999, 101)

This class specificity does not map onto Asencio's sample, as the scholar describes gay diasporic Puerto Rican men from a range of social classes expressing hostility to *locas*. It does seem to correlate to Decena's (2011) work.

Ramírez's early scholarship can be seen as indebted to the leading exiled gay Cuban writer Reinaldo Arenas's landmark description of *locas* in his 1992 autobiography *Antes que anochezca* (*Before Night Falls*). In the well-known chapter "Las cuatro categorías de las locas," unfortunately presented in Dolores M. Koch's 1993 translation as "The Four Categories of Gays," Arenas states his motivations for his taxonomy as one based on observation, analysis, and the desire to explain variation: "Atendiendo a aquellas diferencias tan grandes entre unos y otros homosexuales, establecí unas categorías entre ellos" (1992, 103) ("Noting the substantial differences among homosexuals, I established some categories" [1993, 77]). Arenas proposes the following four: *la loca de argolla*, *la loca común*, *la loca tapada*, and *la loca regia* (1992, 103–4), which Koch translates as "dog collar gay," "common gay," "closet gay," and "royal gay" (1993, 77–78).[18] Sadly, this translation flattens the Spanish-language vernacular category of *loca*, unwittingly contributing to the internationalization of an American-specific, historically bound concept ("gay"), a term that Arenas rejects in favor of *locas* and *homosexuales*.[19] Arenas reserves the most severe critique for the *locas regias* ("royal gays"), that is to say, individuals who are integrated into the Cuban revolutionary regime and who receive state protection.

In Julian Schnabel's 2000 biopic *Before Night Falls*, the Spanish actor Javier Bardem appears as Reinaldo Arenas, fully tropicalizing himself to offer an extraordinary performance in which he describes the four categories of *locas*; the American actor Johnny Depp portrays a *loca de argolla*, the most abject *loca* of all, in his role as the incarcerated drag queen Bon Bon (AFI 2017).[20] Locas are also central to other Cuban film representations such as *Strawberry and Chocolate* (Gutiérrez Alea and Tabío 1993), *Butterflies on the Scaffold* (Gilpin and Bernaza 1996), *Las noches de Constantinopla* (Rojas 2002), *Fátima o el Parque de la Fraternidad* (Perugorría 2015), and *Viva* (Breathnach 2016).[21] While *locas* are key to Arenas and to Schnabel's film adaptation, it is notable that in later publications, the Puerto Rican Ramírez and his coauthors Víctor I. García Toro and Luis Solano Castillo (2005, 2007) also minimize the usage of the term *loca* in favor of the term "gay."

The complex negotiation of local or vernacular categories alongside new terms emanating from the global North also appears in Horacio Federico Sívori's ethnographic study *Locas, chongos y gays: Sociabilidad homosexual masculina durante la década de 1990* (2004). Here the anthropologist maps out three subject positions or labels for men who have sex with men in the city of Rosario, Argentina, in the 1990s: (1) the stigmatized *locas*, referring to effeminate homosexuals, but also used by militant (activist) gays as a sign of affirmation, along with the equally stigmatized term *putos*; (2) *chongos* (the equivalent to the Puerto Rican category of *bugarrón*), a term used by *locas* and others to describe men who perceive themselves to be masculine, not stigmatized by effeminacy, and who are not socially recognized or self-identify as homosexuals, but who have sex with *locas*; and (3) "gays," who adopt international or cosmopolitan models of public self-identification and masculine behavior, at times reject effeminacy, distance themselves from the label *locas*, and demand civil recognition. Sívori refrains from offering value judgments on these positions and is more interested in the interplay between the three.

Asencio, Ramírez, Arenas, and Sívori complement Ochoa's analytic interest in *loca*, mapping its use in Puerto Rico, Argentina, Cuba, and Venezuela. The term is also relevant elsewhere across the Americas, as other scholars have shown. The Ecuadorian anthropologist María Amelia Viteri, for example, dedicates a chapter in her ethnographic study *Desbordes: Translating Racial, Ethnic, Sexual, and Gender Identities across the*

Americas to "The Meanings around 'Loca'" (2014, 21–48), analyzing interviews with several Central American immigrants in Washington, DC, with an activist in El Salvador, and with several informants in Ecuador, about how they use English- and Spanish-language vocabulary to mark sexual and gender identities. Viteri is interested in ascertaining whether *loca* can serve as an alternative to the English-language term "queer," ultimately arguing against translation, signaling the complexities of the term and how it varies according to context. As an unstable signifier, *loca* (along with *machorra, las fuertes,* and other geographically specific terms) signals difference, particularly for diasporic or migrant subjects who live in translation.

Closer to Ochoa, the Puerto Rican sociologist Salvador Vidal-Ortiz (2011) discusses the use of the terms *maricón, pájaro,* and *loca* by diasporic Hispanic Caribbean people in the United States, signaling how new usages for stigmatized language arise among Puerto Rican and Cuban practitioners of the Afro-Caribbean religion of Santería, particularly but not exclusively among sexual minorities. Vidal-Ortiz indicates that there is "an inherent resignification of the terms commonly used as detrimental" (902) in which both queer and nonqueer persons use these terms as in-group, neutral, or nonjudgmental terms, which are seen as useful, nonstigmatized ways to relate to each other.

Other symbolic and quotidian valorizations of *loca* also occur among Cuban American drag queens and gay men, particularly in Florida, as Lázaro Lima (2005) and Susana Peña (2013) insightfully demonstrate. While Lima focuses in his article "Locas al Rescate: The Transnational Hauntings of Queer *Cubanidad*" on a memorable mid-1990s appearance by the drag queen Mar Tini as the Virgen de la Caridad del Cobre (Our Lady of Charity), the patroness of Cuba, in the midst of a South Beach gay dance club as a way to challenge Cuban American homophobia, Peña capitalizes on the centrality of the term *loca* in the title of her book, *¡Oye Loca! From the Mariel Boatlift to Gay Cuban Miami,* referencing the term as a marker of vernacular Cuban expression that is resisted, condemned, and transformed in the diaspora, for example through the recuperative (at times radical, at times conservative) performances of monolingual and bilingual Cuban and Cuban American drag queens.[22] Peña also documents the social organization of same-sex attractions and identities exemplified through the taxonomy of *locas, papis* (masculine men), and "muscle queens," an identity that comes closer to the American category of gay (2013, 133–56).

The two final scholarly examples I will discuss serve to reassess and emphasize the vexed complexity of *loca* and its centrality for literary, cultural, and performance analysis. In his ethnographic study *Tacit Subjects: Belonging and Same-Sex Desire among Dominican Immigrant Men*, the Dominican American scholar Carlos Ulises Decena (2011) offers one of the most extensive and nuanced discussions available of *loca* in a Latinx context. Similar to Asencio, Peña, Sívori, and Viteri, Decena notes resistance and anxiety around male effeminacy and the category of *loca*. At the same time, he proposes *loca* as central to self-conceptualizations, interpersonal relations, and community identity, seeing the term as an ambivalent signifier that masculine and feminine gay Dominican men and trans women move through in their daily lives as they interact with others in New York City and in the Dominican Republic. Drawing on the work of Ben. Sifuentes-Jáuregui (2002) on literary representations of transvestism in Latin America and on J. L. Austin's and Judith Butler's discussions of performativity, Decena presents *loca* as "a *gynographic performative*, an 'imagined form of femininity' staged as excess on a male body" (2011, 115). As he indicates, "La loca is not the abjected and repudiated identification for the production of coherence in the informants' subject positions . . . La loca operates in disparate ways that give shape to the boundaries the informants established with others and to their sense of comfort or discomfort with their surroundings" (2011, 115–16).

Building on the linguistic concept of code-switching (moving from one register, dialect, or language to another), particularly as analyzed in diasporic Puerto Rican settings by the anthropolitical linguist Ana Celia Zentella (1997), Decena also proposes the term "code swishing" as a way to describe and understand the contextual, performative nature of multiple forms of self-presentation in a patriarchal context that stigmatizes effeminacy. As he writes:

> *Code swishing* names communicative practices the informants deployed to engage the worlds and the others who surrounded them . . . it implicates gender dissent—in the invocation of la loca or of the humor, or *mariconería*, associated with that performative—as a communicative practice with a polyvalent expressive potential in daily life. La loca may be the target of ridicule but also often is a performative invoked to index proximity and affective intimacy. (2011, 142)

For his study, Decena interviewed men who identified as *locas* as well as ones who rejected this category and monitored each other's behavior. The scholar also offers ethnographic observations of multiple groups of men, including younger, darker-skinned, working-class men "engaging in pretty flamboyant behavior" (161), who were simultaneously dismissed and admired by older, middle-class, lighter-skinned Dominican men. These interviews and ethnographic observations confirm the centrality of the *loca* and "the political implications of effeminacy as communicative practice" that "extends well beyond foundational narratives of homosexual abjection" (2011, 171). Most importantly, Decena's theorization of the complex, slippery, central role of *locas* captures the oscillation between rebellious transgression and abjection.

Finally, it is valuable to highlight how the valorization of *loca* as an untranslatable epistemological category or liberatory *devenir* (becoming) and as a performative stance that appears in the work of Decena, Peña, and to a certain extent Sívori, also profoundly marks Latin American literary and performative representations and their critical analysis. Literary scholar Paola Arboleda Ríos identifies the centrality of *la loca* in the work of the Chilean Pedro Lemebel (perhaps the Latin American writer most closely associated with the category of *la loca* in recent times), the Argentine Néstor Perlongher, and the aforementioned Reinaldo Arenas, seeing *loca* as a way to move toward or come in dialogue with US theorizations of "queer" as rupture and dislocation in a Latin American context, a phenomenon also present in the work of the leading gay Mexican intellectual Carlos Monsiváis (2010).[23] Inspired by Perlongher's engagement with Deleuze and Guattari, Arboleda Ríos writes about the recuperation of madness, of becoming a mad/woman ("del devenir *loca*-mujer," 2011, 115) and of "*incontables devenires no-heteronormativos*, que sencillamente no caben dentro de ciertos modelos teóricos y que requieren de discursos propios que sean a-locada y dis-locadamente *queer*" (innumerable non-heteronormative becomings that simply do not fit within certain theoretical models and that require their own mad and dis-located *queer* discourses) (2011, 120). Arboleda Ríos's analysis highlights how literary texts and declarations by writers and performers can serve as a complement or counterpoint to social science research, as seen earlier in Ramírez's reinterpretation of Arenas's taxonomy.

Arboleda Ríos's interest in Lemebel's literary ruminations on *loca* was greatly expanded through Lemebel's performative practice, both his public self-presentation as a mestizo *travesti* writing subject and his performance collaborations with Francisco (Pancho) Casas as part of the ensemble Las Yeguas del Apocalipsis (The Mares of the Apocalypse), whose artistic creations were structured around the material embodiment of *loca* subjects as political actors defying Augusto Pinochet's dictatorship in Chile in the late 1980s as well as the heteronormativity, conservatism, and racism of Chilean society during the early 1990s transition to democracy. The ample photographic and video documentation of Las Yeguas del Apocalipsis highlights the crossings of leftist politics and gender transgression (Franco 1999; Richard 2004b, 2018). This is also a mark of the scholarship and performance work of artists such as the Peruvian Giuseppe Campuzano (2008, 2013), the Dominican Waddys Jáquez (Stevens 2019), the Spaniard Ocaña (Preciado 2011), the Mexicans Tito Vasconcelos and Lukas Avendaño (Gutiérrez 2010; Prieto Stambaugh 2000, 2014), and numerous others such as the Brazilian group Dzi Croquettes and the Mexican Lechedevirgen Trimegisto (Felipe Osornio) analyzed by Antonio Prieto Stambaugh (2019).

I began this chapter by citing Arboleda Ríos in an epigraph: "What does *queerness* need to become *locura*, in the Latin American style, in the style of Perlongher, Lemebel, or Arenas? It needs race, class; it needs social reality and politics; and seemingly, it needs love" (2011, 121). In her statement, Arboleda Ríos coincides with some of the central arguments of the queer- and trans-of-color critique, namely the contention that American mainstream gay, queer (and to a different extent, trans) theory has resisted recognizing race and social class as relevant determinants for social experience.[24] She also highlights the centrality of love, a critical stance in line with thinkers as diverse as Dr. Martin Luther King Jr., Bob Marley (famous for his song "One Love"), and the Chicana scholar Chela Sandoval (2000); this invocation of love, a hallmark of the transloca astrologer Walter Mercado's signature blessing "mucho, mucho amor," will reappear later in this book, for example in the Puerto Rican trans performer Lady Catiria's conceptualization of community and survival in the face of AIDS (chapter 7). Love, in this context, is an affect of solidarity and a sign of strategic embrace that encourages collaborations and resists paranoid animosities and hatreds; it is a rhizomatic gesture that envisions new possibilities. Arboleda Ríos's invitation that we surpass the limitations of queerness through *locura* leads us to broader consideration of *transloca epistemologies*, or ways of knowing, and of *transloca embodiments*, as I will now explore in chapter 2.

TWO

Transloca Epistemologies

Nina Flowers, Jorge Steven López Mercado, and Kevin Fret

Llámate a la loca.
Búscate a la loca.
¿Dónde está la loca?
Work it, loca!
   —Nina Flowers, "Loca" (2009)

Who is the transloca? What does she know? How does she know? What transloca are we talking about? The transloca who displaces herself, who dances in a club, who sings and earns her living entertaining an audience. The one who theorizes and gives academic talks at international conferences, who teaches at the university level, who writes and publishes books and who sometimes takes her medications for HIV and AIDS. The one who goes to school and works the streets at night and then hangs out with friends at a bar, except that one night that she got into the wrong car or said hello to the wrong person. The effeminate, feminine, rebel one; the one who laughs too much and loves without control. The one who records songs and makes videos and appears on reality television programs. The one we celebrate and hate and recognize or ignore: the assassinated, beheaded, dismembered, or burned one.[1] The transloca I carry inside. The transloca I do not or you did not want to be. The feared transloca. The transloca of alterity. The capitalist transloca, inserted in the neoliberal logic of the market. The transloca that escapes, challenges, and defrauds capitalism; the one who disappears with her debts and spends money without control, like "la Loca," the protagonist of Ángel Lozada's (2006) critically acclaimed novel *No quiero quedarme sola y vacía*.[2] The transloca as a sign of the unwanted, of breakdown, of failure, of the unspeakable.

The transloca as negation or as a sign of liberty. The transloca as a consumer product. The transloca as Other. The transloca who I am, who we are. The transloca who nobody wants to be.

Knowing Joy: Nina Flowers or "La Nina Loca"

At the heart of thinking about Puerto Rican translocas, of transloca performance as a critical practice, and of *translocura* as an analytic or epistemology, is the central paradox of contradiction: *la loca* as a sign of life and death, joy and suffering, mediated through violence. I will first address this paradox by focusing on two very different individuals called Jorge: one, a globally recognized drag entertainer, Jorge Flores, better known as Nina Flowers, who achieved international recognition in 2009; the other a murdered nineteen-year-old, Jorge Steven López Mercado, whose body was brutally dismembered by their assailant in Puerto Rico, also in 2009. I will then move on to a more recent case of violence, that of the openly gay, effeminate trap singer Kevin Fret, who was shot to death in Puerto Rico at the age of twenty-five in January 2019. These figures, read as resisting and succumbing to the violent logics of "queer necropolitics" (Haritaworn, Kuntsman, and Posocco 2014) and "trans necropolitics" (Snorton and Haritaworn 2013), illuminate as much as complicate the arguments of my book. In this context, staying alive is a major accomplishment.

The first case is that of transloca success: Nina Flowers, a self-described "fierce . . . fabulous . . . and unique" queen who sings and dances the *loca* and serves as a maximum exponent of *transloca jouissance*; a transnational transloca who became a transglocal signifier of Puerto Rican queer and drag *eleganza* and "extravaganza."[3] Born in Bayamón, Puerto Rico, on February 22, 1974, Jorge Luis Flores Sánchez started out as a makeup artist who did drag in the early 1990s with a group of friends and went to the clubs; "This woke up a monster, because after that I was really into performing" (WOWPresents 2013). Similar to the renowned artist Antonio Pantojas (Laureano 2007), Flowers initially appeared on stage using her birth name of Jorge Flores but transitioned to the name Nina Flowers in 1999, when she participated in her first drag pageant. As Flowers has indicated, her drag name is a tribute to the German punk singer and actress Nina Hagen combined with a translation of Jorge's last name to English (Logo 2013); she credits 1980s British artists such as Boy George, Pete Burns, and Annie Lennox as the biggest inspirations for her androgynous drag style, which incorporates numerous punk and "freak" elements such as mohawk hairstyles and foam horns, linking her performance to the monstrous and freakish cases Analola Santana (2018) discusses in *Freak Performances: Dissidence in Latin American Theater*.[4]

Flowers became a global mass-media transloca in 2009 thanks to the first season of the television reality competition *RuPaul's Drag Race*. This happened after a fifteen-year career in Puerto Rico, having already won the Miss Puerto Rico Continental drag pageant twice, serving for seven years as the host of a show at Krash/Eros nightclub in San Juan, and after moving in 2008 to Denver, Colorado, where she went to live with her partner (now husband), the Panamanian American public health worker and bodybuilder Antonio Purcell de Ogenio, with whom she had previously maintained a long-distance relationship.[5] In videos available on YouTube and in several episodes of *RuPaul's Drag Race*, Flowers stresses her positive relationship with her family, whom she describes as extremely loving and supportive (Logo 2013).[6] And, as she explains, "I like to be different. I like to be authentic. Ah, my God, I've been called so many names. I've been called clown, I've been called this, I've been called that. I really don't care" (WOWPresents 2013).

American reality television can be a treacherous site for racialized, gender-nonconforming Puerto Ricans who do not speak Standard American English (Anthony 2014; Mayora 2014). A case in point: Nina Flowers is best known as the first runner-up (and not the winner) of her season of *RuPaul's Drag Race*, and her inclusion and exclusion was determined as much by her unusual gender presentation as by her limited command of the English language and generous use of the exclamation "¡Loca!" in a predominantly monolingual American TV program. As the scholar Matthew Goldmark has carefully pointed out, "Nina sheds light on the linguistic requirements of *Drag Race* by signaling English proficiency as part of the competition itself. . . . Nina's language thus paradoxically amplifies and minimizes her potential disruption" (2015, 512); Nina's language racializes her unfavorably and marks her as Other, in a context in which language becomes a marker for exclusion (Rosa 2019; Zentella 2014).[7] Flowers made it onto the show thanks to the internet votes of her admirers, bringing her *locura* and conquering hearts. While she lost the crown to the Cameroonian American first-generation immigrant contestant BeBe Zahara Benet (Nea Marshall Kudi Ngwa), who came to the United States in her early twenties, had a more normative feminine gender presentation, and spoke English with a French accent, the Puerto Rican contestant did win the Miss Congeniality prize, also selected through the online votes of her fans.

Flowers's first appearance on *RuPaul's Drag Race*, her entrance to the

Fig. 3. Nina Flowers at Spin Nightclub in Chicago, May 2010. Photo by Anthony Meade, Bear Lens Photography.

competition workroom in episode 1 ("Drag on a Dime") first transmitted on February 2, 2009, was marked by her very particular androgynous style and by her costume, which honored the floral motif in her performance name: she appeared wearing a bright orange and red, Pucci-like sunflower-patterned pantsuit with a wide collar, cinched at the waist with a corset-like large orange belt; large, sparkly, ornate gold costume jewelry; and dramatic makeup, including very pale white foundation and dark orange eyeshadow that extended in a harsh diagonal line well beyond the eyelid onto the side of the head, which was clean-shaven and sported a compact, nearly foot-high, blond, straight-hair wig attached to the top, coiffed to look like a solid mohawk that culminated in one strand on her forehead, as if a tiny horn.

Flowers's self-presentation, including her nearly bald head, was in dramatic contrast to the more traditional feminine style of other contestants, such as the white American performer Shannel (Bryan Watkins), who reacted to Flowers's appearance cattily, saying: "You're painted! Painted out of your mind," a throwaway comment invoking *translocura* as a sign of mental illness or madness.[8] This first episode then cut to a confessional-style, private declaration by Flowers in which she stated: "I don't consider myself as a female impersonator. I like to be more androgynous. It's an extravaganza," an invocation that pointed precisely to the exaggerated, dramatic, and unnatural dimension of her appearance.[9]

Flowers's complex gender negotiations were further emphasized later on in the same episode when all of the contestants changed out of their initial outfits. In this sequence, we hear another contestant, the African American drag queen Akashia (Eric Flint), say: "Nina surprised me because she is covered in tattoos," or as she said more directly to Flowers, "All right! You all tatted up." We also overhear someone say, "She's rough trade over there," a campy reference to working-class masculinity, specifically to men who have sex with men for pay and do not self-identify as gay; here, the contrast between the female pronoun "she" and the male descriptor "rough trade" marks humor. Finally, in a private confessional, the southern, white contestant Victoria "Porkchop" Parker (Victor Bowling), the oldest member of the group and the first eliminated, said: "The largest transformation to me was Nina Flowers. When she got out of drag, she had on a wifebeater [a sleeveless undershirt] and was tattooed from head to toe. She looks like a dude!," an affirmation that further extends the perception of Nina as a possibly threatening, racialized, and perhaps sexualized, attractive working-class man, as if she were a gang member, in contradistinction to her solidly middle-class family background, as illustrated in multiple childhood photos that appear in episode 7 ("Extra Special Edition").[10]

Nina is portrayed in the same inaugural episode as very aware of the reactions she generates: "I'm pretty sure that some people are not very comfortable about the kind of drag that I do, but that's exactly what makes me stand out, that I'm different." The judges also leveled this accusation of harshness, associated with masculinity, regarding the second outfit Flowers presented as part of the "Drag on a Dime" episode, which consisted of a challenge to create a glamorous drag look using hand-me-downs and "a whole lot of crap from the Dollar Store." While some judges celebrated and fetishized her, as in fashion designer Santino's comment, "Oh, *mami*! I can't get over your outfit. It's got like that real aggression and real twisted beauty about it," lead judge and host RuPaul Charles (better known by the moniker RuPaul) advocated for more femininity and gender conformity: "Your image is so strong. I'd love to see a softer side of Miss Flowers. I want to see the flower." Flowers proceeded to win the challenge, in spite of this tension, with celebrity guest judge and fashion designer Bob Mackie describing her outfit's "hard edge and . . . drama" combined with "sweetness, little flowers cascading on the shoulders," or as judge Merle Ginsberg put it, with a touch of exoticization: "It's dramatic and it's a little scary and I like that." Nina Flowers's fear-and-anxiety-inducing difference had to do with her appearance and style in and out of drag but also extended to her disruptive language use on the show, marked by the insertion of Spanish words and by difficulties with English.

Curiously, Flowers was never portrayed saying "loca" in the first six episodes of season 1, although she was featured dramatically using the term as early as episode 3 ("This Is Your Name. Good Night!") of *Under the Hood* (2009), a "behind the scenes" miniseries available on the Logo TV website and on YouTube that by the next season became known as *Untucked*. The lack of inclusion of clips of Nina saying "loca" in the first six episodes suggests that the producers of the show wanted to minimize linguistic difference, particularly the use of Spanish, perhaps afraid of its potential impact on ratings; Latinx presence on mainstream English-language American television has consistently been minimal and has been marked by stigmatizing stereotypes (Beltrán 2017; Valdivia 2010), and while Puerto Rican contestants frequently appear on *RuPaul's Drag Race*, there is an effort to contain their difference and to make them fit into pre-established roles.

It is only in episode 7 of *Drag Race* ("Extra Special Edition") that RuPaul introduces *loca* as Nina's distinctive catchphrase, competing with the multiple sayings the show's creator is famous for. RuPaul begins the segment by stating: "In my opinion every great television show has a catchphrase. This one has several. And they're all mine." We then see a montage of clips featuring some of these, including RuPaul's insistence on the need for "charisma, uniqueness, nerve, and talent," whose initials unabashedly spell out the word "cunt," a vulgar synonym for vagina that is also used as an insult for women, but that here is proposed as an edgy reference in RuPaul's gender play predicated on double entendres, benefiting from the Black gayspeak or slang meaning of "cunt" as fierce, used "to denote when another gay man is displaying a strong, favorable and diva demeanor" (Shay 2012).

RuPaul promotes hyperattention and repeated use of his catchphrases in the show as a means to hook participants and spectators, part of his strategic use of a personal philosophy as part of his brand.[11] "But the one contestant who gave me a run for my money was Nina, or should I say La Nina Loca," RuPaul indicates, as we transition to see a quick montage of eleven short clips, eight of them with Flowers using the term, and three with two other contestants: the Filipino American immigrant Ongina (Ryan Ong Palao) and BeBe Zahara Benet. The four queens will continue to be portrayed using the term *loca* in that episode and in the additional two of the season (number 8, "Grand Finale," and number 9, "Reunited!"); the two other Puerto Rican contestants, Jade (David) Sotomayor and Rebecca Glasscock (Javier Rivera), who are US born and/or raised, English-dominant, and younger, never appear using the term, highlighting a potential linguistic, generational, or diasporic divide.

RuPaul's transformation of *loca* from a noun used as an interjection ("¡Loca!") to an adjective ("La Nina Loca") is unsettling inasmuch as it shifts potential meanings away from Puerto Rican Spanish vernacular queer community usage toward more standard, pathological understandings, specifically that of seeing the subject (Nina) as crazy (*loca*). The pairing *la Nina loca* also suggests a homophonic variant, *la niña loca* (the crazy girl, an echo of *la vida loca*, or the crazy life), that is potentially unfavorable. The variation is not necessarily malicious and is most likely carried out in the spirit of jest and camp humor, but is nevertheless mediated by RuPaul's limited command of the Spanish language; in other instances, RuPaul has been shown as explicitly resisting any attempt to school her about Latinx queer culture, for example when Flowers portrayed the legendary Cuban diva and gay icon La Lupe (Guadalupe Victoria Yolí Raymond) in the first season of *RuPaul's Drag Race All Stars* in the episode titled "RuPaul's Gaff-In," which was first transmitted on October 22, 2012; Flowers's impersonation of La Lupe was met with little enthusiasm, and the contestant got eliminated from the show on that day, along with her partner Tammie Brown (Keith Glen Schubert).[12] Flowers was never portrayed repeating RuPaul's usage of *la Nina loca*.

Episode 7 of the first season of *RuPaul's Drag Race* also revisits an early use of *loca* that occurred during the filming of the third episode ("Queens of All Media") but was not included (an outtake), tied to Flowers's dramatic mistake while interviewing celebrity guests Tori Spelling and Dean McDermott in a mock talk show segment.[13] In this Oprah Winfrey–inspired challenge, Flowers stumbled with her cue card: Instead of asking Tori Spelling to tell her about her "hit TV show" *Tori & Dean: Home Sweet Hollywood*, she asked her interviewee to "tell me about your HIV." This linguistic faux pas or malapropism was met with humor by the celebrity guest couple but inserted a moment of abjection, mediated by linguistic incompetency.[14] Backstage, Flowers's dramatic exclamation, "*Loca*, I screwed up, *loca!*" stated directly into the camera as she took off her wig, created complicity and sympathy, causing the entire room to laugh; in a sense, Flowers was hailing her fellow cast members and the global audience of *RuPaul's Drag Race* as *locas* who can understand, even if also criticize, make fun of, or dismiss her for her mistake.

Capitalizing on her popularity after the end of season 1, Flowers released her first dance single titled "Loca" in December 2009, in collaboration with Ranny, a Brazilian DJ located in Boston who has worked with Lady Gaga and Britney Spears. This was followed by another dance single titled "Locas in Da House" in 2010, produced with William Umana. Subsequently, Flowers went on to appear in two additional TV programs: *RuPaul's Drag U* in 2010 and *RuPaul's Drag Race All Stars* in 2012. Since 2009, Flowers has triumphed as a DJ, appearing in her masculine attire, as a strong, muscular, shaved-head gay man heavily covered in tattoos; as a makeup artist; and as a drag performer who frequently lip-synchs her own songs and who serves as emcee in numerous clubs around the world. She has also appeared as a guest artist in a variety of music videos and songs, for example in Fior's "Backstabber" video on YouTube (Fior 2016).

As I have highlighted, Flowers's open and insistent affirmation of her *translocura* occurs mostly through the second-person nominative act, which is to say, the act of calling another person a *loca* with drama and flair, with the expectation that there will be a reciprocal act of naming, a phenomenon similar to the one that Horacio Federico Sívori (2004, 77–98) discusses in his book *Locas, chongos y gays*; as Sívori explains, "Locas 'produce themselves' . . . they 'become embodied' through language while also 'establishing' a context and a series of concrete references" (78).[15] This embodiment through language includes the repetition of specific words and the feminization of subjects, intonation, pitch, and volume, and transcends the oral register, integrating hand gestures, facial expressions, and other types of bodily enactments that make the declaration of the word "loca" an out-of-the-ordinary event, a break in everyday conversation, as if always accompanied with exclamations marks, even if simply whispered.

With Nina Flowers, there is no first-person affirmation of a condition such as "Soy o estoy loca" (that is to say, "I am a *loca*") similar to RuPaul's invocation of "la Nina loca," but rather the enunciation of "loca" as the interpellation of an/other: I call you *loca*, fully expecting you to call me *loca* back, even if you do not speak Spanish, as occurred when Ongina (who also sported a much-criticized shaved-head look) and BeBe called Nina *loca*, as Goldmark (2015) points out, even when BeBe was unable to pronounce Jorge's name in Spanish, a failure that led Flowers to exclaim, "¡Ay, loca!" in frustration.[16] Here, *loca* becomes the equivalent of the Anglo-American "girlfriend" or "girl," as if a queer interjection, or a queering of the more masculine "dude," a catchall term whose inflected repetition signals mutual recognition and community building, or what the sociolinguist Scott F. Kiesling (2004) refers to as "cool solidarity," but that can also be used to express other emotions.[17] The use of *loca* as a sign of solidarity was also apparent in the same episode when Flowers comforted Benet after the season winner collapsed to the ground at the news of her triumph; given Benet's lengthy immobility, Flowers eventually lost patience and said: "¡Ay, loca, please, come on, stand up!"

I am fascinated, intrigued, and perhaps even slightly disconcerted by the recuperation that Flowers effects on the word *loca*, entailing the destigmatization of the term and by extension of Puerto Rican queer drag practice, similar to RuPaul's more subtle destigmatization of the word "cunt." *Loca* is what you call me but also what I call you, repeatedly and insistently, what we dance to, the word that sticks like a label or a stamp. Or if not, *loca* becomes the word I use to speak of others in the third person when I describe what they do. It is the word that RuPaul and several other *Drag Race* contestants along with English- and Spanish-speaking transnational television audiences memorized and learned and went on to execute and pronounce in their joy and celebration, at least in 2009 (when the show was first aired) and since, although for many years only when the series was rebroadcast or viewed on clandestine websites or through pirated downloads that circulated among *RuPaul's Drag Race* connoisseurs.[18] For unclear reasons, season 1, also known as "The Lost Season" when it was rebroadcast on Logo TV in 2013, was not available on streaming platforms until 2019 (and is still not available in DVD format) and was fairly hard to see, which made the nine contestants from this season much less known that subsequent competitors, as season 1 winner BeBe Zahara Benet has observed (Desta 2017a).[19]

Nina Flowers's *loca* linguistic phenomenon represents a short circuit or jump over the traditional Hispanic and Spanish-language cultural and religious stigmatization discussed in the previous chapter, a leap above the unease associated with the epithet that circulates close to worse insults such as *pato, pájaro, joto,* or *maricón.*[20] The term *loca* arrived at *RuPaul's Drag Race* and elsewhere without the pain, as the most normal thing in the world, the symbol of the celebration of a very particular spectacular transfeminine alterity that did not correspond to a traditional reproduction of the feminine but rather to drag or transvestism as an aesthetic monstrosity, the "monster" Nina Flowers carries inside (WOWPresents 2013), something slightly frightening but not for this reason less beautiful; an embodiment and affirmation of androgyny and an illustration of a disconcerting yet simultaneously fascinating Other, a hybrid, possibly the graft of multiple animals or mythological beings or even extraterrestrials, decidedly not a conventional human.

> Ese ritmo caliente,
> el ritmo que te traigo,
> ese ritmo sabroso.
> El ritmo de la loca.
> All the locas in the house, can you hear me?
> Work, work, work, work!
>   (Flowers 2009)

In a 2009 YouTube video titled "Shannel and Nina Flowers at Drama Drag LOCA," recorded by an audience member at the Tracks Nightclub in Denver, Colorado, and uploaded by the user identified as LPATWCT (a possible acronym for country singer Keith Urban's album *Love, Pain and the Whole Crazy Thing*), we see Flowers's effusive interaction with her fans,

the collective euphoria, the marked contrast between the Boricua performer's beautiful, yet monstrous, hybrid appearance while lip-synching
her first musical hit "Loca" and that of the slender, ultrafeminized, seminaked white drag queen that preceded her, Shannel, the fellow *RuPaul's
Drag Race* season 1 contestant who appears lip-synching Fedde Le Grand
and Ida Corr's song "Let Me Think about It."[21] While Shannel represents
more typical notions of spectacular, erotic femininity, highlighted through
costume (a fetish-inspired, skimpy one-piece, black shiny women's bathing suit with multiple dangling silver chains that reveal a highly sensual
body, complemented with black gloves and high heel shoes with leather
straps going up her calves, an outfit that Shannel had already worn on
Drag Race in episode 4, "Mac Viva-Glam Challenge," while juggling on the
runway), Flowers's slightly more modest transloca aesthetics come closer
to those of the carnival or circus: she becomes a dwarf, a clown, a shaman, or a mythological figure decorated with her signature dramatic eye
makeup and sporting huge green Styrofoam horns that burst from her
clean-shaved head, as if a tiny minotaur or unicorn, like the Greek deity
Pan or the Roman Faun that leads her audience in a Dionysian celebration
in which music, lights, dance, and the consumption of diverse inebriating
substances lead to euphoria.[22]

At the same time, Flowers is a bilingual economic transloca who incites
her listeners to work or to exercise (on the runway, on the dance floor) and
who is working while she entertains us; a transloca who receives dollars
from her fans, who rush up to tip her in the midst of her performance
while she is dressed as a US dollar or perhaps as the Statue of Liberty in a
green, highly ruffled minidress with eyelets in the back, as if a corset, and
thigh-high gold boots, substituting the face of President George Washington from the dollar bill's front for her own and the incomplete pyramid
and eye-in-a-triangle that appear on the reverse of the Great Seal of the
United States on the dollar bill's back side with her horns, all in emerald
green foam covered with glitter (see figure 3).[23]

There is a certain magic in approaching a drag performer, in offering a
tribute of appreciation through cash and perhaps receiving a special touch
or a kiss or a look to be captured in a cell phone video or photo; audiences
enthusiastically tip drag entertainers while they perform, at least in the
United States and Puerto Rico, and the exchange entails sensual as well as
economic dimensions (Hankins 2015). At the same time, the exhortation
to work and the visibility of money (and perhaps of the American aspiration to "Life, Liberty, and the pursuit of Happiness") remind us that we

are witnessing a capitalist process: the desire for the neoliberal absorption of difference, under which Nina Flowers, a gay colonial subject and artist from the periphery who lives from performing in drag and deejaying, becomes a participant in the global entertainment industry, a fact that changes the impact and reception of her marginal art, even when she is doing exactly the same thing that she did when she was only known in the US colony, which is to say, present herself in small and large gay/queer clubs.

The public exchange of legal tender visualizes the political economy of transloca performance, transforming a gift into a metaphor that sustains and creates community at the same time that it commodifies and capitalizes popular culture (Marez 2017). Then again, if we see Flowers as the Statue of Liberty, her exhortation to work acquires different connotations, mediated by Puerto Ricans' complex colonial situation, as highlighted by the US Supreme Court's Insular Cases (1901); the 1903 case of Isabel González, who was seeking clarification of her right to enter, live in, and marry in the United States (*Gonzalez v. Williams*); Bernardo Vega's narration of first seeing the statue in New York Harbor in 1916 as he arrived from Puerto Rico; Pedro Pietri's 1969 lament in "Puerto Rican Obituary" about how "They worked / They worked / They worked / and they died" (2015, 3); and the Puerto Rican nationalist takeover of the statue and placement of a Puerto Rican flag on Lady Liberty's forehead in 1977.[24] In this context, *loca* serves as a sign of identity, community, and resistance, as much as a transnational or transglocal signifier of capitalist-oriented neoliberal entertainment.

Unknowing Death: Jorge Steven López Mercado

each time you repeat *iván* three times into the mirror,
he'll come back as a specter to wreak vengeance on his assassins.

each time you repeat *iván* three times into the mirror (2),
he'll be joined by the specter of jorge steven.
　—Raquel Salas Rivera, *The Tertiary / Lo terciario*

Violence marks transloca experience as much as work and money.[25] Nina Flowers's partial mass-media absorption and subsequent global success do not guarantee the full physical safety of all translocas (or even of Jorge

Flores), as we remain equally vulnerable to the homophobic and transphobic attacks and murders that we continue witnessing, for example, that
of Flowers's Puerto Rican namesake, the young Jorge Steven López Mercado, the nineteen-year-old gay/*loca*/*perra* subject from Caguas who was
killed and whose body was burned and dismembered and found in Barrio
Guavate, Cayey, Puerto Rico, on November 13, 2009, or more recently, the
murder of gay trap singer Kevin Fret, which occurred in San Juan on January 10, 2019.[26] López Mercado, known by his family and friends as Steven
and who self-identified on social media as "Stephen Miller" in honor of
the British-American actress Sienna Miller, was a working-class, light-
skinned, and conventionally pretty young activist and college student with
interests in fashion and in being a makeup artist who was described as
being "openly gay" by leading Puerto Rican LGBTQ activist Pedro Julio
Serrano (CNN 2009) and by Steven's partner, who also identified him as
nonbinary (Conti 2020). As news sources indicated, Steven was the son
of Miriam Mercado and of Jorge López, the nephew of Rubí Mercado, the
partner of Luis Conti (identified at the time in the press as Luis Rivera),
and the friend of José Alicea and Kiara Hernández (*El Nuevo Día* 2009a).
López Mercado presented themselves as a feminine gay subject, performing their preferred gender for others and for the camera, as documented
in photographs shared widely on the media after his murder and in tribute videos; in gay clubs and bars in San Juan such as Krash in Santurce;
and at drag pageants such as Road to Diva (Figueroa Rosa 2009). He was
friends and hung out with transgender women who engaged in sex work
in Caguas (Conti 2020), including at their sites of employment, and was
accused by his murderer of passing as a woman and of soliciting money
for sex (Rosario and Colón 2009). Steven was an avid fan of Lady Gaga,
and after his memorial service in Toa Alta, over one thousand mourners
listened to Gaga's anthem "Poker Face" en route to the cemetery (*El Nuevo
Día* 2009a).

López Mercado's death—and the murderer's grotesque dismember-
ment and disposal of the body—received significant local and transnational media and activist attention, was understood to be a hate crime, and
generated great anger after local police officer Angel Rodríguez accused
the victim of being responsible for his own death (Figueroa Rosa, Rivera
Quiñones, and Hernández 2009). The dramatic nature of the violence
was seen as the counterpart or backlash to LGBTQ legislative, social, and
cultural gains in some very specific locales.[27] It was, as the Puerto Rican
cultural studies scholar Licia Fiol-Matta wrote, "a crime with expressive

Fig. 4. Jorge Steven López Mercado circa 2009. Photographer unknown.

characteristics as his body was dismembered with the clear intention of sparking terror and reinstating a threatened masculinity (a gesture not that distant from the 'monster subjectivity' or *subjetividad endriaga* Sayak Valencia theorizes in her *Capitalismo gore)*" (2016, 228).[28] It was a killing that anticipated an audience as well as profound affective responses from horrified witnesses and spectators; a manifestation of necropolitics and (trans)femicide (Mbembe 2003; Rizki 2019; Snorton and Haritaworn 2013; Valencia 2019). The memory of the event still provokes profound emotions and pain more than ten years after it occurred.

Jorge Steven López Mercado's murder, like that of many queer, trans, and gender-nonconforming persons, such as the Puerto Rican Italian American Venus Xtravaganza, portrayed in the 1990 documentary *Paris Is Burning*, bears witness to the extraordinary violence lesbian, gay, bisexual, and particularly transgender subjects face, particularly (but not exclusively) when engaging in sex work, a constitutive violence that is at the very heart of transloca subjectivity and has generated extensive theoretical debates in the field of LGB and trans studies, in addition to activist and community responses.[29] In the case of Xtravaganza, her 1988 death went mostly unnoticed by the press when it occurred, only becoming a major focus of journalistic and academic debates due to its representation in Jennie Livingston's documentary; this death marks *Paris Is Burning* as a whole, tempering the exuberance and joy represented in the film.

The substantial mainstream media exposure and activist responses generated by López Mercado's death in 2009 were comparable to those that the murder of gay white cisgendered American Matthew Shepard received across the United States in 1998, even when the Puerto Rican victim was identified (correctly or incorrectly) as a person who was offered money to engage in sexual activities (Figueroa Rosa, Rivera Quiñones, and Hernández 2009).[30] This media attention also marked the subsequent murder of the Puerto Rican publicist José Enrique Gómez Saladín on November 30, 2012, and of the homeless transgender woman Alexa Negrón Luciano, also known as Neulisa Luciano Ruiz, who was killed on February 24, 2020. In the case of Gómez Saladín, homophobic sensationalist coverage in Puerto Rico by the drag puppet La Comay (a character embodied by the puppeteer Antulio "Kobbo" Santarrosa) on the television program *SuperXclusivo*, which included blaming the victim for his own death, provoked an activist media boycott that ultimately led to the television show's temporary cancellation (Avilés-Santiago 2014; Pina Girona 2013; Vega 2012). Alexa's murder, tied to her use of a women's bathroom in a fast-food restaurant, led to widespread reporting and artistic interventions, including a performance of the song "Ignorantes" by the gender-queer trap singer Bad Bunny (Benito Antonio Martínez Ocasio) with the singer Sech honoring her on *The Tonight Show Starring Jimmy Fallon* on February 27, 2020, in which Bad Bunny wore a black skirt and a T-shirt that said, "Mataron a Alexa, no a un hombre con falda" (They killed Alexa, not a man in a skirt). Meanwhile, in Puerto Rico, queer artists created a short video ("Yo siempre quise viajar") featuring spoken word narration and images of reflections in mirrors; the video was produced by Asuntos Efímeros and directed by the transgender artist María José, and was released two days later (on February 29) on YouTube, the same day that a public vigil was held on Calle Resistencia (Fortaleza Street) in Old San Juan near the governor's mansion.

In 2009, some portrayals of Jorge Steven, including tribute videos on YouTube, tended to sanitize the victim and deracinate them from their context (particularly from their contact with the sphere of sex work), as if a sterilizing amnesia or limited vision was necessary for political recuperation and collective mourning.[31] Working against this normalization and closer in spirit to activist and writer Mattilda Bernstein Sycamore's (2012) radical embrace of the term "faggots," to Cathy Cohen's (1997) embrace of "punks, bulldaggers, and welfare queens," and to Paco Vidarte's (2010) embrace of *marica* and *política perra* (bitch politics), the Puerto Rican cultural critic Rubén Ríos Ávila offered a transgressive *cuir* Spanglish recuperation of Jorge Steven as a "homo freak bitch" and as "la Alpha Bitch de una jauría fierce" (2010a), or the "Alpha Bitch of a fierce pack of bitches" (2010b), inspired by the singer Lady Gaga and by young Puerto Rican drag queens such as April Carrión, Queen Bee Ho (now known as Queen Bee), and Zahara Montiere (Alberic Prados), all from the Doll House, who celebrated Jorge Steven's life in their shows as a type of "dragtivism" (Fitzsimons 2019; Voynovskaya 2019) that combined drag and activism as a form of personal empowerment.[32] These multiple subversive gestures of remembrance can be seen as modified instantiations of what the Mexican theorist Sayak Valencia calls "postmortem/transmortem politics" (2019), in which the necropolitical regime is overturned by the dissident subaltern subjects who refuse to comply with its dominant logics, in this case through the celebration of life.[33] In his essay, Ríos Ávila insists that López Mercado was not simply an innocent, family-oriented, gay cisgender man, but rather a radical subject, one whom we can envision embracing what trans scholar Jack Halberstam has called "gaga feminism," that is to say, a posture that "strives to wrap itself around performances of excess; crazy, unreadable appearances of wild genders; and social experimentation" (2012, xiv).

In his critique, Ríos Ávila attempts to recuperate and transform the highly stigmatized term "bitch," similar to the way it has been reclaimed in third-wave feminism, perhaps in a way similar to how I have been engaging the term *loca*, but also hinting at the queer Cuban and more broadly Latin/x American slang usages of the term *perra* (female dog) in Spanish as a synonym for "fabulous" or "fierce" (Peña 2013, 86–90).[34] As Ríos Ávila wrote,

> It's in Jorge Steven's pictures that his true body appears to me, his fierce body. His plump red lips, his hair (flaming red is my favorite), his plucked eyebrows, striking a pose with two fingers framing an eye. It's obvious that Jorge Steven was no Little Red Riding Hood. He was the Alpha Bitch of a fierce pack of bitches. That's the body that his murderer tried to vanish. The body of desire. His desire. But he only was able to tear it apart and multiply it. A body that becomes animal. A body that becomes female. A fascinating, powerful, and dangerous body. (Ríos Ávila 2010b)

Echoing Arboleda Ríos's "devenir *loca*-mujer" (becoming *loca*-woman) (2011, 115), discussed in chapter 1 (a Perlongher-inspired envisioning of the potential for transformation and multiplicity that exceeds traditional identity politics), Ríos Ávila goes on to contextualize Jorge Steven's murder in relation to a much longer history, for example the killing of the effeminate social columnist and model Iván Frontera in San Juan in 1985 by the serial killer branded by the media as "El Ángel de los Solteros" (The Angel of Single Men), less than a block away from where I grew up in Miramar.[35]

Ríos Ávila concludes his powerful "Homo Freak" essay with a critique of the contemporary mainstream LGBTQ movement, particularly of its embrace of "equality" in the framework of liberal (as opposed to radical) and civil rights politics, presenting "la defensa de la diferencia" (the defense of difference) as a more desirable alternative (Ríos Ávila 2010a, 2010b). For the Puerto Rican theorist, it is the "body that is neither female, nor male," the "trans body," the "borderline body, porous, a multiple body in constant transformation, like a fierce pack of queens," the "naked, impudent, explosive body," the "homo freak bitch," that we must all defend. It is a body that exceeds containment, much as Nina Flowers's, and as we will now see, much like that of Kevin Fret.

Flirtations of Violence, Repetitions of Death: Kevin Fret

Jorge Steven López Mercado was not well known at the time of his death, but this did not impede the dramatic outpouring of grief, including vigils in San Juan, Chicago, Philadelphia, and New York City endorsed by national organizations such as GLAAD (Hannah 2010). The murder of the openly gay Puerto Rican trap singer Kevin Fret ten years later presented a poignant contrast to that of López Mercado and highlighted the continuing precarious position of transloca subjects.[36] Fret was an up-and-coming singer who had begun his career participating in televised competitions such as *La Banda* and *Solo Tu Voz* (Roiz 2019a). He was starting to receive significant media attention because of his provocative self-presentation and the novelty of his pose as the first openly gay trap singer in Puerto Rico, in a professional context that is notably homophobic and sexist. Fret was shot to death while riding a motorbike through San Juan in the early morning of January 10, 2019 (Guy 2019).

It is not my intention to dwell on the facts of Fret's murder or its homophobic reception. The crime immediately became the focus of major international news, generating a range of responses, including accusations of extortion from Puerto Rican reggaeton and trap singer Ozuna; the public revelation of a widely available solo porn video filmed while Ozuna was underage that Fret had threatened to publicize; and offensive remarks from the singer Don Omar, a rival of Ozuna, who tweeted a photo of himself accompanied by a caption with a double entendre in Spanglish on January 22 using emojis and hashtags to convey a homophobic message employing the well-known metaphor of *pato* (duck) as a signifier for male effeminacy or queerness, announcing that it was time for a "Lunch break!," asking his fans if they ate duck, and indicating that he didn't because it was tough, which generated numerous angry responses.[37] The murder also prefaced a widely criticized meeting between singers Bad Bunny and Residente (René Pérez Joglar) with the governor of Puerto Rico, Ricardo Rosselló Nevares, on January 11 (Exposito 2019b), approximately six months before Rosselló was forced to resign his post after massive protests, in part about his homophobia. As of this date, the crime of Fret's death has not been solved.[38]

Rather, I am much more interested in how Fret openly built his

Fig. 5. Kevin Fret, image capture from "Diferente—Mike Duran ft Kevin Fret (Video Oficial)," July 18, 2018, YouTube.

translocal/transnational career and persona on a fearless, almost aggressive transloca subjectivity, clearly expressed in his two best-known songs and videos, "Soy así" (released on April 7, 2018) and "Diferente," by Mike Durán featuring Kevin Fret, which was released on July 18, 2018.[39] I am also fascinated by the way in which Fret forcefully articulated his persona in an April 10, 2018, video interview with El Guru on *Rapetón*, available on YouTube, in which he stated that he preferred the designation "el primer trapero abiertamente gay," the first openly gay trap singer, emphasizing "el trapero gay. Porque eso es lo que me gusta, la calle" (the gay trap singer. Because that's what I like, the street).[40]

Being *loca* and "street" entailed negotiating physical aggression, whether as victim or perpetrator, and perhaps trying to soften the potentially controversial nature of this aggressive pose by invoking the American English-language term "gay." To be clear: Fret engaged in violence that was covered by the media and presented as a response to homophobic attacks; aggressive or confrontational behavior characterizes the public self-presentation of many (male and female) hip-hop artists. One event occurred in June 2018, when Fret stated that he was "struck by someone angry that his butt was exposed while tanning by a pool" in Miami (Jackson 2019).[41] Shortly afterward, Fret was arrested for battery charges "after a fight in an elevator that left another man bloodied" (*NBC Miami* 2018); the singer explained to the judge that he had moved to Miami from Massachusetts four months before the incident, highlighting his translocal displacements.

DON OMAR aka KONG ✅
@DONOMAR

Lunch break! Alguno de ustedes come 🦆? Yo no 👎
#dígalenoalacarnedepato #esdura

Fig. 6. Text of homophobic tweet in Spanglish by Don Omar posted on January 22, 2019, stating: "Lunch break! Do any of you eat [duck emoji]? I don't [brown thumbs down emoji]. #saynotoduckmeat #itshard."

In tension with his embrace of the term "gay," Fret also stated in his *Rapetón* interview that he lived with the concern of being seen as "el pato ridículo" (a ridiculous faggot), claimed the label "la bichota" (the female drug queenpin) and "la mamá" (the mother), wore makeup, felt he had "la loca adentro" (the *loca* inside), did not identify as transgender, was raised in a conservative religious household, and stated, "Mi objetivo es crear la diferencia" (My objective is to create difference), emphasizing his desire to be "la bichota de crearle el flow de vamos a salir del closet, puñeta, vamos a romper el closet" (the drug queenpin creating the let's-get-out-of-the-closet flow, motherfuckers, let's break the closet) and to be considered among the best, not as a female performer but as a performer in general.[42]

Fret's differential articulation of his femme ("bitchy," "sassy," "puta") gender and sexuality was marked by his use of Puerto Rican vernacular expressions such as *pato* and *mala mala* in his songs and by his references to *loca* in his interviews, as well as by his self-presentation and his public disclosure of his "cirugía de lipomarcación," or liposuction procedure.[43] Claims of authorship and intentionality in Fret's musical compositions are complicated by the fact that Fret explicitly acknowledged that his songs were collaborations and by the ways they are profoundly linked in their reception with the highly produced YouTube videos. In this sense, his unscripted online interviews can be seen as giving us slightly more direct access to the image he wished to convey, one marked by greater spontaneity and the mediated innocence of an artist who was still new to fame; it is worth remembering that Fret's brief mainstream recognition all occurred within the space of a nine-month window, from April 2018 to January 2019.

The lyrics to Fret's best-known song, "Soy así" ("I Am This Way") present an empowered, potentially violent, lyrical speaking subject (the collective Kevin Fret, mediated by his collaborators) who affirms their identity faced with a space of confrontation, hatred, and jealousy (Fret Family 2018). As the singer proclaims, "Por más que me quieran odiar" (No matter how much you want to hate me), "es que soy así" (that's the way I am), an affirmation that seems to echo Lady Gaga's 2011 "Born This Way." Fret's "this way" or "the way I am" translates to being a fashion clothes horse who references luxury designer labels (Gucci, Marc Jacobs, Prada, Tory Burch), who has a weapon ("la buchi armá," represented in the video as a pink plastic automatic assault rifle), and who dresses and applies makeup and confuses and seduces his ostensibly male enemies, who suffer cognitive impairments as a result of Fret's appearance. The juxtaposition and braggadocio expressed in the first verses correspond to but also transform typical hip-hop/reggaeton masculine posing emphasizing wealth, women, and guns, except that here Fret transforms himself into the object of desire for masculine listeners, partaking of the "queer future" or "queering" of hip-hop that the Canadian scholar Rinaldo Walcott (2013) describes, at the same time celebrating the "irreverence . . . misbehavior . . . bad manners . . . immorality . . . lack of respectability or restraint . . . [and] illicit embrace of overabundance and excess" that the American cultural studies scholar Jayna Brown (2013, 147) identifies in the musical genre. The lyrics of reggaeton and trap songs should not be taken literally; as the anthropologist Yarimar Bonilla (2018a) has highlighted in relation to the Puerto Rican middle-class, college-educated trap singer Bad Bunny, "Exaggeration reigns among young people seeking to represent themselves as heroic protagonists of what is in reality a banal and stifling day-to-day existence."

As "Soy así" progresses, Fret's speaking subject positions himself as a musical authority whom others try to emulate for free, a situation Fret decries, demanding royalties; he claims he charges for everything he does, including his kisses. To those who claim they are not his female fans he says, "Bitch, please!" calling their bluff, that is, their ingenue poses as "mosquitas muertas" (a colloquial expression that translates as "tiny dead flies"), to be dealt with by applying Flit-brand insecticide. The master of a posse of armed females ("las babies mías"), he claims mastery of nightclubs ("la disco"), which they close, and brothels, which they burst with money ("los puteros lo explotamos en chavos"). Speaking to the implicit female (or perhaps queer/*cuir*) listener, Fret announces that the listener's boyfriend is looking at him, potentially changing sexual orientation and even calling him, even when Fret did not give the boyfriend his phone number. Fret then warns this implicit listener to stay calm and lay low ("no frontees") because Fret has power and authority comparable to that of the major transnational Colombian female drug lord Griselda Blanco (1943–2012), also self-identifying in a rather unusual juxtaposition as a reincarnation of the Mexican painter Frida Kahlo.[44] As "la puta bichota de esta cabrona selva" (the drug queenpin ho of this fucking jungle), Fret declares himself "Mejor que tu mujer / Mejor que tu marido" (better than your wife / better than your husband).

Toward the second half of the song, Fret transitions to affirming a series of traits or attributes that define him, offered in queer Spanglish couplets:

Easy, trashy
Mis amigas me dicen que soy classy.
Bitchy, freaky
Pa' tumbarles los machos yo tengo el tricky.
Sassy, Saucy
Los labios siempre los tengo glossy.
Puta y hecha
Mi culito es importado de Colombia.

These (mostly) rhymed verses are marked by the juxtaposition of suggestive self-referential word pairings in English (easy/trashy, bitchy/freaky, sassy/saucy) with Spanish-language phrases that include intrasentential code-switching: "My girlfriends tell me that I am *classy*"; "To steal their machos I have the *trick*"; "My lips are always *glossy*." The couplets end by moving away from Spanglish to Spanish-only affirmations, in which the word pairing stands for sexual promiscuity (*puta*) and an affirmation of bodily transformation (*hecha*), as Fret affirms that he is a well-made (surgically transformed) "ho" whose "little ass [was] imported from Colombia."

Much as in season 4 of *RuPaul's Drag Race All Stars* (2018–19), where season cowinner Trinity "The Tuck" Taylor expressed pride over her plastic surgery and gluteal implants, Kevin Fret insists on and celebrates his feminizing physical transformation, stating that he received his buttock enhancement in Colombia, tying the drug trafficking referenced via Griselda Blanco to the cosmetic surgery industry. Fret also references a well-known criminal investigation in Puerto Rico, that of Ana Cacho, a suspect in the unsolved murder of her eight-year-old son Lorenzo González Cacho in 2010 (Pina Girona 2013). The singer then states that he is as controversial as Bad Bunny ("el Conejo Malo"), and that he knows why the global hit "Despacito" by Luis Fonsi and Daddy Yankee did not win a prize at the Sixtieth Annual Grammy Awards in 2018, where it was nominated in three categories.[45]

Fret's feminization and alternate embodiment culminates in a stanza in which Fret speaks of himself as a goddess, demands acts of reverence, and warns rivals that life is not a movie and that he has a license (i.e., street credibility), culminating with the affirmation, "¡No es amenaza, es advertencia!" (It is not a threat, it is a warning!). Finally, in the outro, or concluding section, Fret reaffirms his name, the title of "bitch," and the moniker *El del meneo* (the one who knows how to shake it).

The video for "Soy así" visualizes the lyrics I have analyzed. All of the song's many claims are accompanied by explicit sensual imagery in which a highly stylized, slender yet muscular, and somewhat androgynous Fret poses with four attractive, seminaked, black-clad, at times masked young women who have long, straight, black hair (one of whom appears carrying a handgun), as well as with his sister Doryann Fret (the only person who appears wearing bright red lipstick) and with two shirtless masked men who appear in a position of subjugation, as if reenacting a scene of sadomasochism or bondage and domination.[46] Fret first appears sitting in an ornate gilded throne, holding his pink plastic machine gun, which comes across as a camp element; he is wearing a texturized, sparkly, zippered silver top with long sleeves that is cut off at the midriff, exposing his ripped stomach, with matching tight, sparkly pants and sparkly silver tennis shoes that have a large black stripe on the side. His short, bleached blond hair is longer on top and cropped on the sides, and he is wearing noticeably shiny lip gloss. Fret also appears wearing other outfits (a zippered black hoodie and a sparking necklace with pink Capri pants or leggings, for example, or shirtless with the pink Capris) and a variety of large sunglasses (a black round pair and square sparkly ones) and sucking on a pink spherical lollipop. At times, he stands and dances, for example gyrating his hips or his derriere seductively; he also slowly gyrates his shoulders while sitting on the throne, and sometimes drapes his body over the armrests. At other moments, Fret appears solo, kneeling on the ground on all fours. He also appears smoking a hookah, as do some of the women in the video, including his sister Doryann. Fret's appearance with the two slightly tanned, perhaps darker-skinned, muscular, shirtless, gold-masked men is particularly noticeable, as he is holding gold chains attached to their necks. The images in the video oscillate between hypererotization (for example, gyrating exposed female butts) and camp parody (a pink plastic machine gun). The combination of the song's references to drug trafficking, plastic surgery, consumer culture, and violence, together with the highly erotic images of the video, place "Soy así" squarely in relation to what trans theorist Paul B. Preciado identifies as our contemporary "pharmacopornographic" regime (2013, 33–36) and as partaking of "sucia" aesthetics (Vargas 2014).

Fret's other well-known song, "Diferente," presents an interesting contrast, as the gay trap artist collaborated with an ostensibly (publicly identified) heterosexual singer, both asserting that they are "different" and that this difference creates challenges. Fret repeats some of his trademark assertions, including insisting on his talent and using vernacular *loca* vocabulary: As he states, "No es ser puta, es hacerse. Bitch!" (It's not about being a ho, it's about being self-made [or having plastic surgery]). He also references expensive watches (Patek Philippe), weapons and silencers ("cortas y tips"), privileged access to VIP lounges, and his fancy expensive clothes, insisting that he is "el primer pato que tuvo el descaro" (the first shameless faggot in his line of business), and that he kills with his "estilo raro" (queer style).

In the video for this song (MalongoMiusiTv 2018), Fret appears with brilliant deep blue hair, female makeup (including eye shadow, very long eyelashes, blush, and lip gloss), a bejeweled forehead, studded earrings, a long-sleeved white shirt that exposes his chest and white hot shorts that alternate with a multicolor mesh dress that doubles as a bathing suit, an expensive diamond and platinum watch, numerous gold chains, a black belt with an oversize, round, bejeweled gold belt buckle, and painted fingernails, coming closer to the sensual self-presentation of the numerous seminaked female dancers (including his sister Doryann Fret) than to the casual, sporty look favored by Mike Durán. The video portrays a mafia- or drug kingpin-inspired scenario with many young men, large amounts of money, and hand gestures simulating guns; Fret and Durán occasionally appear sitting side by side on a living room sofa. Toward the end of the video, Durán briefly places his right arm over Fret's shoulders in an act of solidarity. This scene is intercut with images of Fret apparently eating of a bowl full of gold chains that he brings up to his mouth with a fork, while Doryann is portrayed making herself a white bread sandwich stuffed with cash, which she then seems to bite. Money, it is clear, is a central motivating element that is symbolized as crucial to desire and success, echoing the phenomenon I identified with Nina Flowers.

While the publicly heterosexual trap singer Bad Bunny flirts with genderqueer postures by painting his fingernails and wearing colorful, whimsical outfits, and has also been seen as "redefining masculinity" (Cepeda 2018) and as an "ally to the LGBTQ community" (Villa 2019), for example in his gesture of radical queer solidarity in relation to the murder of

Alexa, Kevin Fret extensively used facial makeup, referred to himself as a *loca* and *pato*, sexualized his body for men, flirted with violence, and suffered the deadly consequences.[47] Fret's murder ten years after that of Jorge Steven López Mercado and almost thirty years after the death of Venus Xtravaganza points to the persistence of violence against translocas and the ways that transloca performance maintains a disruptive character that destabilizes and threatens dominant sexist, homophobic, and transphobic frameworks. Fret's fearless confrontational stance coincided with and has been furthered more recently by the over-the-top queer Puerto Rican rap singer Villano Antillano (Legarreta 2018; Jackson 2020a), who credited Fret for leading the way in what is referred to as "rainbow [or queer] rap" (Ayala 2019). Villano Antillano is best known for his 2018 song "Pato hasta la muerte" ("Faggot until Death"), for self-identifying as a "bilingual bitch" in his song "Nunca" ("Never"), and for featuring the emerging drag queens Ubi Aaron, Anoma Lía, and Ana Macho in the video for his song "No confío," released on October 29, 2019.[48]

The contrast and continuities between Jorge Steven López Mercado's and Kevin Fret's brazen, youthful, confrontational style, which has been furthered by Villano Antillano in his songs, videos, and social media presence (for example, on Instagram), and Nina Flowers's equally disruptive yet somehow more palatable transnational mass-media performance on *RuPaul's Drag Race* provide a window into Puerto Rican transloca embodiments and knowledges. Flowers's, López Mercado's, Fret's, and Villano Antillano's *translocura* (and that of young queens such as Ubi Aaron, Anoma Lía, and Ana Macho) oscillates between English and Spanish, capitalist neoliberalism and its negation, femininity and masculinity, sanity and lack of reason, and the Caribbean and global "mediascapes" that frame what Jossianna Arroyo (2015), building on the foundational work of Joseph Roach (1996), has termed mass-media "cities of the dead," referring to film, television, and internet representations of violence, death, and mourning in the Spanish Caribbean. The communitarian and assimilable jouissance of Flowers's and Fret's music and performances cannot be thought of independently from neoliberal absorption and of the horrifying and absolutely unacceptable violence of López Mercado's and Fret's deaths; they become a type of gore capitalism (Valencia 2018). All transform lives. All confuse. All threaten, although at different scales and in different registers. The epistemology of the transloca comes about in its complexity and contradictions, in its movements and displacements, in the joyful and tragic negotiations of the transdiaspora.

THREE

Diasporic Welfare Queens and the Transloca Drag of Poverty

Welfare Queens are the drag queens for the next millennium.
—Erika Lopez, *The Welfare Queen*

Poverty is an everyday reality for many Latin American and Latinx *travestis, transformistas,* and trans subjects, including many Puerto Rican translocas.[1] It is as prevalent and central as social exclusion or stigma (chapter 1) and as violence and jouissance (chapter 2). It influences the reception of all Puerto Ricans and of transloca Latinxs in the United States, regardless of actual socioeconomic status, and extends to their portrayal in anthropological and sociological research (Bourgois 1995; Glazer and Moynihan 1970; Lewis 1966), in independent and mainstream media productions such as *West Side Story* and Andy Warhol's *Trash* (Negrón-Muntaner 2004), and in national politics, for example, in debates about poor mothers referred to as "welfare queens."[2] It is also at the heart of Nuyorican and diasporic Puerto Rican literary and cultural poetics, where poverty is portrayed, embraced, and denounced by multiple foundational artists such as Piri Thomas, Nicholasa Mohr, Miguel Algarín, Miguel Piñero, Pedro Pietri, Luz María Umpierre, Tato Laviera, and Sandra María Esteves, as scholars such as Frances R. Aparicio (1988), Juan Flores (1993, 2000), Lisa Sánchez González (2001), Frances Negrón-Muntaner (2004), Urayoán Noel (2014), Sandra Ruiz (2019), and Patricia Herrera (2020) have noted. How do diasporic translocas cope with this situation? One way is through the *transloca drag of poverty*, a multifaceted, resourceful drag of resistance and negotiation, involving contradictions, invention, and inversion.

Puerto Rican transloca performers such as Erika Lopez, Holly Woodlawn, and Monica Beverly Hillz engage in complex and at times parodic tactics and strategies regarding sexualized and racialized poverty in the United States, participating in and counteracting governmental practices and neoliberal commodification and exploitation; these strategies are different from the ones that impoverished radical transloca activists such as Stonewall veteran Sylvia Rivera historically espoused, which more often entailed rejection and/or contestation of state practices, favoring political organizing and direct-action work. In this chapter, I discuss Erika Lopez's solo performance *The Welfare Queen* (2002–11); Holly Woodlawn's (1991) autobiography *A Low Life in High Heels: The Holly Woodlawn Story* (coauthored with Jeffrey Copeland) and her appearance in Andy Warhol and Paul Morrissey's film *Trash* (1970); and Monica Beverly Hillz's participation in season 5 of the reality television competition *RuPaul's Drag Race* (2013) as three examples of strategic negotiations of poverty, in which transloca performance serves to engage with and challenge neoliberal abjection. I then juxtapose these examples to Sylvia Rivera's very notable radical antiauthoritarian politics—a different type of transloca performance—which span from 1969, the year of the Stonewall revolt, and 1970, when she participated in a Times Square petition drive that led to her arrest, to 2002, the time of her death at age fifty.[3] I do this as a way to acknowledge a different, equally valuable strategy for dealing with poverty and marginalization.

In Rivera's case, her transloca performance entailed a denunciation of police practices, particularly of the incarceration of drag queens, transvestites, and trans women for loitering or engaging in prostitution, along with a severe critique of antitrans violence by state and nonstate actors and a calling out of racism, classism, and antitrans bias within the mainstream lesbian and gay movement. This was accompanied by a focus on issues of social inequality related to housing, employment, and health care. Notably, Rivera did not advocate for welfare as a solution, calling instead for revolution, radical social change, "Gay Power," government reform, and community-based support such as housing and food distribution for homeless trans youth and adults, a stance that can be considered a *jaiba*, or street-smart, decolonial transloca politics of a different kind.[4]

What is the relationship between the stereotypical pejorative representation of women on welfare and the transloca drag of poverty? Here it is useful to understand the phrase "welfare queen" as a provocative oxymoron, engaging a literary trope that is particularly appropriate for multiple queer Puerto Rican colonial paradoxes, as Arnaldo Cruz-Malavé argues in "The Oxymoron of Sexual Sovereignty," where the Puerto Rican scholar discusses "the oxymoronic nature of sovereignty itself" (2007a, 58). According to the Merriam-Webster dictionary, "oxymoron" refers to "a combination of contradictory or incongruous words . . . ; broadly: something (such as a concept) that is made up of contradictory or incongruous elements."[5] Oxymoronic drag elements define the depictions of the African American Linda Taylor, the first woman maligned in the United States in the 1970s with the sobriquet of "welfare queen" after she committed welfare fraud, among other crimes. According to the journalist Josh Levin, a "*Jet* [magazine] article depicted her as a shape-shifting, fur-wearing con artist who could 'change from black to white to Latin with a mere change of a wig'" (2019, x). Other so-called welfare queens have been envisioned as "Cadillac-driving, champagne-sipping, penthouse-living" abusers of the system (Zucchino 1997, 13). So how does "welfare" relate to royalty, as suggested by the word "queens," which is also used as a synonym for homosexuals?

The term "welfare," in spite of its roots in conceptions of well-being ("the good fortune, health, happiness, prosperity, etc., of a person, group, or organization"), currently entails mostly stigmatized associations of poverty and government assistance,[6] as well as undertones of biopolitical control and abjection in a neoliberal scenario in which only private enterprise is celebrated and where faith-based organizations (particularly US Christian charities) are favored as service providers, substituting in the role formerly occupied by the state, where the rationality of the contemporary Homo economicus led by an obsession with financial gain trumps the values of democracy (W. Brown 2015, 9–11).[7] "Queen," on the other hand, implies nobility, prestige, recognition, and validation (as in the "queen of the home" or the even more glamorous "beauty queen"), although it also has "disparaging and offensive" slang connotations as a "contemptuous term used to refer to a male homosexual, especially one who is flamboyantly campy or effeminate," as indicated by Dictionary.com.

Since the 1970s, users of the phrase "welfare queen" in the United States have enacted a juxtaposition of terms that distorts an experience of poverty; the phrase is used to accuse a woman, usually of color, particularly a cisgendered, heterosexual single mother and head of a household, of deception, of exploiting the government, and of unfairly trying to gain access to undeserved wealth for herself and for her children at the expense of hardworking, honest, tax-paying yet ultimately duped, ostensibly cisgendered, heterosexual, mostly white citizens and corporations.[8] For the scholar Laura Briggs (2002, 75), the vilification of poor, working-class

Puerto Rican women as "welfare queens" is directly tied to the social scientist Oscar Lewis's portrayal of Puerto Ricans as "hypersexual, as bad mothers, and responsible for their own poverty" in his book *La Vida: A Puerto Rican Family in the Culture of Poverty—San Juan and New York* (1966), which includes representations of gender and sexual nonconformists or, to use Lewis's terms, "queers," "fag[s]," "effeminate men," "lesbians," and "pans[ies]," as well as prostitutes and drug users.[9]

Welfare queens are, in many ways, the exact opposite of beauty queens: racialized, vilified, criminalized, and undesired. Even if the actual subject in question is attractive, their persona is diminished and their aesthetic choices are questioned through the racist and classist critique of style (hair, clothing, makeup, jewelry), which is at times labeled as being "ghetto" (poor or marginal), a highly charged put-down; in this sense, and following the French sociologist Pierre Bourdieu (1984), taste is mobilized to enforce class and, we can add, racial and ethnic hierarchies. Dominant representations typically do not present "welfare queens" as partaking of mainstream (i.e., white, Anglo-Saxon, Protestant, middle class) visual norms, moral standards, or bodily stances. They are portrayed as disorganized bodies that rupture conventions and irritate due to their profound difference and as people who use their children in an instrumental, amoral way.

In gay parlance, "queen" (an English-language equivalent of *loca*) is a polysemic signifier, a slang word for effeminate male homosexual, at times serving as a synonym for trans woman, drag queen, or gay man, in addition to cisgender female pageant winner, a multiplicity captured by Marcia Ochoa (2014) in the title of her book *Queen for a Day*: Transformistas, *Beauty Queens, and the Performance of Femininity in Venezuela.*[10] This multiplicity also appears in the titles of diverse US drag and trans pageant documentary films, ranging from the pioneering New York City–focused *The Queen* directed by Frank Simon (1968), which features white American performer Flawless Sabrina, African American queens Crystal LaBeija and Dorian Corey, and Puerto Rican performer Mario Montez, among other contestants, all the way to Henrique Cirne-Lima and Josué Pellot's 2010 *I Am the Queen* and its 2012 sequel, *The Other Side of the Queen*, which follow several working-class Puerto Rican participants in the Vida/SIDA-sponsored Paseo Boricua Cacica Queen Pageant in Humboldt Park, one of the main Puerto Rican neighborhoods in Chicago.[11]

Conservative Republicans and equally conservative Democrats in the United States who accuse poor or working-class mothers of being welfare queens usually do not imply the double meaning of "queen" as homosexual, in spite of the fact that numerous gays, gender-nonconforming persons, and trans women are extremely poor, may even be homeless, may have children, and are barely recognized by the state or by social service organizations, as the African American political scientist Cathy Cohen (1997) pointed out in her highly influential "Punks, Bulldaggers, and Welfare Queens: The Radical Potential of Queer Politics?" In her article, Cohen criticized the biased exclusions inherent in 1990s Anglo-American queer theory and political organizing, which tended to downplay or simply ignore the specificity of persons of color, poor persons, and other marginalized queer groups, failing to contemplate the possibilities for coalitions with these disenfranchised communities on the grounds of race and class. Contrary to dominant perceptions that frame LGBTQ populations in the United States as predominantly white, middle to upper class, and obsessively focused on marriage, military service, and assisted reproduction, actual LGBTQ persons demonstrate remarkable heterogeneity and multiple conflicting priorities, as Sylvia Rivera insisted throughout her thirty-plus years of activism.[12]

In this chapter, I present a new meaning for the term "welfare queen" and also elaborate on what I call the *transloca drag of poverty* or, following Sylvia Rivera, what could be referred to as the *transvestism of poverty*, as Rivera at times rejected the use of the term "drag," opposing its episodic and performative/camp nature in favor of lived experience;[13] Holly Woodlawn also expressed her opposition to the term "drag," identifying its stigmatized charge.[14] "Drag," in this context, means a challenge, a difficulty, or something undesired, similar to and profoundly linked to the *transloca drag of race* that I will discuss in chapter 5. But "drag" is also the cultural practice of cross-dressing that often implies humor and camp sensibility, and that in fact might entail aspiring to the recognition and glamour of the pageant beauty queen even when one is abjectly poor, as we will note particularly in our discussion of Lopez, Woodlawn, and Hillz.[15]

What does it mean to consider drag or transloca performance as a political act (as a type of "dragtivism") that has the power not simply to challenge binary gender norms but also to question other social formations and power structures in society? What does it mean to see drag or trans performance as something more than mere entertainment? Or, more pointedly, to recognize the dire life conditions of specific drag queens and trans persons, for example those referred to as "street queens" (*locas pobres, callejeras,* or *deambulantes*) in the 1960s, so carefully documented by Esther Newton in *Mother Camp* (1972), a situation that continues to our days?

Jennie Livingston's influential documentary *Paris Is Burning* (1990), which was rereleased theatrically and received significant national recognition in 2019, highlights how drag can serve as a lived, embodied practice that achieved gender and class crossings for African American and Latinx queers and queens in New York City in the middle to late 1980s, even if these crossings are only momentary, as in a drag ball.[16] Livingston's film, which includes numerous Puerto Rican trans women and gay men of the House of Xtravaganza, highlights the aspirational quality of drag, its ability to project fantasy and allow for a momentary or more permanent embodiment: to appear as or become through self-fashioning.[17] The documentary also highlights the alternative kinship systems referred to as houses (a type of surrogate family) that serve to create support networks and to maintain complex emotional ties, a type of social structure that the performance studies scholar Moe Meyer compellingly likens to the houses of the Afro-Caribbean religion of Santería (2010, 105–39), which also emphasize a holistic system of care and reciprocity in the diaspora among people related by faith and not by blood.[18] It is precisely the Puerto Rican richness of *Paris Is Burning* that led Puerto Rican Sicilian American queer author Joseph Cassara to make the House of Xtravaganza the focus of his first novel, *The House of Impossible Beauties* (2018), which centers on the life of Angel, a fictionalized representation of trans performer and sex worker Venus Xtravaganza, whom I briefly discussed in the previous chapter.[19]

Paris Is Burning has also been seen as a fundamental predecessor for Sara Jordenö and Twiggy Pucci Garçon's engaging film *Kiki* (2016), which documents the contemporary African American and Latinx ballroom scene in New York City, a comparison that director Jordenö apparently dislikes.[20] It is also a crucial precursor or intertext for the well-received drama television series *Pose* (2018–19), which features a large cast of queer- and trans-of-color actors portraying characters in the same late 1980s New York City scene, including the Puerto Rican trans actresses Mj Rodriguez and Indya Moore.[21] *Pose* is also notable for its significant queer-of-color creative team, including screenwriter and executive producer Steven Canals (who is Afro–Puerto Rican), African American writer and transgender activist Janet Mock, and choreographer Twiggy Pucci Garçon.[22] The show has also been lauded for its frank depiction of antitrans violence, perceived to be a landmark in American television history.[23] *Pose* is profoundly tied to and literally unthinkable without Livingston's cinematographic referent.

When *Paris Is Burning* first came out, its reception was decidedly mixed. Critics of the film such as bell hooks (1992) and Coco Fusco (1995) quickly denounced what they perceived to be its false consciousness, deception, or delusion, that is, its buying into the myth or ideological fantasy of the American dream that the film's subjects articulated; critics also accused the film of cultural appropriation.[24] Fusco and hooks chastised the documentary film's subjects for their ideological positions or lack of radical politics and also criticized the director for her portrayal of their opinions and for not subjecting this discourse to a more explicitly Marxist, antiracist, feminist, or decolonial critique. Instead of recognizing many of the featured drag queens, trans women, and gays and lesbians as Gramscian organic intellectuals—that is to say, as transloca performers who articulate a complex analysis of their life experiences from outside of academia or from other more traditional and recognized knowledge-producing spaces—detractors such as hooks and Fusco saw the film's protagonists as foolish dupes, except perhaps in the case of interviewee Dorian Corey, whom hooks (1992, 155–56) misidentifies as "Dorian Carey."[25] Trans-of-color activists also denounced the film and called for boycotts, for example at the Celebrate Brooklyn! Festival (Dockray 2015), at times based on accusations that Livingston unfairly exploited the documentary subjects; trans theorist Jay Prosser (1998, 21–60) offered a mixed assessment of the film and of the critical debates it generated, siding with some of hooks's critiques.

Other scholars, such as Jackie Goldsby (1993), Judith Butler (1993, 81–98), Chandan Reddy (1998), E. Patrick Johnson (2003, 76–103), Marlon M. Bailey (2013), and Lucas Hilderbrand (2013), however, have seen *Paris Is Burning* as a rich archive of lived experience; as a document of a vibrant subculture; as a transformative portrayal of art forms and strategies for survival in a racist, homophobic, and transphobic world. Bailey, for example, credits the documentary for inspiring the Detroit ballroom scene, which he believes would not exist (at least not as it developed in the 1990s) without it. Hilderbrand, on the other hand, has carefully explored and challenged the accusations of financial exploitation and highlighted the film's collective process, for example the central role of the narrator and of the editor, offering important contextual information that leads to a better understanding of its development and execution.

The contrast with Susana Aikin and Carlos Aparicio's *The Salt Mines* (1990) and its sequel, *The Transformation* (1995), is notable, in that these lesser-known documentaries portray a much more sordid experience of abjection—particularly *The Salt Mines*—with bilingual, diasporic Puerto Rican, Dominican, Cuban, and Anglo-American individuals living in extreme poverty outdoors, in a homeless encampment in abandoned garbage trucks in New York City.[26] Curiously, one of these trans women, the Dominican Giovanna, wears a discarded winter coat trimmed with fur: a possibly upper-class garment that serves multiple purposes, including providing warmth and glamour to a subject who considers herself elegant and beautiful in spite of her surroundings. The subjects in *The Salt Mines* take pride in their appearance and work to maintain it, at times to be able to engage in sex work and generate an income, at the same time that they struggle simply to survive.

In contrast, documentary footage of Sylvia Rivera shot by white gay activist Randy Wicker in 1996, when she also lived in a riverfront West Side homeless encampment in Manhattan very close to the ones portrayed in *The Salt Mines*, does not focus on any elements of glamour whatsoever; Rivera is not portrayed applying makeup or wearing fancy clothes and even states that she has no gowns. This important footage appears in several documentaries, including in trans white filmmaker Tara Mateik's tribute video *Sylvia* (2002) and in gay white cisgender director David France's more recent *The Death and Life of Marsha P. Johnson* (2017), shown on Netflix, which has also generated accusations of appropriation, in this case by African American trans filmmaker Tourmaline.[27] In this footage, Rivera describes how her alcoholism, her isolation in Westchester, New York, and the news of the death of Marsha P. Johnson (who died under mysterious circumstances and was possibly murdered) led her to lose interest in life, to move back to New York City, and to drift into homelessness. This and later footage showcase Rivera explaining that she felt a renewed sense of self in the homeless encampment, seeing herself as a "mother" to the residents, many of whom were dealing with issues of substance abuse and HIV/AIDS; she was inspired by the legacy of Johnson and believed she was carrying on her friend's struggle.

Mayra Santos-Febres's novel *Sirena Selena vestida de pena* (2000b); Rashaad Ernesto Green's feature-length narrative film *Gun Hill Road* (2011), starring the Puerto Rican–Dominican transgender actress Harmony Santana; Carmen Oquendo-Villar and José Correa Vigier's mid-length documentary *La Aguja / The Needle* (2012); Vivian Bruckman Blondet's Neo-DIVEDCO documentary short *Desmaquilladas* (2013); Antonio Santini and Dan Sickles's feature-length documentary *Mala Mala* (2014); Sean Baker's film *Tangerine* (2015); and the aforementioned TV series *Pose* (2018–19) are additional twenty-first-century cultural productions that negotiate Puerto Rican transloca drag and poverty in a context marked by aspirations of class mobility, glamour, and female beauty.[28] All of these cultural productions demonstrate the transloca drag of poverty as something undesired, burdensome, tedious, annoying, boring, and even potentially violent and dangerous, but also funny, endearing, quirky, authentic, and vernacular; something to be overcome, negotiated, traversed with skill and cunning, survived, challenged, fought against, and perhaps even celebrated. As a socially stigmatized category with very real material implications, it requires a response, particularly when it entails a lack of basic necessities required for well-being: shelter, food, health care, clothing, and warmth.

Erika Lopez: Performing Puerto Rican Welfare Abjection in California

Cisgendered women can also be translocas or engage in transloca performance, for example when they adopt explicitly queer, over-the-top gender performance strategies and invoke the figure of the drag queen, participating in "same-sex masquerade and gender parody" (Gutiérrez 2010, 118) or becoming "female impersonator[s]" (Sandoval-Sánchez and Sternbach 2001, 123). What happens when an impoverished transloca empowers welfare queens and resignifies this figure's meaning, but in California? For the San Francisco–based, Afro–Puerto Rican, bisexual novelist, cartoonist, and performance artist Erika Lopez, welfare queens become the drag queens for the twenty-first century, or more accurately, "for the next millennium" (2010, 104). At face value, Lopez's outrageous assertion does not account for the complexity and multiplicity of lived experiences and social locations of individuals who practice drag or of women who are on welfare; but then again, Lopez specializes in shock value as part of her aesthetic project and humor, which can in some ways be linked to third-wave feminism's irreverent take on social issues.[29]

Lopez's assertion that "Welfare Queens are the drag queens for the next millennium," proclaimed in her solo show *The Welfare Queen*, performed from 2002 to 2011, highlights the performative aspects of the social image of poor women of color who receive government assistance and are demonized as undeserving criminals, and also emphasizes the possibility of reenvisioned welfare queens becoming performers who appear on stage and share their radical, highly politicized, empowering story in a tragicomic way, even integrating music. As a single, unemployed, cisgendered queer woman-of-color artist with no children who describes receiving welfare in two different moments (in 1995 and then again in 2002), Lopez drew on her life experiences and challenged her stigmatization through exteriorization: a performative excess, demonstrated through drawn images—those of the sultry Welfare Queen and of the elderly yet empowered Grandma Lopez—and storytelling (on paper or on a computer screen, with words or lines), all seen as iterations of the self, and through autobiographical performance as the character Kitten Lopez, entailing a humorous and poignant rant that shares in the tradition of queer solo performance that Holly Hughes and David Román (1998) highlight in their anthology *O Solo Homo*, akin to the queer Latina solo performances of Carmelita Tropicana, Monica Palacios, and Marga Gomez that Alberto Sandoval-Sánchez and Nancy Saporta Sternbach (2001, 95–126) analyze in *Stages of Life: Transcultural Performance and Identity in U.S. Latina Theater* and to the Nuyorican feminist performances discussed by Patricia Herrera (2020). For Lopez, drag—the exaggerated performance or conceptualization of identities, or the actual experience of appearing before an audience and provoking emotions—serves as a strategy of attack and a means of empowerment.

Here the social category of "woman" is eminently understood as linked to facade, costume, mask, or performativity, building on Joan Riviere's classic essay "Womanliness as Masquerade" (1929), in which the English psychoanalyst described the stratagems of dissimulation women must perform in order to fit circumscribed social roles, for example by not challenging male authority, even when a woman is more knowledgeable or skilled than a man. Simone de Beauvoir's procedural conceptualization of womanhood—her eminently quoted phrase, "On ne naît pas femme: on le devient" (One is not born, but rather becomes, a woman)—as articulated in her classic *The Second Sex* (1949), and Judith Butler's theorization in *Gender Trouble* (1990) regarding the performativity of gender that serves to constitute womanhood (that is to say, the iterative enactment of femininity that builds and consolidates the socially recognized category of woman) explain the physical and mental process of living *as if* one were a welfare queen, processing the stigma of being considered lesser than, unworthy, or broken.[30] As such, Erika Lopez imagines herself and creates varied alter egos such as Kitten Lopez, Grandma Lopez, and the Welfare Queen as iterations of performative excess. Being a Black Puerto Rican bisexual woman artist on welfare becomes a performance of drag. And here "drag" is understood as abject but also intrinsically marked by humor and camp: a parody that is world-making or utopian, as José Esteban

Muñoz (1999, 2009) would argue, that destabilizes and envisions different alternatives through mockery and fun but also through anger and rage.

The countercultural work of Erika Lopez, particularly her performance *The Welfare Queen*, serves as a way to contextualize Holly Woodlawn's appearance in Andy Warhol and Paul Morrissey's film *Trash* (1970) and gives us tools to better understand Monica Beverly Hillz's portrayal in season 5 of *RuPaul's Drag Race* (2013). Lopez emphasizes the spectacular nature of human misfortune in a neoliberal context in which many artists of color (for example, the Haitian–Puerto Rican Jean-Michel Basquiat) are not valued while they are alive and in which there is rampant gentrification.[31] In this context, welfare is a stigma but also a form of creative subvention: an alternative for poor/unemployed artists. And, as I mentioned, Lopez ultimately proposes welfare queens as the drag queens for the new millennium, what I would describe as *translocas de la resistencia* (resilient, resisting translocas). What happens, then, when we take the word "queen" at face value, as a sign of distinction, nobility, or achievement, or as a proud affirmation of queerness? Or when we resignify the term "welfare queen" as a traumatic badge of pride, a complex multivalent condition, or even an ironic countercultural aspiration?

Born in 1968 in New York City to a German American mother and a Afro–Puerto Rican father and raised by her lesbian mother in southern New Jersey near Philadelphia, Lopez first performed *The Welfare Queen* (initially called *Nothing Left but the Smell: A Republican on Welfare*) in 2002 at the Douglass Student Center in Rutgers University, New Brunswick, New Jersey, and went go on to present it in other cities in the United States and in Europe, including at Theatre Rhinoceros in San Francisco and at the feminist WOW Café Theater in Manhattan in 2003, culminating in a final run produced by the Bronx Academy of Arts and Dance (BAAD!) in 2011.[32] She also published the performance text in a variety of formats, at times incorporating her drawings.[33] In her performance, Lopez interrogates and challenges dominant notions about contemporary class relations in the United States, particularly in California, as she comments on race and sexual politics. *The Welfare Queen* is structured as an act of autobiographical storytelling or personal confession, in which the artist tells a cautionary tale related to what she describes as her professional downfall: the story of how a successful writer who thought she was on top of the world after publishing three novels with the leading American publishing house Simon and Schuster ended up extremely poor.[34]

Lopez begins her monologue by describing her art-school days in

Fig. 7. Erika Lopez as Kitten Lopez in *The Welfare Queen*. Text reads "Kitten Lopez, one of the puerto rican girls that's just dyin' to meat ya." Photo by James Swanson. Art direction by Jeffrey Hicken.

Philadelphia and her aspirations for professional success, which led her to a reenvisioned career path as a writer and to a move to San Francisco, a somewhat unusual but not unheard of action for a queer Puerto Rican.[35] Penniless, she applied for food stamps; her foray to the welfare office led to a surprise encounter with other Black persons—as she describes, "the last of the city's tenacious black people were hiding out in the food stamp line before they had to pull out of this foofy biscotti city of latte people"

(2010, 55)—and to the humorous yet somewhat cynical description of the courting rituals of two African American individuals: the large-gold-hoop "bagel-earring girl" and the white-nylon-suit "yeast infection boy," who is also described as a "food-stamp, Mac-daddy" (2010, 59). The speaker soon admits that her condescending attitude is a foil for not acknowledging her own stigmatized status as a Black Puerto Rican welfare recipient, an attitude perhaps based on her class background and educational status.

After describing the commercial success she experienced with the publication of her three mainstream books, Lopez zeroes in on her "downfall" in 2002, which led back to the welfare office. This experience is described in more abject terms, including identification with a homeless, cross-dressing man she knew from her neighborhood, "a craggy little old WHITE MAN with one big matted dreadlock flapping against his back like an old screen door," whom she describes wearing "a long straight black skirt found on the street" and labels as "the neighborhood scary monster man" (75); this man lives on her block in his Datsun and greeted her in the welfare office with a nod. The narrator/speaker/performer then offers a grotesque description of a government employee sitting behind a window, also portrayed as a "scary monster neighbor in her own neighborhood" (81).

Abjection is signaled throughout the performance through smell, specifically the profound psychological effect certain odors have on her in the welfare office:

> The smell that all economic realities came down to when I was a kid. You could dress it up or turn it around and spank it, but you couldn't run from the truth. It wasn't the musty smell of Old People, or the garlic smell of Spicy People from faraway lands. It wasn't the missed litter boxes smell of the Cat People. It wasn't even the hampery people smell. No! Not even the Tofu Breath People Smell. No, no, no . . . it was *The Poor People Smell.* (82–83)

The smell of poverty is also a major plot element in Bong Joon-ho's award-winning film *Parasite* (2019), where it marks social differences and leads to interclass violence, specifically to the working-class father Kim Ki-taek's (Song Kang-ho) gruesome murder of his boss, the wealthy Park Dong-ik (Lee Sun-kyun), after Park expresses his olfactory disgust.[36] To counteract the stigma and potential trauma of smell, Lopez comically proposes starting a line of "welfare colognes to cover up the truth . . . for we will smell like the middle class" (92), a type of DIY (do it yourself) artisanal business strategy that negotiates stigma through humor, but which also could be seen as condescending.[37] Much as in Patrick Süskind's best-selling 1985 novel *Perfume*, the capacity to perceive social odors causes profound psychological states that at times can tap into misanthropy, but does not turn Lopez into a murderer, as in the case of the German novel's protagonist; the ability to harness and transform smells through the use of perfume has a broader social impact.[38]

Abjection can be a valuable tool to destabilize and challenge preconceived norms. In *Abject Performances: Aesthetic Strategies in Latino Cultural Production*, the Chicana scholar Leticia Alvarado focuses on a group of Latinx artists characterized by the "deployment of abjection as an irreverent aesthetic strategy" who "cohere their aesthetic gestures around negative affects—uncertainty, disgust, unbelonging—capturing what lies far outside mainstream, inspirational Latino-centered social justice struggles" (2018, 4). Alvarado's interest is precisely in "those who do not desire to move from abject to subject but instead perform an abject collision that threatens to reveal the inequalities of a national body insistent on a legacy of freedom and equality" (9). Lopez's work fits squarely with the examples Alvarado focuses on, which include the Cuban American multimedia artist Ana Mendieta, the Chicanx collective Asco, and the Chicana performance artist Nao Bustamante, among others.

After a friend's suicide and her own suicidal ideations, the narrator/protagonist of *The Welfare Queen* describes an abject physical metamorphosis—the literal drying out of her own body—and as a result declares, "*I was the new scary monster now*" (99). This realization (*devenir monstruo*, becoming monster), a gesture also similar to the Latin American cases the scholar Analola Santana (2018) explores in *Freak Performances*, leads Lopez to embrace her new, self-proclaimed identity as a "Welfare Queen" and to discourage others from choosing a writing career. The performance ends with Lopez reiterating her suicidal thoughts and offering a soulful a cappella rendition of a song about a traffic accident in which her motorcycle was destroyed, in which Lopez sings, "Oh there's nothing left / Nothing left but the smell" (111). While the song's lyrics seem to advocate resignation, despair, and acknowledgment of a hard situation, the actual performance comes across as an act of survival and resistance, and as such the song allows her to culminate a collective cathartic experience in which the solo performer is working through multiple traumas on stage: her personal economic difficulties and precarity; her traffic accident; the death of one of her closest friends (Kris Kovick); the dramatic racist (anti-Black) gentrification of the place where she lives, overtaken by anticigarette capitalist baby boomers, or, as she says, the new denizens of the "foofy biscotti city of latte people," where she feels marginalized and excluded, the same anti-Black city portrayed in Joe Talbot and Jimmie Fails's film *The Last Black Man in San Francisco* (2019).[39] This catharsis is accomplished through the embrace, demystification, and reconceptualization of the stigmatized category of the welfare queen, which is envisioned as a manifestation of Latinx abjection.

Lopez's performance enacts a critique of racism, albeit mostly focused on Black/white relations, in spite of the particularity of the Anglo-American white supremacist dynamics that have been in place since the nineteenth-century US westward expansion, consolidated after the 1846–48 Mexican American War, as Tomás Almaguer (1994) discusses in his book *Racial Fault Lines: The Historical Origins of White Supremacy in California*. These broader dynamics entailed the displacement of Mexican elites and the subsequent racialization (following Omi and Winant 1994) of all Mexicans, seen as lower-status whites (or nonwhites), as well as the open persecution of Indigenous populations, identified as savages and marked for annihilation. It also included the denigration and subjugation of African-descent slaves and freedmen and of Asian immigrants (Chinese, Japanese, Filipino), marked as racial inferiors. Lopez's performance does not account for this historical complexity.

Nothing Left but the Smell: A Republican on Welfare, sub-subtitled *She's Not a Republican, She Just Has the Self-Entitlement of One* and then renamed *The Welfare Queen*, is an attempt to understand the lived experience of poverty in a society where poverty and homelessness are constituted as the most abject state, what Lopez identifies as every community's "scary monster neighbor," a status that she also self-ascribes. Here humor functions as a strategy for the negotiation of fear and horror, taking advantage of but also displacing Julia Kristeva's theorization about abjection, of the fear generated by "one of those violent, dark revolts of being, directed against a threat that seems to emanate from an exorbitant outside or inside, ejected beyond the scope of the possible, the tolerable, the thinkable" (Kristeva 1982, 1).[40]

Lopez's phenomenological narrative of embodiment, her "somatic transaction" of racialization (Fetta 2018), particularly focused on what she describes as the "smell of poverty" but eventually engulfing all of her senses and her entire body, and her vocal and physical performative experience—the shouts of rage during the performance, the intensity in

the delivery of the monologue, the occasional tears and emotional interruptions by the artist on stage who is not professionally trained, the soulful song with which the performance ends—makes us question the way
discourses of poverty are deployed by dominant classes as strategies of
social control, and leads us, in fact, to understand an interpretive struggle:
Who gets to speak for the poor? Are the poor spoken about, or do the poor
get to speak for themselves? What does poverty mean for translocas and
for others, beyond the manipulations of often-unreliable statistical analysis? What are the multiplicities of poverty? Specifically, what does poverty
mean to Erika Lopez as she elaborates an autobiographical rant about the
failure of the American dream, or more precisely, about the nefarious and
insistent racialization or war on people of color? As Lopez acknowledges,
she embodies, performs, and speaks of these issues on stage in "the Self-
Consciously Post-Modern way of my people" (2010, 63), marked by "the
hip, detached, and ironic way that my generation deals with everything.
Sure, it's arrogant—and even extremely annoying—but if we actually cared
about all the shit that's going on, we'd be heartbroken" (62). Avoiding or at
least negotiating heartbreak is a valuable skill of transloca performance, as
Holly Woodlawn also shows.

Holly Woodlawn's Puerto Rican Drag of Poverty

Impoverished Puerto Rican translocas who receive welfare have made
their mark since the late 1960s and early 1970s. For the self-described
"well-bred, Southern-raised, Puerto Rican Jew[ish]" trans performer
Holly Woodlawn, welfare became a strategy of survival in a context of
limited opportunities marked by prostitution, rampant drug use, incarceration, failed suicide attempts, and homelessness.[41] Born in Puerto Rico
in 1946 to a Puerto Rican mother and an American soldier of German
descent, and raised in New York and Miami Beach by her mother and
by her Polish American immigrant Jewish stepfather, Woodlawn experienced early teenage rejection and institutionalization due to her gender and sexual transgressions, followed by dramatic downward mobility
and impoverishment after she ran away from home at the age of fifteen
and "hitchhiked her way across the U.S.A.," as famously described in Lou
Reed's (1972) song "Walk on the Wild Side," where Reed documents the
lives of several Warhol superstars.

Woodlawn's 1991 memoir *A Low Life in High Heels*, which she coauthored with Jeff Copeland, describes Woodlawn's limited employment opportunities in New York City in the early 1960s as a trans adolescent who did not have a high school diploma; as she states, "At the age of sixteen, when most kids were cramming for trigonometry exams, I was turning tricks, living off the streets, and wondering when my next meal was coming" (1992, 60). Once off the streets, Woodlawn's employment consisted mainly of clerical/filing and modeling/sales jobs, which she was able to hold as long as she passed as a (cisgender) woman, at a time when cross-dressing was against the law and punishable by imprisonment, as well as deemed socially unacceptable and accompanied by moral and religious censure: a triple stigmatization by the state, civil society, and the church. This rejection was once again at work when Holly got kicked out of beauty school for coming to class while wearing female makeup and women's clothing, and when she lost a job as a go-go dancer in Albany, New York, after being perceived to be a man.

In the late 1960s, Woodlawn's contact with and integration into the predominantly white New York avant-garde theater and arts scene, particularly with Andy Warhol's Factory and with figures such as Jackie Curtis, Candy Darling, and John Vaccaro of the Playhouse of the Ridiculous, created opportunities for fame and exposure, but still did not provide basic sustenance; in fact, Woodlawn describes her relationship with Warhol as one of exploitation. Intent on being glamorous (as the title of chapter 3 of her memoir indicates, "Born to Be a Beauty Queen") and emulating Lola Flores and Lana Turner, and adopted by Puerto Rican queens when she first arrived in New York, she even became Miss Donut 1968 in Amsterdam, New York.[42] As a denizen of a bohemian demimonde marked by exclusion and by the copious consumption of drugs, Woodlawn also turned to theft as a means to survive, and experienced incarceration in 1970. Later, she would explicitly mark a distance between herself and the working-class "Puerto Rican queens" she had lived and interacted with, identifying them as "vicious" and "psychotic," as the scholar Frances Negrón-Muntaner (2004, 92) has pointed out in Boricua Pop, highlighting the tensions and negotiations of a stigmatized colonial, ethnic, and racial identity. Negrón-Muntaner also emphasizes that "even when [Woodlawn] repeatedly calls attention to the fact that she is 'very proud of being Puerto Rican,' the publicity for Holly's memoir stresses her association with Andy Warhol and her transvestism, not her ethno-nationality" (92).[43]

In her memoir, much like Erika Lopez, Woodlawn humorously presents welfare as a legitimate social alternative, describing a historical shift:

from a moment when welfare was relatively easy to receive (although not universal or permanent) in the middle to late 1960s to a period when it became highly bureaucratized, entailing lots of "red tape." After a second period of homelessness, Woodlawn moved in with white gay friends who received Social Security checks, and decided to follow suit:

> I thought it was a grand scheme and soon I was on welfare too. It was easy to get welfare then, since all a person had to do was stand in line, plead for help, and sign on the dotted line. Today there's so much red tape it's not worth the hassle. Welfare, Häagen Dazs, Crystal Meth, Vitabath, and a scrub brush were the essential elements in the tiring life of this speed queen. (1992, 115)

In this tongue-in-cheek depiction, welfare becomes a source of revenue for a "speed queen" (understood as "[a] person, female, who uses and/or is addicted to uppers," according to the online *Urban Dictionary*) whose drug consumption (whether crystal meth or other narcotics) complements her elevated culinary taste (Häagen-Dazs ice cream) and personal hygiene routine ("Vitabath and a scrub brush").[44]

In the 1970 Andy Warhol / Paul Morrisey film *Trash*, Holly Woodlawn plays the lead character of Holly Santiago, a transloca protagonist with entrepreneurial spirit who collects garbage for resale and serves as a go-between for clients, specifically for young men who want drugs, referred to as "junk."[45] As Woodlawn describes, she "was given the part of a down-and-out trash collector/connoisseur whose big motivation is to get laid by her impotent junkie boyfriend and obtain welfare. What perfect typecasting!" (1992, 6). The film highlights two economies: a libidinal one in which sex and affect serve as currency, which has the goal of emotional and sexual fulfillment; a material (political) one, which entails selling junk/trash/garbage (drugs or undesired objects) as participants in a secondary, parallel, or underground economy that is not recognized by the state as legitimate, and at the same time, trying to remedy the deficiencies of this poorly paid parallel economy by receiving government assistance.

As young, drug-using, sexually marginal subjects, the film's protagonists Holly Santiago, her boyfriend Joe Smith (played by Joe Dallesandro), and Holly's sister Diane (interpreted by Diane Podlewski) are at the threshold of mainstream society. Their situation is reminiscent of the three options available to Puerto Ricans in the United States that the poet Miguel Algarín (1975) proposes in the introduction to the *Nuyorican*

Fig. 8. Joe Dallesandro and Holly Woodlawn scavenging for junk in *Trash* (1970). Screen capture.

Poetry anthology: to labor for low wages, which actually does not seem to be a possibility; to hustle and work at the margins of the law, engaging in what is perceived as criminal activity; or to become an artist and transform society and the self through the invention of a new language and a new culture.[46] How do translocas negotiate these historical options?

In *Trash*, Holly and Joe do society's "dirty work," serving as a class of "untouchables" in a caste system that stigmatizes poverty and drug use but that does not disavow them; as the critic Jon Davies indicates, Holly and Joe "are not only desperately poor, but sexually frustrated as well, as the heroin has left him impotent—despite many women's concerted efforts to turn him on" (2009, 14). Upper- and middle-class people are portrayed in the film as constantly amused by and in need of these untouchables, be it as a form of entertainment or to actually obtain products, whether it is to buy drugs or to obtain objects such as Holly's silver high-heel shoes, which the corrupt welfare caseworker Mr. Michaels (interpreted by Michael Sklar) identifies as prized camp objects and tries to extort from her.

Mentions of welfare appear throughout *Trash*. The first occurs in a conversation between Holly and her pregnant sister Diane, who does not know who the father of her baby is and does not want to raise a child. Holly expresses her desire to care for the baby, and Diane responds, "We'll be able to get on welfare," which elicits an enthusiastic reaction from Holly. In the next scene, we see Holly naked and asleep in bed, as Joe and his dog walk in. Once awakened, Holly attempts to sexually arouse Joe while simultaneously telling him of Diane's pregnancy and of their plans. Holly also dreams that Joe will "kick dope" (get off drugs) and that Diane will move in with them. Holly starts to become frustrated because of Joe's drug-related impotence, to which Joe replies "Listen, just use the beer bottle." Holly then proceeds to simulate masturbation, crying out, "Oh God I want welfare!" In her memoir, Woodlawn has indicated that this over-the-top sordid scene generated unwanted attention and stigma.[47] As a plot device, welfare becomes tied to sexual pleasure, loneliness, and drug-related impotence; it becomes the substitute for desire and material well-being. Transloca performance facilitates the absurdist representation juxtaposing government sustenance, a potential orgasm, and a cold glass bottle.

Further discussion of welfare occurs in a later scene in *Trash*, when Holly walks into her apartment after trying to make money in front of the Fillmore East theater to discover her sister Diane making out with Joe naked in bed. When Joe proceeds to ask Holly for fifty cents, she declares: "I'm mad! It's my fucking home. I wanted to try to get back on welfare. Be respectable. Have a nice place so welfare could take care of us. Now I'm gonna feel like a piece of garbage. Welfare wouldn't take me!" Interestingly, here welfare is associated with a politics of respectability that somehow affords the individual a sense of self-worth. After Joe indicates that Holly "should feel like a piece of garbage with all the garbage you bring home," Holly defends her practice, seeing it as a legitimate form of employment that generates income, leading her to declare: "I need welfare. I deserve it. Shit. My family has a right to be on welfare. I was born on welfare, I will fucking die on welfare. I don't need you to help me. Fuck you and your dog."

The third and final welfare scene in the film is one of the best known; here, the transloca drag of poverty stresses humorous creativity as a tool of survival. In this scene, we see a complex, failed scenario of deception, framed by the seminaked figure of Joe, who is wrapped in a blue blanket, and by the protagonist Holly Santiago, who is pretending to be a pregnant woman who perceives welfare as an entitlement. The scene is largely structured around improvised dialogues; as the scholar Maurice Yacowar notes about this and the previous one, "In two wholly improvised scenes, Holly

articulates a dignity and self-respect that deny her identification as trash"
(1993, 41). After Mr. Michaels enters their basement apartment, Holly
attempts to convince him of her need and worthiness:

> MR. MICHAELS: Well, we need welfare, don't we?
> HOLLY: Sure do!
> MR. MICHAELS: You applied for welfare yesterday, Miss Santiago.
> HOLLY: Yes.
> MR. MICHAELS: Why did you apply for it?
> HOLLY: 'Cause we need it.
> MR. MICHAELS: Yeah.
> HOLLY: I'm gonna have a baby.
> MR. MICHAELS: Yeah, I can see. When are you expecting it?
> HOLLY: Next week. (*Looking at Joe, with confusion or doubt.*) Soon.
> MR. MICHAELS: Have you been on welfare before, either one of you?
> HOLLY: No. But we need it, though.
> MR. MICHAELS: You certainly should be eligible for it, there's no reason
>   not to.
>
> (*Mr. Michaels then begins to ask about the furnishings in the apartment,
> which Holly obtained from the garbage, and asks Miss Santiago and Mr.
> Smith what their parents do. Holly then reorients the conversation.*)
>
> HOLLY: When are we going to get welfare?
> MR. MICHAELS: There are a lot of things we have to consider.
> HOLLY: Aren't we entitled to it? (My transcription)

At this moment Mr. Michaels asks about her silver high-heel shoes,
and Holly indicates that she picked them up in the garbage. Mr. Michaels
then tries to extort them from her: "Those are really great shoes! You think
they look like the shoes Joan Crawford always wore. . . . Would you consider selling these, Miss Santiago? They would make a great lamp." Holly
is not amused by his proposition and refuses to comply; Mr. Michaels's
reference to a female Hollywood star, a centerpiece of white American gay
camp aesthetics, does not have the intended effect. While the scholar Moe
Meyer has defined camp as "the total body of performative practices used
to enact gay identity, with enactment defined as the production of social
visibility" (2010, 52), *Trash* evidences a transloca clash, in which a Puerto
Rican character resists potential identification with dominant gay views,
particularly when marked by power differentials.

Holly and Joe are not successful in their quest for welfare, exemplifying the mediated failure of the transloca drag of poverty but also highlighting its antiracist potential. As the interview proceeds, Mr. Michaels states that Joe is not on a methadone program, but he proposes ignoring this issue, if Holly will acquiesce to his request for her shoes. In the midst of their conversation, Mr. Michaels makes a racist generalization about welfare: "Look, I've dealt with the Negroes that crank out kids every nine months. Like bars they have children," suggesting that Black persons are not only promiscuous (as indicated by high fertility rates) but also alcoholics. At this moment, Holly becomes more agitated and argumentative, stating, "I was raised on welfare, and any woman who is pregnant has to have welfare. And you still can't have my fucking shoes!" inadvertently also confessing that she sells the garbage she collects, generating an income. "Just give us welfare!" she proclaims, stressing. "I'm entitled to it!" Angrier and angrier, she tells Joe: "I'm not going to give him the fucking shoes and I'm not going to stand for any of this fucking screaming in my own house!" And, as she stands up to kick Mr. Michaels out, she accidentally drops the pillow that she was using to simulate her pregnancy, forfeiting any chances for government assistance.

In her memoir *A Low Life in High Heels*, Woodlawn describes receiving welfare on and off, but also indicates the profound anger she felt during the filming of the semi-improvised scene with Michael Sklar, given his racist utterances. As she indicates,

> Michael was my first experience with a professional, unionized actor. . . . When we weren't filming, we would be yukking it up in the back, but when we did the scene, he suddenly became this pain-in-the-ass welfare worker who didn't like me at all. I was so intimidated and at a loss for words, until Michael made a crack about the Negroes cranking out babies every nine months to get on welfare. Well, honey, I was livid! Beverly Johnson was the top model of the year and he's talking about negroes cranking out babies to get on welfare? The NAACP was going to picket this movie for sure! I became so upset by this racial slur that I actually began to take him personally. I was no longer Holly Woodlawn playing Holly Santiago in a movie. I had made the transition, and this was real. Needless to say, we got into a big uproarious fight, with everybody yelling, screaming, and carrying on. The scene had to be shot five times! (Woodlawn and Copeland 1992, 145)

Failure has been described by Jack Halberstam (2011) as a "queer art."
Woodlawn's failure is precisely the triumph of a view informed by social
justice, which sees the transloca drag of poverty as a radical tool for
social critique.

While Holly Santiago was not successful in her quest for welfare in
Trash, in her memoir Woodlawn describes receiving an alternate type
of support from Andy Warhol and his Factory: limited handouts that in
many ways compensated for labor exploitation; the fact that Holly was
paid approximately $150 total salary for starring in a film that eventually
grossed four million dollars, one million in the United States and three
million in Europe. As she states,

> Every now and then, usually after too many drinks, I would feel like
> an exploited fool. But then, all the Superstars were Andy's fools. We
> acted like lunatics on film and he made millions off of it. Sometimes
> I felt cheated and sometimes I didn't, but when I did, I would be-
> come totally unraveled and incensed with anger. So, to release my
> frustrations, I'd march over to the Factory, snort flames, stomp my
> feet, and carry on like a mad banshee. "That goddamn son of a bitch
> is making millions off of me and I'm living in poverty!" I screamed.
> (1992, 163)

In many ways it comes down to the valuation of art and the exploitation of
labor—something Erika Lopez also highlights, in relation to Jean-Michel
Basquiat and to herself—and to the role of the government in a capitalist
economic system structured around inequality, which limits employment
possibilities and stigmatizes the poor and the marginal but which also
depends on and exploits many individuals' artistic production, whether it
is in the form of entertainment through performance or through the creation of works that can be capitalized and sold in the market. In this context, the general public has no qualms about most artists and performers
being poor, exploited, and marginalized. Woodlawn's status as an impoverished Jewish Puerto Rican Warhol superstar, entailing a mix of celebrity,
media attention, and glamour accompanied by exploitation, poverty, and
neglect, makes for a complex and contradictory welfare queen: the Queen
of Trash, the transloca queen of low. She also becomes, in her campy, over-
the-top dramatic way, a symbol of the potential of the transloca drag of
poverty, and of transloca performance more widely conceived.

Monica Beverly Hillz and the Reinscription of Puerto Rican Welfare Queens

Plus ça change, plus c'est la même chose. More than thirty years after Wood-lawn's participation in Andy Warhol's *Trash*, and several years after Erika Lopez's last performance of *The Welfare Queen*, Monica Beverly Hillz's (Monica DeJesus Anaya's) appearance in season 5 of *RuPaul's Drag Race* in 2013 extended the trope of the racialized Puerto Rican welfare queen—the *transloca pobre*—giving it a new inflection, as a "ghetto" or "banjee" queen competing for the title of "America's Next Drag Superstar."[48] Here Warhol superstardom was exchanged for the notoriety produced by participa-tion in one of the country's highest rated reality-based television contests, especially popular among gay and female audiences, including significant numbers of young viewers; one that by 2013 had a cash prize of $100,000 for the top winner, as opposed to the modest cash prize of $20,000 that Nina Flowers (discussed in chapter 2) competed for in 2009. *RuPaul's Drag Race*, produced by World of Wonder and transmitted on Logo TV from 2009 until 2016 and since 2017 on VH1, also owned by Viacom, pits contestants against each other, demanding expertise in sewing, costume design, makeup, hair or wig styling, lip-synching, acting, dance, female impersonation, knowledge of popular culture, and humor, or what RuPaul coyly synthesizes as CUNT ("charisma, uniqueness, nerve, and talent").[49] The first eleven seasons (2009–19) were marked by the presence of at least one and at times as many as three Puerto Rican contestants, and season 12 (2020) was the first to feature no Puerto Ricans; as of December 2020, no Puerto Rican had ever won, although Nina Flowers was the first runner-up of season 1 and won the Miss Congeniality Award.

The careful selection of *RuPaul's Drag Race* contestants based on the potential for conflict and jarring juxtaposition (in other words, the inclu-sion of contestants for shock value as opposed to genuine talent) high-lights a tension identified as early as 1972 by Esther Newton in *Mother Camp*, namely the difference between middle-class, predominantly white, well-educated professional female impersonators ("stage impersonators") who master camp comedy and cabaret singing, on the one hand, and working-class, frequently homeless, "street queens" and "street imper-sonators" (*locas pobres* who embody the transloca drag of poverty) who occasionally work in prostitution and who mostly do lip-synching. The divide in *RuPaul's Drag Race* is not quite as Manichaean, but does evidence disparities of educational and professional background, class status, skills, and linguistic proficiency. Similar to Warhol's Factory, the program positions RuPaul as a type of benefactor who can provide patronage (a grand prize) and global fame not only to the lucky winner but to all the "Ru girls" who participate on the show and acquire a somewhat temporary notoriety, at least immediately following the broadcast of their season.

While Monica Beverly Hillz was announced in preliminary advertising in late 2012 and early 2013 as a Latina bombshell or beauty queen—a "fishy" queen, a category of high praise used to indicate striking verisimilitude, an ability to pass as what we would now identify as a cisgendered feminine woman—after the show began, Hillz was quickly racialized as Black, working class, poor, "ghetto," and "banjee" (an urban, ballroom culture, hip-hop term popularized by *Paris Is Burning*), evacuated of the signifier of Latina and particularly of Afro-Latina, which was more clearly assigned to other transloca contestants in her season, such as the dark-skinned Panamanian American Serena ChaCha (Myron Morgan), from Tallahassee, Florida, and the Black Puerto Rican Lineysha Sparx (Andy Trinidad), from San Juan, who spoke with a strong accent and who on occasion did not understand English, but not to the light-skinned, "thick and juicy," or large-bodied, Cuban–Puerto Rican Roxxxy Andrews (Michael Feliciano) from Orlando, Florida.[50] Instead, Hillz was expected to participate in a dominant Black/white binary outside of Latinidad in which Black equals poor or "ghetto," even while the show's creator and arguably main star, the African American performer RuPaul Charles, who was identified in the show's credits as coming from Detroit's Brewster Housing Projects (but is actually from San Diego and then Atlanta), performs hegemonic white movie star glamour, particularly through the use of extravagant blond wigs and highly stylized gowns, signaling the class mobility best exemplified by celebrity entrepreneur billionaire Oprah Winfrey.[51] Monica Beverly Hillz's racialization and de-Latinization highlights the unpredictable racial dynamics among the show's contestants and/or the producers' use of difference as a strategy to create narrative tension and viewer interest, for example the tension between two pageant queens in season 5, the African American contestant Coco Montrese and her former friend, the white contestant and rival Alyssa Edwards, who are presented as social equals and highly polished given their participation in the professional drag pageant system.

Of course, it can be said that in many ways the producers of *RuPaul's Drag Race* simply took advantage of the aspirational status of the contestant's performance name, particularly of her stylized middle and last name, "Beverly Hillz," which references the extremely well known, predominantly white, very affluent city in Los Angeles County—the setting for the 1990 film *Pretty Woman*, Hillz's favorite—transforming the spelling in what comes across as a hip-hop-inspired move, exchanging the final *s* for a *z*, resonating with performers such as Jay-Z, but also subtly echoing Audre Lorde's *Zami: A New Spelling of My Name* (Neal 2013) as well as the "graffiti grrlz" (women graffiti writers) discussed by the scholar Jessica Nydia Pabón-Colón (2018).[52] The contrast between Monica Beverly Hillz's hip-hop style and the anti-Black stereotype of what Beverly Hills represents, for example in the television series *Beverly Hills 90210*, which ran from 1990 to 2000, perhaps made it inevitable that the contestant would be challenged on the grounds of race, class, and social location.

The divergence between early promotional publicity materials and the actual representation that began in the first episode of season 5 ("RuPaullywood or Bust"), first transmitted on January 28, 2013, was dramatically reconfigured a week later in the second episode ("Lip Synch Extravaganza Eleganza") as a result of Monica Beverly Hillz's distanced and anguished presence, which eventually lead to an on-camera breakdown and the dramatic confession of her self-identification as a trans woman in the midst of her transition who did not identify as a gay man. This redirection aligns with other dramatic confessions, for example Ongina's disclosure of her HIV-positive status in season 1, and with the postshow disclosure of former contestants such as that of the US-born Puerto Rican Peruvian American Carmen Carrera, who now self-identifies as a trans woman and who created significant anti–*Drag Race* sentiment in 2014 through her criticism of the usage of the word "trannie" and the pun "She/Mail," which echoed the disparaging term "shemale" on the show.[53] Monica Beverly Hillz was soon eliminated after her disclosure in the next episode ("Draggle Rock") transmitted on February 11, but she was not disqualified, a situation experienced by other non-rule-complying contestants such as Willam Belli in season 4.

Monica Beverly Hillz's pre- and postshow interviews—for example, on the *Feast of Fun* podcast (Felion 2013), where she appeared with *Drag Race* season 1 contestant Jade Sotomayor, another Puerto Rican transloca working-class queen from Chicago, and in a later episode of *Cooking with Drag Queens* (Feast of Fun 2019)—have expanded our knowledge about her life, particularly about the economic and work struggles she has faced as a feminine Puerto Rican gender-nonconforming individual; these inter-

Fig. 9. Monica Beverly Hillz in *RuPaul's Drag Race* season 5 (2013). Screen capture.

views highlight the profound challenges entailed in the transloca drag of poverty, which at times can seem almost unsurmountable. Born in Chicago in 1985, Hillz grew up in Humboldt Park and was later adopted by her aunt at age eleven, as her birth mother was unable to care for her due to substance abuse.[54] As a teenager, Hillz later became homeless, lived in the Indiana/Kentucky border region with her birth family, was bullied in high school, contemplated suicide, ran away to Chicago, started performing in drag, developed a cocaine addiction, became involved in prostitution, and eventually moved back to Kentucky.[55] At some moment, she began to take female hormones (Hillz 2018). In late 2019, she announced that she was in the process of having her legal name and her sex changed (Feast of Fun 2019), which she later confirmed on Facebook. At no moment has she publicly discussed receiving any type of government assistance; she has also not spoken about her family receiving welfare. Most of these extremely serious issues were not discussed in season 5 of *RuPaul's Drag Race*.

In a 2013 SocialScope interview available on YouTube, Hillz expanded on her drug use and work as an escort, detailing the violence she was subjected to and how she continues to experience nightmares as a result, a condition that can be interpreted as post-traumatic stress disorder.[56] The interview is notable for her candidness and willingness to discuss challenging topics with the interviewer (Joss Barton) in a less confrontational setting, for the interviewer's sympathy, and for the notable sisterhood we see between Hillz and her close friend Jade Sotomayor, who also appears in the video. Hillz's pioneering role as the first trans woman to publicly disclose her gender identity on *RuPaul's Drag Race* has kept her in the public eye, particularly after RuPaul made trans-exclusionary comments in 2018.[57] In this sense, Monica Beverly Hillz has used the national and international exposure she obtained by performing in drag as a platform to advocate for trans rights, particularly those of trans women of color; like Lopez and Woodlawn, she has used the transloca drag of poverty as a space for engaging politics of exclusion and the experience of precarious life.

Sylvia Rivera's Radical Performance of Politics

I have chosen to conclude this chapter on *translocas pobres*, welfare queens, and the drag of poverty by discussing the activism of Sylvia Rivera because of the ways it resonates with the world-making performances of Erika Lopez, Holly Woodlawn, and Monica Beverly Hillz, and because it is a radically different option that carries significant weight. I struggled for a long time as to how to integrate a discussion of Rivera in a book that is intrinsically about artistic performance and not about activism.[58] Yet, watching videos of Rivera's impassioned 1973 speech at the Christopher Street Liberation Day rally in New York City, I was reminded that the strength of her message had to do as much with her physicality and with her portentous voice as it did with the actual words she spoke.[59] That is to say, her delivery (her political performance as a *transloca pobre*) as an ora-

Fig. 10. Sylvia Rivera and Marsha P. Johnson at Christopher Street Liberation Day March 1973. Leonard Fink Photographs, Box 3, Folder 24, LGBT Community Center National History Archive.

tor who literally had to fight to get to the microphone, and whose physical and emotional exhaustion and profound frustration were captured by those video cameras, motivates me. That, and the fact that she has become the subject of controversy: while ostensibly one of the most famous translocas in the United States, with streets and organizations such as the Sylvia Rivera Law Project (SRLP) in New York City named after her, she is also the subject of elision.[60] To top it off, Rivera has been the focus of numerous artistic representations, whether in documentaries, animated films, or narrative films such as Nigel Finch's *Stonewall* (1995), Roland Emmerich's similarly named 2015 film, or Tourmaline and Sasha Wortzel's 2018 *Happy Birthday, Marsha!*, where Rivera is played by a range of different cisgender and transgender actors.[61]

Rivera was born in 1951 in New York City to a Puerto Rican father and a Venezuelan mother and raised by her maternal grandmother.[62] Much like Holly Woodlawn and Monica Beverly Hillz, she ended up running away from home at a young age, in Rivera's case, when she was ten years old; like Woodlawn, Rivera went on to live and hustle in the Times Square area of Manhattan, where she engaged in sex work as a minor and was adopted, so to speak, by older Puerto Rican drag queens. She became politicized in the middle to late 1960s in the context of the civil rights struggle, the anti–Vietnam War movement, the women's and gay liberation movements, and the Puerto Rican cultural and political movement led in New York City by the Young Lords Party.[63]

There is considerable debate as to whether Rivera was actually at the Stonewall Inn on the first night of the riots in 1969 or if in fact she participated in any of the activities that transpired in the two subsequent days.[64] As in other famous interpretive struggles regarding truth-telling and sociopolitical activism (most notably, that of Guatemalan Nobel Peace Prize winner Rigoberta Menchú, who was also accused of lying), defenders support her claims, while detractors try to discredit and minimize her role.[65] Rivera stated in numerous occasions that she was at Stonewall during the riots and used the authority and respect that she received as a Stonewall veteran to raise awareness of the needs of gender-nonconforming people, which she referred to in different ways throughout her life, including using the terms "street queens," "drag queens," "transvestites," and, toward the end of her life, "transgender."[66] She also used Spanish-language terms such as *pato* and *maricones* (Marcus 1993, 188) to reference this stigmatized population.

Rivera had extensive knowledge about the incidents that transpired on the first night of the Stonewall riots in 1969 and was able to narrate these in the first person without a script, as she did when I invited her to a meeting of Latino Gay Men of New York (LGMNY) in June 2001.[67] Rivera frequently explained why she marched in the New York City Pride March with the Stonewall Veterans Association, and many people recognized her for her involvement, for example historian Martin Duberman (1993) in his definitive account about the event, even if journalist David Carter (2004) chose not to mention her in his book on the same topic. Rivera is also included in Jason Bauman's *The Stonewall Reader* (2019) and in Marc Stein's *The Stonewall Riots: A Documentary History* (2019). It is also clear that Rivera is a key figure for trans activists, artists, and scholars such as Leslie Feinberg (1998), Jessi Gan (2007), Jack Halberstam (2018), Tourmaline (Gossett 2012a, 2012b), and Riki Wilchins (2002), all of whom stress her foundational role in the trans rights movement.[68]

Soon after Stonewall, Rivera became extremely involved in the gay rights struggle. She was arrested in 1970 while petitioning for signatures in Times Square. That same year she participated in a building takeover at New York University.[69] Around this time, she published a short piece titled "Transvestites: Your Half Sisters and Half Brothers of the Revolution" (Rivera 1972), which appeared in *Come Out*, the periodical of the Gay Liberation Front.[70] In 1970, she also established STAR (Street Transvestite Action Revolutionaries) and STAR House, a homeless shelter for young street queens, together with her comrade in arms, the African American activist Marsha P. Johnson.[71]

Rivera's participation in the 1973 New York City Christopher Street Liberation Day March and in the rally held immediately afterward cemented her position in trans history. According to Randy Wicker, Rivera experienced several confrontations during the march route and narrowly missed being arrested.[72] Rivera's subsequent speech, documented and included in films and videos such as *The Question of Equality* (Dong 1995), *Sylvia* (Mateik 2002), and *The Death and Life of Marsha P. Johnson* (France 2017), portrays an absolutely committed activist hell-bent on challenging racist, classist, and gender-based exclusions within the lesbian and gay movement.[73]

Rivera's speech is structured around complex rhetorical strategies, focusing on the situation of incarcerated street queens who wrote to STAR and who were ignored by the leading gay and lesbian groups; Rivera's critique is extremely compelling, engaging in what the scholar Ruth Osorio (2017) calls the "delivery of *parrhesia*," or truth-telling. Rivera goes from describing the experiences of incarcerated trans women subjected to abuse (institutional violence, including sexual assault), to speaking from personal experience ("I have been beaten, I have been raped, I have lost my apartment for gay liberation") and challenging those who are listening to her, the same ones who booed her when she got on stage. She culminates her speech by getting the audience to participate in a collective cheer, inviting them to spell out the words "gay power," her voice faltering in exhaustion toward the end. Rivera employed similar rhetorical strategies but in a less confrontational setting in her 2001 LGMNY speech at the Lesbian and Gay Community Services Center, juxtaposing her personal experience and that of her community to the experience of her listeners, this time speaking to a group of predominantly Latinx gay men that included some trans women and drag queens.[74]

In none of the available documentation about Sylvia Rivera is there ever a mention of welfare queens, although at least one scholar uses the term "welfare" when identifying Johnson's and Rivera's activism, specifically their "foundational antipolicing, anti-prison, welfare and shelter organizing" (Tang 2017, 379). Rather, Rivera advocated for the radical transformation of existing structures, whether they were the police or the lesbian and gay movement. She supplemented this with an impetus for the creation of alternative structures such as STAR House, as well as organizing the homeless encampments on the West Side of Manhattan in 1996. By the late 1990s, she embraced the possibilities of effecting change and offering services through a religious organization, the Metropolitan Community Church (MCC), and also committed herself to antiviolence work, for example demanding justice in relation to the murder of the African American trans woman Amanda Milan.[75]

Rivera's life, thought, and activism remind us of the limitations of "welfare queens" as a strategy for the advancement of poor, disenfranchised drag queens and trans women of color, and as such serves as a counterpoint to the dramatic and at times humorous strategies of transloca artists such as Erika Lopez and Holly Woodlawn, coming closer to the explicit activist stance that Monica Beverly Hillz has adopted of late. All four demonstrate the radical potential of the transloca drag of poverty to challenge social structures in the context of inequality. All four expose the profound imbrication of race, class, gender, and sexuality in America and belie the myth of social equality and full democracy implicit in dominant narratives of the "American dream." Honoring, remembering, and understanding their predicament and their strategies of survival is a valuable and necessary endeavor.

FOUR

Freddie Mercado and the Ultrabaroque Drag of Rasanblaj

In the introduction to the catalog for the New York City Museo del Barrio exhibit *Here and There: Six Artists from San Juan*, the art scholar and curator Deborah Cullen (2001, 6–19) takes up Elizabeth Armstrong and Víctor Zamudio-Taylor's (2000) provocative categorizations of *ultrabaroque* and *post-Latin American art* to discuss the work of six (at that time) young contemporary Puerto Rican visual artists based predominantly in Puerto Rico, including Freddie Mercado Velázquez, the transloca performer who is the focus of this chapter.[1] By "ultrabaroque," the three critics refer to an intensification of the *barroco de Indias*, or New World baroque, that has characterized (and, some would argue, limited and pigeonholed) Latin American art; it is a profoundly queer baroque, I would add, one that was taken up by numerous Latin American authors, artists, performers, and scholars in the twentieth century and recast as *neobarroco* (neobaroque) in the Hispanic Caribbean and as *neobarroso* in the Southern Cone (Argentina, Chile, Uruguay) to resignify and transform dominant notions of culture.[2] Simultaneously, through their use of the term "post–Latin American art," Armstrong, Zamudio-Taylor, and Cullen wish to displace the centrality of questions of national identity and attempt to locate these productions in an international, cosmopolitan setting, one in which an artist's place of birth and ethnonational identification are only one among many other constitutive marks.[3]

There is always a risk with critical gestures like that of *post-Latin American art* that distance artistic production from its site of origin, even while also highlighting the local. It becomes very easy to favor the former over the latter and to lose the specificity of origins, particularly in a neoliberal context that is only too happy to absorb cultural productions, homogenize local specificities, and neglect the particularities of minoritarian subjects and cultures through the market-oriented logics of a multiculturalism destined to manage and absorb difference in order to maximize profit. Transloca performance, I contend, insists repeatedly on the value of the local, even when artists simultaneously combine, juxtapose, or filter it through the translocal, transnational, or transglocal, or what the Trinidadian American scholar Rosamond S. King (2014) has referred to as the "Caribglobal." It does not inhabit the realm of the "post," but rather insistently dwells, negotiates, and disrupts the here and now, as it attempts "to think and feel a *then and there*" (Muñoz 2009, 1) through the lens of the "trans" and in relationship to the body (Aranda-Alvarado 2012).

One possible conceptual alternative to *post-Latin American art* is the framework of *rasanblaj*, theorized as "Catalyst. Keyword. Method. Practice. Project" by the scholar Gina Athena Ulysse (2014), using a word from Haitian Kreyòl that envisions an "assembly, compilation, enlisting, regrouping."[4] For Ulysse, rasanblaj is an invitation to engage with the multiplicity and complexity of the Caribbean, not in an effort to move away from it, but rather to dirty metropolitan models: to make them engage the radical, communitarian, erotic, decolonial, utopian, profoundly historical present and future of the region. A transloca practice, rasanblaj is a feminist, queer, contemporary rearticulation of Édouard Glissant's notion of *Créolité*, a questioning of postidentities, a political recuperation that Ulysse envisions valorizing the groundbreaking and transformative work of intellectuals such as Audre Lorde, Mimi Sheller, C. L. R. James, Michel-Rolph Trouillot, Brian Meeks, Suzanne Césaire, José Esteban Muñoz, and M. Jacqui Alexander.[5] For me, rasanblaj serves in understanding the profoundly queer, ultrabaroque, transloca performance of Freddie Mercado, highlighting a type of Caribbean *rasquache* project based on poverty, improvisation, recycling, and reuse, or what Laura G. Gutiérrez defines as "a resourceful, working-class, neo-baroque [Chicanx] aesthetic sensibility" that finds parallels in other Latinx contexts (2017, 184).

How does one queer the ultrabaroque as an aesthetic and political practice, or is it already queer? A historical style from the seventeenth century, the baroque "is marked generally by use of complex forms, bold ornamentation, and the juxtaposition of contrasting elements often conveying a sense of drama, movement, and tension" (Merriam-Webster). It is a style that moves away from classical lines and simplicity to embrace exuberance, exaggeration, and opacity. Critics have debated it politics, seeing it as a reentrenchment of conservative values or its opposite, a practice of resistance and critique.[6]

Rubén Ríos Ávila, among other scholars, has highlighted how certain twentieth- and twenty-first-century Latin American queer artists drew from the baroque; he calls Néstor Perlongher and Pedro Lemebel "locas barrocas" (baroque *locas*) (2009) and sees in the work of Perlongher and José Lezama Lima "una compartida vocación por el delirio," or a shared vocation for delirium (2013, 177), where "delirium" (a state close to madness, or *locura*) enables a critique of Western rationality. According to Ríos Ávila, "Perlongher has referred to the baroque, thinking specifically of Góngora and Lezama, as 'the most scandalously anti-Western art derived from the very West' (Perlongher 113). It is from the Westernness of the *logos*, the womb of Westernness, its *mother nature*, that delirium departs" (2013, 177). Yet Perlongher marks a difference between the classical baroque and its appropriation in the twentieth century, in a period in which the belief in the "transparency" or legibility of realist forms has collapsed (quoted in Ríos Avila 2013, 182). For Ríos Ávila, the *barroco de Indias* is a reparative strategy of inversion that overturns the European colonial gaze: "It is a baroque that returns to the gold of the Conquest the original brightness of its blinding light, that returns the gold to the river" (184). As such, this decolonial baroque (or rather, the neobaroque) enables an interior critique, much like rasanblaj. The baroque becomes an enabling gesture of transloca performance, an aesthetic practice of exuberance that challenges received truths.

Meeting Freddie Mercado

Mercado scares, delights, and offends; he is a Puerto Rican postmodern doll, a performative Caribbean embodiment, an ultrabaroque disruption: profoundly creole in his infinite local references, and only partially post–Latin American in his universalizing appeal. A master of Caribbean rasanblaj and of the Caribglobal, Mercado's transloca performance and visual arts production centers uncanny (freakish, monstrous) manifestations of drag as part of his exploration of transgender, translocal, and transnational phenomena, and bridges the "trans" to account for the multiplicities of gender, sexuality, race, species, and geography. Mercado's constant, transformative, always surprising, and sometimes upsetting queer hybridations are an ultimate example of what translocas can be or do: purveyors of an artistic practice that crosses the line between sanity and madness, the known and the unknown, and the real and the imaginary.

A consummate visual/performance artist, Mercado's life and work are all intimately enmeshed in a project of staging and rearticulating a complex trans-Caribbean identity, one deeply marked by his questioning of multiple identity categories and conceptual binaries—such as human/nonhuman animal, human/monster, and life/death, or what Mel Y. Chen refers to as "the fragile division between animate and inanimate" (2012, 2)—frequently through humor and the grotesque and through the exaltation of androgyny, hybridity, and eroticism. He does this with limited resources, as an artist who has never been commercially successful and whose production is generally not purchased by institutions or by wealthy individual collectors. Mercado's work was first discussed by art historians, art critics, and media scholars, but was mostly neglected by Caribbean theater and performance studies scholars until rather recently, perhaps because of Mercado's training as a visual artist and the predominant lack of a written or linguistic component in his work or maybe because of its sexually transgressive, queer ultrabaroque nature in a profoundly socially conservative context.[7]

In this chapter I will build on diverse theoretical and methodological frameworks, including art history and art criticism, but also position Mercado in relation to theater and performance scholarship, particularly given his importance as a collaborator and participant in what Lowell Fiet, Vivian Martínez Tabares, and Carlos Manuel Rivera, among others, have identified as alternative or marginal theater in Puerto Rico, in other words "el 'otro' teatro puertorriqueño" (the "other" Puerto Rican theater), or what José O. Rosado has called the "liminal" works of "la 'nueva' nueva dramaturgia puertorriqueña" (the "new" new Puerto Rican dramaturgy), which is to say, works that truly challenge Roberto Ramos-Perea's self-named (yet somewhat staid) "New Puerto Rican dramaturgy."[8] My placement of Mercado, his *loca*-lization—to employ Lisa Sánchez González's (2001) and Marcia Ochoa's (2008) clever word play—corresponds to Dorian Lugo Bertrán's (2002) inclusion of the artist in the contemporary Puerto Rican avant-garde anthology *Saqueos*, where Mercado appears together with other island-based, experimental performers, such as Eduardo Alegría, Ivy Andino, Javier Cardona, Teresa Hernández, Nelson Rivera, Ivette Román, and Bernat Tort. It also corresponds to the great affinity between Mercado's work and that of Latinx and Latin American performance artists and groups, such as the ones included by Coco Fusco (2000) in *Cor-*

pus Delecti, by Diana Taylor and Roselyn Costantino (2003) in *Holy Terrors*, and by Deborah Cullen (2008) in *Arte ≠ Vida*. Finally, it has to do with the long-standing links between visual artists and the Puerto Rican performing arts that Nelson Rivera (1997) has so carefully documented, and to the fact that Mercado has participated as an actor or collaborator in productions by María De Azúa, Zora Moreno, Mickey Negrón, and Awilda Sterling Duprey, among many others.[9]

Much like the Mexican painter Frida Kahlo, Mercado highlights his own corporeality, in this case, that of a large-bodied, overweight, androgynous or effeminate, light-skinned Puerto Rican man who is frequently confused for a woman and at times thought to be of African descent or *jabao* (light-skinned mixed race) because of his curly hair and body type; Mercado's racial indeterminacy causes anxiety in Puerto Rico and has led to debates about his work and to accusations of cultural appropriation. Mercado also highlights his hybrid cultural milieu, and turns it and himself and his collaborators such as Mickey Negrón and Héctor Torres (and even myself, that is to say, Lola von Miramar) into his own greatest creations, displacing two- and three-dimensional representations from walls and gallery spaces and challenging traditional, conservative, Puerto Rican audiences as he transforms his own body and those of others into living works of art.[10] As he has stated, "My work is a constant performance," one that is achieved by wearing intricate female, animal, or monster costumes; engaging in long dressing sessions; making public and private appearances, at times transformed into famous historical female characters such as Felisa Rincón de Gautier and Myrta Silva; painting self-portraits in multiple disguises and costumes, perhaps the most direct link to Kahlo, but also to other contemporary painters such as the Puerto Rican Arnaldo Roche Rabell and the Mexican Nahum B. Zenil; and creating self-dolls.[11]

Process and transformation are integral parts of Mercado's work: being and becoming, or, to quote Elin Diamond's succinct definition of performance, "a doing" and "a thing done" (1996, 1). Like Kahlo, Roche Rabell, Zenil, and contemporary performance artists such as the Yeguas del Apocalipsis, Giuseppe Campuzano, and Lukas Avendaño, Mercado directly foregrounds issues of gender, sexuality, race, ethnicity, and self-fashioning. In his paintings, drawings, installations, and dolls, he documents and deconstructs his creations and imagines alternative racial and gender possibilities. Yet, quite unlike Kahlo and Zenil, Mercado's world has not so far included masculine objects of affection. While his eternal transformations are at times accompanied by the solitary self-generated birth of his doll "children," they are most often about the here and now of his ever-changing masculine/feminine, androgynous, freakish, or monstrous presence in time and space.

Mercado's "constant performance" occurs whether he is holed up in an apartment, visiting a random space, or appearing at an art gallery or museum in Puerto Rico, the Dominican Republic, Amsterdam, or New York City; dressed up as a fantastic or grotesque female character, perhaps with one of his doll creations in tow; or perhaps wandering down the streets of Old San Juan or Santurce or Río Piedras in his habitual manner, wearing large, loose tunics crowned by his long unfurled curly hair. At other times, he is transformed into a divine apparition for *Noches de Galería* (*Gallery Nights*): a mobile public work of art, transportable, eternally changing, wandering from place to place, being inside and out, simultaneously part of city street life and of the rarefied indoor environment of the arts; a cultural streetwalker, working the sidewalk with a combination of explicit sensuality and art, the opposite of an anonymous Baudelairean flâneur or of Michel de Certeau's citizen-subject (1985); a standard-bearer of a very, very queer democracy, nomad-like like Gilles Deleuze and Félix Guattari's theoretical subjects (1986b), disruptive and uncontainable; an ultrabaroque transloca creature of the night that appears at all hours of the day.[12]

There are other Freddies that I wish to highlight: those of the cultural citation or appropriation, of invented characters that reference global cultures not necessarily associated with Puerto Rico, for example a veiled Muslim woman opposing the war in the Persian Gulf in the early 1990s, decorated with a tiara of military green plastic toy soldiers, showing up to class at the Escuela de Artes Plásticas and photographed by a friend in a context in which there are few veiled women, except perhaps for traditional Catholic nuns and pious female churchgoers; a historical character of the colonial West Indian baroque, posing in an elite museum inside of a gigantic ornate gilded wooden frame; an Italian Renaissance damsel.[13] Here Freddie becomes mysterious, pseudo-orientalist, and, at times, orientalizing (Said 1979)—not due to prejudice or cultural insensitivity, but as a strategy of the weak, an inverted reenactment of schizoid mimicry à la Henry Louis Gates (1988), what Josefina Ludmer (1985, 1991) calls, in reference to Sor Juana Inés de la Cruz, a *treta del débil* (a tactic or feint of the weak).

With Mercado, the insular, claustrophobic space of Puerto Rico suddenly becomes the creative citational space of the *One Thousand and One*

Nights (Freddie/Scheherazade) or an encyclopedic catalog, marked by its sharp, critical, sociopolitical bent, visible to those who can read between the lines; an opaque practice comparable to Lezama Lima's baroque "sistema poético del mundo" (poetic system of the world), populated by myriad, uncontainable associations and references that can be quite maddening and confusing (Cruz-Malavé 1994; Ríos Ávila 2013). This is something that escaped the *New York Times* art critic Holland Cotter (2001) in his otherwise insightful review of *Here and There: Six Artists from San Juan*, when Cotter stated: "Minimalism isn't their scene; nor, in any overt way, is politics."

Mercado represents a mystery somewhere between absurd and perfectly recognizable, which fragments the Puerto Rican "insularism" of the canonical intellectual Antonio S. Pedreira (1934) in an unexpected, almost Borgesian, way that confuses trivial matters with the sociological referent.[14] The exotic other is mixed with the exaggerated localism in an aesthetic where everything counts and has value (a baroque Caribbean rasanblaj as bricolage or assembly), and everything can be indexed or referenced, if, after all, the very ontological being operates at the margins, outside of the accustomed order and within the sphere of those rejected and violently censored by intolerance and conservative petit bourgeois provincialism. Curiously, living exclusively on the island and avoiding migration provokes a radical distancing option.

Mercado's strident performances achieve their highest complexity and posit their very own liminal frontiers with his not-quite-human characters that lead to the disintegration of the subject, to his literally becoming an animal, a monster, a freak, or a doll. These include Freddie as chicken or hermaphrodite rooster/chicken, a female creature that lays eggs and looks for her rooster (himself), cackling down the halls of a museum, as in the opening of the 2001 *Here and There* Museo del Barrio show; as a six-eyed creature with exposed breasts bearing eyes as nipples and multiple foam heads sprouting from his headpiece in the 2002 ARCO International Contemporary Art Fair in Madrid (Robinson 2002), a performance that became the image on the cover of a book published in Puerto Rico (Torrecilla 2004); and as *La Vaca Maja* (The Spanish Maja Cow), a mantilla-wearing creature that milks herself and feeds cold yogurt to spectators—particularly to children—out of a cow udder prosthetic, as at the CIRCA 2007 International Art Fair in Puerto Rico.[15] He also becomes an ostrich at the Museo de Arte Contemporáneo de Puerto Rico (MACPR) in 2010; an anthropomorphized black swan / duck / ballerina, a perverse homage to

Fig. 11. Freddie Mercado Velázquez as an androgynous, anthropomorphized bald eagle in *Viaje . . . Sé* (MACPR, San Juan, 2013). Photograph by Luzmar Soneira, courtesy of Marina Barsy Janer.

Darren Aronofsky's 2010 film *Black Swan*, playing with the double valence of *pato*, or duck, in Puerto Rico as a stigmatized euphemism for faggot and with Hans Christian Andersen's "The Ugly Duckling" in Mercado's *El Black Patito Swan Feo*, performed at the Asuntos Efímeros Cabaret hosted by Mickey Negrón in Río Piedras in 2011; and a grotesque, oversexualized, burlesque, female doll/fetish creature with a giant multicolor head and enormous foam penis, also at Asuntos Efímeros (2011).[16]

In his performance *Viaje . . . Sé* presented in Santo Domingo and San Juan in 2013, Mercado became an anthropomorphized, large-breasted, female American bald eagle crowned with a dozen large green and light yellow plastic toy soldiers (see figure 11).[17] In the video documentation of his performance at the MACPR (Mercado 2013), which was part of a panel discussion, "The Recent History of Puerto Rican Performance Art (2003–2013)," organized by the performer and curator Marina Barsy Janer, we see the costumed artist in a museum exhibit room, moving his head as if he were a bird, shaking his gloved and long-red-fingernail-bedecked hands, making the small bells at his wrists jingle; the creature then caws at the audience, generating laughter. Mercado wears a large headpiece that includes a caricaturesque eagle's head sculpted out of foam with distinctive white feathers on top, whose yellow beak protrudes and slightly covers the performer's femininely made-up face; the creature also seems to wear a somewhat matted (perhaps dreadlocked), auburn-colored, humanlike wig. As the performer raises his arms, we see two large, naked, pink-flesh-colored, plastic baby dolls that dangle from his wrists, attached by S-M-like black leather straps, as well as large, exposed, light brown breasts with nipples that contrast with the bird's dark brown plumage. We also see two pink human mannequin hands tied to the performer's waist; the creature proceeds to nurse the dolls at her breasts. Mercado then raises a bedazzled, black-feather-adorned, handheld mirror that has a beautiful human female countenance painted on its back, which becomes a type of mask.

As the performer moves the hand mirror, the creature now has two faces: its own and the idealized depiction on the back of the performance object. Suddenly, the artist turns the mirror, and now the reflective surface faces the audience, and we become its face. Then the performer turns his back to the audience and we see that the bird's large, humanlike derriere, which seems to have a black-lined simulated vagina, is framed by two huge black-and-white eyes made out of foam, as if tail feathers, framed by long black feather eyelashes; the huge brown derriere stares at us and jiggles, as we hear more audience laughter. We then discover that the creature has a huge brown foam penis that dangles between its legs, as if a fertility symbol, which had been hidden behind a brown skirt or apron, and yellow foam talons attached above the performer's feet. The mysterious creature then walks toward the back and proceeds to leave the room.

In *Viaje . . . Sé*, Mercado transforms an endemic creature of North America (the bald eagle), highly venerated by Indigenous populations but also a national symbol of American imperialism, through a transloca performance invoking caricature (the animal's head resembles a Muppet), militaristic childhood objects (plastic toy soldiers), and femininity and motherhood (the baby dolls, which almost seem like a human sacrifice or the creature's offspring) in a hypersexualized, androgynous framework of exposed human adult female breasts, hyperbolic buttocks, possibly a vagina, and a large penis, all made with low-cost materials. The hybrid creature (half-bird, half-mammal) interacts strangely with the audience, as if a shaman, employing onomatopoetic sounds and staging tableau-like scenes, obliquely embodying a critique of masculinist, heterosexual, foreign political domination (American colonialism in Puerto Rico) by virtue of the performer's identity and the performance's location in Puerto Rico in a museum (MACPR) housed in a former high school designed by the American architect Adrian C. Finlayson and built in 1916 in the Georgian Revival style, almost as if a southern plantation, during a period of Americanization in the public education system.[18] The performance is ultrabaroque in its effusive attention to sensory and kinesthetic semiotic details and in its hermetism or opacity; it includes ritual elements that are beyond easy comprehension. It embraces the practice of rasanblaj in its juxtaposition and recycling of materials, images, and references, and allows for a multiplicity of interpretations.

In addition to becoming a rooster/chicken, swan/duck, eagle/human, and cow, Mercado has also been other animals and unknown creatures, such as a Zika- or chikungunya-laden mosquito at the Quiebre International Performance Festival, held in San Juan in 2016, as well as a surrealist crab—as a symbol of Santurce, also known as Cangrejos—that is also a female doll and a monster for the *Resistencia en fractura . . . desnuda* performance at the Juliette Jongma Gallery in the Netherlands during Amsterdam Art Week (Romero 2017; Santiago 2017b).[19] Finally, Mercado has performed as the blue elephant-headed Hindu deity Ganesh, for example in the video *Boricuas: Freddy M.* (Viguié 2003), in which Mercado appears with six eyes (four of them painted on his face) singing and then lip-synching a song by the Mexico-based Argentinean performer Liliana Felipe (the bolero "A Nadie"), playing with a similarly decorated, self-made doll head with the same exuberant curly long hair as the performer (his doll child), placing a large picture frame over his head and becoming a framed portrait, and finally donning a self-made large blue foam mask and becoming a dancing Ganesh.

This Freddie blurs the distinction between male and female, but also human and nonhuman or divine, subject and object, individual and sexual fetish or charm: Freddie as a baroque surrealist doll, *esperpéntica*, with sinuous curves and overcharged sexuality, reminiscent of Caribbean sexpot vedettes, such as Iris Chacón, dressed up for Halloween; Freddie as a double doll who masturbates: a critique of the Peruvian talk-show host Laura Bozzo and her syndicated show *Laura en América*, broadcast in the United States by Telemundo; Freddie as a prosthetic made of mannequin arms and legs, with a sculpted and painted foam head, decorated with ribbons and fabrics, as for his performance at the Hemispheric Institute of Performance and Politics' Encuentro in Lima, Peru, in July 2002 as part of Ivette Román's *Círculo* cabaret.[20] This is the Freddie of sexual effrontery, of voluptuousness created by hip, buttock, and breast prosthesis mainly made out of foam pads but also from his own flesh, seemingly closer to a Latin American *travesti* than to a good ole' drag queen or cross-dresser. These iterations of self are mediated by Mercado's dolls, that is to say, by his sculptures and visual creations that at times become performative objects with a life of their own: the objects he sells and exhibits in galleries; the small Freddie miniatures, more recently including *Freddilicias*, small-scale portraits he has been creating since 2013, that select collectors and friends snatch up, which barely subsidize his life.[21]

There are other performative Freddies that surface at cabarets: historical figures such as doña Fela and Myrta Silva, for example, when he performs with Ivette Román or Mickey Negrón; at rock concerts, and in music videos, for example with the leading Puerto Rican alternative rock singer Fofé (José Luis Abreu), with whom Freddie has appeared as a baroque postmodern adornment, first on the stage of Fofé's rock band El Manjar de los Dioses (The Delight of the Gods),[22] and later with Fofé's subsequent band, Circo,[23] not to mention Mercado's appearances in music videos such as Calle 13's "Tango del pecado" (2007) and more recently in Macha Colón and the Okapi's "Si Superman se deprime" (2017), where he appears as a giant humanized tree frog, or *coquí*; these collaborations sometimes entail a paycheck but more frequently are done for free or for low pay given the extremely limited budget of alternative arts in Puerto Rico. There is also the backstage Freddie, an apparition, a participating specter, as costume designer for a performance of the modern dance troupe Andanza, with whom he has also performed,[24] or for his former teacher, the enormously talented Awilda Sterling Duprey.[25] Finally, there is Freddie as a demented sunglass-wearing housewife, head full of hair curlers, dancing with a masked wrestler, the painter, sculptor, and performance artist José Luis Vargas, in a video titled "El Santo de Santurce, Episode 5," alluding to the rich tradition of Mexican *lucha libre*—and particularly to Mexican films starring *El Santo* (Rodolfo Guzmán Huerta)—in the context of Santurce, a working-class San Juan neighborhood recently characterized by the heavy presence of Dominican immigrants (Vélez 2002). Mercado's hair-curler-wearing, loud-gum-smacking character Chiwanda Sánchez (Reyes Franco 2007), who makes occasional unexpected appearances at museums, as well as at dive bars such as La Grilla, a liquor store / pool hall located on Fernández Juncos Avenue in Santurce, which has a portrait of its female owner by Mercado, is a parodic drag antecessor to the better-known and, to some, more cruel, class-biased, and somewhat controversial character of Francheska or Frenchy "La Caballota," a contemporary *yale*, or working-class young woman, interpreted by Natalia Lugo in numerous YouTube videos (Marrero Rodríguez 2014).

These are some of Mercado's multiple transloca incarnations, his ultrabaroque assemblage of types, his living rasanblaj. They range from the individual and collective performances to visible and invisible (unmarked or unacknowledged) collaborations with other artists, and I have listed them in a demented stream—my own critical, ultrabaroque transloca rasanblaj: the free association or rhizomatic explosion of the transloca theorist/critic—a Puerto Rican and transnational archive and life. With the exception of the music and collaborative videos, however, these performative interventions are mostly ephemeral works, recollected in memory, as a sensory experience, reconstructed and portrayed in the artist's own work, whether in paintings or sculptures, or salvaged through incidental photographs (and now videos) or through the scenes choreographed for the camera lens of other artists, such as the Brazilian Fernando Paes (one of Mercado's earliest photographic collaborators), of ADÁL / Adál Maldonado (for example, the extraordinary 2016 *Retratus Puertorriquensis* featuring Mercado with six eyes, all bedecked in pearls, as well as images in the 2016 *Underwater / Los ahogados* and 2018 *Los dormidos / The Sleepers* series), and for others such as Aarón Salabarrías Valle, whose installation, performance, and photo series titled *Paraíso ter-*

renal (1999–2001) is exhibited at the Museo de Arte y Diseño de Miramar and features Mercado with the artists Rolando Esteves and Brenda Díaz.[26]

The ephemeral character of these pop-up performances leads to complex archival strategies: Mercado greatly relies on the photos taken by friends and acquaintances, a practice that has greatly increased since the advent of mobile phones with cameras that is also enhanced by social media platforms such as Facebook and Instagram. The artist's Facebook page served in the 2010s as an important repository of his work. At the same time, Mercado has become a key collaborator with leading conceptual art photographers such as ADÁL and Salabarrías and has also benefited from the interest of younger curators and performance artists such as Marina Barsy Janer and Marina Reyes Franco, who have documented Mercado's work and publicly shared their video recordings (Mercado 2013).

Life as (Strange) Art

Freddie Mercado Velázquez was born in Santurce, Puerto Rico, on September 24, 1967. He received a bachelor of arts degree from the Escuela de Artes Plásticas y Diseño de Puerto Rico in San Juan in 1994 after nine years of study. He has never lived outside of the island.[27] He has presented his work since 1987, but only started to receive more sustained critical recognition toward the mid-1990s.[28] His performative and visual work acquired an international dimension through his participation in important expositions and shows in the Dominican Republic (1995, 2013), Spain (1998, 2000, 2002), the United States (2001, 2002, 2008), and Peru (2002), as well as in major international art fairs, such as ARCO 2002 in Madrid, Spain, and CIRCA 2007 and MECA 2017, both held in San Juan.[29]

In spite of his notoriety, for most of his career Mercado has not been a commercially successful visual artist and for the most part has not been represented by any gallery, although he had solo shows in spaces such as La Pintadera (2007) and =Desto (2007) in San Juan (Rodríguez Vega 2007; Weinstein 2007); in the Dominican Republic (2013) (Rosario 2013; Grullón 2014); and at the Productos Gostosos cafeteria and exhibit space in Río Piedras in 2016. Since 2017, he has been represented by Roberto Paradise Gallery, which has featured his work in art fairs in Germany and the Netherlands, in addition to exhibiting his work in August 2017.[30]

The ephemeral, performative, and essentially anti-assimilable character of Mercado's oeuvre, marked by its explicit sexual content and by the artist's stigmatized persona, has frequently made it hard for the artist to live off of his work and has implied at times economic impoverishment, which has even included temporary homelessness in 2001. Mercado's lack of a steady income and of comprehensive medical insurance (traits of the transloca drag of poverty analyzed in chapter 3) also created major complications when the artist required two hip replacement surgeries in 2018, which led the filmmaker Carla Cavina to start a GoFundMe campaign that raised over four thousand dollars.[31] Mercado has addressed this situation of precarity through frequent collaborations with other artists and by working in interior design and costume design and as an extra or technical assistant in film and video productions; he has also taught introductory painting classes at his alma mater on Saturday mornings, and has received limited financial assistance from his family.

Mercado's "strangeness" and his importance was first remarked upon by the Puerto Rican art critic Manuel Álvarez Lezama, who is credited with having coined the term *los novísimos* (the newest ones) to describe the group of young artists (in their twenties, at the time) that appeared on the island in the 1990s. As Álvarez Lezama wrote in 1995:

> Freddie Mercado is probably one of the best-known characters in our local arts scene. You will find Freddie exotically dressed as a woman at every opening night of our San Juan Galleries. He is indeed a one-man show, a happening, a walking work of art. His costumes are fascinating artistic creations that go from the aristocratic to the bizarre. One day he is in the XIXth century and the next day he will be exploring Zeffirelli's *Romeo and Juliet*. (1995b)

In another article, Álvarez Lezama added:

> Mercado cannot pass unnoticed because he is, in the context of our extremely conservative culture, a constant provocation, a disturbing work of art, a walking "happening," a celebration of the absurd, a threat to some of our deceitful moral values and our confined sexuality, and an existential tribute to the carnival we unfortunately do not have in Puerto Rico. (1995a, 16)

Álvarez Lezama affirms that Mercado's costumes have a very clear intentionality and purpose, and are not merely frivolous distraction; he insists that their finality is "to amuse us, to teach us, and to make us think" (1995a, 16). The critic also acknowledges his fear and initial wariness and suspicion, which is to say, the discomfort he experienced when confronting the transgressive figure of the artist: "At first, I was somewhat uneasy with Mercado's exuberance, but then I became accustomed to his presence, to his parodies, to his threats. Now if he does not appear in an important activity, I feel as if something is really missing" (1995a, 16).[32]

Álvarez Lezama's reaction corresponds to that of many critics and, in fact, to my own personal process of approximation to and familiarization with the artist, mediated through the initial shock of what Freud ([1919] 2003) identified as *unheimlich* (the uncanny): that which disorients and challenges one's views.[33] I remember my initial fascination with Freddie, always accompanied by my fear of approaching him—a fear due in part to my own shyness about open displays of sexuality or, specifically, about nonparodic, hypersexualized female embodiment, but also in part to the aura of the artist and his monstrous hybridity. These are sentiments that came with an enormous desire that he always make an appearance wherever I was; that forced me to engage my own fears and biases, the monster, freak, or transloca I carry inside.

Rituals of Dress: Process and Intersectionality

Mercado's transvestic uniqueness has to do with the materials he employs, his compositional process, and the ways in which he self-documents his own work and reuses or recycles these self-representations. The journalist Dyanis de Jesús (2001) has commented on Mercado's compositional and exhibition technique, on the shifting, transformative nature of his work, what I would call his *transpictorial* oeuvre: living paintings, images on canvas that make it onto the body as much as onto the exhibit wall. As de Jesús observes, Mercado's plastic work, specifically his paintings or self-portraits and images of dolls, become performative objects and/or costumes for his performances: "Freddie Mercado exhibits his painted works converting them into pompous skirts which he himself wears as part of some extravagant woman's dress. The enormous canvas becomes a skirt to later go on and become a canvas once again." De Jesús, among others, has also identified the artist's ritualistic composition technique of quick assemblage, which consists of tying fabric and presewn clothes with knots, which he generally does not sew together.[34] Recycling and speed are fundamental elements of this process of experimentation. As Mercado points out: "Some of the pieces are sewn by my uncle [who is a tailor]. I make things by hand. I recycle a lot. I like to transform pieces, use a [woman's] slip on a pant leg, things like that" (quoted in Ramírez 1999, 17).

Mercado's process of creation—*transvestire*, to transform not only gender norms, but the normative act of dressing itself, as if an eternal, cyclical repetition—also becomes, or perhaps is always already part of, his performance. On occasion, this constitutive process, his intrinsic, vital, life-process-performance, takes center stage, with an audience or without. A key example: Freddie engages in a four- or perhaps even nine-hour-long process of transformation in private, dressing and undressing at home on a *Noche de Galería*, and becomes so caught up in this play that he forgets to leave the house and make his appearance, losing all conception of time. On another occasion, he stages this process behind the lit gallery window of the now-closed Joaquín Mercado gallery in Old San Juan, so that it clearly becomes a performance that is visible to the public on the street (Cullen 2001, 56).[35] At other times, such as in *Telas presento*, the performance consists precisely of dressing and undressing in front of an audience in a gallery or museum, and then dressing a mannequin or doll that will remain in place; in his cabaret acts, Mercado dresses and undresses while the musicians and singers perform, transforming himself consecutively into different people and creatures.

The compulsive autobiographical nature of his self-referential paintings and dolls approximates his work, as I have mentioned, to that of Frida Kahlo, turning both of their faces into recognizable icons, but also to other contemporary Latin American gay, lesbian, and trans visual artists who paint or photograph themselves obsessively, at times in drag, such as the Mexicans Nahum B. Zenil and Lukas Avendaño and the Puerto Ricans Arnaldo Roche Rabell and Ángel Rodríguez Díaz,[36] as well as to the Chilean trans performance collective Las Yeguas del Apocalipsis (The Mares of the Apocalypse) formed by Francisco Casas and Pedro Lemebel, who in fact recreated Kahlo's 1939 painting *Las dos Fridas* (*The Two Fridas*) as an installation in 1990.[37] It also connects him to the work of the large-bodied, Chicana lesbian photographer Laura Aguilar and to the performance transcriptions of the Cuban American Ana Mendieta, which Charles Merewether has called "performing the self" (2000, 134).[38] Other relevant comparisons are to the gay Chilean painter Juan A. Dávila's enormously controversial transvestite portrait of the Latin American liberator Simón Bolívar,[39] to the more recent queer portrait of Mexican revolutionary leader Emiliano Zapata by Fabián Cháirez,[40] or perhaps to the Anglo-Australian enfant terrible, club kid, and performance artist Leigh Bowery, whose large body was often the subject of Lucian Freud's paintings and etchings.[41] Mercado's uniqueness resides in how his images of himself and other dolls become layers to be worn on his own body, turned into clothing, so that in effect he carries with him, on him, a referential transcription, a history of his own production: he is his work, and that work is literally and figuratively on his skin. All of this exists in a profoundly Caribbean context, in dialogue with Puerto Rican history and culture, as what we can identify as a practice of ultrabaroque *translocura* and rasanblaj.

Corpus Tabula Plena: *Racial Ambiguity and Gender Androgyny*

A great deal of the impact of Mercado's work has to do with the very corporeality of his ample androgynous body, which is perceived as violating norms of weight, masculinity, and propriety, and the fact that his long, curly hair, light skin, sartorial practices, and physical voluptuousness complicate easy readings of his race, ethnicity, and gender in a country (Puerto Rico) where people are obsessed with distinguishing between whites and Blacks and between males and females, as well as with denying the persistence of racism, and where racial mixture ("fusion") was in fact believed to bring about "confusion" (Pedreira 1934).[42] As Gladys M. Jiménez-Muñoz (1995, 2002), Yeidy M. Rivero (2005), and Jade Power-Sotomayor (2019) have shown, some popular artists have taken up noxious racial stereotypes as a form of uncritical comedy, as in the blackface and cross-dressing 1950s televised performances of Ramón Ortiz del Rivero, better known as Diplo. Mercado's racial/ethnic and sex/gender indeterminacy, for example the fact that his chest is often read—and presented by the artist—as large, exposed female breasts, and that his hair is extremely curly, provokes multiple forms of anxiety regarding his presence, which he very successfully exploits in his performative and pictorial work, partaking in what I call in the next chapter the *transloca drag of race*. This challenge to dominant racial/ethnic and sex/gender norms is a common trait in the work of several contemporary Puerto Rican performers, particularly Javier Cardona and Marcus Kuiland-Nazario ("Carmen") (both discussed in chapter 5), as a number of writers have observed, including Jossianna Arroyo (2002) in her superb analysis of Black identity politics and "cultural drag" (a term she borrows from Kuiland-Nazario) in Puerto Rican translocal culture, and, more recently, in the work of artists such as Mickey Negrón, Macha Colón (Gisela Rosario), Awilda Rodríguez Lora (La Performera), Lío Villahermosa, and Las Nietas de Nonó (Mulowayi Iyaye Nonó and Mapenzi Chibale Nonó). Performance art, it would seem, is a privileged site for this critique and for the invention of alternate possible orders. Then again, Mercado's insistent use and perhaps misuse of global cultural referents further complicates his work, rendering him a rather slippery subject.

Mercado inserts himself within a cultural tradition of transvestism (a word I have been using interchangeably with drag) but resignifies this practice in a radical manner, since it is no longer a question of recreating typical images of female beauty, but rather alluding to and engaging it in a strange, distorted, visual and aural but for the most part not linguistic way that at times includes elements of burlesque. His "monstrous," "freakish," psychedelic, or surreal appropriation of femininity is reminiscent of other drag performers, such as the "drag terrorist" Divine (Glenn Milstead), whom John Waters has referred to as "the Godzilla of drag queens."[43] Mercado shares with Divine the spectacular, disorienting use of his large body, a penchant for humor, and the resistance to glamorous makeup, using cosmetics as a tool for making strange rather than for beautification. Both shock yet also seduce and entertain audiences, creating memorable impressions, and thrive in the context of artistic collaboration. Mercado can also be placed somewhere between what João Silvério Trevisan describes as a Brazilian drag queen and a "caricata de carnaval," or carnival cross-dresser, both defined by their "postura escrachada," or messy (nonmimetic) appearance and by their distance from silicone-injecting *travestis* who more commonly aspire to conventional or hyperbolic female beauty (2000, 379).[44]

It is for these reasons that I feel obliged to state my discomfort with some critics' dismissal of Mercado's link to transvestism, evidenced in comments such as Deborah Cullen's observation that "Mercado is not a drag performer" (2001, 56), which echoed Haydee Venegas's (1998, 280) opinion. While I appreciate Cullen's attempt to place Mercado in the context of feminist women artists such as Valie Export, Adrian Piper, and Orlan—and I would add Ana Mendieta, Laura Aguilar, and Cindy Sherman—and in fact agree with the validity of reading Mercado's work in relation to feminism as well as to critical race and ethnicity theory, I do not think this excludes his location in the tradition of gay male drag; this comes across particularly strongly in Mercado's appearance on actor and drag legend Antonio Pantojas's television show *Estoy Aquí* (2005), a

program that in many ways serves as the coming together of two generations of transgressive Puerto Rican drag performers.[45] I embrace Marjorie
Garber's assertion: "*Transvestism is a space of possibility structuring and
confounding culture*: the disruptive element that intervenes, not just a category crisis of male and female, but the crisis of category itself" (1992, 17).

Mercado's performances differ from those of typical, entertaining
Puerto Rican cabaret actors or gay disco drag queens and trans performers, like Antonio Pantojas, Ruddys Martínez, Alex Soto, Johnny Ray, Víctor Alicea, and Zahara Montiere (Alberic Prados) or the television personality Dreuxilla Divine (Nelson Roldán), who joke with the audience
as a means to weave a web of complicities and effect parodies and self-
effacing critiques, as perverse clowns or comedians who make raunchy
comments, use vulgar or lewd terms, and make the most out of insinuations and gossip.[46] For starters, Mercado generally does not talk while
performing. He also does not follow the particular visual style or highly
affected, effeminate metaphysical speaking style of the extremely well-
known Puerto Rican queer astrologer and performer Walter Mercado, in
spite of the coincidence of their last names, although he can be said to
share the ethics of *relajo* (as a Caribbean twist on camp and *rasquache*
aesthetics, a type of irreverent humor and glee) that Diana Taylor (2003,
110–32) identifies as a defining trait of the astrologer's performance.[47]

Freddie Mercado places himself outside of these dominant models:
neither a transgender sex worker, nor a beauty queen wannabe, nor the
malicious and perverted entertainer, nor an astrologer to the masses—
even when he maintains and borrows much from all. He does not lip-
synch very much, except perhaps by chance, such as the time I saw him
casually grab a *pernil* (pork shank) bone at a Three Kings' Day party in
Fernando Sosa's kitchen in Santurce and imitate the *merenguera* Olga
Tañón, using the carcass as a pseudomicrophone; this improvised performance reiterated the unexpected and at times grotesque character that
much of Mercado's work takes, even his more structured and carefully
put together appearances, which frequently include audience interactions that can go in multiple directions. It is much more common to hear
the performer emit small onomatopoeic or musical sounds, as Santiago
Flores Charneco (2002) has observed: the abstract laments of a geisha;
the cackle of a domestic bird; perhaps one laugh or another.[48] His voice, a
regular or modified human speaking voice, that is, somehow would seem
to break the artifice or illusion, and as such it seems Mercado wants to
distort sound as much as image: to provoke a discontinuous aural rupture,

in synchrony with his visual dissonance; a frequent refusal to talk that also places him closer to the nonunderstandable, the mysterious, impenetrable Other, what is construed by him as the culturally unintelligible or foreign, the animal, the mute; a surface to be read but which avoids or displaces easy interpretations; a practice that causes great discomfort among Puerto Ricans, who frequently tend to be very conservative and at times xenophobic.

Mercado's disruption is most pronounced when he is dressed as a hybrid animal, for example the cackling rooster/chicken or *gallo/gallina* in his performance at the Museo del Barrio exhibition opening in 2001, or some other not exclusively human form, such as the *gallina/samurai/androginoide* (chicken/samurai/androgynoid) he portrays in *Coco Barroco*, as a *criatura cacareante*, or cackling creature: "Croooo, cro cro cro croooo. Cro crooo cro cro cro croooooo" (Flores Charneco 2002). This is certainly the case for Mercado's performance of *En esta vida de reciclar me trans-formo* (*In This Recycling Life I Trans-form*), carried out on December 15, 2019 at the "Burlesque Bottomless Brunch" organized by María De Azúa at Señor Frog's Puerto Rico in Old San Juan as part of Winter Pride Fest 2019, which also featured Yulietta (Yulie Padilla) and April Carrión, in which Mercado appeared as a glittering pink vision (a divinity or monster) with a giant sparkling eye / elephant-like foam headpiece decorated with costume jewels, his face painted half charcoal black, the other half with traditional drag makeup, with a voluminous skirt that included several self-portraits, wrist bells used to create music in a ceremonial context, a scene in which Mercado turned into a Christmas tree, and a disorienting soundtrack featuring recordings of the Peruvian camp icon Yma Sumac. Photo documentation of Mercado's face makeup circulated on social media, generating angry denunciations mostly from white, university-age viewers who did not see the performance, critiqued what they identified as "blackface," demanded that Mercado "pedir perdón a la comunidad negra" (ask the Black community for forgiveness), felt his images were "triggering," and accused anyone who did not agree with their position of being "boomers" (out of date, older, and politically incorrect). The unwillingness or inability to acknowledge the complexity of the performance, the impetus to reduce it to a decontextualized fragment, the lack of interest in engaging in a conversation with persons who tried to foster a critical dialogue, and the violent rhetoric of some of Mercado's supporters, was quite painful. The rift was a disservice to actual struggles to combat biased representation. It assumes that racially ambiguous subjects do not have the right to question, explore, challenge, or transform dominant norms, and that audiences do not have the capacity to engage unsettling representations.

Race is not the only point of friction in Mercado's representations. Freddie's sexual and gender identity has been described (and pathologized) in multiple ways: from hermaphrodite (Barragán 1998) to possessing a "non-sexuality" (Verguilla Torres 1999). "He suffers from androgyny" (6), the same author later affirms, as if androgyny were an illness or medical condition. The Afro–Puerto Rican writer Mayra Santos-Febres (2003), one of his most subtle critics, has affirmed that Freddie "blurs the division between the sexes"; the author celebrates his androgyny in a positive manner, similar to the way Nina Flowers celebrates androgyny in chapter 2. It is an interesting androgyny, frequently reiterated by Mercado in interviews and self-documentation (Forbes 2011; Pantojas 2005; Viguié 2003), one caused by bulk (large body mass) and not by thinness, the dominant 1970s female beauty standard. Mercado explicitly mixes male and female sexual signifiers, as evident in the performance *Viaje . . . Sé* (2013), refracted through the femininity of what, when speaking about women, are often called Rubenesque or zaftig bodies: an excess that tends to be read as antimuscular and antitestosteronic softness and that is shunned in mainstream conceptions of female beauty (Gay 2017), as well as in mainstream gay male culture, which is dominated by conceptions of thinness, on the one hand, and excessive muscularity, on the other (Whitesel 2014). It is also an androgyny that a number of critics (Barragán 1998; Venegas 1998) have likened to the political situation of Puerto Rico itself. Spanish arts curator Paco Barragán has referred to Mercado's performance as "transgresor, travestido y hermafrodita . . . metáfora del propio Puerto Rico: americano de pasaporte, caribeño de corazón" (transgressive, transvestite, and hermaphrodite . . . a metaphor for Puerto Rico itself: with an American passport and Caribbean heart).[49]

Mercado has explored his racial/ethnic and sex/gender hybridity in a major performance/installation piece called *Telas presento* (1999), shown at the University of Puerto Rico, Río Piedras, as part of his *Entre telas* exhibit, where he created a Janus-like, biracial, multifaceted, free-standing figure with two faces, one in front and another in back: half Black, half white, as a double who rescues the experience of slavery and its traces inscribed on the body in a game of front and reverse (see figure 12).[50] The name of this piece is a linguistic pun with two meanings. The first, "cloth or fabrics I present," is a hyperbaton, alluding to a salesperson, perhaps,

Fig. 12. Freddie Mercado Velázquez. Detail, face and self-portrait mask, *Telas presento*, University of Puerto Rico, Río Piedras, 1999. Photo by Freddie Mercado Velázquez.

or to a seamstress showing material for dressmaking. The second, "I present them to you" (*te las presento*, in which the "them" possibly means his identities, the women he portrays), refers to the acts of artists as the ones who introduce, show, or bring to light new things. Both play with the links of sewing and painting, specifically through the materiality of the canvas and of clothes.

Telas presento involves Freddie dressing and undressing in front of an audience, and eventually dressing a large cardboard paper doll that remains as an installation, surrounded by sculpted and painted foam dolls and other constructed objects. The life-size two-dimensional (flat) mannequin has two faces: one in front, which is very pale white and in sharp focus, while the other in back is Black and somewhat fuzzy.

They are not self-portraits. The large cardboard doll is dressed in several layers of cloth skirts (an underlying white petticoat and an outer skirt made out of painted canvases), which give it three-dimensionality. The main skirt is actually made out of self-portraits and images of dolls sewn together. This pictorial front/back opposition suggests multiple readings, particularly as a self-portrait of Mercado hangs at the neck with a huge sewing needle to its side, as if it were a carnival mask to be held up to the face with one hand. The two women can be read as that which is behind the mask: a woman paler and a woman darker than Mercado's self-representation, the images of two mothers and two races. The fact that the Black woman is in the back and fuzzy can be read as a comment on the invisibility of racialized labor (African slavery, for example) or as a metaphor for racial anxiety, that which is inside or in the shadows (not visible but still there), particularly in relation to how dominant processes of racial "whitening" in Puerto Rico attempt to efface and minimize African and Indigenous ancestry, as in Fortunato Vizcarrondo's (1942) well-known poem "¿Y tu agüela, aonde ejtá?" ("Where Is Your Grandmother?"). It can also mean that this Black woman (the hidden grandmother of Vizcarrondo's poem) is the shadow, soul, or guardian angel; the orisha or divinity that mounts the artist, turning him into who he is. The Janus-like character of the sculpture suggests that these are one and the same woman, as they share the same body; Mercado's inclusion of both should be seen as a tense and contradictory affirmation of what is visible and invisible and of the potentially deceptive character of the visual to reveal deeper truths.

Mercado highlights maternity in another important visual representation, an untitled carnival or ball scene self-portrait of a light-skinned Freddie in a green dress holding a chocolate-brown baby or perhaps a doll dressed in white lace dress and headdress, a typical Santería or Yoruba ceremonial garment (see figure 13). The baby or doll is actually held with a set of mysterious extra black arms that sprout from Mercado's shoulders and back. We can also see one of his white arms, resting on the ballooning skirt. In this painting, it is impossible to tell if these extra arms belong to Freddie or to a person standing behind him whose face is not visible. It is also impossible to tell if the arms are black because of their skin color or if they are covered with long opera gloves, or, for that matter, if the subject is holding a "real" or a prosthetic baby. In addition, there is a large black shape to the left of the main figure's face, which could either be her hair or some unidentified form.

Fig. 13. Freddie Mercado Velázquez. *Untitled* (self-portrait), oil on board.
Photo by Freddie Mercado Velázquez.

These visual ambiguities make the painting somewhat disconcerting upon closer analysis, and suggest a possible fantastic or monstrous configuration. The serene look on the main figure's face and the baby's wide-open eyes and mouth convey a more tranquil image. Over all, the juxtaposition of strong primary colors (blue, yellow, red) in swirls in the background competes with what seem to be black flames that complement the black arms and black hair. This backdrop to the two central figures saturates the painting with energy and movement, presenting a contrast to the figure's stillness. Who or what is this possibly four-armed, multi-colored, possibly biracial figure? The presence of a white adult holding a Black child also inverts the traditional role of Black nannies, milkmaids, and caretakers minding white babies (see Arroyo 2003b) and possibly even suggests the fantasy of birthing a child with a Black father, or envisions the pair (mother/daughter) as an allegory of orishas in Santería or of souls in Kardekian Espiritismo (Spiritism).

It is important to explain why and how Mercado's work, which is grounded in a position of difference, marginality, and abjection, does not participate in what Jossianna Arroyo has termed "cultural transvestism" (2003b), which is to say that it is not a discourse of integrating *mestizaje* of the white authorial subject who appropriates the other in his discourse, but rather one of *mestizaje* as radical rupture: of Blackness within, carried on one's back or in one's DNA and genetically predisposed to reappear in a queer act of progeny, perhaps closer to the utopian impetus of Gloria Anzaldúa (1987) in her landmark *Borderlands / La frontera: The New Mestiza* (obviating Anzaldúa's celebration of José Vasconcelos's problematic *La raza cósmica*) or to the phenomenon explored by Alicia Arrizón (2006) in her influential *Queering Mestizaje.*

Arroyo (2003b), in fact, distinguishes between the concept of "cultural drag" used in her essay on Javier Cardona (2002) and the notion of "cultural transvestism" that grounds her book *Travestismos culturales*. For Arroyo, cultural drag implies a voluntary political adoption of drag as a tactic that questions race, gender, and sexuality, while cultural transvestism implies a type of sleight-of-hand by a hegemonic (white, male, heterosexual) writing subject that ventriloquizes or appropriates the voices of minoritarian individuals rendered as objects. While I appreciate the distinction Arroyo makes between different types of cultural engagements, the critic might be overestimating the difference between the words "transvestism" and "drag," which to some are simple synonyms, while to others, such as Sylvia Rivera and Holly Woodlawn, they are incommensurate, particularly when "transvestism" (or the descriptor "transvestite") is understood as equivalent to what we now identify as transgender and "drag" is seen as eminently theatrical.[51]

In his work, Mercado's light-skinned or white-passing, queer, transgender "mother" figure potentially gives birth to multiracial children out of her own mixed background, like a multiracial Athena springing forth from the head of her father, or becomes the "mother" or "godmother" in religious systems that valorize dolls (inanimate objects) as ceremonial objects for ritual practice (Barsy Janer 2019). There are no visible love stories or sexual partners in Mercado's work; Mercado is the father and mother of his doll children, or a stand-in for a tacit relationship that remains obscene (offstage, but also stigmatized and perverse). And, as we will see, Mercado further explores racial ambiguity in his representation of Myrta Silva, a white Puerto Rican female singer and composer associated with Afro-Caribbean and tropical music.

Historical Performative Dolls: Temporalities of Cabaret

> Niña, no hables tan duro, que lo más lindo que le ha dado Dios a la mujer es la voz.
> —Doña Felisa Rincón de Gautier, recalling what her mother used to tell her as a child[52]

Amid the enormous and ever-changing list of characters that Mercado has represented, he has portrayed a very select number of real women, engaging in what David Román (2005) has identified as *archival drag*: the representation of figures from the past, whether in a camp, parodic, or serious and admiring way; a gesture that echoes Hélio Oiticica's celebration of Mario Montez's "resurrection" or embodiment of the glamorous Dominican Hollywood actress María Montez, a gesture that recuperates past Latin American divas, "reciting and recycling them for the present" (Cruz-Malavé 2015a, 604).[53] Two of Mercado's most famous female impersonations are those of white grande dames of the Puerto Rican collective memory, specifically the populist aristocrat Felisa Rincón de Gautier (1897–1994), better known as "doña Fela" (using the Spanish-language female honorific *doña*), the notorious cofounder of the Popular Democratic Party, right-hand woman of Governor Luis Muñoz Marín, and ex-mayor of San Juan, a position she occupied from 1946 to 1968, who is best remembered for flying in snow for the children of Puerto Rico in the early 1950s;[54] and the popular singer, composer, television host, and impresario Myrta Silva (1924–1987), nicknamed La Gorda de Oro (The Golden Fat Woman), whom I would like to call *la sandunguera guarachera*, the queen of low-brow or popular entertainment, who anteceded Celia Cruz as lead singer with the Sonora Matancera in Cuba in 1949–50 and was credited with authoring some of the most successful *guarachas* and *boleros* of her time.[55] This is the Freddie of the collective trance, of spiritual ecstasy, of *espiritista* channeling; the one that leads people to confuse him with historical grande dames when he performs as part of Ivette Román's *Círculo* cabaret or in Mickey Negrón's *Asuntos Efímeros* or as part of Alegría Rampante's concert at the Teatro Tapia in 2016, or just when he walks down the street or appears at unexpected places; the one that allows him to celebrate grande dames for being *damas grandes*, that is to say, physically large (white) women like himself.[56]

Mercado's performance of doña Fela is spectacular: she is the lady of overflowing, intricate wigs, turbans, and old-style Spanish fans; the one who gave her name to a large, multistory parking lot in Old San Juan; the one adored by the people. According to Mercado, people saw him dressed in her style at her funeral and believed he was her relative: As he describes in his appearance on Antonio Pantojas's (2005) TV show *Estoy Aquí*, onlookers spoke to him, took his photo, and ran off. Accordingly, we can say (as Freddie does) that it was the crowd, the popular mass, *el pueblo de Puerto Rico*, that made him into doña Fela, consecrating their similarity and hailing her reappearance.[57]

Mercado's impersonation follows in a long tradition of drag appropriations of doña Fela's image, carried out even while she was still mayor of San Juan, in spite of the fact that she was also known (at least according to one source) for incarcerating working-class, effeminate homosexuals (Soraya 2014, 93). One memorable example of doña Fela drag is the 1965 Mexican feature-length coproduction *Puerto Rico en carnaval* (dir. Tino Acosta), where the noted gay female impersonator and night-life impresario Johnny Rodríguez, who owned the well-known El Cotorrito nightclub, appears dressed as her in a scene shot at the Isla Verde International Airport.[58] Rodríguez is also known to have performed as Myrta Silva in New York City nightclubs.[59]

Doña Fela's unique history gives us some insights as to why Freddie Mercado chose to represent her and why she is a camp transloca icon par excellence. In spite of her elite upbringing, Felisa Rincón de Gautier was an accomplished seamstress and pattern designer who trained in New York and dreamed of opening clothing factories, and who even briefly had a very successful store named Felisa's Style Shop in Old San Juan. She is invariably described as motherly, obsessed with children, and heavy-set, always wearing ornate hairpieces, turbans, and dangling earrings.[60] In her youth she occasionally dressed in men's clothes and hunted with her sister Finí (see photo in Gruber 1972), although she was also adept in the very feminine "language of the fan" used to court male suitors. She was a pioneer of women's participation in politics, being one of the first women to vote in 1934 and having had to struggle against her father and her husband to gain permission to run for office.

Ruth Gruber (1972) indicates that Rincón de Gautier was influenced by the Puerto Rican lawyer and writer Nemesio Canales, a pioneering defender of women's rights, and that Rincón had contact with the suffrage leader and novelist Ana Roqué de Duprey. Rincón married Popular Democratic Party colleague Genaro Gautier when she was forty-three, and they had no children. She was also notorious for changing outfits several times a day while performing her many tasks as mayor of the capital, and was constantly referred to as a woman with a feminine disposition and masculine virtues and political skills: "She combines the grandeur of a Spanish *marquesa* with the bumptious energy of [New York City mayor] Fiorello La Guardia," said *Life* magazine (Norris 1969, 73). Or a less flattering portrayal: "'She's a combination,' her enemies charged, 'of Marie Antoinette holding court and a tough Tammany Hall politician'" (Gruber 1972, 209), combining references to aristocratic French despotism and Democratic Party corruption. What's even more astounding is that there were even dolls made of her in life, as well as a musical comedy.[61]

When performing silently as doña Fela, Freddie Mercado successfully embodies the demeanor of this distinguished figure through her iconic look, ever-present wigs and fans, and gracious comportment, which the performer then tweaks and disrespects, introducing a camp element that challenges hagiographic depictions and highlights humor. Since Mercado does not employ words or verbal cues in his performance, the artist relies on costume, body gestures, and semiotic signifiers to achieve his impersonation; at times he uses a photographic reproduction of her face made into a fan. Successful reception of Mercado's performance is greatly predicated on audience recognition of the historical referent. This is clearly easier for older audiences, but continued reverence of this popular figure (for example, through a very colorful and well-executed 2015 large-scale

Fig. 14. Freddie Mercado Velázquez performing as Myrta Silva at Cabaret Círculo, Nuyorican Café, Old San Juan, Puerto Rico, 2001. Photographer unknown. Collection of Freddie Mercado Velázquez.

mosaic mural by Celso González and Roberto Biaggi prominently displayed on Luis Muñoz Rivera Avenue in Puerta de Tierra, clearly visible as one walks or drives to Old San Juan, and through a major museum exhibit in 2019) ensures that doña Fela's iconic face maintains currency for younger generations.[62]

The second historical figure that Mercado has consistently embodied, Myrta Silva, the divine *gorda* who was also known as La Bomba Atómica Puertorriqueña (the Puerto Rican Atomic Bomb) and La Vedette Que Arroya (The Run-You-Over Vedette), as Frances R. Aparicio points out (1998, 177), is almost the polar opposite of Felisa Rincón de Gautier; Mercado's portrayal of Silva is equally contextual but leads explicitly to the world of music and entertainment, as opposed to that of politics and civic culture. Silva was a mythical singer who began her career in Puerto Rico in the 1930s when she was only ten years old, and who was already performing in New York City by 1939.[63] She was not a descendant of the "refined," Spanish and French creole island aristocracy, as doña Fela was, but rather a poor, rural, migrant subject from Arecibo who went to New York City with her family at an early age. Echoing a popular misperception that privileges male agency, Ruth Glasser states:

> In the late 1930s . . . Rafael Hernández discovered Myrta Silva, who became one of the first Puerto Rican female singers of popular music. When Hernández saw her, she was barely into her teens, a former dishwasher and chambermaid who was performing twenty-one shows weekly at the Teatro Hispano for twenty-five dollars. (1995, 116)

As the queer scholar Licia Fiol-Matta (2017) highlights, the description neglects to mention that Silva had already managed to get herself broadcast on the radio before this apparent "discovery." Commenting on her body and physical presence, Aparicio has observed:

> Mirta [*sic*] Silva was not the sensual, sleek vedette that Latin America saw in Tongolele, nor was she a motherly, tender figure. Through her irreverent humor, singing style, and physical overendowment, she self-parodically subverted popular expectations of the delicate, fragile, and even sexy female singer. Although matronly, she was not at all a maternal figure but rather more of an androgynous image on television, her body and voice a social space of conflicting gender expectations. (1998, 177)

Aparicio's perception of Silva as androgynous helps to explain the singer's appeal to Mercado.

Licia Fiol-Matta's groundbreaking analysis in *The Great Woman Singer: Gender and Voice in Puerto Rican Music* (2017) goes even further in highlighting the entertainer's radical rupture and challenging received notions, presenting Silva as a Puerto Rican woman who triumphed in the genre of the Cuban guaracha and as a well-known lesbian who specialized in singing risqué songs full of double entendres highlighting heterosexuality as well as queerness.[64] For Fiol-Matta, Silva's life is encapsulated in the tension between several characters or personas: the initial "Myrta," child ingénue who went on to become a transnational sensation, and the later "Chencha" and "Madame Chencha," a grotesque, obese figure who negotiated her own abjection and became feared as a television personality known for publicizing malicious gossip. In fact, Fiol-Matta describes Silva's character of "Madame Chencha" as a *loca* and a drag queen (2017, 59), also affirming that "Chencha's intent was to speak truth to power" (2017, 47).

In many ways, Freddie Mercado's recuperation of Myrta Silva (his archival drag performance or resurrection), in which the performer exaggerates the popular entertainer's persona, serves as a way to propose a genealogy of Puerto Rican abjection, of women that audiences love to hate. Mercado's Myrta Silva is larger than life, overflowing with Caribbean exuberance, rhythmical and musical even while voiceless (Mercado never speaks while embodying this character), and identifiable because of the artist's physical similarity, his use of maracas or other instruments, and his passionate movement in synchrony with music.

It is in the space of the cabaret where Freddie Mercado has found a most welcome environment to play with his recreations of what we can now see as quite transgressive historical grande dames. I will conclude this chapter by chronicling a memorable *Círculo* cabaret night that I attended at the Nuyorican Café in Old San Juan (2001). On that occasion, Freddie began by playing on the stage with Japanese paper parasols while the experimental vocalist Ivette Román sang and the renowned musician Luis Amed Irizarry played the electronic keyboard, accompanied by other invited guests. Gradually, Freddie abandoned his exoticizing divertissement and began to add elements to his costume: a silk scarf on his head, dark Jackie O. sunglasses, a large black patent leather handbag that perfectly matched his black high heels, a dress and long black gloves, a dramatic fan. Suddenly, Freddie had become doña Fela before our very own eyes, silently waving hello to her audience with great dignity, moving her hand from side to side, generating the glee associated with acts of magic, when something unexpected happens that defies easy explanations. We all knew that we were now in the presence of doña Fela, that is, that Mercado had become the deceased mayor of San Juan, and that in effect he had brought her forth to live and breathe among us.

Subverting the refined manners of this historical character, Mercado then humorously shocked the audience with unexpected actions. After several uncharacteristically provocative crotch-shot leg movements and tongue flickering insinuations, the now hypersexualized doña Fela took off her sunglasses, put the fan away, changed her head wrap, pulled a maraca out of her purse, fixed her lipstick, and quickly became Myrta Silva. A diva has been conjured from the great beyond; another memorable figure was now before us, brought back to life in all her glory and with all her *picardía* (mischief). Myrta is the inversion of doña Fela, a new and improved version: grotesque and scandalous, delightful and obscene. After engaging in a delightful rumba, Myrta disappeared before our very own eyes, and Mercado became a gigantic white doll wearing women's underwear and gauze veils, a strange unexplainable creature, turning around provocatively and showing her derriere. Her head was a gigantic foam sphere, a cubist work of art that portrayed multiple competing perspectives of a female face, which sat atop a white fringed silk lampshade: A toy or a monster? A ghost? A tropical Picasso? The doll then played with her veil as if it were a cloud, accompanying a song ("Rabo de nube") written by the Cuban Silvio Rodríguez, which was performed by Ivette Román, while Mercado seemed to become a visualization for the lyrics, as if a tableau vivant.

Mercado inhabits and appropriates these characters, giving credence to performance studies scholar Joseph Roach's observation that "the voices of the dead may speak freely now only through the bodies of the living" (1996, xiii). In the aforementioned ultrabaroque progression, Mercado went through multiple incarnations of the feminine: he began by gesturing toward Asian archipelagos and islands (Japan) with paper parasols, perhaps as a citation of a geisha or as a critical act of Orientalism as a strategy to decenter local patriarchal heteronormative paradigms, in which a citation of an unfamiliar cultural element distracts or negotiates sexism (Hedrick 2013); he then moved toward emblematic historical white Puerto Rican womanhood; and ultimately became a nonhuman creature, a performative, theatrical, hybrid, monstrous, playful doll that disconcerts and confuses. These characters were achieved through costume changes that were clearly visible to the audience, but also through the use of (invisible) prosthetic padding in the hips, buttocks, and chest that might have been taken by some to be real. This is also true of Mercado's 2019 performance as "Madame Chencha" in *¡Se va armar la Gorda! Una noche de performance por artistas de peso* (Reyes Franco 2019), in which Mercado embodied a profoundly abject Silva, now missing some teeth (the teeth Mercado has lost due to dental illness, specifically to a hereditary type of gum disease), as a means to comment on the massive protests that brought down the administration of Governor Ricardo Rosselló Nevares that year, participating in the Latin American tradition of *cabaret político* (political cabaret) that Laura G. Gutiérrez (2010, 101–31) carefully analyzes.

Mercado's ability to inhabit these characters has a lot to do with camp (or with "Caribglobal tropicamp," following King and Oiticica), and with the way that doña Fela and Myrta Silva lend themselves to simultaneous parody and reverence and were unwittingly campy themselves. Mercado's scandalous recuperation of these figures, an iteration of the transloca drag of poverty as much as of ultrabaroque rasanblaj, is thus a monstrous gesture of love, of what the Chicana feminist theorist Chela Sandoval has termed "a hermeneutics of social change, a decolonizing *movida*" (2000, 139), and an example of what Paola Arboleda Ríos (2011) suggests the English-language term "queer" needs to approximate Latin American *locura*. Mercado's deconstructive reordering, assemblage, and reconstruction propels transloca performance into unexpected dimensions and disorders the racial schemas that we will now discuss in the next chapter.

FIVE

Javier Cardona and the Transloca Drag of Race

To be black is to *have been* blackened: this is how I am describing a central thesis of Fanon's.
—Darieck B. Scott, *Extravagant Abjection*

Envision stepping into a theater and hearing the story of a young, handsome, Afro–Puerto Rican actor—the performer Javier Cardona—who goes to a casting call and is expected to speak in exaggerated tones, move his body in a supposedly "Caribbean" or highly expressive fashion, and don a synthetic, curly-haired, partially braided, dark wig for a toothpaste commercial, all of which leave him feeling profoundly unsettled. Flip this image: now imagine him asking diverse audience members in a theater to do the same, or showing us photographic slides in which he is dressed up as a female maid or as a Santería madam or as a male basketball player or as a sugarcane field worker. Imagine him traveling to the United States and being told that he "doesn't look Puerto Rican." See him eventually put on that wig and darken his face (as if performing in blackface, or perhaps as a *loca* or a *viejo* in the Fiestas de Santiago Apóstol in Loíza) and hear him speak to us in multiple voices and registers, and then see him rip off the wig as he dances madly by himself (also like the *loca* in Loíza or in other Puerto Rican carnivals), all framed as a retelling of the "Snow White" fairy tale.

This is the *transloca drag of race*: the burden of performative expectations, of having to play a gendered, sexualized, and racialized part that does not correspond to your lived experiences or desires. It is a drag that also entails the empowering, perhaps playful subversion of those expectations; an ambivalent, self-critical *transloca performance* that negotiates treacherous grounds, that is willing to engage gendered racist stereotypes as a way to destabilize them, but that potentially has undesirable psychic effects, different from yet also similar to the more joyful release and pointed social commentary that characterizes religious and carnival play.[1]

Understood as a burden, an embodiment, a subversion, or a failure, here the transloca drag of race exposes the arbitrary nature of race as a socially constructed category, particularly when employed as a structure of oppression.[2] It also tells us about the nature and limitations of Puerto Rican cultural nationalism in a multiethnic, multiracial society; the performative gendered and racialized dimensions of social experience; and the power of outsiders (whether interlocutors, viewers, or audience members) to question and destabilize the subjectivity of an individual, that is to say, to lead someone (a specific Puerto Rican exponent of transloca performance such as Javier Cardona) to experience a failed sense of belonging to a larger collectivity such as a nation, a group, or a community due to the interlocutors' bias, ignorance, lack of knowledge, or prejudice.[3] Cardona's performative embodiment is somewhat different from Freddie Mercado's exploration of race and of decolonial *mestizaje*, as I discussed in the previous chapter, inasmuch as Cardona's explicit critique of racism takes center stage, coming closer to Sylvia Rivera's, Erika Lopez's, and Holly Woodlawn's openly-antiracist postures explored in chapter 3.

Typically understood as the male-to-female gendered inversion of clothing and behavior for theatrical or cabaret entertainment, although also perceived as a practice that as Judith Butler (1990, 1993) and Marjorie Garber (1992) argue, destabilizes categories and creates crises, drag (*transformismo*)—reenvisioned as the transloca drag of race—here refers to an ambivalent movement: the external imposition or personal choice to use clothing, makeup, wigs, and/or behavior to present an idealized or exaggerated perspective of racial and, by extension, ethnic or national belonging, as a way to actualize an inevitably gendered and sexualized stereotype; the inversion of the Martinican psychiatrist Frantz Fanon's (1967) concept of "white mask" as elaborated in *Black Skin, White Masks*, an opposite scenario in which a Black subject adopts a black mask that is equally dissonant than that of the dominant or hegemonic group.[4] Potentially a type of disidentificatory practice when done as an act of personal volition (Muñoz 1999), the transloca drag of race can be an act of racial violence, when imposed upon from the outside. As an ambivalent practice potentially marked by melancholia, sadness, and critical awareness—in other words, one that benefits from the competing meaning of "drag" (as a verb and a noun) as "to draw or pull slowly or heavily" or "to cause (as oneself) to move with slowness or difficulty" or as "something that retards

Fig. 15. Javier Cardona as maid. Image from *You Don't Look Like*, 1996. Photo by Miguel Villafañe.

or impedes motion, action, or advancement" (Merriam-Webster)—we can envision the transloca drag of race in dialogue with, but also distinct from, and even in opposition to masquerade, blackface, cultural transvestism (Arroyo 2003b), or other racial impersonations, as a potential questioning of authenticity, a type of "racial performativity" engaged in by Black and other LGBTQ subjects as a strategy of survival (Johnson 2003, 9), or as a performance of "realness" (Bailey 2013, 55–68) with its concomitant limitations. It can also be an affirmation of knowledge, as in drag performer Dorian Corey's deep awareness of the complexities of American racism in Hollywood and in the entertainment industry and how these complexities filter down to local, working-class, New York City communities of color, as portrayed in Jennie Livingston's documentary *Paris Is Burning* (1990). It is a counterpoint (and complement) to the *transloca drag of poverty* that I discussed in chapter 3; part of the dyad of race and class that structures oppression in Puerto Rico and elsewhere.

Javier Cardona's critically acclaimed solo performance *You Don't Look Like . . .* (first performed in 1996, later restaged in 2003) is a decidedly non-traditional drag show in which the transloca drag of race is enacted as the drag of *negritud* or of Afrodiasporic experience, the drag of Puerto Ricanness, and the drag of colonial subjectivity.[5] At stake is what all of these should look like, specifically Puerto Rican Blackness, assuming it is even recognized as something that exists and is not misread, constantly elided as "foreign" (*de las islas*, from other islands in the Caribbean or from the United States), or fixed (localized) in one specific Puerto Rican municipality (for example, Loíza), caught up in stereotypes and racist visions, notwithstanding the crucial contributions of scholars, activists, and artists who have shown the centrality of the African diaspora to Puerto Rican culture.[6] It is a part and a performance—the conscious act of crossing a line, a type of *translocura*—that might, in fact, drive you crazy (*loca* or *loco*), or at the very least make you feel caught in a schizophrenic nightmare where meaning-making is out of your hands (see chapter 1), part of the Caribbean and metropolitan scene of racism and colonial subjugation that Fanon and the Puerto Rican author Piri Thomas lucidly articulated (Martínez-San Miguel 2014, 99–124). At times, it is an imposition that goes against personal notions of authenticity, of expressing what one perceives to be one's true self. At others, it becomes a possibility for recognizing and challenging conventions, particularly through artistic practice, as if it were a game, albeit one with very high stakes. Finally, it is a strategy of resistance, as Trevante Rhodes's performance suggests in the third part of Barry Jenkins's film *Moonlight* (2016, based on a play by Tarell Alvin McCraney), in which the frail, innocent child known as Little (performed by Alex Hibbert) and the awkward adolescent Chiron (Ashton Sanders) become the strong, muscular man called Black (Rhodes), an embodiment of African American masculinity whose aggressive pose is questioned in Miami by his lifelong friend and object of desire Kevin (André Holland), who asks Black what is behind the facade while serving him savory pork chops and Cuban-style rice and beans.[7]

Contemporary Puerto Rican artists, activists, and scholars have rigorously challenged canonical conceptions espoused by leading intellectuals such as Antonio S. Pedreira ([1934] 1973), who argued in his foundational essay *Insularismo* (*Insularism*) that Puerto Rico was marked by the "confusion" generated from its racial "fusion," and by Tomás Blanco ([1942] 1948), who defended an idealized view of harmonious and peaceful coexistence of racial groups in Puerto Rico. These antiracist challenges have included Julia de Burgos's ([1938] 1997) poetic lament in "Ay ay ay de la grifa negra" ("Grief of the Black Woman"), Isabelo Zenón Cruz's (1974–75) wide-ranging exploration of Afro–Puerto Rican experience in his *Narciso descubre su trasero: El negro en la cultura puertorriqueña* (*Narcissus Discovers His Rear: Blacks in Puerto Rican Culture*), and José Luis González's ([1980] 1989, 1993) architectural metaphor for Puerto Rican society, envisioning the superposition of layers over one another in his very influential *El país de cuatro pisos* (*The Four-Storeyed Country*), which privileges African slavery and Black populations as the base of Puerto Rican culture at the expense of Indigenous and diasporic populations, as Juan Flores (1980) pointed out. In the diaspora, figures such as Piri Thomas (1967) in his landmark *Down These Mean Streets* have challenged how anti-Blackness manifests itself in migrant communities.

The contemporary persistence of racist limiting stereotypes is also highlighted by Bárbara Abadía-Rexach (2012), who shows in *Musicalizando la raza* (*Musicalizing the Race*) and in her frequent newspaper columns and radio programs how Black Puerto Rican culture is pigeonholed into specific musical formations and how prejudice insidiously continues to manifest itself, for example when the leading white actress Ángela Meyer indicated her desire in 2016 to once again perform her signature TV character of Chianita in blackface.[8] Blackness is minimized, elided, and joked about to this day, as Arlene Torres (1998), Gladys M. Jiménez-Muñoz (1995, 2002), Yeidy M. Rivero (2005), and Isar Godreau (2015) have demonstrated; segregated in accordance to social class, as Zaire

Dinzey-Flores proves (2013); ultimately silenced, as the historian Ileana Rodríguez-Silva (2012) has shown. Javier Cardona proposes tackling these racist elaborations head on and building upon diverse forms of resistance: problematizing stereotypes, documenting exclusions, "dragging" (cross-dressing) and dancing through this dilemma.

*Translocating (*Transloca-lizando a*) Javier Cardona*

Not frequently thought of as an exponent of transloca performance because of his generally normative masculine self-presentation, the queer actor, dancer, performer, choreographer, and community educator Javier Cardona has explored issues of race, gender, and sexuality and their links to conceptions of the nation in homoerotic duos with Eduardo Alegría such as *Tipos del paleo* (1989) and *La cruel tortura de trepaparedes*, which was part of *Mencheviques* (1995); in one-man shows such as *You Don't Look Like . . .* (1996, 2003); and in his choreographic and group perfor-mance work, including *Ah mén* (2004) and *Hasta el cuello* (2016–17), staged in Barrio Gandul, Santurce, a central part of San Juan.[9]

Initially trained at the University of Puerto Rico by the director Rosa Luisa Márquez and by the visual artist Antonio Martorell as part of Los Teatreros Ambulantes de Cayey, Cardona has also worked with renowned international theater artists including Miguel Rubio (Grupo Cultural Yuy-achkani, Peru), Osvaldo Dragún (Escuela Internacional de Teatro de la América Latina y el Caribe, Argentina and Cuba), Augusto Boal (Theater of the Oppressed, Brazil), and Peter Schumann (Bread and Puppet The-ater, United States), as well as with numerous Puerto Rican generational cohorts.[10] Consistent with this training, Cardona is fully committed to the pedagogical use of art, including interactive games with audiences as a strategy for social change, following the models elaborated by many of his mentors, including Boal (1974) in his classic *Theatre of the Oppressed* and Márquez (1992) in her *Brincos y saltos: El juego como disciplina teatral*; Boal's and Márquez's influence is visible in *You Don't Look Like* and in other pieces Cardona has appeared in.[11]

Cardona has complemented his theater work through his participa-tion in experimental dance, training with Gloria Llompart and Viveca Vázquez in Puerto Rico and dancing with the choreographers Sally Silvers and Jennifer Monson in New York City ("Javier Cardona" n.d.).[12] In addi-tion, Cardona holds a master's degree in educational theater from the New

York University Steinhardt School and was an adjunct instructor in their Department of Music and Performing Arts Professions, also doing extensive theater work with incarcerated youths.[13] In 2017, he began a PhD program in the School of Education at Indiana University, Bloomington, and has been collaborating with local youths in performances that challenge racism, specifically "the diverse events that continue to shape and reshape actions related to the removal or permanence of confederate monuments around the country."[14] He has also participated in *QUEER ALIENation*, "a free, interactive evening of visual art, installation art, performances, conversation, and community solidarity" that featured "six local scholars, artists, educators, and activists as they play with issues of time, space, equity, and identity . . . about their experiences as queer im/migrant graduate students within the United States" (Luish 2018).

In a previous publication (La Fountain-Stokes 2011b), I proposed reading Cardona as a transloca, that is to say, as a gay Puerto Rican performer who uses drag as a means to question sociocultural norms and to generate a critical dialogue in a markedly transnational/translocal colonial environment. Subsequently, Cardona was interviewed by Jossianna Arroyo, who asked him: "Do you consider yourself transloca?" (2016, 281). In his response, Cardona reflected on the multiple meanings of "trans" and *loca* in the Puerto Rican archipelagic and diasporic context and concluded by posing his own set of queries:

> What do you think? Am I transloca or not? Is it the transvestism of the loca or the local? I think it is Larry La Fountain's task, and that of other critics, to "loca-lisarme" (locate or place me). What I do know is that I am not loca as in crazy. But there may be critics and other folks who might read me that way. I would love to dialogue with [La Fountain-Stokes] more to find out if he thinks of his own work as a critic as fitting the label of "transloca." (Arroyo 2016, 281)

Cardona's provocative response proposes a circular return: the inversion of the critical gaze; an exhortation to continue a dialogue begun many years before, that of the scholar who wishes to *transloca-lizar*, or transloca-lize, the artist by using playful (yet potentially offensive) critical metaphors, and of the artist who invites the critic to position himself more explicitly.

Like the Puerto Rican scholar Juan Flores (2009) in *The Diaspora Strikes Back*, Cardona sees a dynamic relationship between the diaspora and the island, based on the sensuality of experience, whether it be culinary, erotic, intellectual, or everyday and *cafre* (tacky). In his interview with Arroyo, Cardona references Flores's term "cultural remittances," indicating the multidirectionality of cultural transfers, and the way that the home country (Puerto Rico) is also influenced by its predominantly US-based diaspora, as archipelagic Puerto Ricans learn about and adopt customs, mores, and values that come to them from elsewhere. In many ways, this is precisely what my chapter will attempt to do: to translocate Cardona's work and explore the queer intersections of Puerto Rican coloniality, gender, migration, race, and sexuality, particularly the seductions of complicity and pain, under the framework of the transloca drag of race. At the same time, this book serves to transloca-lize myself as an antiracist queer cisgendered diasporic feminist Puerto Rican transloca scholar, a self-identified white person of color (Pabón-Colón 2019; Vidal-Ortiz 2004), in dialogue with Cardona and with a broader bibliography on the topic.[15]

You Don't Look Like . . . : *Race and Cultural Drag*

In *You Don't Look Like . . .* , Cardona engages stereotypes about Afro–Puerto Ricans and how the dominant racial system excludes and marginalizes those who supposedly "don't look Puerto Rican" because of their skin color and hair texture. The title of Cardona's piece refers to a common situation experienced by many whose phenotype does not correspond to Puerto Ricans' own notions of race—idealized as the harmonious mixture of Indigenous, African, and European peoples, but favoring whiteness through the process of *blanqueamiento*, or whitening (Godreau 2015; Rodríguez-Silva 2012)—or to the homogenizing vision of US racial categories that insist on stark divisions between Black and white that also racialize Latinxs (Cobas, Duany, and Feagin 2016) and make "Afro-Latin@s" invisible (Hernández 2017; Jiménez Román and Flores 2010). To be told that you "don't look Puerto Rican," as the queer Puerto Rican theater scholar Alberto Sandoval-Sánchez has indicated (1999, 91), is a misrecognition or denial of identity; Sandoval-Sánchez identifies the phrase as a racist utterance, and as such an act of violence.

Cardona's multimedia performance integrates music, most notably, a deconstructed version of the popular song "El Africano" ("The African Man") with which the performance begins and which Cardona later hums, as well as spoken narration, props, audience interaction, visual slides, and dance, and lasts a little over twenty minutes. The piece is not explicitly presented as a drag show and does not have a straightforward plot, but rather a set of interlinked short scenes that juxtapose direct exposition (first-person testimony) with representation (including choreography), and in which the dramaturgy of the body is in direct dialogue with and at times more important than the text or script, as scholars Vivian Martínez Tabares (2004) and Yeidy M. Rivero (2006) have pointed out.

The opening bars of "El Africano" play in the darkness of the theater and immediately signal to knowing audiences that this performance will be in some way about Afro-Hispanic Caribbean masculinities and femininities or at the very least about the Caribbean and its culture, but also that this will be an unusual interpretation or questioning, as the song's vocals are highly distorted and the track seems to be slowed down.[16] As the lights come up, we see Cardona running in circles, perhaps as a symbol of constraint, of the inability to go anywhere, or as a sign of his athletic fitness. Cardona is wearing a large backpack that has a small Puerto Rican flag patch, strongly positioning national identity as a central theme: it is a performance of national drag (Berlant 1997, 145–73; Goldmark 2015; La Fountain-Stokes 1998), in which explicit signifiers are mobilized and worn to signal allegiance. The actor looks like an average young adult, in a sleeveless white T-shirt and khaki pants, similar to or perhaps slightly older than many of the audience members in attendance.

"El Africano" was originally composed by the Colombian Wilfrido Carmelo Martínez Mattos, better known as "Manduquito," and recorded as a cumbia by Calixto Ochoa y su conjunto in 1983; it was later popularized internationally as a merengue by the Dominican performer Wilfrido Vargas, who rerecorded it in 1984.[17] The transnational song is well known for its falsely naive refrain of "Mami, ¿qué será lo que quiere el negro?" (Mommy, what does the Black man want?), a double entendre ostensibly repeated by a young woman to her mother through the male singer's voice, in a type of vocal drag, as the young woman purportedly does not understand the reason for the man's sexual advances. The song plays with Hispanic Caribbean stereotypes of Black male hypersexuality and cultural Otherness; for example, Wilfrido Vargas's recording of the song begins with guttural linguistic utterances meant to resemble seemingly unintelligible African speech. This suggests that popular racist perceptions exist not only in elite spheres of power but also in widely shared popular cultural forms (García-Peña 2016), and, alas, that pleasure can be derived from grotesque but potentially parodic representations, perhaps through techniques of ironic reception or distancing (Aparicio 1998). It also plays with Hispanic Caribbean women's strategies for negotiating social conventions that privilege sexual abstinence or virginity. The song's popularity in Puerto Rico has to do, in part, with the presence of a substantial, somewhat marginalized Dominican community in the archipelago but also with the workings of the transnational Latin music industry.[18]

You Don't Look Like is based on a personal experience Cardona had while attending a casting call for a toothpaste commercial, and presents an Afro–Puerto Rican actor who is looking for work and is only offered television and theater roles that reinforce stereotypical images most often found in the dominant Puerto Rican racist media imaginary (Rivero 2005, 2006); these limitations of typecasting have a demoralizing psychological effect on the performer. The performance includes direct audience interaction; further testimonial narratives, including a description of travel to the United States; an enumeration of diverse examples of blackface or stereotyped Puerto Rican television representations such as the characters of Chianita, Pirulo el Colorao, Ruperta la Caimana, Cuco Pasurín, and Willy el Merenguero; a slide presentation; a hyperexaggerated counter-performance of blackface; and an expressionistic dance performance with potentially disintoxicating, ritual character.[19]

Cardona's performance is subtly framed as a retelling of the "Snow White" fairy tale in which the protagonist embodies the role of a reenvisioned, now sympathetic Evil Queen, much as in the rewriting of the Wicked Witch of the West from *The Wizard of Oz* in Gregory Maguire's (1995) novel *Wicked* and in Stephen Schwartz and Winnie Holzman's musical theater adaptation of the same name (Wolf 2008) or in Walt Disney Pictures' reenvisioning of the wicked fairy godmother from "Sleeping Beauty" in the 2014 film *Maleficent* (dir. Robert Stromberg), but also possibly (and rather abstractly) the role of Snow White's seven dwarves, presented as iterations of the self in a photographic slide show.[20] While feminist scholarship has debated the possibilities of empowering recuperations of fairy tales (Bacchilega 1997; Haase 2004), here we have a Black, queer, Puerto Rican transloca enactment that suggests the limitations and perhaps impossibility of such an endeavor, closer to the radically cynical rejection articulated in the African American photographer Carrie Mae Weems's well-known image *Mirror, Mirror* from the *Ain't Jokin'* series (1987–1988), in which the lighter-skinned/pale-faced fairy godmother in the magical mirror violently denies the darker-skinned Black woman's aspiration of beauty ("Looking into the mirror, the black woman asked,

'Mirror, mirror on the wall, who's the finest of them all?' The mirror says, 'Snow White, you black bitch, and don't you forget it!!!'").[21] As Deborah Willis explains, "The subtext to *Mirror, Mirror* is Weems' desire to show the holder of the mirror other avenues through which to recognize beauty. The photograph reads as a counternarrative to the history of racist images" (2012, 38).

Cardona's adaptation of a classic tale is similar to but perhaps more understated than that of other queer Puerto Rican artists such as Arthur Avilés and Elizabeth Marrero, who have queered *Cinderella*, *The Wizard of Oz*, and *The Ugly Duckling* in a more explicit fashion.[22] It is also different from the more explicitly referential postmodern fairy-tale dance choreographies that Sally Banes (1994, 280–90) has analyzed. In Cardona's counternarrative, there is an inversion of good and evil predicated through the transloca drag of race: Puerto Rican hegemonic racism and US colonialism (the preference for whiteness, the enforcement of white supremacy, the elision of Blackness or minimization of *lo negro*, and dramatic ignorance about Puerto Rico) stand in for Snow White (Puerto Rican racial elites; Uncle Sam), while the Evil Queen's vanity (her desire to be the most beautiful of them all) is figured as an affirmation of Otherness, of the right to be oneself, and an experiential search for self-identification. In essence, in this performance, the Evil Queen has become—to benefit from critical post- and decolonial, feminist reappraisals of Shakespeare's *The Tempest*—a resignified Caliban (Fernández Retamar 1989), or even better, Caliban's "woman" (Wynter 1992), or his mother Sycorax (Lara 2007), no longer simply a monster, an invisible figure, or a witch that threatens the European colonizers, but now a human subject. This act of becoming Other entails a rejection of hegemonic European whiteness and civilization, represented in Shakespeare's play through the characters of Prospero, his daughter Miranda, and the spirit Ariel, and the privileging of the marginalized inhabitants of the island where the play is set.

Here it is worth highlighting the German (or Hessian) origins of the "Little Snow White" story, including the implicit racial dimensions of the Brothers Grimm's fairy tale (or at least of the version they collected and edited) as first published in 1812 with the title *Sneewittchen*.[23] Also known as "Little Snow-Drop," the story begins with a queen who is sewing by a window with an ebony frame, who pricks her finger with a needle, and upon seeing three drops of blood on the snow wishes for "a child as white as this snow, as red as this blood, and as black as the wood of this frame!" And thus, "Soon afterwards a little daughter was born to her, who was white as snow and as red as blood, and whose hair was as black as ebony" (Grimm 1921, 172). This whiteness, marked by the natural or cosmetic touch of red, perhaps in rosy lips and cheeks, and by dark hair, becomes the ultimate representation of beauty.

European racial discourses positing hierarchies of civilization and concomitantly of aesthetics were already firmly in place in what was to become Germany by the middle to late eighteenth century. As Emmanuel Chukwudi Eze (1997) demonstrated in his analysis of Immanuel Kant's *Anthropology from a Pragmatic Point of View* (1798), the leading Prussian philosopher and foundational intellectual figure who has been seen as an impartial rationalist in fact harbored prejudicial racist views.[24] While major German colonial expansion in Africa did not begin until 1884, anti-Black sentiment and awareness of European global imperialism justified by notions of racial superiority were part and parcel of German thought.[25] Walt Disney's influential 1937 filmic reconceptualization of *Snow White and the Seven Dwarfs*, based on the Brothers Grimm's tale and made in a country (the United States) marked by legal segregation, antimiscegenation laws, and lynching, should also be seen as profoundly racialized and particularly relevant to the Puerto Rican colonial experience, particularly when considering Disney's explicitly racist early work.[26]

How do the symbolic elements of the "Snow White" tale become visible and audible in Cardona's performance? They do so through props, visual projections, audience interaction, and discourse. Mirrors and reflections play a crucial part in *You Don't Look Like.* Cardona's first line is a rescripting of one of the Evil Queen's most famous phrases: "Espejito, espejito" (literally, a repetition of "little mirror"), followed by a variation: "Necesito saber si yo también soy . . ." (I need to know if I am also . . .), spoken as the performer looks at himself in a small hand mirror that he pulls out of his backpack; the phrase will be repeated and challenged toward the end of the performance, when there is a verbal declaration (but not a physical staging) of the breaking of the mirror, also a feminist fairy-tale liberatory strategy (Harries 2004).[27] After the first scene, Cardona will proceed to point his small mirror at audience member's faces, pretending it is a television camera; he also looks at himself in another mirror that doubles as a tray surrounded by small packages of white sugar and artificial sweetener that he will distribute among the audience, a "commercial" or publicity-related interruption that in fact serves to highlight the relationship of sugar to slavery and thus to the African presence in Puerto Rico (Cuchí Coll 1969; Rodríguez-Silva 2012); the performer, serving as a waiter, jokingly mentions that he has no brown sugar ("Caramba, morena no tenemos, no, la compañía no la está trabajando" [1997, 48]), negating the option of a symbolic third space that might point to Blackness (in Puerto Rico, *morena/o* is a racial term that indicates African descent).

Cardona's engagement with mirrors as performative objects and as part of the scenery highlights the role of visuality, both of the act of self-reflection and that of being seen by others, and complements the narrative component of the performance. *You Don't Look Like* proposes a double play of seeing and being seen; describing and enacting the act of vision, whether of self or of the Other. Cardona's initial quotation of the central question of "Snow White" is left unanswered; the tacit subject of Blackness becomes that which is unspoken, apparently almost unspeakable.[28] He then turns to the audience to narrate his autobiographical casting experience, including an awareness of inherent bias and exclusion in the Puerto Rican advertising field, stating, "Ustedes saben quién hace este tipo de anuncio" (You know who typically appears in this kind of ad). As Yeidy M. Rivero (2006) observes in her incisive analysis of this performance, this statement can be seen as a comment on the politics of casting in Puerto Rican television and the preference for white or light-skinned actors. The unwillingness or inability of Cardona to openly name the source of exclusion (Blackness, being Black or Afrodiasporic or *negro*) in these opening lines hints to social practices that prefer elision as a strategy of politeness and social control.

Cardona dresses as he talks, putting on the hand mirror as if it were a necklace or chain with a saint's medal and an orange cotton or linen button shirt. When he describes the other "talent" at the casting, he once again uses euphemism and elision, saying, "Todos los talentos, porque así es que los llaman en este ambiente, éramos . . . este . . . este . . . tú sabes . . ." (All the talents, because that is what we are called in this environment, we were all . . . umm . . . ahh . . . you know . . .), indicating that they were different from the young woman directing the casting, who we assume was light-skinned or white. He then describes noticing that they all spoke in a strange fashion, and discloses his assumption that they had a diction or speaking problem. The performer confesses that he thought they were Nuyoricans, recognizing that he stereotyped them because of their language use, a biased observation that points to prevailing negative attitudes in the archipelago regarding return migrants.[29] He then states that he realized that they were doing what they were directed to do.

Direct interaction with the audience allows Cardona to breach the typical audience divide, breaking the "fourth wall," or imaginary dividing line, that characterizes bourgeois realist theater and lightening the tone of the performance while also highlighting the presence of mirrors; he turns the collective experience of witnessing the performance into a communitarian event, in which individual audience members have to speak out loud, follow physical instructions, and literally participate in an enactment of the transloca drag of race. Using the hand mirror as if it were a television camera, Cardona tells different audience members to look into it, say their name, and repeat the line "Bunga, bunga, agua" but increasing their expressivity and supposedly Caribbean nature.[30] As audience members do this, others laugh out loud, particularly when Cardona praises them for their performance, perhaps experiencing joy or embarrassment. Cardona then takes left- and right-profile shots of the willing or unwilling subjects, asks them to smile wide and thanks them, telling them he will be calling them back. In addition to the other mirror, which becomes a tray to serve sugar packets to the audience (and allows spectators to partake in the sense of taste and to experience the perhaps minor thrill of receiving a gift), there is the stage mirror that frames Cardona's blackface performance and occasionally reflects his choreography as he moves across the performative space.

The image of an Afro–Puerto Rican looking and not discovering him- or herself in the mirror or in a mirrorlike reflective surface is also central to Isabelo Zenón Cruz in his landmark two-volume treatise *Narciso descubre su trasero* (1974–1975), where the (closeted) Puerto Rican scholar and activist retook the Greek myth of Narcissus to argue that when Black Puerto Ricans try to see their reflection, they do not see their face, but rather their rear; this dissonance requires a process of consciousness-raising that can shatter centuries of prejudiced preconceptions. In his celebrated short story "En el fondo del caño hay un negrito" (1959), the renowned Puerto Rican writer José Luis González focuses on a young, poor Black boy, "el negrito Melodía," who stares at himself in a pond and eventually drowns while reaching out to his perceived new friend; here, reflections are seen as treacherous to Black Puerto Rican subjectivity.[31] As a reference to "Snow White," the mirror is also a sign of female vanity, of seeking self-assurance but also knowledge, of trusting in the magical or paranormal: a speaking mirror with the ability to gauge relative beauty across a geographical expanse. Mirrors are also central in many film representations of drag queens and trans performers, who are invariably shown looking at themselves as they transform their appearance, for

example Dorian Corey in *Paris Is Burning*; the mirror is cinematographi-
cally invested with truth-telling power. In Cardona's piece, negating the
mirror opens up possibilities for progress, but also creates obstacles and
troubles a relationship with the self.

Mirrors play complex roles in numerous Puerto Rican representations
of race and gender. One of the most striking scenes in Luis A. Maissonet's
1959 short didactic film *Juan sin seso* (*Witless Juan*), produced by the Puerto
Rican Division of Community Education (known as DIVEDCO, its acronym in Spanish) with a script by the renowned playwright René Marqués,
is structured around a mirror.[32] Here we see a poor, rural, dark-skinned
woman who is missing her front teeth (Juan's wife) and who watches an
advertisement for beauty soap on television and believes the claim that by
using it, she will have "una cara más blanca, más aterciopelada, más bella"
(a whiter, more velvety, more beautiful face). We then see her wash her
face and stare in a mirror with her back toward us; as she turns around
and smiles, she reveals her unchanged, still dark-skinned, toothless countenance, and we hear dramatic music as well as the narrator loudly proclaiming, "¡No!" The framing suggests that Juan's wife is deceived by all of
the images she sees, including by her reflection in the mirror, and that it
is only the outside, authoritative, paternalist, masculine speaking subject
who can articulate the truth in a context in which rapid modernization
and industrialization has confused people, in a sense making them unable
to perceive the real (Colón Pizarro 2011; Esterrich 2018; Marsh Kennerly
2009). Whether as a sign of a fractured or false conception of subjectivity,
as elaborated by the French psychoanalyst Jacques Lacan, who identifies
gazing in the mirror as a crucial yet flawed stage of identity formation; as a
sign of race in Puerto Rico (Zenón Cruz; González), or as a sign of gender
and race ("Snow White"; *Mirror Mirror*; *Juan sin seso*), the mirror, or one's
reflection, is seen as complex and problematic.

The Seven Dwarves Become the Ten Embodied Selves

One of the most notable ways in which Cardona addresses and counteracts potentially noxious, limiting, racial and gendered stereotypes and in
which he highlights the transformative potential of the transloca drag of
race is through the parodic incorporation of a series of photographs that
show the performer dressed in multiple costumes; the multiplicity of these
ten images critiques racist stereotypes but also mirrors the differential

attributes of the seven dwarves associated to Snow White in her fairy tale, not in the early Brothers Grimm version but in twentieth-century reelaborations such as in Walt Disney's 1937 film.[33] Unlike the fairy-tale dwarves, however, the ten variations do not provide shelter or support for an innocent protagonist; they function in the realm of postmodern fragmentation and distancing, and can also be thought of as iterations of the tarot's Major Arcana or as diverse manifestations of the orishas from Santería, whether a range of multiple, different divinities or varying aspects of just one. As a list of noxious stereotypes, the slide show plays a similar role to the exploration and critique of US anti-Black stereotypes such as the sambo, the mammy, the coon, the pickaninny, and the Uncle Tom presented by the queer filmmaker Marlon Riggs in his well-known 1987 documentary *Ethnic Notions* (Kleinhans 1991; Kleinhans and Lesage 1991); the more poetic, assemblage-like, and testimonial organization of *You Don't Look Like* is closer in style to Rigg's classic 1989 film *Tongues Untied*, except that it does not include an open discussion of sexuality.

The ten images of Cardona taken by the photographer Miguel Villafañe are quickly projected as extremely large background slides during Cardona's discussion of an interaction with "un amigo de la cultura" (a friend of the arts) who gets him "una parte bien sencillita" (a minor, simple role) and tells him to do an outstanding job "because there are no minor roles."[34] The projection is so fast that the images are more like brief flashes that sear audience members' eyes and generate a cumulative effect; individual reactions to each photo are combined with the overall impact of the series. Careful attention to each image, which are now freely available on the internet as part of the documentation of the piece, allows for more nuanced appraisals.

Villafañe's images include Cardona dressed as a tribal, premodern, or savage African, identified in the published script as "un negro salvaje" (perhaps a direct reference to "El Africano"); as a colorful *rumbero*, or rumba dancer or musician; as an urban rapper (*un rapero*) sporting the mid-1990s most advanced communications technology (a beeper), an image also associated with that of drug dealer; as a *jíbaro* or farmworker in the coastal sugarcane field; as a biblical Black magus, or wise man (in Puerto Rico, Melchior and not Balthazar);[35] as a *santero* or perhaps Palo Monte Afrodiasporic religious practitioner; as a potentially Afrocentrist reggae or salsa fan, who is identified in the script as a Rasta, or "stoned Rastafarian"; and as a basketball player.[36] There are also two female representations that appear toward the end of the sequence: Cardona as a *madama,* or Santería (or perhaps Espiritismo) madam, clothed in white with multicolor necklaces, alluding perhaps to popular entertainers Myrta Silva or Carmen Miranda, who is portrayed as a washerwoman (see figure 16); and as a *sirvienta* (maid or domestic worker), looking intently at the spectator (see figure 15).[37]

If in Disney's 1937 *Snow White and the Seven Dwarfs,* each dwarf represented a particular temperament, affect, or trait (whether that of the leader Doc or of the additional six: Grumpy, Sleepy, Happy, Bashful, Sneezy, and Dopey), the ten photographic characters enacted by Cardona present a mix of attributes, some parodic and highly exaggerated, some seemingly realistic or lifelike, and some eroticized and noble. While the image of the grimacing, seminaked, African tribesman who wears an animal print loincloth and holds a cane in midair and that of the *rumbero* might be parodic or even offensive, they also reveal a very handsome, fit man; for example, the rumba musician's photo suggestively shows a triangle of flesh above the pants and below the billowing red and multicolored sleeves of the musician's outfit. The next image (the rapper) is rather contemporary and has Cardona wearing a baseball cap backward, black sunglasses, a black-and-white striped referee shirt, gold chains, blue jeans, and very fashionable black-and-silver sneakers; in spite of the stylized hand gestures, the representation is not intrinsically over the top compared to some of the other photos, and highlights attractive youth-oriented urban masculinity that might coincide with the style preferences of some of the persons in the audience. The transition to the next image, that of the machete-wielding, straw *pava* hat-wearing, Black peasant or *jíbaro,* who appears wearing stained white clothes, is notable because of the incongruity with the previous photo; it is seemingly a historical reenactment that feeds into but also challenges nostalgic, idealized recuperations of countryside life. Subsequently, Cardona's serious, theatricalized pose as King Melchior, wearing a bejeweled gold crown, a purple turban, a seemingly fake black beard, a Walter Mercado–like black cape decorated with golden stars, and a box of fake plastic jewels, departs from the realm of verisimilitude except as a citation of religious and commercial enactments of biblical Magi that are ever-present during Christmastime and that tap into popular Puerto Rican Catholic beliefs; it can also be seen as a reenactment of the Burger King, a popular American fast food hamburger restaurant's mascot.

The juxtaposition of the regal (although also slightly ridiculous) Black magus image with the one that follows of a sexy, uncouth, laughing *santero* (perhaps a *babalao,* or religious leader) pits two religious systems against

Fig. 16. Javier Cardona as *santera*. Image from *You Don't Look Like*, 1996.
Photo by Miguel Villafañe.

each other, emphasizing masculine embodiment through its representation of a man with an exposed hairy chest covered with bead necklaces in muted colors that embodies the spiritual and magical beliefs of Afro-diasporic religions; the *santero* appears sitting at a table possibly drinking rum and smoking a cigar, partaking of the pleasures of the body, perhaps in ritual form. This image is immediately followed by the sitting *madama*, perceived as a *santera* or washerwoman: it is a haunting, upper-body or three-quarters portrait in which we see a potentially unhappy, stoic, or simply tired character looking slightly downward away from the camera, wearing a beautiful white lace dress and colorful plastic or Lucite bead necklaces, green grape-like earrings, a knotted white headwrap, and perhaps a touch of red lipstick, and holding a bundle of clothes wrapped with a black maid's uniform. The dignified countenance, framed by large, black eyebrows, suggests labor and seems to distance the portrait from more exuberant representations of *madamas*, for example those of Brazilian *baianas* appropriated and globalized by the entertainer Carmen Miranda, who subsequently became a camp icon and the object of frequent drag parody and homage.[38] The image also marks a gendered difference or distance from the laughing *santero*.

The other female representation is quite different: it is a full-body portrait of a smiling, hairy-legged, barefoot maid, her head slightly tilted, who stares straight into the camera and holds an empty wine glass on a beautiful silver tray; her exuberant black curly hair is held back with a broad white kerchief, causing her locks to fall behind her neck (see figure 15). The maid is wearing a black uniform trimmed at the neck and sleeves with ornate white lace, and also wears a spotless lace-trimmed white apron; she is not wearing a slip, and we can see her naked legs underneath the slightly translucent black fabric of her uniform. She is also wearing orange and gold circular clip-on earrings and seems to have red lipstick. Her bare feet interrupt the formality of the service uniform, perhaps suggesting incivility or strategic resistance to conventions and norms. The overall composition is that of an attractive person who irradiates beauty. It is a noble, well-lit portrait that ostensibly ennobles the subject and the profession portrayed, but that also perhaps activates stereotypes of compliant, happy domestic workers.

These two female representations disarm the audience and generate laughter. After the maid, we then see the so-called stoned Rastafarian, perhaps meant as a detrimental stereotype, portraying a handsome, pensive man who holds his hands behind his head; he is wearing a colorful

African-inspired red print shirt, has black oval eyeglasses, and sports a five-o'clock shadow. The last image of the series is that of Cardona as a serious, perhaps taciturn or angry uniformed basketball player wearing shorts, whose red-trimmed, sleeveless white shirt says "Edson 12" (perhaps a reference to the Brazilian professional basketball player Edson Bispo dos Santos), who also stares straight into the camera, and whose quietly simmering rage counteracts the apparent joy expressed by other characters such as the *santero* and the *sirvienta*.

In her important essay on *You Don't Look Like* titled "Mirror, Mirror on the Wall," Jossianna Arroyo (2002) offers detailed analysis of these images and suggests the idea of "cultural drag" as a mechanism to read Cardona's piece as an exploration of race, nationality, gender, and sexuality. Arroyo borrows the term from the Los Angeles–based Puerto Rican performance artist Marcus Kuiland-Nazario, who became well known in the 1990s through his drag alter ego of Carmen, a loud-mouthed, Latina HIV/AIDS prevention warrior who thought nothing of storming into bars and other locales to share her bilingual Spanish-English sex-positive message of virus prevention (Martínez 1994). For Kuiland-Nazario—similar to the queer Latinx Teatro Viva! artists studied by scholar David Román in his 1998 book *Acts of Intervention: Performance, Gay Culture, and AIDS*— ethnic or Latino-inflected, multilingual, over-the-top drag performance that plays with and at times risks reenacting stereotypes can serve as a radical political tool in a minoritarian context. This vision of the radical political potential of drag also coincides with the "terrorist" drag interventions of African American Chicana performer Vaginal Davis (Muñoz 1999, 93–115), where drag performance is used as an antiracist tool that operates through the parody of militarized white supremacy (Davis's character of Clarence) and with other explicitly political uses of drag, for example Empress José Sarria's unsuccessful electoral bid in 1961 for San Francisco Board of Supervisors (in male drag) and drag performer Joan Jett Blakk's Queer Nation Party campaign for US president in 1992 and 1996, portrayed on the stage in 2019 by Tarell Alvin McCraney and the Steppenwolf Theatre of Chicago in the play *Ms. Blakk for President*.[39] This is also true of the New York City–based drag legend Lady Bunny's constant, acerbic, left-leaning political jabbering (Schulman 2018); of Sister Roma of the San Francisco Sisters of Perpetual Indulgence's long-standing political advocacy and activism (Fitzsimons 2019; Signorile 2014); of the internationally renowned Taylor Mac's "radical faerie realness ritual" performances involving incisive antiracist and antihomophobic political commentary (Román, Westerling, and Venning 2017); of Miss Chief Eagle Testickle's (Kent Monkman's) Indigenous interventions in the art world (Cousineau-Levine 2017); of Panti Bliss's activism regarding marriage-equality in Ireland (O'Toole 2017); and of the drag performer Pissi Myles's appearance at the impeachment hearings of President Donald Trump in Washington, DC, on November 13, 2019 (Fitzsimons and Kacala 2019).

For Arroyo, Cardona's varied gender representations help in the identification of the arbitrary nature of racial constructs. Arroyo argues that Cardona's two female (cross-dressing or drag) images as a *santera* and as a maid create a more radical rupture of any illusion of verisimilitude that spectators might have, even if Cardona never actually cross-dresses in feminine clothes in front of his audience. For Arroyo, racial performativity becomes that much more apparent when filtered through the lens of gender and its possible implications for sexuality, even while she stresses that the two female images represent a type of "imperfect drag" (2002, 167). As Arroyo states,

> This black maid is not an incarnation of the feminine body, nor does she have the "perfection" and the "illusion" of the feminine required of drag. Her hairy legs, bare feet, and erotic innuendos work with the "masquerade" of the feminine, a pose that relates directly to cultural construction, power relationships, and meaning. (2002, 164)

While I agree with the iconic value of these two images, particularly as the result of their simultaneous and later circulation as part of the documentation of the performance in print and online spaces, and with their "imperfect" nature (Cardona wears almost no female makeup, for example), "conceptual" or figurative drag (for example, embodying the Evil Queen from "Snow White") begins with Cardona's very first utterance in the show; the highly charged images of maid and *santera* form part of a more complex drag system present in the performance. It is true that the audience's reaction to seeing the two drag images is loud, raucous laughter, a stronger reaction than that observed for many of the other slides. It is also true that perceptions of Afro-Caribbean women as domestic workers, laundresses, and Santería or Espiritismo practitioners are firmly enmeshed in dominant imaginaries that frequently refuse to envision other potential labor possibilities (Alegría Ortega and Ríos González 2005). At their heart, the ten representations highlight Cardona playing dress-up, embodying difference, and envisioning theatrical staging for the photographic camera as a potential space for critique. Villafañe's photos enable Cardona to explore complex stereotypes and diverse realities, highlighting the performativity of race and gender as forms of drag. At the same time, each image potentiates uncontainable varied audience engagements and fantasies.

Blackface Drag, Minstrelsy, and the Transloca Drag of Race

Some of the most dramatic representations of the transloca drag of race as an imposition, a pain, or a burden occur when Cardona discusses the television commercial casting agent wanting him to wear a wig, which he says he refused to do, and when we actually see him darken his face with black-colored makeup and put on a wig cap and then a black curly hair wig, both of which he will then rip off during his dance, a classic move in the drag repertoire meant as a magic reveal of the "truth" behind the facade. The staged act of blackface by a Black performer here serves as a reenactment of trauma (social expectations) but also as a potential site of parody and Bakhtinian carnivalesque inversion, much as the Afrodiasporic blackface performances of the *loca* and *viejo* in the Feast of St. James the Apostle in Loíza question and challenge the authority of the ostensibly white caballeros and engage differently with the *vejigantes*. The gesture visualizes the masquerade of race, its performative aspects, its drag, and stands in tension and dialogue with blackface or "brown skin" performances by diaporic Caribbean blackface minstrels such as Bert Williams (Stephens 2014, 31–70) and by non-Black queer Hispanic Caribbean performers such as Rita Indiana Hernández (García-Peña 2016, 155–69; Quinn 2016).

It is precisely while in blackface that Cardona goes on to describe personal experiences in which his national identity as a Puerto Rican was challenged in the Caribbean archipelago and abroad. As Cardona's character states in the performance, it was during a trip to the United States that the protagonist was told, "You don't look like . . .":

> Bueno, si por ahí me ven bailando en zancos siempre hay alguien que me pregunta si soy de Loíza. Si entro a una tienda en el Viejo San Juan se creen que soy de Saint Thomas o de las Islas. Si voy a coger un avión me hacen preguntas moronas buscándome un acento "extrañito". Y si estoy en Estados Unidos me preguntan la clásica: que qué soy yo. Yo les contesto a la rajatabla, casi a la defensiva: puertorriqueño. Rápido fruncen el ceño y como si fuera un halago

me dicen: You don't look like. . . . Entonces como que los ojos se me
van pa'trás, los colmillos como que me empiezan a crecer, la cabeza
con todo y cuello se gira discretamente hacia la izquierda, el pecho
se me hincha y bien dentro de mí me pregunto: a qué centella se
supone que yo look like. I don't look like Puerto Rican, I don't look
like black, I don't look like this, I don't look like that. What am I
supposed to look like? (Cardona 1997, 49)

Well, if I'm dancing or performing something on stilts, there's always someone who asks me if I am from Loíza Aldea. If I enter a
store in Old San Juan, they think I come from St. Thomas or from
"the Islands." If I'm boarding a plane, they ask me all kinds of stupid
questions, looking for a "strange" accent. And if I'm in the United
States, they ask me the classic question: What am I? I tell them in a
straightforward, almost defensive way: Puerto Rican. Immediately,
they frown in amazement and, as if they were complimenting me,
say: "You don't look like a . . ." Then I squint my eyes, my fangs start
to grow, my head and neck turn discreetly to the left, my chest sticks
out, and deep inside I ask myself: what the fuck am I supposed to
look like? I don't look . . . Puerto Rican, I don't look . . . black, I don't
look like this, I don't look like that. What am I supposed to look
like? (Cardona 1998, 15)

In this scene, we witness a displacement of anger and frustration from
racial prejudice in Puerto Rico toward the manifestation of American
ignorance and racialization, specifically that of the homogenizing vision
that nonofficial segregation imposes on subjects in the United States
(Cobas, Duany, and Feagin 2016). This misidentification is not exclusive
to Black Puerto Ricans, but occurs across the board.

The bilingual scene also reveals a complex relationship as a colonial
subject marked by language. As noted, the protagonist early on indicates
biased perceptions about diasporic Puerto Ricans when he believes the
fellow actors at the toothpaste ad casting are Nuyoricans who don't know
how to speak Standard Puerto Rican Spanish (Arroyo 2002, 160–61). Both
the Puerto Rico–based scholar Lowell Fiet (1998) and Cuban theater critic
Vivian Martínez Tabares (2004) have pointed out the linguistic struggle
present in the piece, which reflects wider tensions related to colonialism
and to the relation between the colonizer and the colonized (Memmi
1965); the very title of the work, which is in English, is symptomatic of
this, as the performance is predominantly in Spanish. Language, as has

been amply noted, is one of the most contentious issues regarding Puerto Rican identity under US colonialism (Barreto 1998, 2001; Zentella 1997).

The final reckoning with others' perceptions of him leads Cardona to become a type of monster, to invoke a figure also referenced by Nina Flowers (discussed in chapter 2) and enacted by Freddie Mercado (discussed in chapter 4): the act of nonrecognition in the United States provokes a process of angry self-bestialization (the eyes rolling inward, the growing of fangs), an engagement with the abject (Alvarado 2018; Kristeva 1982) and with the legacy of imaginations of Black racial monstrosity (S. Johnson 2015), but also a process of truth-speaking. This conundrum, the self-reckoning that one can never satisfy others' expectations, that one will inevitably be the Other (Sartre 1964), leads to a moment of myth-busting, the (linguistic) breaking or shattering of the mirror, a declarative utterance spoken directly at the mirror ("Espejito, espejoto, siempre tú has estado roto"): an acknowledgment of the mirror's inability to speak the truth or to grant totality. This revelation goes hand in hand with the recognition that people will constantly assume things: "Pero, como la gente siempre asume cosas. Mira, si me sacudo por calor, por piquiña o por coraje ya estoy en un despojo" ("But, since people always presume things . . . look, if I shake because I'm hot or because something itches or because I'm angry, they already think I'm possessed" [Cardona 1998, 16]). Any type of movement, whether it is provoked by heat, an itch, or anger, will be misinterpreted as an Afro-Caribbean or religious ritual cleansing, an act of magic or superstition, the sign of wildness, of the savage.

If this is the case, the performer seems to suggest, he might as well engage in movements that might have this effect: as a disintoxicating ritual, a disorienting ceremony of unusual, jarring poses and physical displacements that do not correspond to the music we hear (at first a single sustained electronic note), which is activated by uttering the word *despojo* (a type of ritual cleansing), or to the silence that follows; perhaps a reenactment of the Evil Queen's final scene in the Brothers Grimm's version of the "Snow White" fairy tale, when the Queen is made to dance to death while wearing fire-hot iron shoes.[40] Cardona's performance thus turns into a dance piece that serves as a type of exorcism of racism, but also as a puzzle and subversion of expectations: initially focusing on strange, repetitive body contortions and on flexing of the knees and elbows while standing in place and looking downward, then progressing to small jumps, walking in a near-squatting position, all downstage left, near the desk, with his movements reflected in the mirror on the side; these movements lead to upright jabs with raised forearms while the hands are held close to the face and to dramatic movement back and forth on a diagonal across the entire stage, to hand punching in the air, and to the simulation of sleepwalking with arms outstretched and then held high in the air, eventually branching out into fuller expressions that incorporate limbs held in awkward angles, pantomime, and jumping, as the music goes from a single note to veer closer to noise with electronic distortions.

In *You Don't Look Like*, dance enables a questioning of the pernicious stereotypes of race. As Cardona moves to the back of the stage, he positions his right hand behind his head, leading to forward and sideways full-body flexes at the waist, guiding his head toward the floor, eventually displacing the wig, which he throws to the side. He then proceeds to take the wig cap off and disposes of it as well. The sudden introduction of conga percussion in the soundtrack leads Cardona to raise his right fist high, move both fists near the face, and release his whole body, allowing it to slightly fall on itself; raise his left leg and left arm high; then move to a mid-squat with spread legs, with both hands resting near the knees. After a pause, Cardona retakes the backward diagonal movement, now integrating a percussive arm gesture that seems to simulate the action of cutting sugarcane, quickly moving to a feet-together displacement led by moving the waist and hips while the hands and arms continue self-contained movements near the upper body, then leading to forward jumps on the diagonal, with the hands cradling the head. Arriving downstage left again, Cardona places one arm forward, the other behind his back, and joins his hands under his torso between his legs, proceeding to walk stiltedly. He then moves toward the back of the stage, where he begins a march forward facing backward, his body led by his percussive buttocks and hips, only to turn around, throw his arms in the air, and move back while looking downward. Another forward run leads to a birdlike stance center stage, with the left foot on the right knee, the simulation of a sleeping pose with the bent upper torso closer to the ground, and more walking, running, and jumping with outstretched arms in a circle above the head. It is fair to say that many of these movements come across as demented, which is to say, as those of a masculine transloca.

Cardona continues to dance even when the music stops; his movements include a pantomime and a long stance with raised right arm, the simulation of flight with outstretched arms conducted on a diagonal accompanied by jumps, dainty steps backward, the repetition of the foot on the knee gesture, walking, the simulation of binoculars with the hands making circular gestures by the eyes, and gazing into the distance, which lead to the final verbal declaration of the piece. The performance ends with Cardona forcefully posing a question before stepping off stage: "¿Ahora me habré visto lo suficientemente negro?" (Am I black enough now?), translated by Annette Guevárez and Lowell Fiet as "And now, do I look black enough for you?" (1998, 16). This conclusion can be seen as a negation of the death of the queen in the Brothers Grimm's fairy tale and as the survival of the Black Puerto Rican transloca.

Unlike Rivero's (2006) assessment, I would argue that Cardona's choreography and gestures are marked by postmodern dance movements that do not neatly correspond with Afro–Puerto Rican folkloric dance or to social dance, modern dance, or ballet, although at times seems to borrow some phrases. The choreography and gestures seem more inspired by the movement vocabulary of Viveca Vázquez, Awilda Sterling Duprey, and members of the avant-garde dance movement Pisotón, as Susan Homar (2010) has documented, some of whom Cardona trained with, as well as by the legacy of Gilda Navarra's Taller de Histriones, which focused on pantomime (Feliciano Díaz 2014). Cardona's movements are marked by athleticism, pauses, strong angles, quick jumps, and decisive phrases. They retake the energy of the initial running scene and bring it full circle. The choreography dialogues with and embraces what dance scholar Clare Croft has proposed as "queer dance": "the pleasures and difficulties of moving between multiple, layered identities. Frustration and diminishment physically reframed as strength. Images that do not immediately make sense, but that somehow gather force" (2017, 1). It also stages a compelling and very particular iteration of what Thomas F. DeFrantz and Anita González (2014, 1) have identified as "black performance . . . as a circumstance enabled by black sensibilities, black expressive practices, and black people."

You Don't Look Like highlights the transloca drag of race: the tensions between perception of a "natural" or unmediated performance of race, specifically of Blackness, and more clearly artificial, constructed, performative versions. This is especially theatricalized through descriptions, actions, images, sounds, flavors, and movements: references to wearing wigs with strange hair textures and curls; the act of putting on blackface onstage, darkening his skin from his natural dark brown complexion to charcoal black, followed by putting on a wig cap and a curly hair wig; the invitation to the audience to eat sugar and to see an opaque, athletic choreography whose meaning is not immediately evident. It also occurs through the projection of photographic images (ten reenvisioned dwarves) that highlight male and female stereotypes that become drag iterations in and of themselves.

Unlike Cardona's early and mid-1990s dance duos with Eduardo Alegría, where the homosocial contiguity of the dancing male bodies wearing women's housedresses (mumus) suggested a homoerotic content that served to question sexual orientation, and unlike later group choreographies such as *Ah mén* and *Hasta el cuello*—which also include male dancer interaction, discussions of effeminacy (in the case of *Ah mén*), and drag performance—there is no explicit mention of same-sex desire in *You Don't Look Like*, and most people believe that the piece is exclusively about race and nationality, a position that the performer seems comfortable with. However, as Arroyo (2002) and others have highlighted, *You Don't Look Like* is also about masculinities and sexuality, which range from the expectations generated by the initial merengue song "El Africano" and the self-presentation of the performer as a masculine, athletic man running on stage, to the negotiation of men in television and theater, artistic/labor practices that have historically been tainted with questionable masculinities. The gendered exploration is pushed further by the allusions to "Snow White" and by the photographic representations by Miguel Villafañe, particularly but not exclusively the images of Cardona in female drag. The donning of makeup and a wig and the participation in a postmodern dance solo also potentially challenge conventional norms of heterosexual, cisgender masculinity, which sees all of these as potentially suspect.

Cardona never openly discusses his sexual orientation or his personal sexual desires or attractions in this piece, something that is unusual in a performance marked by confessional disclosures regarding employment, travel, and daily life, aggressive assertions of Puerto Rican cultural nationalism, and the defense of the Spanish language. This reticence differs from other Black Puerto Rican queer representations such as Josean Ortiz's *La última plena que bailó Luberza* (2013–15), a forthright drag enactment of a short story by Manuel Ramos Otero about the renowned madam or brothel owner Isabel la Negra, which was staged in San Juan and New York with Ortiz playing the female lead, and Charles Rice-González's exploration of intergenerational dialogues and Black gay diasporic Puerto Rican identity in the Bronx in his play *I Just Love Andy Gibb* (2016), staged by the Pregones Theater, which focuses on how queer Afro–Puerto Rican males can overcome their idealization of white masculinity and learn to love themselves.[41] Cardona's reticence is reminiscent of the contextual negotiations that Carlos Ulises Decena (2011) analyzes among Dominican immigrant men in New York City, a discretion that Decena describes as a "tacit subject," referring to the avoidance of particular disclosures for the sake of safety and well-being or to maintain family harmony. It also echoes Wesley Crichlow's (2004) description of the silences of Black gay Canadian men as portrayed in his book *Buller Men and Batty Bwoys: Hidden Men in Toronto and Halifax Black Communities.*

One could ponder if the title *You Don't Look Like* suggests an additional type of anxiety: that of not looking effeminate (or like a *loca* or *maricón* or even gay), an issue fleshed out in *Ah mén*. It is perhaps the end of *You Don't Look Like*, when Cardona dances in an unencumbered manner (the queen's death dance transformed into a dance of survival), that produces the most profound sense of liberation and possibility, where the seduction of the dancing body ruptures the impasses of language, race, and identity. Choreography by itself would perhaps be insufficient; as the queer African American literary scholar Darieck B. Scott writes about Fanon's analysis of social dance and its relation to muscular tension as a physiological or somatic response to dehumanization, "Muscular tension, as literal physical condition that is also a psychic state, is worked out and released in ritual performances that fail to address the root cause of the tension, and the tension perpetually recurs because of that failure" (2010, 66). But *You Don't Look Like* is not simply ritual performance; it is a lot more.

A holistic reading of Cardona's piece, including its narrative text, choreography, music, props, and visual projections, suggests a richer, nonassimilable vision, one that comes closer to *translocura* or to the radical potential of combining a critique of fossilized racial conceptions, racial prejudice, and white supremacy with an exploration of alternate gender and sexuality. Cardona's performance, which is centered on Puerto Rico, presents the United States as a hostile location and diasporic Puerto Ricans as symbols of alterity. In the next chapter, I will discuss how diasporic Puerto Ricans also create community through transloca performance, challenging hegemonic notions of gender and sexuality, particularly through the use of music, theater, and lip-synch performance.

SIX

Bolero, Translocation, Performance
Jorge B. Merced and the Pregones Theater of the Bronx

The Latin American bolero is a music of seduction: slow, danceable, with sorrowful, lovelorn lyrics, in a 2/4 time signature.[1] The director Wong Kar-Wai knows it well, and that is why boleros accompany Maggie Cheung and Tony Leung as they become desperate lovers in Wong's *In the Mood for Love* (2000), a nostalgic film set in 1960s Hong Kong, interlaced with classic Latin American songs interpreted in a heavily accented Spanish by none other than Nat King Cole. A movie for the new millennium, marked by its postmodern vanguardist style, but at the same time profoundly conservative, as Stephen Teo (2001) points out in relation to its traditional melodramatic romantic plot; a film in Cantonese and Shanghainese, with a soundtrack performed by an African American heartthrob well known for conquering many hearts, here and there.[2]

Wong's attraction to all things Latin American is well known. Earlier, in his deceivingly titled *Happy Together* (1997), the director presented Leslie Cheung and Tony Leung as two melancholy gay male transloca Hong Kong expatriates in Buenos Aires whose amorous travails anticipated those of *In the Mood for Love*. Among the first images in *Happy Together* is a stunning aerial shot of the imposing Iguazú waterfalls accompanied by the music of the Brazilian Caetano Veloso, not in Portuguese, but in Spanish, as in his 1994 album *Fina estampa*; a linguistic gesture reproduced by the Spanish film director Pedro Almodóvar—a faithful lover of the bolero and of Latin American songs—in *Talk to Her* (2002), where we see a Spanish lady bullfighter and her male Argentinean reporter friend listening to Caetano, who sings "Cucurrucucú Paloma" before their very eyes. It is noticeable that it is the same *huapango* (a different musical style) in the Spanish film as in Wong's movie, a song by the Zacatecan composer

163

Tomás Méndez that was immortalized by the great Lola Beltrán. But here it is the androgynous Caetano, who years before had openly declared his attraction to a young, sun-drenched, male Bahian surfer in his song "O leãozinho" ("The Lion Cub"), the same Brazilian singer whose large musical production is marked by ambiguity and sexual/gender games, as César Braga-Pinto (2002) has observed; the same Caetano who sang "Burn It Blue" with Lila Downs in the film *Frida* (2002), directed by Julie Taymor, where the grande dame of female masculinity Chavela Vargas (a most extraordinary *transmacha*) also appeared.[3] It is about a slow, melancholic song ("Cucurrucucú") that describes one lover's lament for his or her absent lover, crying, suffering, singing, moaning, not eating, finally dying of "mortal passion," after which his or her soul turns into a bird; love and death, tied by the musical form.

Accompanied by Caetano and the tango, the homosexual lovers of *Happy Together* reconstruct their transloca lives as fleeting immigrants in Argentina and become local in their passion for *fútbol* (soccer), *mate* (the herbal infusion), and beef, although as the scholar Francine Masiello points out, the process is marked by the disjunctures experienced by Asian migrant workers in the Southern Cone, suffering from linguistic alienation and economic poverty (2001, 141–43). This homoerotic passion is mediated by the dance that the protagonists engage in in the privacy of their small rented room, without need, for one instant, of words: a dance similar to that of Salma Hayek (who plays Frida Kahlo) and Ashley Judd (appearing as the Italian photographer Tina Modotti) in a scene from *Frida* in which the two women dance and kiss while Lila Downs sings "Alcoba Azul," with the difference that (in the latter) a group of people including Albert Molina and Antonio Banderas watch and desire them in silence.

This musical passion is no coincidence: the tango is, in many erotic and sentimental ways, the Buenos Airean equivalent of the Mexican-Caribbean bolero, of the Portuguese fado, of the southern blues, and of many other explicit songs of passion, as Iris M. Zavala (2000) suggests in her book *El bolero: Historia de un amor*. All of these twentieth-century musical forms, clear markers of modernity and of its inherent contradictions, are intercrossed with a profound desire for the impossibly perfect love: the longing for the painful recognition of that which is farther away than one can reach. The Latin American bolero (a particular genre of slow song with origins in Cuba and its accompanying dance, not to be confused with the folkloric Spanish bolero) is the music of the androgynous voice, deep in the case of women, ethereal, close to the falsetto in the case of men (think of the Cuban singer Bola de Nieve); a music of indeterminate love objects, of ambiguity, of the you and the me, in spite of your sex, or precisely because of your unnamable sex. When danced, it is the music of two bodies intimately embracing each other, moving slowly in close proximity, publicly or privately sharing a carnal delight.

For José Quiroga (2000), the bolero is a nostalgic diasporic recuperation of a Cuba that no longer exists: the musical equivalent of the homoerotic photo by Benno Thoma that graces the cover of Quiroga's *Tropics of Desire: Interventions from Queer Latin/o America*. For the Puerto Rican writer Luis Rafael Sánchez (1988), the bolero is transformed into the motivation for a transloca pilgrimage through the Caribbean in his novel (or *fabulation*, as he prefers to call it) *La importancia de llamarse Daniel Santos*, which is to say, as Ben. Sifuentes-Jáuregui once told me, the importance of being, or rather, of loving, not the Ernest of Oscar Wilde, but a tropical music singer; in Sánchez's book, the bolero becomes "a common *locus*, a code that appeals and unifies all social classes" (Cortés 2015, 77).[4] This popularity is retaken by Mayra Santos-Febres in her novel *Sirena Selena vestida de pena* (2000b), where the young transloca protagonist seduces her audiences by singing boleros (Arroyo 2003a; Cuadra 2003). Meanwhile, for the Chicana scholar Deborah R. Vargas (2008, 2012), the bolero creates a space for the negotiation of gender and sexuality in the US/Mexico borderlands, in which "dissonant divas" like the Tejana singer Chelo Silva can express themselves and cultivate audiences that appreciate their subversion.

Some time ago, an Italian American artist-turned-poet from New Jersey broke my little transloca heart; let us say that he was something between an angel and a demon. I confess that in my state of profound depression, I couldn't find greater relief than to hear recordings of boleros and rancheras sung by Paquita la del Barrio, that Mexican institution which "dresses like the torch singers of yesteryear" (Foster 2000) and sings about squashing men as if they were vile insects.[5] Contrary to Zavala's interpretation of Paquita, whom Zavala catalogues as a pseudo- or counter-bolero singer ("the one who elaborates the transvestism of the bolero"), for me, Paquita's art is pure emotion, by which I mean the distilled or condensed intensity of affect that breaks forth, free of social convention, and speaks its truth as cruel hyperbole, and that sees the world as a stage for the taking and the subject as a star. Who knows: perhaps it is precisely Paquita's inversion or transvestism that attracts me so much. *Tres veces te engañé, tres veces te engañé, tres veces te engañé: la primera por coraje, la segunda por capricho, la tercera por placer.*[6] But of course I didn't deceive him, at least not that I remember (and certainly not three times!), although it doesn't really matter. The only thing that does is that I felt that Paquita could say all of those things that I couldn't, like: *¿Me estás oyendo, inútil?* (Are you listening to me, you good-for-nothing?). And suddenly, I felt myself back in Monterrey, Nuevo León, attending the *Shakira* drag queen cabaret that Jorge B. Merced had recommended, seated at a lonely table in the nearly empty Fréber Concert Theater, hypnotized by a drag queen identical to Paquita that impeccably lip-synched her songs to the great delight of the small audience.[7] So much so that for me, Mexico became a world all about women: not only María Félix—may she rest in peace, she who died during her sleep the day of her eighty-eighth birthday; Doña Bárbara, Agustín Lara's María Bonita, the one to blame for poor Jorge Negrete's burning in hell—but also Paquita la del Barrio and Paulina Rubio, La Pau, whom I saw much later in Mexico City interpreted by another, rather ugly drag queen, on a stage in El Zócalo, directly across from the cathedral and under the shade of an enormous tricolored flag, after the city's twenty-third annual gay pride parade in 2001.[8] The bolero is thus about memory: of body, place, space, and time. It marks our lives and organizes our experiences, creating a referential transcription of love. Transvestism itself, especially the drag queen who sings or lip-synchs boleros, recreates and reanimates these worlds using deceit as an accessory: it makes us live them again, with some distance, without a doubt, but with great emotion and intensity, with the enthusiasm that marks the affective ties of a good spectator.

To speak of the bolero as a genre is to summarize personal transloca stories of music, drag performance, and translocality, mine and others, and that is why I have begun this chapter with so many digressions, with the maps of my own migratory musical, performative, and geographical emotiveness.

El bolero fue mi ruina: *The Bolero Was My Downfall*

What happens when the bolero becomes the structuring element in a theatrical play about a transloca that murdered her lover in Puerto Rico? And when this play is presented in New York City by a diasporic transloca? In *El bolero fue mi ruina* (1997–2002, restaged in 2005 and then presented in 2017 as *The Bolero Was My Downfall*), the Puerto Rican actor and director Jorge B. Merced and the Pregones Theater of the Bronx offer a musical play centering on the experiences of the unforgettable Loca la de la Locura (The Queen of Madness), an incarcerated bolero singer and teller of love stories.[9] Jailed in Puerto Rico, Loca meditates in her cell in the no-longer-standing Río Piedras State Penitentiary, colloquially known as "Oso Blanco" (White Bear), about why she killed her lover Nene Lindo (Pretty Baby), a sexist *bugarrón* or masculine-acting man who had sex with *locas*, whom she was afraid would abandon her.[10] The play is a generally faithful adaptation of the short story "Loca la de la locura" by Manuel Ramos Otero (1948–90), the leading openly gay Puerto Rican author of the late twentieth century, who lived in self-imposed exile in New York City for most of the last twenty-two years of his life.[11] "Loca la de la locura" was first published in the Puerto Rican magazine *Reintegro* in 1980 and was reprinted posthumously in *Cuentos de buena tinta* in 1992, and also appeared as "The Queen of Madness" in a 1990 translation by Amy Prince.[12] Merced, who is one of the two associate artistic directors of Pregones Theater, received a photocopy of the short story from José Olmo, a friend of the deceased author; Merced shared it with the company and spearheaded its theatrical adaptation.

My analysis of this piece, which premiered in Spanish in 1997, was in repertoire until 2002, was later restaged with new costumes and backdrops in 2005, and was most recently reenvisioned and restaged in 2017 in translation to English and with four actors, allows me to further expand the discussion of music, drag performance, and translocality with which I began this chapter; to talk about transloca performance, migration, sexual and erotic games, auditory and stereophonic stimuli, and desire, in the context of theater, of the Puerto Rican diaspora, and of the redefinition of the sexual and affective (emotional) identities that have become characteristic of the last five decades, at least since 1968, when Ramos Otero first arrived in New York City. Concretely, it allows me to argue for the connection of music, gender identity, and migration, and to see how one particular diasporic Puerto Rican play created a space for imagining a different world: one where Hispanic Caribbean gender and culture are central. In the following sections, I will elucidate how Ramos Otero's short story was transformed into a theatrical performance, highlighting the narrative's intrinsic performative and discursive dimensions. I will also analyze Jorge B. Merced's biographical experiences and personal background as an actor and dramatist who, with the director Rosalba Rolón and other company members, collectively transformed the text into a particular type of solo

Fig. 17. Jorge B. Mer-
ced performing as
Loca la de la Locura
in *El bolero fue mi
ruina,* 2006. Photo
by Erika Rojas.

show with live, interactive musical accompaniment, and twenty years later
made it into a play for four actors and two musicians.

Merced's performance of Loca la de la Locura and Nene Lindo lead
me to think of the actor as a transloca but also as a *transmacho,* that is
to say, a hyperaestheticized or exaggerated representation of masculinity, highlighting the male performativity and swagger that characterize
not only the *bugarrón* but many iterations of Hispanic Caribbean and
Latin American masculinity, which can also be embodied by *transmachas,* that is to say, by masculine women such as the aforementioned
Mexican / Costa Rican Chavela Vargas or by others such as the Puerto
Rican singer Lucecita Benítez, the Cuban / Puerto Rican performer Marga

Gomez when donning a tuxedo to "cross-dress into her father's persona, Captain Willy Chevalier" (Sandoval-Sánchez and Sternbach 2001, 125), or by contemporary drag kings and male trans performers in Puerto Rico such as Chris Griandher (Christopher Korber) and Pó Rodil.[13] Merced's *transmacho* embodiment, which privileges a counterpoint between loud and expressive yet also suave and seductive hypermasculinity as a function of machismo, sexuality, and vulnerability, sharpens the performative and signifying valence of his transloca (feminine) enactment.[14] As several Puerto Rican spectators have pointed out to me, to see Merced perform the role of Loca la de la Locura is to relive memories of Manuel Ramos Otero in his bohemian nights or even in his drag escapades in the Condado in San Juan, where he was nicknamed "Miss Condominio" (Miss Condominium) because of his statuesque height in and out of heels. To see and hear Jorge B. Merced is to recall a series of boleros, and the role of the bolero, in the darkness of the theatrical night.

The Textual Base: Transloca Discursiveness in "Loca la de la locura"

Manuel Ramos Otero's departure from Puerto Rico in December 1968 and his semipermanent migration to New York City were two of the most important events in his life, captured and reiterated throughout his career in his narrative, poetic, and essayistic writings, many of which were extremely autobiographical.[15] In fact, Ramos Otero lived for most of his adulthood (practically until his death in 1990) in a self-imposed exile due to what he perceived as the sexual intolerance of Puerto Rican society, a migration that Manolo Estavillo (Guzmán 1997) has suggestively named *sexile*, also explored by Frances Negrón-Muntaner in her hybrid film *Brincando el charco: Portrait of a Puerto Rican* (1994), as I discuss in my book *Queer Ricans: Cultures and Sexualities in the Diaspora* (2009). In New York City and New Jersey and in his occasional return trips back to Puerto Rico, Ramos Otero honed his poetry and fiction writing but also became very involved in theater as well as in staging performances of his poems, as the cultural journalist Carmen Graciela Díaz (2018) carefully shows.

While Ramos Otero's writing was frequently autobiographical, we also have what Arnaldo Cruz-Malavé has called the creation of "personas" (1993, 240), or what Jossianna Arroyo (2001) identifies in other instances as *máscaras*, or masks, that is to say, self-referential fictional projections that the author constructed with great care. In fact, transvestism and the use of the female voice, as much as the creation of feminine characters, were central elements of Ramos Otero's poetic and narrative work: he evidenced a clear performativity, an effort to establish the centrality of the body in the act of writing, specifically in a writing that questioned, problematized, and challenged a rigid, conservative, and dominant canonical vision of Puerto Rican culture regarding gender, sexuality, and the colonial situation.[16] To this we can add the exploration of forbidden topics such as homoerotic sexuality, sadomasochism, and the consumption of drugs, especially heroin, distinctive traits that many critics and readers have used to identify Ramos Otero as a radically marginal figure or *poète maudit*. Many of the most sordid and scatological references in Ramos Otero's "Loca la de la locura," including all suggested mentions of drugs, were excised in the Pregones Theater adaptation, which led some audience members in Puerto Rico to express frustration and to see the adaptation as a conservative, assimilationist, or sanitizing play.[17]

The original narrative form of "Loca la de la locura" is already inclined toward theatrical performance. The short story's first-person narration is directed at an implicit reading or listening audience; it is a speaking voice that centers Loca, the transloca protagonist who is a singer of boleros, but also integrates her lover, Nene Lindo, mentioned through indirect discourse, and Loca's deceased mother, who is voiced through the repetition of citations. Ramos Otero's short story proposes a collective narration, one that also appears in other stories by the same author, for example in "El cuento de la Mujer del Mar" ("The Story of the Woman of the Sea") (Ramos Otero 1979). This occurs through the figure of the *cuentero*, or storyteller, a figure reminiscent of Walter Benjamin's (1968a) storyteller, who has the ability to create communal cohesion through narration.[18]

Like Scheherazade in the *One Thousand and One Nights*, Loca seems to propose that one *is* because one *narrates*, and narrates as a *loca*, coming closer to queer *testimonio* or life storytelling (Cruz-Malavé 2007b, 2017b) as the experiential documentation of marginalized experience by subaltern subjects with a greater perception of the impact of affect (and of madness) on thinking. To echo an earlier discussion from the introduction of this book, Loca speaks with the authority of experience, of what Cherríe Moraga identified as "theory in the flesh," a practice of "naming our selves and . . . telling our stories in our own words" (Moraga and Anzaldúa 1983, 23), with the caveat that it is a voice full of irony, aware of its instability and artificiality, and with our knowledge that Loca is a literary character and not an actual person.

In the first page of the text, Loca declares: "Tendré que confesar que mi ruina fue el bolero" (I will have to declare that my downfall was the bolero) (Ramos Otero 1992, 233), a hyperbaton or inversion that the Pregones Theater reorders to name its theatrical production.[19] In this world, the bolero creates, destroys, and confuses, as it mediates between generations, states of sanity, gender perceptions, and body relations. The centrality of *loca* and *locura* is displaced in the title of Pregones's adaptation, which privileges the musical form of the bolero and the concept of *ruina* (ruin, decay, failure), or "downfall" mediated through camp humor, as opposed to the explicit queerness and madness highlighted by the Puerto Rican author.[20] At the same time, Pregones's title invites audiences to perceive the potential irony in Loca's utterance, which is mediated by melodrama.[21]

The importance of the bolero in the short story comes across not only through the lyrics and meanings of the songs and the implicit positioning of the "you" and "I," which already implies discursive locations, but also as a result of its referential geography, which alludes to a broader Pan-American and even Pan-Hispanic world, entailing music from across Latin America, the Caribbean, and Spain, creating a transatlantic sonic bridge. Ramos Otero cites at least ten songs in the short story, but only some of these appear in Pregones's adaptation. Some are integrated as contextual or background music ("Dos cruces"); some become Nene Lindo's lip-synch performances ("El reloj"); some are simply titles that are mentioned in the story and the play ("La múcura" by Bobby Capó); in some cases, lyrics are quoted in Loca's speaking voice ("Ansiedad"). Most notably, there is the integration in the play of songs that do not appear in the short story and that Loca listens to (for example, Lucho Gatica's recording of "Si me comprendieras") or lip-synchs on stage, such as Toña la Negra's interpretation of "Oración Caribe" and Myrta Silva's "La vida es un problema" and "Qué sabes tú." There is also the incorporation of Sylvia Rexach's "Olas y arena" and of a rather sexist song performed by Ismael Rivera ("Si te cojo") that do not appear in Ramos Otero's text, as well as the unfortunate omission of any reference to the 1950s Spanish singer, film star, and camp icon Sara Montiel and to her song "Es mi hombre (mon homme)" ("He Is My Man") from the film *La violetera* (1958), which is quoted in the short story.[22]

While there isn't a direct mention of overseas migration in Ramos Otero's short story, the theme of sexile appears in the displacement of the protagonist from the countryside to the city. In fact, Loca leaves Hormigueros,[23] a small town in the southwest of the island, and moves to

San Juan because of electoral harassment: she is a member of the Popular Democratic Party (the commonwealth party) and is accosted by *un independentista* (a male advocate of independence for Puerto Rico) who violently tries to impede her vote.[24] As a result, Loca leaves her hometown, creating a parodic echo of René Marqués's classic drama *La carreta* (*The Oxcart*): "Harta de subir y bajar la misma cuesta de Hormigueros . . . en una carreta de bueyes dejé aquel pueblo de mierda para buscar la ciudad, los muelles podridos de salitre extranjero y el dólar que para una mujer sufrida siempre ha estado desvalorizado" (Fed up with going up and down the same hill in Hormigueros . . . I left that shitty town in an oxcart, to look for the city, the piers rotten by foreign saltpeter and the dollar, which has always been undervalued for a suffering woman) (Ramos Otero 1992, 236). Loca's *partida* (her departure, but also a vernacular term for male effeminacy), caused in part by leftist intolerance of gender and sexual nonconformity, places her in the realm of tropical cabaret. And while the story doesn't mention migration to the United States, the North American presence on the island is registered through language use and through mentions of foreign products and stores that mark Puerto Rican life, presented in counterpoint to the extensive use of colloquial Puerto Rican phrases, vernacular words, and local references; Pregones faithfully integrates this heteroglossic discourse created by colonialism.

Finally, it is important to point out the centrality of violence and of transgressions of the law, of the prison cell where almost all of the narration takes place, and of the crime (the murder), specifically, one committed by a female-identified transloca who had also been the victim of violence perpetrated by Nene Lindo, who slapped her for questioning his masculinity and later shot and wounded her when she tried to sexually penetrate him; incarceration and the state's punitive role are precisely the focus of Radost Rangelova's (2007) analysis of this short story.[25] Here it is valuable to ponder what happens when a transloca is not only the victim of violence but also the perpetrator, perhaps similar to the case of Kevin Fret discussed earlier in this book. Loca is incarcerated in a men's prison; as we learn in the story, Nene Lindo was born in 1943 and murdered in 1968, specific dates that are not highlighted in the play. At least ten years have gone by since the violent incident, and Loca is about to be released from Oso Blanco, placing the narration in the late 1970s or in 1980, the year the story was first published. The references are to another historical moment, curiously marked by the continuity of Puerto Rican political parties that still monopolized discussions about the territorial status throughout the late 2010s. It is notable that Loca killed Nene Lindo by slitting his throat; she killed him precisely by destroying that which produces voice.

Trans/forming the Transloca: Approximation, Incorporation, and Diaspora

The dramatic force of *El bolero* depends on and is nourished by Merced's presence (his body, voice, gestures, physical choreography, and marked rapport with the audience) as much as his life experiences, very concretely by his activist history and approximation to Latinx drag and trans life in New York City, and by being, just as Ramos Otero, a Puerto Rican first-generation gay migrant or sexile that left the island in 1982 in part due to his sexuality.[26] For Merced, *El bolero fue mi ruina* functions as a recreation of the queer Latinx world of New York City, even when the text centers on the island of Puerto Rico; the diaspora becomes central in the space of the theater, given the large number of English- and Spanish-speaking queer Puerto Rican and Latinx migrants who went to see the play over its many years in repertoire, sometimes multiple times, and who reacted effusively to the performance, in effect participating in Latinx queer "worldmaking" (Muñoz 1999, 195–200) or in a space of "utopia," following Jill Dolan, who has stated that "live performance provides a place where people come together, embodied and passionate, to share experiences of meaning making and imagination that can describe or capture fleeting intimations of a better world" (2005, 2). As diasporic phenomena, "Loca la de la locura" and *El bolero* partake in what Jossianna Arroyo (2001) has described in reference to Ramos Otero's work as a "transit between Norzagaray Street and Christopher Street," meaning a multiple referentiality toward two localities or central points, one in the Caribbean and the other in North America, as a type of bridge.[27] In this sense, the parallel between Merced and Ramos Otero is crucial.

Jorge B. Merced was born in 1965 in Carolina, Puerto Rico, and moved to New York City at the age of seventeen.[28] He studied piano and composition at the Escuela Libre de Música in Puerto Rico; theater at the City College of New York and at the EITALC International Theater School in Cuba; dance and choreography at the Alvin Ailey School; and forum theater technique with Augusto Boal.[29] He did not complete a college degree. He joined Pregones in 1987, later becoming one of the two associate artistic directors, together with Alvan Colón Lespier, both of whom work with artistic director Rosalba Rolón.

Pregones, a celebrated company established in 1979, has been a bastion of Puerto Rican artistic production in New York City, and very particularly in the South Bronx, for decades, as Eva C. Vásquez (2003) has carefully documented.[30] The group is characterized by its community-centered vision, collaborative practice, long-standing tradition of literary adaptations, bilingualism, affordable ticket prices, and integration of live music. In 2013, Pregones merged with Miriam Colón's historic Puerto Rican Traveling Theater (PRTT) of Manhattan and is now known as Pregones/PRTT.[31]

Merced has also participated actively in Puerto Rican and Latinx LGBTQ culture and activism in New York City, collaborating extensively with artists such as Arthur Avilés, Eduardo Alegría, Charles Rice-González, Pablo García Gámez, and Aravind Enrique Adyanthaya, among others. As a self-reflexive and documentary practice, Merced has written about his experiences with Pregones's theater-forum piece *El abrazo / The Embrace*, an AIDS community education project based on the theories of Augusto Boal that ran from 1987 to 1993 (Merced 1994a, 1994b).[32] He has also written about LGBTQ Puerto Rican and Latinx activism in New York City (Aponte-Parés and Merced 1998) and about Pregones's LGBTQ-themed theater initiative called Asunción, which he spearheaded (Merced 2007).[33] The actor was also crucially involved in Pregones's theatrical initiative called *Máscaras* (*Masks*), a piece for women dealing with sexual violence and abuse.[34]

How did Merced come to drag? It is useful to understand his transloca performance as involving two distinct processes, those of *transloca approximation* and *transloca incorporation*, which occurred simultaneously in the transit between Puerto Rico and New York, culminating in *El bolero fue mi ruina*. By *transloca approximation* I mean to reference spectatorship and interaction with a concrete, visual, and emotional "repertoire" of living, culturally significant performance practices—what Diana Taylor refers to as a "nonarchival system of transfer" (2003, xviii)—and with a personal and collective queer "archive of feelings," what Ann Cvetkovich describes as "an exploration of cultural texts as repositories of feelings and emotions, which are encoded not only in the content of the texts themselves but in the practices that surround their production and reception" (2003, 7). In this context, transloca approximation refers to the experience of seeing drag queens and trans women or other trans/genderqueer artists perform, whether on television or in person, as much as to the personal contacts that occur through conversations and friendships, also marked by traumatic happenings, for example by the incarceration of trans women who were close friends, as Merced described in a 2002 interview.[35] Approximation is the comprehension of the phenomenon through witnessing, embracing what Horacio N. Roque Ramírez called "a living archive of desire" (2005).

By *transloca incorporation*, which can also be understood as *transloca embodiment*, I wish to reference the bodily process of drag or trans performance in the flesh (echoing but also questioning and expanding Cherríe Moraga's theorization), through one's own praxis: the corporealization or personification that occurs when one cross-dresses or transforms one's body, as one partakes in a potentially transgressive, dangerous, or joyful action. The analytic distinction between approximation and incorporation/embodiment is subtle, but recognizes that there is a difference between the potentially extremely rich experience of viewership and dialogue, on the one hand, and an actual physical, theatrical, or performative practice; that "theory in the flesh" (experiential knowledge) occurs differently for translocas when you actually dress up in drag or get beaten up because of your interest in or identification with drag and trans culture. In this sense, trans Puerto Rican / Colombian poet Morgan Robyn Collado's (2012) and trans Chicano scholar Francisco J. Galarte's (2020) challenges to Moraga's (2011) more recent transphobic statements (specifically, to Moraga's unease regarding male trans experience), serve to recuperate and transform her earlier generative theorizations.

My focus on incorporation/embodiment (building on the Latin root of *corpus* and *corpore* for "body," which is more apparent in the Spanish language word *cuerpo* and in English-language adjectives such as "corporal") coincides with the scholar Susan Stryker's assertion that "transgender studies considers the embodied experience of the speaking subject, who claims constative knowledge of the referent topic, to be a proper—indeed, essential—component of the analysis of transgender phenomena; experiential knowledge is as legitimate as other, supposedly more 'objective' forms of knowledge, and is in fact necessary for understanding the political dynamics of the situation being analyzed" (2006, 12). For me, "incorporation" also distantly echoes (as if geological sediment) and perhaps turns upside down the nineteenth-century German activist Karl Heinrich Ulrichs's conceptualization of *anima muliebris virili corpore inclusa* (a female soul enclosed in a man's body), in which it is no longer just a soul, but a body that registers as female (Silverman 1992, 339–88).[36] A chronological retelling of Merced's life experiences reveals that transloca approximation and transloca incorporation occur simultaneously, with very particular meanings for the actor. We can identify this process in two fundamental moments: before and after his migration to New York.

Merced's childhood in Puerto Rico was marked by his early play with his mother's clothes, a game he sees as typical of *loquitas*, or homosexual boys—what we could refer to as an early stage of transloca incorporation—as well as by a later experience of transloca approximation, that of viewing a television show hosted in drag by Antonio Pantojas, the island's best-known drag performer of the 1970s and 1980s.[37] In an interview that I conducted in 2002, Merced praised his youthful experiences, seeing them as typical behavior of boys who question their sexual orientation and/or gender identity:

> As a boy I went through that stage where I also dressed up with my mother's wigs. I literally felt pleasure in that delight. I think that all gay boys or many *loquitas* (fairies, queers) [do that]. I think that is divine, to give ourselves the liberty of being able to explore occasionally and put on the girdles and wigs and other *pendejaces* (worthless or foolish things). (La Fountain-Stokes 2018e, 145)

It is significant that Merced describes this childhood gender play in terms of enjoyment, as something "divine," a gesture of freedom, but also devalues it by describing the women's clothing as "other *pende-jaces*," possibly minimizing the importance of the episode. The celebration of the act as a common experience, as a rite of passage, and as a moment of freedom marks this episode as central in the constitution of a boy labeled as different. However, his possibly misogynist devaluation potentially reinscribes a masculinist positioning and signals the anxiety transloca embodiment creates.

It is worth highlighting this tension, regardless of how minimal it may be. While Merced takes advantage of and maximizes the opportunity of performing in drag on stage, it isn't something that he assumes as a definitive characteristic of his daily experience or overall artistic identity, and this might explain the simultaneous effusiveness in the representation of the character of Nene Lindo, a hypermasculine *bugarrón*, as if Merced was negotiating the potential stigma of effeminacy by also hyperbolically portraying ultramasculinity, highlighting the camp exaggeration that both entail. Merced's staged female drag is very particular, given that the performer's baldness (or shaved head) and his hirsute, muscular body are clearly visible to the audience. Yet, while feminine drag does not constitute Merced's primary artistic practice, Merced cross-dressed on several occasions when he first moved to New York, particularly on Halloween and in the theater. In both cases, his drag did not entail high-femme verisimilitude (a simulacrum of conventional female beauty), but rather a type of feminine referentiality that functions as an index or trace: he dressed as the character of Miss Piggy for Halloween and as a municipal building (*una alcaldía*), conceived as an effeminate character in the play *Migrants*. In this sense, it is worth clarifying that like Javier Cardona (the focus of the previous chapter), Merced isn't associated with drag in the way other transloca performers are who assume this practice as distinctive of their art, such as Nina Flowers and Freddie Mercado.

In addition to his early childhood cross-dressing in Puerto Rico, Merced also highlighted in his 2002 interview his teenage experience of seeing the well-known drag queen/actor Pantojas on television (as Merced describes, in his family's "family room"), which provoked a major confrontation with his father, a crisis that culminated with Merced's migration to New York. In the interview, Merced described how his father slapped him when he insisted on his right to see Pantojas on TV at home and dared to suggest that the drag performer was a legitimate artist: "All I know is that my father felt absolutely offended that I was comparing him to a *maricón*, to a *vestida* (a cross-dresser), to a man who was there with a *plumero* (effeminate mannerisms) on television. And he slapped me" (La Fountain-Stokes 2018e, 145). For Merced, his father's act of censorship and rebuke (turning off the TV set) interrupted a potential moment of mass media or televisual identification with a drag queen who negotiated a complicated public subjectivity: the rejected, abject figure that was able to occupy center stage, at least on television, a paradox that media scholar Félix Jiménez has analyzed (2004, 246–65), highlighting the long-standing tradition of drag televisuality in Puerto Rico.

It is noteworthy that Pantojas's style was characterized by spiteful, mordacious satire, in other words, that of a *loca mala* (evil queen), to cite the characterization that Efraín Barradas (2003) offers of Ramos Otero and Pedro Lemebel, that of a vicious and defensive individual from whom one must protect oneself, but also that Pantojas was radically political since the early 1970s, a committed leftist who believed in independence for Puerto Rico and in gay liberation (Irizarry 2019; N. Rivera 2018), who openly asked, "¿Dónde está mi lugar en la Revolución?" (Where is my place in the revolution?) in an interview in the *En Rojo* cultural supplement of *Clari-*

Fig. 18. Antonio Pantojas on the cover of *En Rojo, Claridad*, November 29–December 5, 1990: 13. Photo by Francesca von Rabenau. Cover by Celia Marina Romano. University of Michigan Library (Special Collections Research Center).

dad (Rodríguez Martinó 1990), having suffered exclusion from the traditionally homophobic Left (see figure 18).[38] Merced's father was disconcerted by the open display of effeminate gender on television (*el plumero*,
quite literally the feathers, a metaphor for homosexuality in Spanish), and
perhaps also by Pantojas's pro-independence politics, and exercised his
authority by turning the TV set off and interrupting the show.

In this context, Merced felt the need to assert his own autonomy and to
question the authority of his father, thus provoking a confrontation. Sig-
nificantly, the violation of norms of masculinity (the introduction of the
image of Pantojas in the "family room") was resolved by an act of physical aggression against the son, captured in the melodramatic phrase "the
only slap that my father has ever given me in my life." This violence made
the event go from one of transloca approximation corresponding to the
world of ideas, visuality, aurality, and mass-media spectatorship, to one of
transloca incorporation, which is to say, the physical pain produced by the
defense of the right to watch drag on television in one's own house. And
as Merced states in his interview, "As soon as he did it, I looked at him and
told him: 'I hope you remember this moment for the rest of your life and
never forget!' and then I left" (La Fountain-Stokes 2018e, 145). The son
responded to his father's act with a campy telenovela phrase, as if invoking Walter Mercado's days as a soap opera star, and with the symbolic
and literal departure from family life, as Merced moved away from Puerto
Rico to New York, a move that can be best understood in the framework
of queer migration (sexile) marked by violence and exclusion.[39] Merced's
retelling of this story reenacts complex personal and family dynamics; his
staging of *El bolero fue mi ruina* can be seen, in part, as a psychic response
to the violence his father exerted and as an homage to Pantojas and to
the televisual drag tradition in Puerto Rico, more than as partaking of
the long-standing tradition of American drag performance on the theatrical stage (Baker 1994; DeCaro 2019; Doonan 2019; Garber 1992; Selenick
2000).

Merced's experiences in New York offer us two different although
interrelated approaches to drag. Transloca incorporation occurs through
three specific events: Merced's participation in the 1986 Village Halloween Parade, or more accurately, in the Christopher Street Promenade, two
extremely important and long-standing alternative cultural events (one
formally organized, the other more impromptu, both held on October 31),
where Merced appeared dressed up as Miss Piggy, which constituted his
first act of public cross-dressing (La Fountain-Stokes 2018e, 144); his par-

ticipation in Pregones Theater's play *Migrants: Cantata a los emigrantes* (1987–90), where he portrayed a feminine, talking City Hall along with Alvan Colón Lespier and José Joaquín García (Vásquez 2003, 99); and finally, his role in *El bolero fue mi ruina*.[40] His process of *approximation*, however, is more complex, and has to do with Merced's frequenting La Escuelita, one of the most important Latinx gay clubs in New York City, and later GT's Bar in the Bronx, as well as with his participation in activist and social groups such as Boricua Gay and Lesbian Forum, Latino Gay Men of New York, and Gay Men of the Bronx, and with his extensive contact and friendship with Latina drag queens and trans women, especially with Barbara Kent, Mari Cuebas, and Ruby Ray Raymond Troche.[41]

Merced feels that these shared experiences with drag queens and trans women are the sources that inform and authorize his embodiment of Loca la de la Locura, and that what occurs in *El bolero fue mi ruina* is the recreation of a queer, gay/trans Puerto Rican space in the United States, a type of transloca space that the actor never experienced during his youth in Puerto Rico except through television and childhood cross-dressing games. Thus, his referential frame is predominantly the queer, trans, Puerto Rican world of New York City, first in Manhattan, then in Jackson Heights, Queens, and later in the Bronx, so much so that when Merced finally did see his first live drag show in Puerto Rico in 1994, what he felt was nostalgia for New York.[42] Merced arrived at Ramos Otero's short story as the direct result of his experiences "abroad": the "local" is "translocal" and queer in its conception and elaboration. Or to phrase it differently, the construction of Puerto Rican authenticity (or of greater accuracy in representation) is to a great extent a direct reflection of the existence of these vernacular, autochthonous practices among New York Puerto Ricans, and the actor and theater company's ability to tap into this rich cultural and performative repertoire (Taylor 2003) or archive of feelings (Cvetkovitch 2003). This does not guarantee complete accuracy in representation, but increases the grounded connection of the play.

Finally, it is worthwhile to highlight Merced's perception that *El bolero fue mi ruina* is a profoundly diasporic, New York–based work, because it is precisely the distance of exile, that space outside of Puerto Rico, that allows for the telling of such tales. This is true as much for the conditions of production of Ramos Otero's story as for the professional and cultural formation of Merced in the gay Latinx bars and nightclubs in New York City, where Merced obtained the gestures and the conceptual imaginary of the piece, his gay Latinx activism, and his friendships with Puerto Rican and other Latina drag queens and trans women in the diaspora. It is also particularly true when compared to the largely derivative works of gay theater produced in Puerto Rico in the 1980s and 1990s, which were to a great extent translations and adaptations of white, mainstream, American and European shows, and not original works based on texts by Puerto Rican playwrights, with notable exceptions such as Abniel Marat's *dios en el* Playgirl *de noviembre* (1986).[43]

El bolero fue mi ruina has more to do with what Puerto Rican cultural theorists such as Juan Flores (1993, 142–56) have identified as early cultural stages of migration, which favor referencing the country of origin and the Spanish language, than with second- and third-generation productions, in which there is more marked use of English and a US geographic specificity. Interestingly, Pregones has in its repertoire both Spanish-centered works and English-dominant ones that are more clearly anchored in the new experience, located concretely in New York City, particularly in the Bronx. At the same time, if we privilege music as a tool for the development of diasporic Puerto Rican identities, as Ruth Glasser (1995) does in her enormously valuable book *My Music Is My Flag*, then perhaps it is not so important to verify whether there is an explicit mention of the migratory condition itself, an "overdetermination" so to speak, as the very enactment or reenactment of the music has its own social purpose and end. Here it is also useful to insist on the different ways in which music interpellates an audience according to its age, sex, gender, sexual orientation, and migration history.

Staging Transloca *and* Transmacho *Performance*

In *El bolero fue mi ruina*, Loca is in prison with her scarce possessions, which include a small makeup kit and a pink satin photo album adorned with lace, where she keeps photos, press clippings about the murder of Nene Lindo, and some of her deceased mother's belongings, including her mother's long black braid.[44] The solitary bed and the empty cell at the center of the stage—the narrative space—are framed by two additional environments: stage right, the cabaret, marked by a small raised stage with sparkling stars, a moon and a golden palm tree between the two musicians (Desmar Guevara and Ricardo Pons) who accompany Loca and Nene Lindo in their performative musical remembrances; stage left, the cemetery, indicated by a profusion of plastic flowers and small white crosses on a slightly inclined ramp that has a larger cross at the top, also framed with hanging stars, which Loca visits at the beginning and at the end of the play.[45]

The performance actually begins in the dark with a recording of "Dos cruces" ("Two Crosses"), a sad, melancholic Caribbean-style Spanish bolero of failed, distant love, as performed by the Mexican trio Los Tres Diamantes, as an androgynous, somewhat feminine unidentified caped figure spins while holding a large bouquet of artificial flowers and then proceeds to drop these on the ground as she walks across the stage.[46] The over-the-top, Walter Mercado–inspired, dark green cape is lined in white satin and has a hood that completely covers the figure's face.[47] Underneath, she wears a white dress trimmed in gold, long satin white gloves, and sparkly silver shoes. The figure emits a loud lament and then moves one of her hands to the top of her head. She crosses the stage and arrives at the cemetery, proclaiming, "A todos nos gustan los entierros" (We all love funerals) in a deep, masculine voice, framed by the small white crosses that echo the lyrics of the bolero. Who is this mysterious figure? Why is she invoking funerals? What two deaths does the song anticipate or reflect? And what is the relationship between her voice and her costume?

As the caped figure walks up the ramp, she starts to undress, revealing an adult person wearing dark long pants, a charcoal-gray ironed short-sleeve shirt with black buttons, and a black hairnet: it is Loca in her prisoner's garb. She then walks down the ramp toward the center of the stage and eventually to her prison cell, where she looks at her keepsake album. Loca's somewhat masculine appearance coincides with Merced's use of a deep, masculine voice for some of her pronouncements but will also be offset by occasional, affected, high-voiced phrases and feminine gestures. The at-times neutral, masculine-inclined stance of the prisoner will allow Merced to embody a more feminine pose for Loca as a cabaret entertainer as well as the dramatic ultramasculine pose of Nene Lindo as a performative *bugarrón*. The performance will oscillate between these three representations throughout, theatricalizing the performativity of gender as a socially constructed, embodied practice that depends on reiteration (Butler 1990, 1993) but also the specificities of Puerto Rican and, more broadly, Hispanic Caribbean masculinities, for which gender enactments are not simply "natural" attributes assigned at birth, but rather depend on specific behaviors in order to succeed (R. Ramírez 1993, 1999).[48]

Loca's first monologue is precisely about the challenges of narration. As she says, "No sé si me será difícil contar esta historia" (I don't know if it will be hard for me to tell this story), to then affirm, "La muerte es un buen comienzo" (Death is a good beginning), which leads her to read the sensationalist tabloid headlines related to her crime. The monologue is marked by melodrama, dramatic exaggeration, (tropi)camp humor, and a proud affirmation of resignation marked by old age. As Loca comically affirms with a masculine voice that is in tension with the feminine grammatical markers of her speech, "Yo estoy tranquila caminando por la vejez como una cucaracha que atraviesa una pared blanca sin miedo a que le den un chancletazo" (I am calm walking through old age like a cockroach that crosses a white wall unafraid of being squashed with a sandal). Her pronouncements, which entail an abject comparison with a cockroach (a long-standing trope in Latinx popular culture), are interrupted by guttural noises made by the musicians to her side, which Loca identifies as the next-door prisoner's masturbation; she indicates that this occurs every fifteen minutes by the clock.[49] This leads Loca to cite her mother for the first time, using a feminine gender marker (*misma*) to refer to Loca: "Bien lo decía mi madre: en la soledad acabarás enamorándote de ti misma" (My mother said it well: in solitude you will end up falling in love with yourself). Merced will not quote the scatological second part of Ramos Otero's sentence, which reads, "El ruido de un peo sonará como un bolero" (The noise of a fart will sound like a bolero) (1992, 233). This sanitizing edit maintains the primacy of bolero, eliminating a potential sophomoric joke.

The neighbor's masturbatory interruption, a gag that will reoccur later in the play, leads Loca to recount her first encounter with Nene Lindo at the Club Medianoche (Midnight Club), to describe her chartreuse taffeta gown ("toda de tafeta verde chatré"), and to the first lip-synch of the evening: a dramatically lit rendition of Agustín Lara's bolero "Oración Caribe" ("Caribbean Invocation") as interpreted by the leading Afro-Mexican performer Toña la Negra (Antonia del Carmen Peregrino Álvarez, 1912–82), and not the tango "Ansiedad" ("Anxiety") that Ramos Otero identifies in the short story.[50] For this scene, Merced stands on the bed, his face illuminated by a direct spotlight, while the rest of the stage is dark.[51] The lyrics of Lara's song posit a speaker who begs for "piedad" (mercy) for those who suffer and cry. Loca performs the better-known melodious second and third stanzas, and not the slow, initial invocation that marks the song as a "salmo de los Negros" (a psalm of Black folks), perhaps unwittingly depoliticizing the song at the expense of highlighting glamour and drama, while simultaneously taking advantage of "the sensuality that is invoked by [Toña la Negra's] throaty voice with its low timbre" (Arce 2017, 257).

Merced's lip-synch as Loca, which clearly invokes Toña la Negra's star power, is quite beautiful; it is extremely contained, focusing on facial gestures, hands held at the neck close to the face, and moving lips. This performance is followed by a crucial description of Loca's makeup, listed over "Oración Caribe" as musical background:

> El rostro de polvo canela cubre las imperfecciones de la piel como una gasa musulmana. Dos soles de colorete coral acentuando los pómulos de odalisca condenada. El pan stick bronce hace que un fósforo inesperado ilumine intermitentemente un lunar. La base permite que el sudor parezca rocío. El blanco de payaso me hace inalcanzable.

> The cinnamon-dust mask covers the imperfections of the skin like a Muslim gauze. Two coral-colored blush suns accentuate the condemned-odalisque cheeks. The bronze pan stick makes an unexpected match intermittently illuminate a beauty mark. The foundation allows perspiration to glisten like dew. Clown white makes me unattainable.

The description is copied verbatim from the short story, with the excision of a final additional orientalizing phrase, referencing a tortured geisha (Ramos Otero 1992, 234), perhaps to fit the time constraints of the song. Face powder, rouge, highlighter, foundation, and clown white makeup are some of the essential cosmetics used in the transformation of a drag queen, feminizing the face and allowing for dramatic embellishment. The mention of "clown white" is especially indicative that it is a description of theatrical or performance makeup, and not of general, everyday women's cosmetics.

This slightly campy citation of the iconic performer Toña la Negra (a Caribbean icon) through the rendition of a bolero that pulls at one's heartstrings is immediately contrasted in El bolero with the deadpan and then exaggerated recitation of the opening stanza of Sylvia Rexach's extremely well-known 1950s song "Olas y arena" ("Waves and Sand"), also not in Ramos Otero's short story, a Puerto Rican classic that Merced performs in alternating masculine and then high, effeminate or falsetto, voice.[52] The effect of the strange spoken quotation is laughter and nostalgic recognition of the iconic composition, particularly since Rexach (who led a rather tragic life) is also considered a camp icon; Loca (or Merced) seems to be parodying the lyrics, which posit the sand as a speaking subject in love with the waves of the sea. At the same time, the citation celebrates Rexach, whose verses "reflect the desolation a human can feel as the result of urbanization, many women's longing for liberty, and women's desires to engage in sexual relationships with banned eroticism" (Vázquez González 2016, 2). It is worth noting that it is the imprisoned Loca, with her gray uniform, who is quoting these songs, suggesting that incarceration has not interfered with her ability to remember and perhaps perform for herself; her ability to cite and recreate glamour is reminiscent of other incarcerated *locas* or *folles* in Jean Genet's (1943) *Our Lady of the Flowers*, Manuel Puig's (1976) *Kiss of the Spider Woman*, and Reinaldo Arenas's (1992) *Before Night Falls*.

Loca follows this scene with a pantomime in which she seems to receive physical blows, which we will later learn were proffered by Nene Lindo when she questioned his masculinity. Loca continues her narration, describing the collapse of beauty (or at least of her drag makeup) as her seven pairs of Woolworth's fake eyelashes begin to come undone. As she states, "Yo era como otras mujeres y no era igual" (I was like other women but was not the same), a phrase ripe with meaning that is actually a citation of lyrics from the tango "Ansiedad." After repeating the warnings she received about Nene Lindo—"Es un bugarrón terrible. De navajitas yen. Te dejará cuando te pongas calva" (He is a terrible *bugarrón*. The razorblade kind. He will leave you when you go bald)—Loca insists on the need to suffer like other women, and quotes her mother for the second time: "Mi madre lo dijo: 'Tú no serás trigo bueno, Loca la de la locura, pero hasta el trigo malo necesita un hombre que a machetazo limpio la derrumbe'" (My mother said it: "You might not be good wheat, Loca la de la locura, but even bad wheat needs a man that will knock it down with sharp machete blows").

Loca's pantomime of violence, her repeated mentions of sharp, cutting objects such as razors and machetes, and her insistence on the inevitability of women's physical victimization highlight a very particular (melodramatic, antifeminist, performative) conception of Puerto Rican womanhood and set the stage for the appearance of Nene Lindo, who is portrayed as a suave, attractive, yet violent Puerto Rican man; an old-school Casanova or Don Juan who seduces the ladies but is also quick with the blows (see figure 19). As the stage lights dim, the audience witnesses Merced's physical transformation, as the actor dons (in the early 1997 production) a white hat, a white jacket or sports coat (later modified to a red jacket

Fig. 19. Jorge B. Merced performing as Nene Lindo in *El bolero fue mi ruina*, 2006. Photo by Erika Rojas.

in 2005), a light solid-color tie, a dark shirt, and black pants to become a dancing hypermasculine Caribbean dandy who stands much closer to the audience than Loca generally has, and who usually receives an effusive and immediate warm response, perhaps a recognition of sorts or a relief brought about by familiarity, or simply the celebration of the embodiment of a traditional masculine object of desire.[53] This enthusiasm is complex for gay audiences, or at least was complex for me.

In his monologue, Nene Lindo describes how he seduced Loca but also how he nearly twisted her arm to get her to sing the tango "Niebla del riachuelo" ("Small River Fog"), a sad, nostalgic song about sailors, decaying ships at port that will no longer sail, and the remembrance of a forlorn romance.[54] He then cites fairly innocuous lyrics from the waltz "Soy marinero" ("I Am a Sailor") made popular by the Chilean singer Oswaldo Gómez, better known as El Indio Araucano, but then states that he has "una puta en cada puerto" (a whore in every port), that he is a "bugar-rón del Caribe" (a Caribbean *bugarrón*), and that he moves between the rhythms of *bomba* and *plena*, two Afro–Puerto Rican popular musical forms. This leads to a citation of lyrics from Ismael Rivera's "Si te cojo" ("If I Catch You"), a popular yet misogynist salsa song from 1977 with music composed by Bobby Capó in which the male singer threatens a female lover with grave physical abuse if she in any way disobeys him, flirts with another man, fails in her responsibilities, or is unfaithful; as Nene Lindo rhythmically proclaims, "Un piñazo en un ojo te voy a dar / palo, palo, puño y bofetá" (I will give you a black eye / multiple blows with a stick, a punch, and a slap).[55] Ramos Otero does not reference this song in his short story. "Si te cojo" represents some of the worst aspects of Puerto Rican machismo, namely a long-standing proclivity to domestic violence that has currently reached epidemic proportions (Proyecto Matria and Kiló-metro Cero 2019; Roure 2011, 2019), and that also affects same-sex couples (Toro-Alfonso 1999; Toro-Alfonso and Rodríguez-Madera 2004).

Nene Lindo claims that this blatant violence contrasts with his pri-vate behavior, inspired by the bolero: "Pero en la intimidad un levan-tador de a bolerito viejo" (But in private [I am] an old-school bolero seducer). He also believes that "el bolero me da autoridá" (the bolero grants me authority). This authority apparently also enables violence, which explains "la gaznatá cálida que la vuelve una virgen que delira entre su asunción y el placer adobado de la carne" (the warm slap that turns her into a virgin that babbles amid her assumption and the well-seasoned pleasure of the flesh), a direct quote from Ramos Otero's short story. Praising the bolero, Nene Lindo proceeds to flirt with a woman in the audience and to flatter tall women, "mares who win a race by one head," "glaciers in the Tropic of Cancer, eternally enveloped by a cloud of 'Malboro'" (Marlboro cigarette smoke).

Nene Lindo's celebration of boleros leads to a lip-synch performance in which he impersonates the well-known, ultrasuave Chilean crooner Lucho Gatica (1928–2018) singing "El Reloj" ("The Clock"), an extremely popular Latin American composition performed by an instantly recogniz-able voice; Ramos Otero quotes verses from this song in his short story.[56] The playful rendition includes two gags. The first occurs when Nene Lindo gets distracted and forgets to lip-synch, missing some of the lyrics, forcing him to recuperate quickly; this generates loud laughter from the audience. The second gag occurs when Nene Lindo goes onto the small cabaret stage, hands the microphone to one of the musicians (Desmar Guevara), and has him take over the lip-synch, bringing down the house with approval and glee. This successful integration of the mostly nonspeaking musicians seemingly breaks representational walls and highlights the artificiality of the representation, integrating the musicians in a more direct way. It is a minor, Brechtian pause, which reminds the audience that it is witnessing a theatrical representation that plays against regular conventions and codes, but also highlights Pregones's distinctive, collective ethos.

The impact of Nene Lindo's lip-synch performance also has to do with Gatica's popularity and with the iconic status of the song. As his *New York Times* obituary indicated, "Mr. Gatica helped enshrine bolero, a style of flowing romantic balladry that had originated in Cuba in the late 19th century, as a midcentury pop craze" (Russonello 2018). The obituary also indicates that "in the process he became a heartthrob who dominated pop radio stations throughout the 1950s and '60s and a leading man in the thriving Mexican film industry." The specific song, "El Reloj," was composed and has lyrics by the Mexican Roberto Cantoral, who penned it in 1956 (Berlanga 2010), and describes the poetic speaker's desire that the clock stop ticking so that the time of love will become eternal.

This performative relay (having Nene Lindo hand the lip-synch over to a musician) also allows Merced to change back into the clothes of the incarcerated Loca and retake the narration of the story, particularly her experiences in prison marked by the anniversaries of Nene Lindo's death in 1969, 1972, and 1978, as well as her earlier experience fleeing from Hormigueros to San Juan. Loca will now proceed to set up a special cabaret performance on November 19 (not coincidentally, the day the first arrival of Christopher Columbus to the island is celebrated in Puerto Rico), carefully describing her clothing as we see her transform into a glamorous entertainer. While she verbally describes putting on a black crepe dress with a cleavage trimmed with black marabou feathers and a tail that reaches the floor, rhinestone earrings, opera gloves, and a twilight-colored wig, Loca actually takes off her prisoner's uniform to reveal that she is already wearing (in the 1997 production) a sparkly, patterned silver top layered over a black undershirt with a sparkly, silver-trimmed short skirt and sparkly silver leggings, which she then complements with sparkling silver shoes, clip-on earrings, opera gloves, and an elaborate cloth headpiece with large flowers that she takes out of a box, but not with a wig. (In the 2005 production, Loca wears a large gold sequin dress and no wig.) Merced faithfully recites Ramos Otero's text but reveals a different, perhaps slightly less glamorous outfit that was more suited for his onstage transformation in full view of the audience, or that perhaps maintains a greater element of androgyny. This moment serves to visually emphasize a moment of discontinuity between the base text and the performance.

The visible costume change leads to Loca's lip-synch of Myrta Silva's 1968 hit "La vida es un problema" ("Life Is a Problem"), followed by her equally popular 1962 composition "Qué sabes tú" ("What Do You Know"), which constitute the central transloca performances of the play, and also involve direct interaction with the musicians, who hand Loca her bejeweled maracas. The two songs are quite different: the first is a lively number that features Silva's emblematic *soneo* (improvisational or conversational skill) in which she talks quickly in the middle of the song, exhorting the listening public to *gozar* (enjoy life) and to live without concerns and even drink alcoholic beverages, since we all know how bad life is ("es un problema sin solución," i.e., it is a problem with no solution), even mentioning the possibility of a nuclear holocaust and the end of the world caused by a hydrogen bomb ("ya la bomba H está inventada y el día menos pensado, ¡pum! El mundo se acaba"), while the second is a slow-tempo bolero, a somewhat spiteful, melancholic song in which the speaking subject incriminates her listener for not knowing what it is like to be in love and to suffer, spending sleepless nights because of unrequited love, to ultimately affirm, "Tú no sabes nada de la vida" (You know nothing about life).[57] Merced lip-synchs both songs impeccably, even the fast-paced *soneo*, also encouraging audience participation for both numbers (getting people to clap and sing along), which is usually met with great enthusiasm. The two songs present valuable philosophical lessons, a transloca pedagogy of sorts, emphasizing the need to enjoy life (a reiteration of carpe diem) but also the validation of bitterness and spite as legitimate reactions to amorous travails.

Myrta Silva, as I highlighted in chapter 4, is a crucial referent for Puerto Rican transloca performance, a leading performer and composer who combined a larger-than-life, charismatic personality, a riveting stage persona, great entrepreneurial spirit, and considerable bolero-writing skills, but who simultaneously experienced social rejection, marginalization, and abjection because of her large body size, age, and lesbian identity, a set of painful circumstances carefully analyzed by Licia Fiol-Matta (2017) in her book *The Great Woman Singer: Gender and Voice in Puerto Rican Music*; she is what Fiol-Matta calls a "thinking voice." Silva is a central Puerto Rican transloca referent, and accordingly, it is no surprise that Merced (and Pregones) would want to invoke her and perform her songs in *El bolero fue mi ruina*. Ramos Otero does not mention any of these songs in his short story, but does refer to a photograph of Silva.

November 19, a national holiday in Puerto Rico marked by Hispano-philia and Eurocentrism, is also the day that Loca ate Nene Lindo's ass out (as she says more poetically, "Me lancé al beso negro como una hiedra que tumba tapias de concreto," referring to the sexual act as "beso negro," or black kiss, a common expression registered in Spanish-language dictionaries)[58] and then had a near-death experience after trying to sexually penetrate her lover: "Traté de virarlo pero Nene Lindo me sacó la pistola" (I tried to flip him but Nene Lindo pulled the gun out on me). This act is significant (and dangerous) given the primacy of anal penetration in so-called *activo/pasivo* sexual dichotomies, which ostensibly allow for the maintenance of hegemonic masculinity for the partner who is not penetrated.[59] This episode left Loca with a scar on her side, which she dramatizes using Marian imagery that invokes motherhood and a bleeding wound: "En el mismo lado del costado por donde María parió como una desalmada está el rasguño imborrable de la bala" (On the same side of the flank where Mary gave birth like a heartless woman is the indelible scratch of the bullet). It is as if Nene Lindo will not only defend his masculinity, but actually further feminize Loca, and she will respond to this at least initially through Christian symbolism that frames her experience in masochistic terms (Silverman 1992, 185–213).

While violence seems to make Loca feel more like a "natural woman," to quote the lyrics of Aretha Franklin's 1967 hit song, the incarcerated protagonist softens the impact of this episode and attempts to create a distraction (or perhaps tries to distract herself) through comedy and gender intensification, by quickly listing a series of cosmetics and other delicate accoutrements that she would enjoy having in prison, including mango peach lipstick, Coty powder, an eyeliner, a silk scarf with scenes of Miami, and some rouge. She also indicates her desire for "Jabones Maja para una Cleopatra criolla" (Maja soaps for a creole Cleopatra), referring to a Spanish brand of beauty and toiletry products that was extremely popular in Puerto Rico, whose label and name invoke folkloric images of Spanish femininity and luxury but that can also be seen as marks of what the scholar Noël Valis identifies as "Not kitsch, not camp, but simply: *cursi* . . . [entailing a] shift from the traditional to the modern, in which pieces of an older culture survive, holding on nostalgically or even ironically" (2002, 3). To be *cursi*, invoking this very Spanish concept, is clearly a defining trait of Puerto Rican translocas.

While she speaks, Loca reclines as an odalisque on the bed, taking her shirt off, as if recreating Francisco Goya's painting *La maja desnuda* (1797–1800), creating an interesting image that contrasts the masculinity of Merced's hirsute, muscular body with the femininity of the outstretched pose, including the reclining head, as if offering her body to the viewer. This creole Cleopatra longs to be Nene Lindo's woman again, but is aware of the clash entailed: "Yo, una jibarita de campo. Él, un jodedor de arrabal. Pero yo era Dalila, por supuesto" (I, a little countryside girl. He, a barrio hustler. But I was Delilah, of course).

Loca's conceptualization of herself as Cleopatra (famously portrayed in a major 1963 Hollywood film by Elizabeth Taylor) and as Delilah and as similar to the Virgin Mary (with a gashing wound on her side) signals a transloca imaginary full of powerful, but also at times treacherous or wounded, historical women. The opposition Loca identifies between herself and Nene Lindo is key: it follows a well-worn twentieth-century developmental narrative of Puerto Rican rural-to-urban migration that brought countryfolk (in this case, *una jibarita*, perceived as perhaps unsophisticated or naive) to the city and thrust them into the midst of urban sophisticates (here, *un jodedor de arrabal*, a street-smart Mack the Knife), particularly during the period of industrial development that started in the 1940s (Esterrich 2018); it is the story (but with several twists) of Juanita in René Marqués's 1953 canonical play *La carreta* (*The Oxcart*), who left the idyllic yet impoverished rural countryside and arrived in the *arrabal* (urban slum) of San Juan, where she was raped, later moving with her family to the Bronx, where she became a sex worker. The affirmation that Loca is Delilah, of course, highlights her power over Nene Lindo, who becomes the vulnerable Samson, whose weakness (his hair) was identified in the biblical story, leading to Samson's death. Loca and Nene Lindo's love story culminates as a failed national allegory marked by murder: an impossible queer foundational fiction or national romance that does not bring together disparate groups (in this case, urban and rural, or *locas* and *bugarrones*) and does not allow for social consolidation, as in the nineteenth-century Latin American novels that Doris Sommer (1991) has analyzed. "Loca la de la locura" and *El bolero fue mi ruina* are not the successful narrative of the coming together of opposites. Rather, they are the survival story of a marginal figure, Loca, an effeminate or androgynous homosexual man or perhaps a heterosexual transgender woman (a transloca), who negotiates her abjection and stays alive. Loca culminates her narration in this scene by citing a *cursi* line—"Pasarás por mi vida sin saber que pasaste" (You will pass through my life without knowing it)—by José Ángel Buesa, a Cuban author derisively referred to as a "poeta de choferes y cocineras" (a poet for chauffeurs and female cooks), as the scholar Gustavo Pérez Firmat (2008) indicates; Buesa's 1936 composition "Poema del renunciamiento" centers on the tortured confessions of an unrequited lover who dreams of his loved one's beauty and suffers in silence.[60]

El bolero fue mi ruina presents a counterpoint between Loca's affection for Nene Lindo and her relationship with her insane mother, who shared her experience of forced institutionalization; it is the story of two *locas*, that is to say, of a *loca* that is the daughter of another *loca*. Loca describes her mother's death as follows: "La pobre, murió en el manicomio sin alcanzar mi fama mucho más loca, mucho más loca que yo" (The poor thing, she died in the insane asylum without achieving my fame much crazier, much crazier than I). This is a striking pronouncement that celebrates infamy and also posits relative degrees of *locura* as it reenvisions mother-daughter relationships. Loca then goes on to describe the assorted possessions she received after her mother's death, some of which she keeps in her pink satin photo album. These include a bottle of Spanish perfume (Flor de Blasón), which Merced pronounces with a French accent; a plastic statuette of the Immaculate Conception; a 78-rpm record of "La múcura" by Bobby Capó; an autographed photo of Myrta Silva; her mother's missal; a newspaper clipping about the capture of the notorious criminal Palomilla (José Gerena Lafontaine, captured in 1949 and then again in 1951 after his escape from prison); a false certificate of adoption; "una de mis primeras fotos vestida como la Verónica en la procesión de Semana Santa en Bayamón" (one of my first photos dressed as the Veronica in the Holy Week procession in Bayamón), a trace of early childhood *translocura* linked to popular religiosity which generates audience laughter; "la trenza" (her mother's braid), which apparently she ripped off after going insane ("se la arrancó de cuajo cuando perdió la razón"); and finally, a revealing letter: "una cartita donde escribía entre carcajadas solitarias y salivones mi nombre. 'Loca la de la locura, loca por falta de hombre'" (a little letter in which she wrote my name amid solitary peals of laughter and drools. "Loca la de la locura, crazy for lack of a man").

As I noted in chapter 1, Latinx and Latin American feminist and queer scholars have highlighted the theoretical overlap between women's madness (and anger) and queer *locura*, for example the contributors to *Translocalities/Translocalidades* (Alvarez et al. 2014). Ramos Otero's story and

Pregones's play combine an interest in *locura* as female madness and male or effeminate queerness, particularly in how both can lead to confinement and to social ostracism, suggesting parallel forms of marginalization, echoing the French philosopher Michel Foucault's (1995, 2006) analysis of institutionalization, whether in the insane asylum (*History of Madness*) or in the prison (*Discipline and Punish*). In the story and the play, the mother offers a folk diagnosis of her child: "loca por falta de hombre" (crazy for lack of a man), an uncertain yet richly suggestive phrase given the speaking subject's compromised mental state. Pregones does not include a more scandalous line from the short story, in which the mother recommends castration as a tool related to seduction, a type of transloca pedagogy perhaps meant to guarantee success in love in a sexist society: "Bien lo decía mi madre, tróncale el bicho a tu hombre si es que te toca la puerta" (My mother said it well, cut your man's dick off if he knocks at your door) (Ramos Otero 1992, 237). This line plays into popular Freudian conceptions of castrating women who emasculate their partners.

Loca's mother/daughter narration leads to the reappearance of Nene Lindo, to a simulated fight scene, and to the reenactment of his murder. The remainder of the play presents Loca trying to explain why she killed Nene Lindo (she insists she is not quite sure; perhaps she is taking her mother's advice to the extreme), as well as her release from prison. At this moment, Loca changes her clothing and drapes a black mantilla over her head as she prepares to visit Nene Lindo's and her mother's tombs at the cemetery.

Why did Loca kill Nene Lindo? She provides a set of plausible answers that illuminate what it means to be an aging transloca:

¿Por qué lo hice? Si lo supiera, pero no lo sé. El miedo a quedarme calva cuando dejaron de usarse las pelucas tuvo que ver con eso. Los juanetes que deformaron mis pies de gacela en pezuñas de rinoceronte tuvieron que ver con eso. Demasiado mondongo de madrugada en el Restaurante Atenas tuvo que ver con eso. Las arrugas y las patas de gallo que no quisieron escuchar los consejos humectantes de Helena Rubinstein tuvieron que ver con eso. Un espíritu atrasado que tal vez se interpuso en el destino. La nostalgia incurable de la maternidad frustrada. Sentirme cada vez que lo clavaba como un carpintero frente a su cruz. Que me volvía vieja como el bolero y él más vigoroso que la salsa. (*El bolero fue mi ruina*)

Why did I do it? If I only knew, but I don't. The fear of going bald
when people stopped using wigs had to do with it. The bunions that
deformed my gazelle feet into rhinoceros hooves had to do with
it. Too much tripe stew at daybreak at the Athens Restaurant had
to do with it. The wrinkles and crow's feet that refused to listen to
Helena Rubinstein's moisturizing tips had to do with it. A delayed
spirit that perhaps got in the way of destiny. The incurable nostalgia
of frustrated motherhood. To feel every time that I nailed him like
a carpenter before their cross. That I was getting old like the bolero
and he was more vigorous than salsa music.

Loca's enumeration highlights typical masculine bodily changes (going
bald) but also ailments that affect women who wear high heels (bunions);
an erratic diet, for example eating *mondongo* (tripe stew, a Puerto Rican
favorite that is associated with the working class) in the early morning;
physical signs of aging that affect beauty (wrinkles and crow's feet); the
failure of American beauty products (Helena Rubinstein); spiritualist or
espiritista beliefs in "delayed spirits"; a complex desire for motherhood,
or perhaps an inner conflict regarding her inability to carry a baby; religious guilt or the use of Christian metaphors to describe the murder (or
perhaps a sexual act, or both); and a fear of old age, metaphorized as the
battle between two popular musical genres: the outdated bolero and the
ascendant salsa.

The final line of the play is an affirmation of liberty: "¡La viuda de Nene
Lindo no tiene tiempo para el miedo!" (Nene Lindo's widow has no time
for fear!), which contrasts with the end of the short story: "Ahora estoy
sin máscara. Con un puñal de huesos para unirme a la revolución" (Now
I am without a mask. With a handful [or dagger] of bones to join the
revolution) (Ramos Otero 1992, 240). In both cases, Loca insists on her
free will and her survivor spirit. If we consider the enormous structural
and personal violence Loca was subjected to (in Hormigueros, from Nene
Lindo, from the state), her survival seems nothing but remarkable. While
it is clear that she has committed a murder and that she has served her
time in prison, it is also true that she is the survivor of multiple forms of
oppression and violence. The play and the original short story ultimately
celebrate her ability to live in the face of adversity. Here, to be a transloca
is to survive, even if it requires killing someone. For Jorge B. Merced, to
be a transloca is to be able to tell this kind of story; to create community
through the performing arts; to celebrate the legacy of a leading queer

transloca writer, Manuel Ramos Otero, who succumbed to the ravages of AIDS in 1990 and was mostly unknown in the late 1990s and early 2000 except by people in very particular intellectual and artistic circles in New York and San Juan. It is also to remember Antonio Pantojas, Myrta Silva, Sylvia Rexach, Lucho Gatica, Toña la Negra, and Walter Mercado and make them part of one's life history, and to celebrate the lives and struggles of New York Puerto Rican transgender women. The bolero becomes the song of survival, a badge of courage, pride, love, and shame for translocas across the seas. Merced's celebration of lip-synch, transforming bodies, and the magic of drag shows such as those he witnessed at La Escuelita nightclub leads us to the next, and final, chapter of this book.

SEVEN

Adoring Lady Catiria, Knowing Barbra Herr

Woman . . . is far more than just the female of man. Rather she is a
divinity, a star.
—Charles Baudelaire, "The Painter of Modern Life"

The body of a transloca drag show or cabaret performer can be a work of
art in and of itself: her own creation, a magical ensemble of Baudelairean
cosmetic devices—beguiling, transformative, illusory, but also hybrid,
unsettling, possibly monstrous (Stryker 1994) or freakish (Santana 2018),
and most frequently not banal; a work of art best appreciated through a
differential perspective, what the Argentine trans theorist Marlene Wayar
refers to as *escorzo* (foreshortening), referring to a technique used in visual
arts to transform perceptions of depth by depicting objects obliquely, as
if rotated on their axis.[1] At times, the transloca's body can be the result of
expensive, painful, and dangerous transformations (diet, exercise, surgeries, liposuction, implants, hormones, and other medications), a collaboration with plastic surgeons, electrolysis technicians, and even underground
hormone vendors and silicone purveyors, but also with makeup artists,
hairstylists, and costume designers or perhaps the result of her own skills
in makeup, costume, padding, and hair.[2] Her body can be displayed on
the stage or dance floor and become the object of admiration and almost
religious worship, covered in a cascade of flowing dollar bills from excited
fans. It can be photographed and filmed in elaborate scenes or become
part of a successful number that includes lip-synching, singing, burlesque,
or dance. It can be a political statement just by the very fact of its existence,
in a context in which trans women are routinely murdered, excluded, and
dismissed. It can also be the subject of verbal discourse, as when a transloca performer talks about her transformations in a one-woman show,
explaining her process, sharing with us her life as a type of testimonial

narrative, or when she answers questions at a pageant or makes an impassioned plea for the recognition of our shared humanity. What is the relationship between body, voice, and transloca performance? How does the Puerto Rican transloca body become a work of art and a sign of the political? And what is our role as members of an audience?

Transloca embodiments (or *transloca incorporations*) can go beyond transvestic costume changes, translational linguistic and musical practices, translocal geographies, and quotidian violence, as I discussed in chapter 6; they can also be about the profound physical transformation of outward appearances to coincide with deeply felt identities and desires. So far in this book I have highlighted how transloca performers such as Holly Woodlawn and Monica Beverly Hillz modified their bodies through the use of hormones while negotiating poverty, and how Freddie Mercado strategically feminizes and transforms himself to create confusion and disorientation among spectators who cannot tell what is illusion and what is real.[3] I have also made an argument for the centrality of embodied experiences for other performers, whether it is through the semiotic and kinesthetic liberation of the subject through antiracist performance and dance, as in the case of Javier Cardona, who combats the violence of somatic racialization (Fetta 2018; Ruiz 2019); the confusion that Nina Flowers's apparently masculine shaved head and multiple tattoos create; the impact of being slapped by your father for watching drag on television (Jorge B. Merced); or the fatal violence that led to Venus Xtravaganza's, Jorge Steven López Mercado's, and Kevin Fret's deaths.

In this chapter I discuss two New York City–based Puerto Rican transloca performers who transformed their bodies and followed different paths regarding their performances and audience engagement. The first is Lady Catiria, a transgender pageant winner and nightclub entertainer who excelled at burlesque lip-synch and drag performance at La Escuelita nightclub (and later at La Nueva Escuelita) near Times Square in New York City in the 1980s and 1990s and who dazzled audiences with her ravishing beauty but who typically did not speak as part of her drag act.[4] The second is Barbra Herr (also a pageant winner), a university-educated trans performer who has distinguished herself through her lip-synchs, singing, and cabaret hosting in New York City (specifically in Greenwich Village, Queens, and the Bronx) as well as in Santo Domingo and San Juan, and who is well known for her engaging conversational banter, whether in her shows, in solo and ensemble theatrical performances, or in documentary and narrative films. The two transgender artists overlap

Fig. 20. Lady Catiria at the Palladium, East Fourteenth Street, New York City, early 1990s. Photo by Brian Lantelme.

in some respects but also represent profoundly different styles; both bring audiences together and create community. In this chapter, I also discuss my own experiences as an awestruck admirer and fan of Lady Catiria and Barbra Herr, at first overwhelmed by their beauty and talent—by the mystery and accomplishment of their self-transformations—who was later able to appreciate their full complexity, including their narrations of self.

Adoring Lady Catiria

Catiria Reyes, better known as Lady Catiria, was a performer, actor, and transgender beauty pageant winner born in Puerto Rico in 1959, who came to the United States as a child with her family and died in New York City in 1999 from AIDS-related causes.[5] As the African American journalist and queer community activist Donald Suggs (1999) wrote, Lady Catiria began her career at the age of nineteen in Jackson Heights, Queens, imitating the well-known Puerto Rican vedette and singer Iris Chacón, an erotic icon for many Caribbean queer men and women.[6] Lady Catiria became most famous for her lip-synch and burlesque dance shows at La Escuelita, a queer Latinx nightclub on West Thirty-Ninth Street and Eighth Avenue in Manhattan, and for her cameo in the 1995 Hollywood film *To Wong Foo, Thanks for Everything! Julie Newmar* (Ayala 1999; Raab 1994), where she briefly appeared in a nonspeaking role. She also obtained great renown for winning the Miss Continental Plus pageant in 1993 (Baim and Keehnen 2011, 445) and the Miss Continental pageant in 1995 (Baim and Keehnen 2011, 442), both in Chicago.[7] In 1996, she became a spokeswoman for people with AIDS, when she used her Miss Continental farewell performance as a vehicle to narrate her personal story of struggle and resiliency and the challenges she faced after learning that she was infected with HIV.[8] She is also remembered for inspiring many transgender and cisgender performers such as Barbra Herr, Candis Cayne, Rosie Pérez, and Angel Sheridan.[9]

Lady Catiria was extraordinarily talented and excelled as an engaging lip-synch performer and dancer who always appeared impeccably dressed with gorgeous makeup and hair and who had notable empathy for her audiences. Yet it was her body, or more accurately, her strategic use of her body, that drove her New York City audiences and myriad fans wild; a body that was not accompanied by her own voice, as Lady Catiria never (or practically never) spoke as part of her cabaret act, but rather served as the conduit for the voices of other (recorded) divas in multiple languages. Her voluptuous body (staged, displayed, transformed) became a language of itself; it was a body that seamlessly blended with the accoutrements of cabaret performance, with her interpretations of songs and choreographies, and with her daring burlesque. Her body was also hard to grasp, and seemed almost like a vision, at least for me, perhaps because of my ignorance or naivete; a body that seemed at a remove, that spoke through visual and tactile and kinesthetic prompts but that stodgily refused auditory communication in public, except that of lip-synch. And it was a populist body, a work of art exhibited in run-down venues with mostly poor and working-class, marginalized patrons, who flocked to La Escuelita in a still-seedy Times Square to adore her; a body that was a combination of cipher and explicit proof of success, of the human ability to transform, to defy nature, to make something different.

With Lady Catiria, there was no distancing of that seamless or monstrous illusion of the "real" of her skin and flesh; no gesture of transcending from the "popular" or from the practices of "everyday life" to high art, except perhaps through the pageant or beauty contest in Chicago, which was mostly unknown to many of her New York City fans in the days before the widespread use of the internet. There was also no effort to make her corporeality into an artistic production in high-class cabarets (for example, as the French transgender performer Coccinelle in the 1960s or the American Christine Jorgensen) or exhibited for viewing and consumption in an art gallery or museum, in a system of international art sales, curatorships, catalogs, grants, all imbricated in a struggle for material wealth and the trappings of fame and immortality through the designation of individual genius, like other body/performance artists that invest substantially in surgical and/or hormonal physical transformations such as the cisgender French visual artist and writer Orlan, the transgender Canadian performer Nina Arsenault, or the Canadian trans performance artist Cassils.[10] And for most of Lady Catiria's numerous fans, this would have been as irrelevant as absurd or incomprehensible, for Catiria was a "populist" artist, shall we say, an artist committed to a group of largely socially marginalized people as well as to many European tourists and slummers who would make their pilgrimage on Friday and Saturday nights to La Escuelita, at least in the 1990s, before Lady Catiria died; much as we can say that Orlan and Cassils are artists that appeal to an elite crowd of the high-art establishment, while Arsenault has been embraced by the queer theater and performance art world.

As a transgender drag show performer who also frequented New York City venues known for sex work such as Sally's Hideaway (Lantelme 2002), Lady Catiria was an "outsider artist," I would argue, an artist separated from the institutional validation mechanisms of art by a matter of steps or degrees but not by the intrinsic quality of her creation, which was valorized artistically, commercially, and emotively in spaces such as the Miss Continental Pageant and at La Escuelita.[11] Much as religious icons and relics can be objects of pious devotion or of frivolous kitsch humor and posing, separated by *degrees* of kitsch, as Celeste Olalquiaga (1992) argues in *Megalopolis: Contemporary Cultural Sensibilities*, the trans performer, particularly the one who barely or never speaks, can be a divinity, a blinding vision, a diva, an embodiment of Otherness, or be perceived as a type of joke.[12] Why is it that this apparent silence can be so powerful? And what happens when that illusion or lack of access is all of a sudden broken through the mediation of technology, for example with the appearance of videos on YouTube documenting Lady Catiria's participation in the Miss Continental pageant, in which she answered questions and gave speeches?

The difference between Orlan, Arsenault, Cassils, and a mostly non-speaking Puerto Rican transgender drag show performer like Lady Catiria is thus not the object (the practice of the body), but depending on the individual, it is the discourse or distance from that body: Lady Catiria's body register seemed mostly private, intimate, familial—a silence about her constructed nature, at least in public in the 1990s, at the very least for her fans at La Escuelita in New York City, which is why the Spanish (cisgender) actress Antonia San Juan's portrayal of La Agrado and her discourse of expenditure (the transgender character's detailed listing of how much she had spent on surgeries to transform her body) in Pedro Almodóvar's 1999 *All About My Mother* was so surprising for Hispanic audiences, particularly since most people incorrectly assumed San Juan was trans.[13] Lady Catiria's onstage silence was also quite unlike the genre of trans testimonial performance pieces pioneered by Kate Bornstein in works such as *The Opposite Sex Is Neither* (Brantley 1993) and more recently by Arsenault in her well-received *Silicone Diaries* (2009) and by Barbra Herr in *Trans-mission* (2017) which I discuss later in this chapter, and decidedly at a distance from Puerto Rican trans memoirs such as Holly Woodlawn's *A Low Life in High Heels* (1992), Soraya's *Hecha a mano: Disforia de género* (2014), and Reyna Ortiz's *T, Stands for Truth* (2017) or from the self-disclosure that occurs in Puerto Rican documentaries such as *Mala Mala* (Santini and Sickles 2014) and *Luis/Lizza* (González-Laguer 2015), in which trans performers, sex workers, business owners, activists, and elders such as Paxx Caraballo Moll, Samantha Close, Ivana Fred, Denise "Sandy" Rivera, Soraya (Bárbara Santiago Solla), Sophia Voines, and Luis Felipe Díaz (Lizza Fernanda) speak about their experiences.[14] Lady Catiria's silence was particular; it was a silence in generative tension with the mouthing of the lyrics of divas.

The Spectacle of Lip-Synch

The apparently disembodied yet actually fully corporeal practice of lip-synching has its own logic, one that does not correspond to singing.[15] The criteria for judgment are not the same. For some, perhaps it is a matter of convenience or practicality, of the conservation of energies, as in a case Esther Newton cites in *Mother Camp*: "As one boy put it to a stage impersonator who was criticizing record acts, 'Records are boring, Mary, but it's the easiest thing you can do'" (1979, 11). Obviously it is not a question of the live voice but of a ghost, the spectral presence of a voice without a body, with an/other body, that becomes embodied in another self: the mimicking mouth, throat, tongue, lips, teeth, chest, shoulders, thorax, diaphragm, stomach, arms, legs, hands, and feet of (that apparent) silence, the kinesthetic body that sways in movements penetrated by a recorded voice and by music perceived and received from the outside, through the ears and skin and muscles and bones of that very real body that we see, a dancing body located in time and space in front of us and dressed or undressed in wigs, makeup, prosthetic, implants, and costumes. The phenomena are simulation and simulacra, to invoke Jean Baudrillard (1988), but a step beyond, as there is nothing fake about having a real person in front of you invoking another (a diva or star), as opposed to a robot, a cyborg, a mannequin, or a hologram. What is the history of lip-synching? When did it begin? How is it related to puppetry, masks, dolls, dummies, and ventriloquism? And what happens when a drag performer such as Lady Catiria transforms lip-synching into a high art, where "the goal is that the copy should *replace* the original" (Evans 2009, 50)?[16]

The drag or trans lip-syncher partakes of the cabaret in the tradition of the musical revue, the space of alterity of nocturnal entertainment, but filters these through the loss of aura and subsequent democratization predicated by Walter Benjamin (1968b) in the age of mechanical reproduction.[17] In this case, the loss of "authenticity," the negation of the "here and now" or "aura" (to use Benjamin's terms) of the original musical performance is recuperated and transformed in the act of lip-synch; this occurs with a different body that instills the song with a new soul.[18] Lip-synch, it seems obvious to state, is an art, but can also become a sacrament or ritual for devotees of drag. And Lady Catiria was a master at lip-synch, one who transformed her songs into unforgettable happenings through her accurate mouthing of the lyrics of frequently well-known musical divas, in combination with choreographies and stunning visuals.

My fuzzy experiential memories of Lady Catiria's specific performances, deeply felt but imprecise, come into sharp focus through technological mediation, that is to say, through the access provided by video recordings of her performances, what now constitutes a more permanent archive. This is especially the case thanks to *Now and Forever: The Best of Lady Catiria*, a limited-circulation VHS tape and DVD produced by La Nueva Escuelita after Lady Catiria's death in 1999 that was available for sale at the venue, which includes recordings of twelve of her lip-synch performances, but also through the official Miss Continental Pageant recordings sold directly by the Continental Pageantry Systems that have now been clandestinely shared by fans on YouTube. Most of the songs that Lady Catiria performed in the Escuelita video are in English, some in Spanish, and some bilingual or in a mix of languages including Italian; most are performed solo, one as a duet and another as a group number. *The Best of Lady Catiria* includes her performances of "Cinque Milla" by Dana International, "Missing" by Everything but the Girl, "Killing Me Softly" by the Fugees, "Lick It" by 20 Fingers featuring Roula, "Cherish the Day" by Sade, "Hastío" by Sophy, "Un-break My Heart" and "Breathe Again" by Toni Braxton, "Cosas del amor" by Vikki Carr (a duet with Jeannette Alexander, who portrays Ana Gabriel), "Where's My Man" by Eartha Kitt, the "Finale (Escuelita Divas)" ensemble piece (a multivoice rendition of the Elvis Presley version of "Let It Be Me") with several Escuelita performers, and "Wind Beneath My Wings" by Bette Midler. There is also documentation on YouTube of Lady Catiria lip-synching "Perfidia" by Linda Ronstadt (in English and Spanish) at the Miss Continental pageant in Chicago in 1995, and of Lady Catiria's 1996 farewell performance, entailing a lip-synch of "It's Never Too Late" by the award-winning gospel singer Tramaine Hawkins from her album *To a Higher Place* (1994).

Most Escuelita numbers follow a conventional pattern (appearance, performance, interruptions, or engagement with audience). One unusual number is a duet that includes making out with another performer. Another one has a notable campy theatrical feel involving extending prosthetic wings ("Wind Beneath My Wings"). Many include reveals, such as Lady Catiria's performance of "Cinque Milla," identified in the video as "This Is My House," a rather apt metaphor, as La Escuelita really was the house that Lady Catiria built.

"Cinque Milla" and Dana International as Diva

Lady Catiria's lip-synch and burlesque performance of a remix of Dana International's provocative 1996 song "Cinque Milla" was quite something; it is identified in the video as Lady Catiria's "last stage performance at La Nueva Escuelita, December 26, 1998," and as such acquires posthumous memorial status. For starters, it is worthwhile to acknowledge the Israeli singer's pioneering role as the first transgender woman to win the

Eurovision Song Contest in May 1998, and the significance that it might have had for Lady Catiria to perform an international musical hit by an award-winning transgender entertainer.[19]

As the valuable scholarship on Dana International indicates, the Mizrahi Jewish pop singer, who is the daughter of working-class Yemeni immigrants and was raised in poverty in Israel, generated varied and complex reactions, including vociferous opposition from ultra-Orthodox Jews and other social and political conservatives. Sharon Cohen (Dana International), who started her career as a drag queen, has positioned herself at the crossroads of linguistic, national, regional, gender, and sexual identities, and publicly promotes political and cultural understanding (for example, in her campaign with Amnesty International), singing in Arabic, English, Hebrew, and Italian (Gross 2013). As Alisa Solomon highlights, citing Lauren Berlant's (1997) concept of "Diva Citizenship," "Though Dana demurs in interviews when questions about the Israeli-Palestinian peace process come up, claiming that she is not at all political, her act of Diva Citizenship has profoundly radical potential because it challenges the very core of Zionism at a moment when Israel is anxiously renegotiating its national self-image" (2003, 151). For Berlant, "Diva Citizenship does not change the world. It is a moment of emergence that marks unrealized potentials for subaltern political activity. Diva Citizenship occurs when a person stages a dramatic coup in a public sphere in which she does not have privilege" (1997, 223). It is also notable that the song "Cinque Milla" ("five thousand" in Italian) comes from Dana International's third album *Maganuna* (1996), which is colloquial Egyptian Arabic for "crazy woman," or *loca* (Ben-zvi 1998, 28).[20] It is possible that Lady Catiria was not aware of these complexities, and that the choice of the song had to do with the new owner of La Nueva Escuelita, Savyon "Big Ben" Zabar, an Israeli.[21]

In her Escuelita performance, Lady Catiria makes her appearance to the verse "This is my house," coming out onto the narrow stage from behind a red curtain, which is quickly drawn to reveal a shiny blue one as backdrop. Lady Catiria is grinning broadly as she reveals her stunning primary-color red and yellow vinyl outfit and outlandish wig. Her shiny dress has a notable cleavage; she accompanies it with a bright red cape with red and yellow sleeves made of the same material, and also wears matching calf-high, high-heel, red plastic boots. On her head she has a gigantic, nearly shoulder-length spherical bouffant two-tone fire-engine-red wig with a flip in the front, underlaid in the back with bright yellow hair (as if an *ombré* effect) that matches her fetish-inspired ensemble. Her makeup is dramatic, including very dark eyeliner, deep black eyelashes, and pronounced contouring of the cheeks.

Lady Catiria's choreography for this number is at first quite simple: side-to-side movements that evolve as she stands still and shakes her breasts in a series of upper-body shimmies, later tilting her body slightly from side to side; she proceeds to mouth the phrase "allora Rola" from Dana International's song, using a colloquial Italian term (*allora*) that serves as an interjection and the Arabic woman's name Rola, perhaps a reference to the Lebanese TV producer Roula Saad. Lady Catiria then looks out and points to audience members as she mouths questions (in English) from the song: "Do you have a reservation?" followed by a simple affirmation: "I have a party in my house." As she proceeds to say, "I serve bananas, potatoes, and some cock," she squeezes her breasts together with her hands, licks her lips, and greets individual audience members as they come up to tip her.

As the song picks up, Lady Catiria's body reflects more animated movements. While the chorus goes on, she purses her lips slightly, makes hand gestures to the repeated lyrics of "la chiquita chiquitita" (the tiny small one) in Spanish; she also repeats "cinquemilla cinquecento" (five thousand five hundred) in Italian numerous times, almost as if stating the price she charges for her performance, the cost of her outfit, or that of her body modifications, as if *pregonando* (hawking her wares). She then points to her ears as she mouths the phrase "Listen to the rhythm," and then takes her coat off and throws it to the side. This leads to a dramatic reveal to the line "This is my house," as Lady Catiria turns around and dances facing the stage, revealing a large red arrow on the back of her yellow body suit with a cutout area at the buttocks which she then shakes like Iris Chacón, first by quickly and repeatedly isolating the gluteus and then by swaying the hips and legs from side to side.

Toward the end of her performance, Lady Catiria gets on the floor, kneels on stage, flexes her back, and once again shakes her butt. The camera captures the moment when a handsome, young, muscular, male audience member wearing a sleeveless T-shirt (perhaps a go-go boy) comes up behind her and attempts to give her a tip but seems at a loss as to where to place the money; we see his indecision as he then squats and proceeds to place it in her cleavage. Lady Catiria, still lying on the stage, later proceeds to do her signature move, which involves putting her right leg over her shoulder in order to place her foot on the floor, as if an erotic contortionist. This whole time, her breasts seem to be nearly popping out of her outfit.

The potentially nonsensical, multilingual lyrics of this song (perhaps about prostitution, perhaps not—five thousand five hundred what?), which has multiple choruses and overlayered effects, poses certain challenges for lip-synch, namely the decision whether to attempt to mouth every unintelligible lyric. It is a song that seems faithful to the Arabic *maganuna* (female craziness) that titles Dana International's album, a transnational gesture of *translocura* that highlights a lighthearted Mediterranean party spirit in stark opposition to exclusionary nationalist politics that police difference, for example Israeli marginalization of queer and other Palestinians (Ritchie 2010), a regime of exclusion based on profound violence (Puar 2017). Lady Catiria negotiates the entertaining and provocative incoherence of the song by selectively choosing only some parts to lip-synch and pursing the lips or simply dancing at other moments; she also perhaps unwittingly participates in "pinkwashing" (queer whitewashing) the Israeli state.[22] This number is more about the outfit, the burlesque dance, and the interaction with the audience than about a seamless reproduction of the song or explicit politics. As the video documents, the audience adored the performance; it circulates widely on YouTube, with more than ten thousand views.

Romantic Ballads in English

While Lady Catiria's lip-synch and dance performance of Dana International's "Cinque Milla" is extremely successful in its combination of costuming, hairstyle, and burlesque, some of her performances of English-language divas such as Tracey Thorn (from Everything but the Girl), Lauren Hill (from the Fugees), Sade, Toni Braxton, Eartha Kitt, and Bette Midler allow for more nuanced attention. To state it simply: slower songs with more coherent or understandable lyrics seem easier to lip-synch, or at least are easier for the audience to follow and appreciate as a lip-synch. At the same time, the Puerto Rican performer maintains her burlesque choreographic movements, particularly the reveal, which generate enormous enthusiasm.

Lady Catiria's performance of Everything but the Girl's "Missing" (identified in *The Best of Lady Catiria* video as "Miss You") is a vision in pink. In this number, Lady Catiria looks like a large Barbie doll or like a little girl's dream of a Disney princess; a grown-up quinceañera, debutante, or young bride, wearing a very elegant yet also explicit dress, a marked contrast from the more sedate style that characterizes Everything but the Girl's lead singer Tracey Thorn. Lady Catiria's gorgeous, sleeveless, open-back, floor-length pink dress, with its ribbons of shiny satin crossing her breasts, exposes and sexualizes the performer's body. Lady Catiria also wears a pink shimmering tiara that holds back her black curly hair, leading it to cascade slightly onto her back. On her ears, she wears long dangling costume pink stone and diamond earrings. Her face is made up with pink eyeshadow and light red lipstick, and her lips are outlined in a darker shade. The two edges of her long skirt are tied to her wrists, and when she moves, her skirt twirls dramatically. The same occurs when she raises her arms.

There is something childlike and celebratory in Lady Catiria's profusion of pink accents, ribbons, and red rhinestones, which are counterpoised with the very explicit, grown-up reveal of her very large breasts that convey multiple semiotic messages (sex object, maternal doll, vulnerable quinceañera). Lady Catiria's joyful costume doesn't necessarily coincide with the lyrics of the song, which are about heartbreak and longing (the refrain of the song is, precisely, "I miss you"); in La Escuelita, these words become an invitation to the audience to envision themselves in Lady Catiria's realm, as the subjects of her enunciation. In the lip-synch of this mournful yet quick-paced, postdisco, electronic ballad from the eponymously titled 1994 British duo's album *Missing*, there is more focus on the careful enunciation of the words, but not at the expense of choreography, which builds on the dramatic nature of her dress. Lady Catiria is a master showwoman who takes advantage of the limited moments she has to perform, negotiating constantly with the fans who come up to give her tips, kisses, and hugs. During her performance, she uses the full space of the club, including the stage near the back curtain and the open dance floor in front of her. Notably, a male audience member wearing a black sports jacket comes up and regales her with a shower of money during her number.

Other interventions embrace eroticism more explicitly. Lady Catiria's performance of the British Nigerian singer Sade's "Cherish the Day" from the 1992 album *Love Deluxe* combines a careful lip-synch (well-mouthed lyrics, expressive movements) with a burlesque performance centered on a dramatic reveal; the performer builds on Sade's sensual musical and kinesthetic style but pushes it into the realm of the openly erotic, embracing the love song's exhortation to "cherish the day" almost as a type of romantic and obscene carpe diem. For this number, Lady Catiria first appears with a semitranslucent shawl (as if a black veil) over her head and chest, goth makeup including black lipstick, a tight black latex or leather dress that reaches the floor and flares at the bottom, long red fingernails, and black, thin-strap, open-toed, high-heel shoes. She then pulls off her veil from her head, revealing her exposed breasts with oversize sparking pasties covering her nipples and a sparkling triangle made of the same material at the bottom of her cleavage holding the skirt. Her dress is also held up by cord-like straps that come down the outer sides of her breasts. Lady Catiria appears with black hair that reaches her shoulders. When she turns around we see her exposed, open back, revealing a small tattoo of a black heart with wings above her buttocks. During the number, Lady Catiria dances provocatively with a curly-black-haired, slightly butch woman in the audience who comes up to give her a tip: they flick tongues at each other and do a pelvic thrust. Performing this song has as much to do with showing her body and interacting directly with the audience as it does with mouthing the lyrics. Lady Catiria's expressions of desire and sensuality are democratic, almost "polymorphously perverse" (Freud 1975, 57) in their multiplicity and visibility, signaling La Escuelita as a space of radical inclusion, at least during certain performances, but also Lady Catiria's embrace of *sucia* (dirty, sleazy, empowered) or *sinvergüenza* (shameless) politics (La Fountain-Stokes 2011a; J. M. Rodríguez 2014; Vargas 2014).

Melodrama (Passion and Comedy) in Spanish

La Escuelita was a Latinx nightclub with "kitsch red-flamed chandeliers, [a] swirling disco ball and blinking Christmas lights" (Raab 1994) that catered to a multilingual and multiracial crowd. It was a space, as the sociologist Manolo Estavillo (Guzmán 1997) discusses at length in his short ethnography, marked by the crossing of Latinxs from varied socioeconomic backgrounds who came together to celebrate community in an adverse context, as Jorge B. Merced has also pointed out (La Fountain-Stokes 2018e).[23] It was a space that initially (in its first decades) challenged the hegemony of English: As the American journalist Vicky Raab proclaimed in 1994, "Spanish is the mother tongue in this queendom." In the early and mid-1990s, the dance floor was dominated by couples twirling across the space to salsa, merengue, and bachata rhythms, at times dancing in intimate embrace, and at other times shaking their ass to house, tribal, pop, and other musical grooves. The drag show, which occurred at

1:00 a.m., prominently featured songs in English and Spanish. Depending on the emcee, the language of presentation would vary, for example favoring Spanish when Mario de Colombia did the honors. This changed somewhat after the club closed in 1995 and reopened in 1996 with new ownership under the management of Savyon "Big Ben" Zabar; the drag performer Angel Sheridan's hosting was English-dominant, and the club started playing more hip-hop than salsa and merengue, as the clientele became more oriented toward African American, Afro-Latinx, and Latinx youth as opposed to the expansive first- and second-generation immigrant Afro-Latinx and Latinx crowd (including entire multigenerational families) that it had catered to earlier. The performance of some Spanish-language lip-synch numbers was maintained in La Nueva Escuelita, but stopped being the show's center.

Lady Catiria's performances of songs in Spanish, whether at La Escuelita or elsewhere, were a crucial aspect of who she was as a bilingual Puerto Rican transloca entertainer. *The Best of Lady Catiria* video only includes two Spanish-language songs; one a solo and the other a duet with Jeannette Alexander. Lady Catiria's contained yet inspired lip-synch performance of the Puerto Rican pop ballad singer Sophy's recording of "Hastío" ("Weariness") from the 1974 album *Yo de aquí no me voy* is masterful and conveys strong emotions. The romantic ballad is by the Mexican Luisito Rey (the father of the well-known singer Luis Miguel) and almost feels like a variation of a bolero; the lyric speaker emphatically asks her lover to speak openly and truthfully ("conversemos claramente"), without fear ("ya no tienes que temer"), unmasking their emotions, to admit the demise of their relationship: "Ya no somos los amantes que ayer fuimos" (We are no longer the lovers that we once were). Lady Catiria benefits in this number from her counterpoint with Sophy's slightly masculine or androgynous self-presentation, including Sophy's marked preference for short hairstyles, and from Sophy's confident lyrical persona.[24]

For her performance of "Hastío," Lady Catiria appears wearing a beautiful, elegant, and provocative floor-length, sparkling black sleeveless dress with a long slit in front of the skirt, revealing both of her legs as she walks, almost as if a Latin bombshell or an inspired Rita Hayworth. The dress has a cutout at the chest, exposing most of one breast and her nipple; it also has an open back. Her very long curly black hair is held back, falling on her shoulders. This song has many quick parlando or enunciated spoken passages in which Sophy directly addresses the object of her discourse. Lady Catiria lip-synchs the song masterfully: she conveys the sense that she feels the words deeply. She stands still in the middle of the dance floor, moving her arms and hands slightly. While she is performing, a parade of people come up to tip her. At times, she addresses them as if they were the person she is singing to. Toward the second part of the song, she moves in a more animated way toward the stage.

Lady Catiria's second Escuelita song in Spanish is "Cosas del amor" ("Love Matters") by Ana Gabriel and Vikki Carr, which Lady Catiria performed as a duet with the Puerto Rican trans performer Jeannette Alexander; the song originally appeared in Carr's 1991 studio album *Cosas del amor.* In the original music video available on YouTube, we see the conventionally feminine Texana singer Vikki Carr at first calmly and then passionately dialoguing with, comforting, and encouraging the distraught Mexican singer Ana Gabriel, who sings of her fear of losing the man she loves. In the video, Carr appears as a blonde, while Ana Gabriel is brunette; both self-present in a feminine manner. The video is melodramatic and seems inspired by telenovelas; it highlights female solidarity in the face of adversity.

In the Escuelita version, Jeannette Alexander lip-synchs Ana Gabriel's part, while Lady Catiria lip-synchs that of Vikki Carr, as they enact a campy butch/femme lesbian couple, bringing to life the homoerotic tension implicit in the song and video and, furthermore, fulfilling in a rather extraordinary way the feminist potential of butch/femme lesbianism as articulated by the performance studies scholar Sue-Ellen Case, who precisely identified bars (here a club) as spaces for liberation: "So the lesbian butch-femme tradition went into the feminist closet. Yet the closet, or the bars, with their hothouse atmosphere have produced what, in combination with the butch-femme couple, may provide the liberation of the feminist subject—the discourse of camp," where camp is defined as "the style, the discourse, the mise-en-scène of butch-femme roles" (1988–89, 59–60), the "space of irony and wit, free from biological determinism, elitist essentialism, and the heterosexist cleavage of sexual difference" (71). Lady Catiria's Puerto Rican transloca twist, specifically a lesbian performance by two trans women, adds a new complexity to Case's extraordinarily generative analysis.

In the aforementioned scene, Jeanette Alexander comes out wearing a shimmering gold lamé dress with a loose gold jacket and held-back, long curly black hair that comes down to her shoulders. Soon after, Lady Catiria appears in a slightly masculine outfit, wearing a sleeveless jumpsuit with a silver zipper in front, large, round, black sunglasses, black shoes with heel, neutral lipstick, and a short black wig (not blond, as in the video), playing up a butch appearance. A somewhat overacted, melodramatic dynamic scene ensues, clearly played more for laughs. (Lady Catiria typically did not do comedy.) Similar to the musical video, it is more like a telenovela that then devolves into a soft porn scene as the women undress. First, Lady Catiria rips Jeannette's cape off, leading Jeannette to reveal her breasts. Then Lady Catiria rips off her own wig, takes off her top, reveals a red plaid bra and boxers, and starts to kiss and make out with Jeannette, culminating in a long kissing scene. At this moment, the audience goes wild, clapping and cheering with great enthusiasm. The number's mix of humor and eroticism made it a crowd-pleaser as it also expanded and reconfigured more established circuits of desire and acknowledges heterogeneity of attractions; it becomes what the scholar Juana María Rodríguez terms lesbian "daddy play . . . engaging directly with forms of dominance—fucking with power, if you will" (2014, 58). And this is done with a song in Spanish.

At the 1995 Miss Continental pageant in Chicago, Lady Catiria also performed a lip-synch number in English and Spanish that led to a sophisticated and quite complex dance number. For the talent component, Lady Catiria did a well-executed, dramatic, bilingual lip-synch of the classic bolero "Perfidia" ("Perfidy"), as sung by the Mexican American performer Linda Ronstadt. The original 1939 song is by the Mexican composer Alberto Domínguez; Ronstadt's version, which appears in *The Mambo Kings* original motion picture soundtrack, moves seamlessly from Spanish to English, an ideal choice for a bilingual and bicultural performer, marking her difference in a positive light. The song conveys profound emotions and a critique of those people who cannot grasp the singer's sufferings due to heartbreak and loss.

For this number, Lady Catiria first appears wearing a gorgeous white satin gown, covered in white feathers with a long tail and huge sleeves. She also has a headdress made out of white feathers. Lady Catiria's lip-synch is very contained, with a still body, highlighting dramatic eye movements, a shifting intense gaze, and the use of her hands, with occasional hip or body shakes to punctuate the music. The stillness is broken when she moves forward onto the runway that abuts into the audience. She then flips the long tail of her dress, and ends with her back facing the public. At the conclusion of the short song we have the dramatic reveal, as she slips out of the white dress and tosses her white feather diadem to reveal a short red dress underneath. This leads to an energetic dance choreography with six male backup dancers to Tito Puente's "Para los rumberos," also from *The Mambo Kings* soundtrack. The dance number has no lip-synch but plenty of group and solo moves, including her signature ass shake. Lady Catiria proves herself to be an accomplished dancer that can perform a large-stage number with great success.

Audiences and Artists

Attending a drag show is akin to going to church or to a religious celebration, particularly if we envision the performers as divinities. As Moe Meyer writes, "When a drag queen is called 'divine,' it is precisely this power to authorize the proceedings around her that is being honored, marked, and recognized" (2010, 105). La Escuelita had its fair share of divinities among its cast members and attendees, and also created a sense of cohesion, unity, and community that approximates dance clubs to sacred spaces (Johnson 1998), full of "queer time" and "queer place" that allowed "transcendence" (Allen 2009), even if it could also be a space of violent confrontations and fights, as Jorge B. Merced has remarked (La Fountain-Stokes 2018e).

The predominantly working-class Latinx, Cuban, Dominican, and Puerto Rican audience of La Escuelita occasionally included Hollywood stars such as John Leguizamo and Rosie Pérez and a variety of middle-class Latinxs who always stood in line in the illuminated darkness of the nightclub, becoming a procession on their way to pay homage to the lip-synching Lady Catiria, men and women desirous to give her money and kisses, wanting to touch and engage in an almost religious ceremony: a gift economy or tribute to a goddess on earth.[25] The audience made its offerings as payment, in appreciation for the visual, Laura Mulvey–esque scopophilic but also tactile and sensory pleasure that the transsexual drag performer offered (Mulvey 2009); it was a symbiotic relationship, as the exchange facilitated the work of art to be—the bodily transformation: the hormones, the surgery; the clothing, cosmetics, and prosthetics; the artist's subsistence: rent, food, medicine, toiletries—while Lady Catiria offered us in return an approximation to the erotic and feminine mystical sublime. This spectatorial physical enactment made the experience one that went well beyond the eye and ear, engaging sight and sound with touch, smell, and perhaps, for some, even taste; that is to say, if you could overcome your sense of unease and nervousness and actually go up to tip her during her performance, something that fortunately I did many times in the 1990s.

Unlike other economic exchange systems between artists and audience, for example, the typical structure by which an audience member pays for a ticket and does not pay again, here the artist has to win over her spectators to ensure a further supply of revenue for that same performance: "While some patrons tip as perfunctorily as if they were mailing a letter, others linger nearby to caress or embrace the goddess, or to briefly and unselfconsciously dance with her" (Raab 1994). Payment is thus directly tied to the immediate satisfaction of the audience, although in Lady Catiria's case, we saw the benefits of a previously established reputation, how having a loyal fan base could be decisive, and how there were preestablished scripts that repeated themselves: an admirer unleashing a rain of dollar bills; the stuffing of paper money in the cleavage and ass by the never-ending parade of other drag queens, transsexuals, butch and femme lesbians, straight women, and assorted men, including highly effeminate, hypermasculine, seriously handsome and not so handsome individuals who interrupted the show; the handing of countless bills, one by one, by an audience member (perhaps Lady Catiria's husband) who all of a sudden would become a twinkling star himself, even if only for a brief moment, in his ostentatious display of wealth. The transgender performer's body earns its keep much as the go-go boy or erotic female dancer does: through a concrete, direct exchange, unmediated by management structures that still might request a cut, accepting money from everyone, without distinction, in this dialectic of exchange that momentarily casts light on the penitent supplicant spectator, for example, me.[26] And as the scholar Sarah Hankins notes in her analysis of "drag tipping," sex work, and the "queer sociosexual economy," "Much US gender performance is organized around the payment of money for erotic behavior . . . the act of tipping itself is just as significant as the form or intensity of the sex that occurs in exchange for money" (2015, 442).

The actor/performer is an extension of the prostitute or sex worker, as has been well noted in historical analyses of the stigma attached to this profession, particularly for women.[27] But the transgender drag show performer is also an Italian Madonna in a procession in Little Italy, much in the way St. Orlan wishes to become the Virgin Mary and receive charity, or a Mexican newlywed bride, who has money pinned to her gown, or a Filipino gay man and his Puerto Rican boyfriend celebrating their twenty-fifth anniversary and receiving ornate garlands of origami-like folded twenty-dollar bills from their Filipina mother in Jackson Heights, precisely the same neighborhood where Lady Catiria began her career imitating Iris Chacón, and where the contemporary performer Barbra

Herr continues (or continued) to appear, at least until the emergence of the coronavirus pandemic.[28] The exchange of money allows for a particular physical intimacy, a special encounter or embrace, a close affective tie, but also commodifies relationships and turns the show into an economic spectacle, as I discussed in chapter 2.

Burlesque and Public Sexual/Erotic Performance

Cabaret performers, sex workers, strippers, go-go boys, and female erotic dancers all share with drag and trans artists the desire to please or shock and in the process somehow gain notice and make a living. Lady Catiria's burlesque lip-synch went far beyond the call of duty, well past the candid interpretation of a singer/songwriter/stylist/song temptress. Here the song became the excuse, the stage and backdrop, the measure of time and rhythm, the frame. Not to say that she did not do justice to her songs; they were transformed, those lyrics in Italian, Spanish, and English, as she would sway and shake masses of flesh clad in vinyl and silk and nothing, as if an almost pornographic Caribbean vedette in the style of Tongolele or Iris Chacón or Ninón Sevilla, a dream out of the Tropicana for eyes more accustomed to Times Square Peeping Tom delights.[29] The song would become an explicit erotic diversion, a means to an end, the end in itself. Other drag queens suddenly would seem G-rated, PG, or R, while Lady Catiria veered toward NR-17, X, and XXX, even when she had not pronounced a single word of her own. Catiria was a master of circus-like contortions whose performances were marked by the inevitable flexing of the leg behind the shoulder and neck, the upturned breast and showing of the nipple, the lick. The occasional shot of her smooth pussy, or so one of my friends would insist. The mystery of the performer: silence.

Lady Catiria was a fleeting star captured by amateur video cameras, well before the advent of cell phones with video-recording capabilities, as her tribute Escuelita VHS compilation and the Miss Continental videos show. She also appeared in an unfortunately all-too-brief cameo in the British filmmaker Beeban Kidron's *To Wong Foo, Thanks for Everything! Julie Newmar*, a 1995 American drag queen movie that feels like a fake, feel-good, *Priscilla, Queen of the Desert* Hollywood remake that would have us believe that Patrick Swayze and Wesley Snipes can outdo Lady Catiria, Laritza Dumont, and Joey Arias (other 1990s New York Latina drag performers) or even the Colombian Puerto Rican American John

Leguizamo, who stars in the film as the down-and-out aspiring performer Chi Chi, an exemplary transloca.[30]

Lady Catiria is fascinating, of course, because as a transgender drag performer who engaged in relatively "explicit" solo-sexual performances but who rarely spoke, she confounds the very useful and subtle distinctions Esther Newton made in 1972 between *street* and *stage impersonators* in 1960s American drag shows, between working-class, strung-out, hormone-taking girls who turn tricks and lip-synch, on the one hand, and so-called respectable middle-class professional men who see themselves eminently as stage entertainers and sing and make campy jokes, perhaps more akin to what I remember Mario de Colombia being like in La Escuelita in the early 1990s, or like Angel Sheridan in La Nueva Escuelita in the late 1990s and early 2000s. My hesitation as to where to locate Lady Catiria does not have to do exclusively with the social and historical changes that occurred over a thirty-year time span (from the 1960s period documented by Esther Newton to the 1990s), although that is obviously important. It has to do, to the contrary, with the persistence of this radical dichotomy predicated on class, race, and respectability, and its particular inflections in a queer, working-class, Latinx environment in New York City (Holly Woodlawn notwithstanding, as I discuss in chapter 3), and on the delicate ways in which transsexuality relates to "mainstream" or "dominant" drag performance, at least in the 1990s, for example, as in the case of the New York–based performer Candis Cayne, unusual in the 1990s and early 2000s among her peers because of her transgender status, which is different from the contemporary experience of Puerto Rican women such as Monica Beverly Hillz, Carmen Carrera, and Lila Star.[31] Perhaps in her celebration of her body, Lady Catiria was more like the renowned New York City transgender personality, model, and performance artist Amanda Lepore, with the difference that Lepore is better known as an image (in fact, as a work of art) or hostess and not as a cabaret entertainer (Lepore and Flannery 2017).

Breaking the Silence:
The Miss Continental Pageant (1995–96) and HIV/AIDS

I never heard Lady Catiria speak the many times I saw her perform at La Escuelita; I also never had the chance to speak to her in private. Lady Catiria did speak in public at least twice, when she competed in the Miss Continental Plus competition in 1993 and in the Miss Continental pageant in

1995 (Fleming 1995); the second speech is currently available on YouTube (bxboi161 2009), as well as in VHS and DVD format from the Continental Pageantry Systems.[32] In her 1995 speech, Lady Catiria highlighted staying off drugs as one of her greatest achievements, to wild audience applause, which nearly brought her to tears; this confessional declaration humanized her and created a counterpoint to her flawless, self-assured visual look. When she turned in her crown in 1996, having completed her year as beauty queen, she presented a previously recorded message in which she disclosed her seropositive status; she also thanked the drag performer John LaFleur "for teaching me how to succeed in this business as well as being such a great friend to me," and also thanked Raúl de la Paz (the original owner of La Escuelita), many additional friends and performers such as Jeannette Alexander and Jeannette Valentino, and "my lover, husband, and friend Jimmy, for sticking it out with me."[33]

The only journalistic article that extensively quotes Lady Catiria is by Donald Suggs (1999) and appeared in *POZ*, a magazine and website that "serves the community of people living with and those affected by HIV/AIDS with daily news, treatment updates, personal profiles, [and] investigative features."[34] In the two-hour tribute video released by La Nueva Escuelita, Lady Catiria is never portrayed speaking except to repeat a person's name during her birthday celebration. Yet awareness of the AIDS epidemic has now become part of Lady Catiria's legacy (Ortiz-Fonseca 2019); the opening of the video indicates that "All profits from the Lady Catiria video will go to directly to God's Love We Deliver," a New York City nonprofit organization that according to their website "cooks and home-delivers nutritious, medically tailored meals for people too sick to shop or cook for themselves," particularly persons with HIV/AIDS.

It is important to recognize that Lady Catiria's friends, family, coworkers, and Chicago audiences did hear her speak, and that individuals have been able to hear her for over two decades through the mediations of technology; that my experience was very particular, or perhaps common but in no way universal, as demonstrated through the testimonies of persons such as Bill Fleming (1995, 1996), who attended the Miss Continental pageant and wrote about Lady Catiria's participation. Lady Catiria's 1996 prerecorded speech on the impact of HIV/AIDS on her life was complemented with a tailored black dress with a rhinestone collar in the form of a red ribbon (the symbol of the international struggle against AIDS) that cost $1,800 (Suggs 1999). Lady Catiria also had her crown dyed red for the event. I am fascinated by this act, which was witnessed by two thousand spectators in Chicago, for while the event centered Lady Catiria's voice, it did so though technological mediation (similar to the departing queen's prerecorded speech in the Miss Universe Pageant) and permitted the star to do what she did best: move across the stage accompanied by music and dance but without pronouncing a single word.

In his article, Suggs quotes Lady Catiria at length, as she speaks about her experiences as a beauty queen, particularly all of the challenges she faced to lose thirty pounds in order to be able to compete in the Miss Continental pageant, and particularly about why she decided to publicly announce her health condition. The article is fascinating and offers interesting observations. Money is frequently discussed: how much Catiria spent preparing for the pageant; how much she paid for the dress she wore that night in 1996. In his news coverage of the impact of the Miss Continental pageant, José Germosén (2001) points out that pageants are one of the few spaces where transgender women who earn their living through lip-synching can overcome their poverty, as winning the contest brings about numerous sponsorships. Finally, drag and trans performers such as Angel Sheridan (n.d.), Candis Cayne (quoted in Germosén 2001), and Barbra Herr (Gomez 2009) have indicated that Lady Catiria was their mentor and friend; in the case of Cayne, it was Lady Catiria who encouraged her to participate in Miss Continental, which Cayne won in 2001. Meanwhile, Herr has identified Lady Catiria as her "gay mother" (Gomez 2009) and as her "trans mom and sister" (Herr 2016).

But, as Angel Sheridan astutely pointed out, Lady Catiria was many things to many people, and different things to each. For a performer who preferred silence over speaking for most of her career, it was precisely the severity of the AIDS crisis, and specifically how it impacted her personally, that led Lady Catiria to fully embrace a public speaking voice, as if subtly echoing the leading activist logo of the late 1980s popularized by the direct-action group ACT UP, "Silence = Death," or emulating the outspoken San Francisco-based Chicana transgender *ranchera* singer and AIDS activist Alberta Nevaerez, better known as Teresita la Campesina (Roque-Ramírez 2005, 2008).[35] For Lady Catiria, recognition and honesty had to do with love and with acknowledging those who surrounded her. As she stated in 1996 in Chicago, "Thank you for teaching me that it isn't how many times we fall, it is how many times we get up that's important. I then thought I was dying of AIDS but I now realize, I'm not dying of AIDS, I'm living with AIDS because you loved me" (That's Entertainment 2018). For Lady Catiria, the politics of love became the politics of survival.

Knowing Barbra Herr

The tension between the (vocal) silence of Lady Catiria's mid-1990s La Escuelita performances and her articulate speaking at the Miss Continental pageant is perhaps unique; other trans Puerto Rican performers have negotiated these spaces differently. Lady Catiria's "trans daughter" Barbra Herr (Barbara Hernández) is another Puerto Rican transloca performer who has transformed her body as part of her trans embodiment.[36] Unlike Lady Catiria, however, Herr's performances are marked by her almost nonstop speech, whether as part of her drag cabaret, for example at Zal Zi Puedes Mini Bar in San Juan or at various locations in New York City; in her documentary *Portrait of a Lady: Story of Barbra Herr* (Gomez 2009) and in her segment in Alberto Ferreras's *Habla Men* (HBO Latino, 2014); in her cabaret/theater piece titled *I'm Still Herr* (2014, 2016); in her one-woman testimonial theatrical show *Trans-mission* (2017); in her performance in Ferreras's short film *Lesson #6* (2017), in which she appeared with the New York–based Puerto Rican drag performer Giovanka De Medici; in her cabaret *Under Construction* (2018); in Nate and Rob Bailey-Millado's documentary *Herr* (in production); or as part of her virtual or online presence on Facebook, where she assiduously posts about everything she thinks and does. In addition, Herr has performed in a variety of plays, including Charles Rice-González's *Los Nutcrackers: A Christmas Carajo* at the Bronx Academy of Arts and Dance (BAAD!).[37] While Barbra Herr shares Lady Catiria's aura and status as a diva, she does not share the impenetrable, outsider quality that Lady Catiria willingly cultivated through her silence, at least in New York City; Herr speaks with the audience, tells stories, and makes jokes, in addition to doing lip-synch numbers in English and Spanish.

Born to Puerto Rican immigrant parents in the Bronx in 1955, Barbra Herr began her artistic career in 1973 as a drag queen in Puerto Rico and New York, appearing with the name Bobby Herr.[38] She performed at bars and clubs such as Bachelor in Santurce and Stars, which was located in the penthouse of the Atlantic Beach Hotel in the Condado, a tourist area in San Juan; at La Escuelita in Times Square and The Monster in Greenwich Village in Manhattan; and at Friend's Tavern in Jackson Heights, Queens.[39] In the 1970s and 1980s, she collaborated extensively in Puerto Rico with the leading drag performer Antonio Pantojas, appearing on television and stage, and also toured as part of a traveling El Cotorrito revue. She also lived in the Dominican Republic for two years. In 1990 (when she was thirty-five), she moved back to New York City, feeling that Puerto Rico was not a welcoming place for her to transition to living as a woman, which included starting to take female hormones. In the 2000s, she went on to participate in pageants, winning the Miss Continental Elite title in Chicago in 2005.[40]

Julio Gomez's 2009 documentary *Portrait of a Lady: Story of Barbra Herr* gives us extensive access to Herr's personal narrative, cabaret performances, and lip-synch numbers; it is freely available on Vimeo and YouTube. The film, which started as the director's school assignment and then became a feature-length piece, opens with clips from a 2005 show at a gay bar in Chelsea, a New York City neighborhood that in the 1990s and early 2000s became a trendy queer hub. In this scene, Herr is extremely at ease and very engaging, sitting on a stool with her bare legs crossed in front of a grid of light panels that display different colors as she casually addresses the receptive audience. Herr speaks with confidence and establishes great rapport. She sports beautiful makeup and a fairly revealing, custom-made red gown with deep cleavage and an open back. Her flattering dress is made of very light material and twirls dramatically when she dances on the small raised stage. The skirt is cut short in front and is much longer in the back, and her sleeves drape dramatically. Her dark blond hair, which is held back, cascades onto her shoulders and flows gracefully when she dances. Herr is also wearing open, high-heel shoes with thin silver straps and has painted toenails; she also has tasteful dangling silver earrings and wears a gold chain with a small pendant around her neck, which comes down in a V. Herr looks very youthful for her age: she indicates during her performance that she is fifty years old, and jokes that she needs reading glasses for small print and that anal sex is not as pleasurable as it was in the past. In Herr's self-presentation, there is a marked continuity with Lady Catiria in terms of privileging beauty and the body and of being stylish but also sexy, which is one of the topics Herr discusses in her show; specifically, Herr indicates her disapproval of young drag and trans performers who do not put much effort into dressing elegantly for their audiences.

In *Portrait of a Lady*, Herr speaks openly about her early experiences as an effeminate boy growing up in the Bronx; her move to Puerto Rico as a teenager; her mother's death in 1973, when Herr was seventeen years old, the same year Herr started to perform in drag; her early career, in which she was typecast as an actor and could only get parts in plays such as *The Kiss of the Spider Woman* and *La Cage aux Folles*; and her subsequent work in television, cabarets, and hotels. She also highlights that she is a college graduate, having studied at the University of Puerto Rico; as she says during her Chelsea cabaret performance, "You know, I'm a Puerto Rican girl from the Bronx but I'm very educated. I do have a BA in Social Sciences so please don't try it. OK, I'm not an idiot." The documentary also includes archival footage from Herr's 1995 appearance on the major television network talk show *Sally*, hosted by Sally Jessy Raphael on NBC, where Herr was featured with six additional trans women in an episode titled "He's So Beautiful, He Became a Girl."[41] In her 2005 and 2007 interviews with Gomez, Herr indicates that (at the time) she had no interest in gender-reassignment surgery. She also outlines multiple health issues and difficult relationships with men marked by violence, and expresses her appreciation for other drag queens and trans women who have helped her develop her career or who served as inspirations, such as John LaFleur, Jeannette Alexander, Jeannette Valentino, Tiny Showbiz, Amazing Grace, Dorian Corey, Chaka Savalas, and many of the contestants in the Miss Continental pageant systems.[42] *Portrait of a Lady* also includes several of Herr's well-executed and very engaging lip-synch performances. Similar to Lady Catiria, Herr performs songs mostly in English but also in Spanish; she appears lip-synching Shirley Bassey's "Diamonds Are Forever" and "Nobody Does It Like Me"; Jennifer Hudson's "One Night Only" from the *Dreamgirls* motion picture deluxe edition soundtrack; Beyoncé's "Listen"; Bette Midler's "Fever" from the *Bette Midler Sings the Peggy Lee Songbook* album; La Lupe's "Amor Gitano"; Barbra Streisand's "Hideaway"; and Yolandita Monge's "Cuando te toque llorar." *Portrait of a Lady* is an extremely valuable archive of Herr's lip-synch performances.

In the mid-2010s, Barbra Herr also starred in a cabaret/theater piece titled *I'm Still Herr* (2014, 2016), which was directed by Luis Caballero.[43] The title plays with the double valence of her stage name as a homophone of the female third-person object pronoun and possessive adjective "her," which can also sound like the adverb "here" (indicating location), to tell the story of how Bobby (now Barbara) Hernández became who she is. In fact, "Herr" is a contraction of her last name and an affirmation of paternal legacy: it indicates "I am still here," as a testament to survival and resilience; "I am still her," an affirmation of gender; and "I am still Hernández," as the rightful claim to family ties.[44]

Herr's performance was structured around various songs interpreted with her own voice. However, Herr does not disavow lip-synch altogether. For example, in Alberto Ferreras's short film *Lesson #6*, Herr portrays a glamorous yet frustrated and angry queer nightlife performer who offers a passionate defense of her art; the character's speech mostly coincides with Herr's own attitudes. As she states,

> Art is getting up on a stage at two in the morning in front of two hundred drunks and not getting a beer bottle thrown at your head. Art is lip-synching to a song that people have heard a trillion-and-one times and yet making it sound fresh and new, so someone will come up to you and say, "You know, tonight I finally understood what Billie Holiday was really singing about." Art is putting up with hecklers and all kinds of homophobic assholes who are both gay and straight, by the way, every single night of the week and yet come up in here with a smile on your face to bring magic to a shit-hole like this one. That is motherfucking art! (Ferreras 2017)

In this impassioned yet humorous declaration, "art" becomes *technē*, a performative skill of survival, and lip-synch becomes a truth-granting tool that sways and moves audiences late in the night, even if it is in a less-than-ideal venue ("a shithole like this one") full of "hecklers and all kinds of homophobic assholes who are both gay and straight"; it serves as a window into the past, or as a key to the artistic sublime, granting access to the true meaning of past diva's performances.

Testimony, Advocacy, and Transparency in Trans-mission *(2017)*

Barbra Herr's commitment to telling her story and raising awareness is represented well in her 2017 autobiographical solo performance *Trans-mission.*[45] At slightly over fifty minutes long, the testimonial piece is mostly in English but includes diverse phrases in Spanish that highlight the bilingual nature of the protagonist's life and of her relationships with her family and friends. The performance includes no major musical or dance numbers, and features Herr simply yet elegantly dressed in an over-sized, long-sleeved, buttoned white blouse with triangular collar, black leggings, black flats, and showy earrings (at least in 2017), her medium-length blond hair held back in a small ponytail. The plot of *Trans-mission* centers on Herr's life experiences at age sixty-one, namely how after per-forming for over forty years and living as a woman for twenty-five, she was getting ready for her sex-reassignment surgery in June 2017, taking advan-tage of the medical access that she received as an out-of-work actor under

Fig. 21. Barbra Herr in *Trans-mission*. Teatro Círculo, New York, 2017. Photo by Peter Eric.

Medicaid, specifically under the Patient Protection and Affordable Care Act (Obamacare) and the laws put in place by Governor Andrew Cuomo of the State of New York, which allowed her access to diverse required health services for transgender persons, including hormone treatment, counseling, and surgery. This historic moment competed with the threats to eliminate these health benefits under the administration of President Donald Trump, which would jeopardize Herr's plans for surgery.

How is the life of persons who do not identify with the sex or gender they were assigned at birth? What challenges do they face with their family, romantic partners, the health system, and with broader society? What clandestine substances (namely black-market hormones and silicone injections) do they use and to what unintended medical dangers do they expose themselves in their search to transform their bodies? And what is the diasporic and Puerto Rican particularity of this experience for a child born in the Bronx in the mid-1950s, who grew up between the Caribbean and the United States speaking English and Spanish and who is recognized for her long artistic career?

Trans-mission is structured as a series of meetings with different psychiatrists to whom Barbra tells her story, sometimes due to emotional problems, at other times to receive the required consent to receive surgery. She begins with Dr. Fishberger, a grumpy adviser whom she saw in 1996 due to panic attacks. She then goes on to describe how in 2000 she saw Dr. Schmitt, a "tall, burly man with a thick German accent," with whom she discusses issues of gender and sexual identity, which lead to funny misunderstandings; for example, he tells her "Let your mind wander" and she asks, "Vanda?," thinking he is referring to another person or to an unknown action. The longest relationship is with Dr. Matthews, a petite blonde woman from the Midwest who saw Herr before she moved on to a final doctor to sign her surgery consent forms. Faced by this last doctor's insistent questioning, she affirms that she identifies as a heterosexual woman who wishes to synchronize her body with her identity and that of course she pees sitting down. The doctors dialogue with Barbra through voice-over recordings; as the program indicates, these are the voices of Cassandra Douglas, Michael Gobberts, and Ranardo-Domeico Grays.

As part of these consultations, Herr tells us anecdotes of her childhood and adulthood, sometimes in chronological order, others not. The therapeutic confession structure is not very innovative at the theatrical level but provides an effective frame for the actress' narration. While Herr moves between the two chairs and the black leather sofa on stage, we imagine those missing authority figures who hold her future in their hands. One anecdote involves a childhood incident when, at age five or six, the young child (perceived as male) put on her mother's wedding dress and fell asleep, receiving a substantial beating when her mother found her later on. She also tells us about the first time she fell in love as a ten-year-old with a boy called Anthony Correa who studied with her at the St. Anselm School in the South Bronx, and then narrates a rather violent episode that took place in 1970 when she was fourteen years old in the locker room of DeWitt Clinton High School, also in the Bronx. On this occasion she was nearly raped by four older boys who grabbed her in the bathroom after their physical education class. As a result, the young protagonist, a delicate, effeminate boy, missed school for ninety days for fear of a repeat incident, thinking that he could not tell anyone what had occurred.

Shortly thereafter, we learn that her family moved to Puerto Rico; here Barbra tells us the tender story of her relationship in 1973 with a white, blond, blue eyed adolescent whom she tutored in English and with whom she made out (or at least kissed) behind her mother's back. "¡Estoy aquí por si necesitan algo!" (I am here in case you need anything!) Barbra says, imitating her mother to the audience's great delight; this first kiss caused a panic attack and she ran away. When she saw him five years later during a drag presentation in San Juan, her former friend rejected her and left without speaking a word. Herr also describes how she returned to New York City in 1973, shortly after her mother's death from a stroke and after graduating from high school, in order to go to beauty school, which led to her first relationship with Leo, another beauty school student who did not know how to appreciate the woman Barbra felt she had inside. In fact, the performer identifies gay men's transphobia as one of the main challenges that has marked her, together with her desire that people stop seeing her as aberrant or monstrous.

One of the main themes of *Trans-mission* is domestic violence, particularly in relationships with unstable and abusive men. Herr makes a long list: Johnny Lee, a lying, drug-using kickboxer who left her for another woman; the romantic Juan Carlos (an angel in comparison with the rest), who later tells her that he named his daughter Barbara in her honor; and a Pentecostal with many personal issues. A hypnosis regression (the only invented plot element, according to the actress) leads her to remember a particularly traumatic relationship marked by the violence of her partner Eddie, who used drugs and alcohol and who made a death threat, an event that Herr successfully recreates on stage; this episode left her hospitalized due to a later suicide attempt by Klonopin overdose.

The best-achieved and most powerful part of *Trans-mission* is the extraordinary final monologue, in which the actress goes over the parts of her body, speaking about her self-knowledge, her political struggles, her desire to simply be able to live her life and accomplish her mission, that is to say, her *trans-mission*, a communicative and life act that has to do with political activism and with personal and social transformation. The monologue, more than simple storytelling, becomes a gesture of truth-telling or parrhesia (Foucault 2001; Osorio 2017) that aspires to transform listeners' opinions through grounded knowledge, or what I have referred to throughout this book as "theory in the flesh," what Gloria Anzaldúa (2002) also refers to as *autohistoria-teoría*, or self-history-theory (Pitts 2016). In this case, Herr knows what she is talking about and has reflected critically about it, because it is her body that is in question and it is center stage. As Barbra states,

So this is my face (*bringing her hands up to her face*) and this is my body. These are my wrinkles (*touching the sides of her cheeks and mouth with her two index fingers and drawing her fingers down*) and this is my pale skin. These are my hands (*she extends her hands in front of her and looks at them, then raises them*) and they are older than I remember them. And they have held the heads of dying friends in their hospital beds (*slightly melodramatic music begins*). And this is my belly (*she crosses her hands and places them on top of her stomach*), and it ingests pill after pill of estrogen in order to maintain myself the epitome of femininity. And these are my breasts (*as she says this, she brings up her hands and passes them over her chest in a downward motion*), and they are augmented. And this is my body, and it is worn and ravaged but I'm learning to love the lines and the rolls and the bigness and the masculine and the feminine of it. And I color my hair and keep it short. And I wear makeup but I refuse Botox. And what I do with my body is for me (*becoming more intense*) and whether that pleases or disgusts you has nothing to do with who I am. And this is my voice. It is deep. And it resonates. And it guffaws. And it makes noise. And it has screamed for help (*raising her voice*) and sung out in passion. And it has whispered in prayer (*switching to a low voice*) and made a quiet noise of joy and celebration. I sound this way and it calls true to who I was by sounding true to who I am. I am Trans gender and this is what I look like at sixty-one years on this planet. This is my face. This is my body. This is not who I am. This is merely where I have been. And it tells the story of a million survivors who live and who I still carry. I no longer need to make myself up in order to assimilate for I am a creation divine that the universe has created and like all of you, I have travelled through it the best way I know how. Yet please know that you cannot make up laws in order to keep me quiet, simply because you recognize me as one outside of your tribe. You cannot keep me out of your schools or your bath-rooms or your churches or your voting booths or your buildings or anywhere simply because of who I am. And because I carry my his-tory here, in my heart space, and because you do as well, we must remember that we are responsible for one another. This is my face, and it is the reflection of how I have lived. And this is my body. And it is the manifestation of a history that deserves to be seen and heard without malice and without judgement. What I am is not a choice. It is a gift! So I do not ask you to approve what I have done. No. I simply ask you to honor who I am becoming as I will always do for you. And this, my friends, is my Trans-mission.

This passionate monologue articulates a theory of transloca embodiment that demands recognition, whether self-acceptance or by others, commu-nally, as a gesture of radical inclusion. It challenges mainstream biases, inviting prejudiced persons to question and transform their attitudes. Part of Herr's effectiveness resides in her repetition of several phrases, such as "This is my face" and "This is my body," almost as a refrain, and in the immediate connection the audience makes with the actual body before us. Herr masterfully employs rhetorical strategies similar to those of Sylvia Rivera (discussed in chapter 3) invoking the "I" and the collective "you" to address and engage the audience as a way to generate compassion and solidarity in the face of social injustice.

Herr has paid a high price for all of these changes, which, as she indi-cated at the very beginning of the performance, included taking dangerous clandestine hormones bought from a "Dirty Bob" in a bar and her femini-zation surgeries in Guadalajara, Mexico, in a context in which many trans subjects engage in transnational cosmetic-surgery-related travel (Aizura 2018); she is no longer as young as she once was, and her emphasis on her age and senior status resonates with other Puerto Rican trans testimonies, whether it is that of Lizza Fernanda (Díaz 2012a, 2012b) or that of Soraya (Bárbara Santiago Solla) in the documentary *Mala Mala* (2014) or in Sora-ya's memoir *Hecha a mano* (2014).[46] Barbra Herr's strategy of fragmenting her body and presenting it part by part resembles the extraordinary monologue by La Agrado alluded to earlier, from Almodóvar's 1999 film *Todo sobre mi madre*; Herr's impassioned version is extremely personal and sincere.

Trans-mission can be thought of productively in relation to the activist and community work of El/La para Translatinas, a transgender Latinx project in the San Francisco Mission District, particularly regarding how El/La challenges narratives of victimization and highlights trans Latinx empowerment, as described by the trans activist Alexandra Rodríguez de Ruiz in conversation with scholar and activist Marcia Ochoa (Galarte 2020; Rodríguez de Ruiz and Ochoa 2016, 164), as well as in relation to the national advocacy work of the TransLatin@ Coalition (TransLatin@ Coalition, Salcedo, and Padrón 2013) and of the Butterflies Trans Foundation in Puerto Rico (La Fountain-Stokes 2018a; Santini and Sickles 2014). While El/La's, the TransLatin@ Coalition's, and the Butterflies Trans Foundation's work is collective, they share with Herr a commitment to reconceptualizing dominant narratives and providing tools for social change. Herr's performance piece can also be seen in relation to the Latin American conceptualizations of *travesti* articulated by Marlene Wayar (2019, 17) and fellow trans activists and artists such as Claudia Rodríguez and Susy Shock in *Travesti: Una teoría lo suficientemente buena*, namely as a questioning of "ser mismidad y nostredad" (to be oneself and a 'collective we' marked by alterity, using the neologism *nostredad*, or "us/otherness") that challenges social exclusion and the medical and psychiatric realms' interest and control over the trans body, also hinting toward the usefulness of *monstruosiarse*, or becoming monster, as a strategy of resistance (Pierce 2020).

I began this chapter by appealing to outdated yet very popular notions of the feminine as mystical sublime, specifically those invoked by the nineteenth-century French writer and poet Charles Baudelaire, as a way to frame some female trans performers' radical transformation of self as an artistic practice that is greatly celebrated by audiences. The careful exploration of Lady Catiria's and Barbra Herr's lives and performances demonstrates the centrality of the body but also its profound interplay with voice and with the politics of everyday life as well as with pressing social issues. Both performers help us to understand and further expand our conceptualizations of Puerto Rican translocas and of transloca performance. Both live and speak through the body in multiple ways.

Epilogue

The exhaustion and/or limitations of widely circulating English-language terms such as "gay," "queer," and "trans," which have acquired certain global homo- and transnormative acceptance, have led many artists, activists, and scholars to explore, recuperate, and/or invent numerous variants, such as *cuir*, "faggots," *folles*, *maricas*, "translocas," and *travesti* (Domínguez Ruvalcaba 2016; Falconí Trávez 2018; Wayar 2019), particularly as a way to resist assimilation. In "We the Enemy . . . ," the SPIT! (Sodomites, Perverts, Inverts Together!) collective bravely affirms,

> We the sodomites, the perverts, the inverts, the faggots, the deviants, the queers, the keepers of spoiled identities, the tribadists, the promiscuous, the popper sniffing fist fuckers, the bottoms and the tops, the vers, the queens and the fairies, the nellies, the nancies and the fannies, the lady boys, the butch lesbians, the leather angels, the dykes, the daddies and the bulldaggers, the crossdressers and the drag queens, the auntie men, the Kikis, the trannies, the celesbians, the clones, the dykes on bikes, the sissies . . . the pansies, the go-go boys, the hustlers, the trades . . . the drag kings, the Tammies, the he-shes, the fishy girls, the cunts . . . the momma's boys, the hot messes, the batty bois, the degenerates . . . are and will always be the enemy. (SPIT! 2017, 3)

Translocas fit right in among these nonconformists identified by SPIT! as "the enemy" in their page-long, countercultural manifesto, which complements the "Faggot Manifesto" (SPIT! 2017, 5) I quoted in chapter 1. Translocas expand this "imagined community" with an explicitly Caribbean or Caribglobal, Spanish-language and Spanglish-inflected, diasporic, and racialized vision that is intrinsically counterhegemonic. As such, translocas, too, "are and will always be the enemy."

In the first chapter of this book I mapped out the critical debates around *loca* in queer and feminist studies, stressing the tensions the term generates and its mediated usages. I then focused on unique case studies, many times recurring to archival technology as much as to repertoires, archives of feeling and desire, and personal recollections, to illustrate, expand, and challenge our understanding of the racial, gender, sexual, economic, and social politics (and necropolitics) of Puerto Rican transloca performance, which can be seen as an identity, a pose, a gesture, a strategy, a reference, or a problem. In *Translocas*, I have documented the lives and cultural production of individuals who have not always been recognized as central to queer or Puerto Rican or Latin American or Latinx projects, and engaged these lives and representations in myriad ways: whether as a spectator of a live performance, of a television program or film, or through the recordings of performances that have allowed me to describe, transcribe, and analyze in a detailed way. I have also posited transloca ethics and pedagogies, strategies of resistance, generational commonalities, and myriad roadblocks, and anticipated objections and potential disagreements. I write about controversial people who do controversial things, as the late 2019 debate about Freddie Mercado's performance *En esta vida de reciclar me trans-formo* demonstrates.

One way of thinking of *Translocas* is as an experimental assemblage; a gathering of voices; an iteration of Caribglobal rasanblaj; a raucous party whose guests include the living and the dead; a simultaneous act of celebration and of mourning; a rite of remembrance for those who have passed or been murdered, whether on the streets of San Juan, Caguas, Cayey, or New York, or at Pulse Orlando on June 12, 2016, for translocas who died as they danced the night away (Kornhaber 2016; La Fountain-Stokes 2018b, 284–92; 2018c; J. M. Rodríguez 2016; Torres 2016). This book can also be thought of as a bridge that marks the work of the body and of its flesh (Moraga and Anzaldúa 1983), its embodied theory and incorporated knowledge, as much as of transatlantic or transoceanic crossings. Sylvia Rivera, Antonio Pantojas, Walter Mercado, Mario Montez, Fausto Fernós, Nina Flowers, Jorge Steven López Mercado, Kevin Fret, Villano Antillano, Venus Xtravaganza and the other members of the House of Xtravaganza, Erika Lopez, Holly Woodlawn, Monica Beverly Hillz, Freddie Mercado, Javier Cardona, Marcus Kuiland-Nazario,

Manuel Ramos Otero, Jorge B. Merced, Lady Catiria, Barbra Herr, and all of the queens and queers and trans women and men documented in *Paris Is Burning*, *The Salt Mines*, *The Transformation*, *La aguja* / *The Needle*, and *Mala Mala* are simply some examples of different possibilities, life experiences, extraordinary achievements, and dramatic tragedies. My engagement with these figures has been marked by extensive contact and collaborations with other performers, such as Arthur Avilés, Eduardo Alegría, Lizza Fernanda (Luis Felipe Díaz), Mickey Negrón, Lío Villahermosa, Awilda Rodríguez Lora, and Macha Colón, and with filmmakers such as Antonio Santini, Dan Sickles, José Correa Vigier, and Carmen Oquendo-Villar. This alternate list is reflected in additional journalistic and scholarly publications (La Fountain-Stokes 2007a, 2009, 2018a, 2018b), as well as in forthcoming book chapters on Fernós and on Sylvia Rivera. My work is also indebted to honorary transloca scholars such as Arnaldo Cruz-Malavé, Rubén Ríos Ávila, Yolanda Martínez-San Miguel, Licia Fiol-Matta, Frances Negrón-Muntaner, José Quiroga, and Jossianna Arroyo, who have frequently reappeared throughout these pages, and aspires to engage more in the future with the writings of Puerto Rican/Latinx transloca chroniclers and theorists such as Manuel Clavell Carrasquillo, Jhoni Jackson, and Jaime Géliga Quiñones.

My analysis has been marked by limitations and constraints, such as my inability to include a more substantive discussion of other female drag and trans performers, for example Johnny Rodríguez, Ruddys Martínez, Alex Soto, Gilo Rosa, Félix Chevremont, Renny Williams, Mirkala Crystal, Putanesca (José A. Guzmán Colón), and Juanita More, and younger performers such as April Carrión, Warhola Pop, Zahara Montiere, Rochelle Mon Chéri, Adi Love, Queen Bee Ho (Queen Bee), Alyssa Hunter, Kriss Du Cecile (with her parodic persona Wanda VazqueT), Amalara Sofía, Ubi Aaron, Tacha Rola, Ana Macho, Misandra Bolac, Machín González, Aldrin M. Cañals, JanpiStar, the many Puerto Rican participants of *RuPaul's Drag Race*, such as Aja, Alexis Mateo (who celebrated the astrologer Walter Mercado in episode 5 of season 5 of *RuPaul's Drag Race All Stars* first broadcast on July 3, 2020, by impersonating him for the "Snatch Game of Love" challenge), Cynthia Lee Fontaine, Vanessa Vanjie Mateo (who is Alexis Mateo's drag daughter), and Yara Sofía, or drag kings and male trans performers such as Chris Griandher, Dingo Konpé, Pó Rodil, and Samy Figaredo (Samy Nour Younes); I hope others will also take up this charge.[1] I have also not fully fleshed out my own embodiment and critical practice as a scholar and performer (or perhaps I have done it in excess), and while Lola von Miramar made some early appearances, she has not been as fully present as she could have been.

Puerto Rican transloca performance negotiates contradictions and envisions new possibilities: it is a practice of critical imagining and not an attempt to assuage all concerns. Marked by hybridity, bilingualism, displacement, prejudice, exclusion, and coloniality, its politics are complex, contextual, and changing. The artists and activists that I have focused on illustrate these tensions and divergences. They are striking in their heterogeneity but also in the overlap of elements such as attention to notable women such as Felisa Rincón de Gautier or divas including Lola Flores, María Montez, Myrta Silva, Sylvia Rexach, Toña la Negra, Sarita Montiel, Iris Chacón, La Lupe, Ednita Nazario, Yolandita Monge, Bette Midler, Eartha Kitt, Madonna, Beyoncé, Britney Spears, and Lady Gaga; in their engagement with (tropi)camp but also *cursi* aesthetics, mysticism, and religion; the invocation of crucial referents such as Antonio Pantojas and Walter Mercado; of musical genres such as the bolero but also reggaeton and trap; and in their investment in community building and in transformational notions of queer Puerto Ricanness and Latinidad in a context marked by colonial relations, racial strife, multilingualism, and economic precarity. Some lip-synch; some dance; some recite long monologues; some give rousing speeches at public events, appear on television and film, or make cooking videos shown on YouTube when not recording podcasts; some paint and make sculptures; and some become monsters or appear nearly naked and radically transform their bodies to match their sense of self. Many disconcert and disorient, while others mostly entertain.

Some questions remain. What multiple new directions will Puerto Rican and Latinx transloca performance take given new challenges and political realities in the Caribbean archipelago and the United States, the constant (almost interminable) appearance of new performers and media platforms, the shifts in technology, the new spaces of neoliberal commercialization and encounter such as RuPaul's DragCon, the growing impoverishment of Puerto Ricans and the depopulation of the archipelago (Negrón-Muntaner 2018), imminent ecological threats, the unsolved problem of violence, particularly against trans women, the persistence and increase of additional homophobic and transphobic discourses and actions, and health crises such as COVID-19, which has led performers to have to shift away from traditional venues and to livestream performances on Instagram and Facebook, accepting tips via ATH Móvil, PayPal, Cash App, and Venmo (Alfaro Pérez 2020)? Is there a Puerto Rican specificity to "translocas"? Will younger translocas share much with the artists I have privileged, or will we be dismissed for not being political in the right way, devoured by the young who are uninterested in the struggles of the past? Or perhaps inspired and transformed, for example by the commitment to dragtivism and the collective spirit embodied by Ana Macho (Bryan Karhu Castro Vega), Misandra Bolac (I. Unanue), and Machín González of the Haus of Vanguardia (Absurdo PR 2019; Jackson 2020b; M. Rodríguez 2019; Vélez 2019a, 2019b)? What is the relationship of trans-feminisms to translocas? How will transloca myths such as Walter Mercado continue to reappear and reincarnate or be transformed? Is transloca performance a useful concept to understand *perreo combativo* (combative *perreo*, or twerking) and the actions of the "queer, trans, and non-binary youth, [that] used *perreo*, reggaeton's dance style, to create a sensuous and liberated communal space" (Dávila and LeBrón 2019) during the protests against Governor Ricardo Rosselló Nevares in Puerto Rico, ultimately bringing him down in the summer of 2019? What would happen if we attempted a broader Caribbean, Latin American, Latinx, Caribglobal, or global South approach? What does the future hold in store for Lola von Miramar? Inquiring, radical, antiracist, and politically committed minds want to know.

Notes

Introduction

1. While etymologically distinct, there are similarities between the English-language term "travesty" and the Spanish terms *travesti* and *travestismo*. According to the Merriam-Webster dictionary, "travesty" refers to "a debased, distorted, or grossly inferior imitation; a burlesque translation or literary or artistic imitation usually grotesquely incongruous in style, treatment, or subject matter" (https://www.merriam-webster.com/dictionary/travesty). This meaning is similar to the second definition of *travestismo* in the *Diccionario de la lengua española* of the Spanish Royal Academy (RAE): "Práctica consistente en la ocultación de la verdadera apariencia de alguien o algo" (http://dle.rae.es/), which highlights hiding or distorting the truth.

2. See Campuzano 2008, 2009, 2013; Menstrual 2012; Pelúcio 2009.

3. As Santos-Febres (2005, 129) writes, "El travestismo caribeño es una treta de supervivencia que no ha sido muy nombrada en las literaturas ni artes de estas tierras." Also see King 2014, 20–62.

4. Haggerty 2000 includes several useful articles on terms used to refer to effeminate homosexuals in the English language such as "faggot," "fairy," "molly," and "queen." For historical perspectives on "fairy," see Chauncey 1994. On *bicha, bichas loucas*, and *viado* in Brazil, see Kulick 1998, 40; Lopes 2002, 89–120; Trevisan 2000, 139. On *folle* as a stigmatized and radical homosexual term in French, see the important and extensive scholarship of Le Talec 2008, 2009. On *massisi*, see Braziel 2008. On "batty bwoys," "battymen," and "buller men," see Crichlow 2004 and King 2014. On *maricas, maricones, mariquitas*, and *mariposas*, see García and Alonso 2001; Paz Pérez 1998a, 1998b; Rodríguez González 2008. On Puerto Rican *patos* and Jewish American *feygelekh*, see La Fountain-Stokes 2007a.

5. All translations not otherwise attributed are my own. Lorca was murdered by fascists in Spain in 1936. On García Lorca in New York, see Stainton 1999. On the "Ode to Walt Whitman," see Walsh 1995.

6. On "tropicamp" see Cruz-Malavé 2015; Hinderer Cruz 2011; Oiticica 2011; Oiticica and Montez 2014; Suárez 2014. On Mario Montez, also see Gregg 2013; Martin 2013; Negrón-Muntaner 2004, 106–14; Suárez 2008, 2014, Willard 1971, 11–15.

7. On the history of Puerto Rican drag, see F. Jiménez 2004; Laureano 2007 and 2016, 31–90. *El Nuevo Día* 2013 focuses on the history of Bachelor, highlighting Anto-

nio Pantojas, Johnny Ray, Ruddys Martínez, Willie Negrón, Barbra Herr, and Alex Soto. Santiago Túa 2015 offers a journalistic account based on interviews with Víctor Alicea, Carlos Esteban Fonseca, and Manuel Clavell Carrasquillo. Clavell Carrasquillo 2013 offers documentation of Zal Zi Puedes, a key site for contemporary drag performance in San Juan. Jackson 2016 offers a survey of contemporary performers in Puerto Rico; also see Jackson 2020b and Martínez 2017. Castro Vega 2019 focuses on the alternative youth-led queer drag scene.

8. The globally distributed television reality competition *RuPaul's Drag Race* included twenty Puerto Ricans among its 140 contestants during its first twelve seasons (2009–2020). See Abad-Santos and Reid 2014; Hanna 2013; "Queens by Category" n.d. For analysis of the portrayal of Puerto Rican contestants, see Betancourt 2016; Edgar 2011; Goldmark 2015; Jenkins 2013, 2017; McIntyre and Riggs 2017; Strings and Bui 2014. Also see several of the articles in Daems 2014, particularly Anthony 2014; Kohlsdorf 2014; Marcel 2014; Mayora 2014; Morrison 2014; and Norris 2014. For discussion of the relationship between the key Puerto Rican drag/trans referent *Paris Is Burning* (1990) and *RuPaul's Drag Race*, see Campbell 2015; de Villiers 2012; Edgar 2012; Goldmark 2015; Levitt 2013; Rodriguez y Gibson 2014.

9. On drag and trans representation in Chile, see Richard 1994, 2004a, 119–42, 2004b, 2018. Analysis of Latin American and Caribbean, Latinx, and Spanish drag and trans performance, lives, and metaphors appears in Arroyo 2002, 2003a, 2003b; Balzer 2005; Barragán 1998; Calderón 2016; Campuzano 2008, 2009, 2013; Contardo 2018; Cornejo 2019; Domínguez Ruvalcaba 2007, 2016; Gutiérrez 2010, 115–26; King 2004–5, 2014; Kulick 1998; Kulick and Klein 2009; Lewis 2010; Lopes 2002, 67–120; M. López 2013, 2014; Muñoz 1999, 2020; Ochoa 2004, 2008, 2014; Peña 2011, 2013; Perkins 2017; Preciado 2011; Prieto Stambaugh 2000, 2014, 2019; Prieur 1998; Robles 2015; Román 1998, 2005; Sifuentes-Jáuregui 2002; Venegas 1998.

10. Wayar 2019 indicates that she steals the phrase *lo suficientemente buena* (good enough) from the psychoanalyst Donald W. Winnicott, who coined it in 1953 to refer to a "good enough mother" (17).

11. See Davis and López 2010; Falconí Trávez 2018, 10; López and Nogueira 2013; Viteri 2017. For a general discussion of "queer theory from the South and its epistemologies," see Lugo Bertrán 2018.

12. Also see Rivera-Servera 2017.

13. J. M. Rodríguez 2011, 2014 and Halberstam 2018 offer useful discussions of the opposition between the "negative turn" in trans and queer studies and more utopian conceptions, for example, those of Muñoz 2009. See Snorton and Haritaworn 2013 on the trans of color critique.

14. On Fernós, see Huppke 2010; La Fountain-Stokes, Torres, and Rivera-Servera 2011; Lewin 2009; Obejas 2000; Shapiro 2006. Fernós and Felion have been posting *Cooking with Drag Queens* videos on YouTube since 2010. Also see "Fausto Fernós" 2018 and Feast of Fun 2018a, 2018b.

15. In this book I will use the term "Latinx" following Alan Pelaez Lopez's 2018 usage and cognizant of the limitations indicated by Richard T. Rodríguez (2017).

16. Stryker and Currah 2016 and Gramling and Dutta 2016 raise these issues in a special issue of *TSQ: Transgender Studies Quarterly* (3, nos. 3–4) dedicated to "Translating Transgender." Also see the issue "Trans Studies en las Américas," *TSQ* 6, no. 2 (2019).

17. Pérez Firmat 1994 analyzes the links between translation and geographic displacement by tracing the meaning of the term *translatio* in Latin. Viteri 2014, citing J. M. Rodríguez's (2003) analysis of queer Latino language, highlights the limitations and at times impossibilities of translation in relation to Latin American and US Latinx sexualities and gender identities. Also see Manalansan 2003.

18. See Stryker and Whittle 2006; Stryker and Aizura 2013.

19. "Diasporican" is a neologism coined by performance poet Mariposa (María Teresa Fernández) in her "Ode to the Diasporican (pa' mi gente)." "AmeRícan" is the title of a 1985 book by poet Tato Laviera. "Artivism" is a portmanteau of art and activism; see Valentín-Escobar 2011. "On "transglocal" see Lawrence 2016.

20. On Antonio Pantojas, also see Abreu 2017; Del Valle 1995; Fiet 1995; Fundación Nacional 2014a; Irizarry 2019; Martínez Tabares 1997b; Millán Ferrer 1994; N. Rivera 2018; J. Rodríguez 2017; Rodríguez Guerra 2006; Rodríguez Martinó 1990; Rosado 1995; Santiago 2017a; Soberón Torchía 1999.

21. For critiques of the universalizing effects of "gay," "queer," and "transgender," see Cruz-Malavé and Manalansan 2002; Falconí Trávez 2018; Falconí Trávez, Castellanos, and Viteri 2014; Guzmán 2006; Meccia 2006; Valentine 2007; Vidal-Ortiz, Viteri, and Serrano Amaya 2014.

22. On Sylvia Rivera, see Bronski 2002; Cohen 2008; Duberman 1993; Dunlap 2002; Feinberg 1998; Fitzgerald and Marquez 2020; Galarte 2020; Gan 2007; Highleyman 2009; Marcus 1993; Mayora 2018; Musto 1995; Retzloff 2007; Reyes 2015; Rivera 1998, 2002, 2007; Shepard 2004a, 2004b, 2013; Stryker 2008; Wilchins 2002. For a discussion of Rivera's use of varied terms, see Sandeen 2014. The Sylvia Rivera Law Project in New York City carries her name; see https://srlp.org/about/who-was-sylvia-rivera/. I borrow the term "Intralatina" from Aparicio 2019.

23. STAR's mission was to provide housing for homeless trans youth of color, referred to at the time as "street queens." On the history of STAR, see Cohen 2008, 89–163. On Marsha P. Johnson, see Cohen 2008, 8–164; France 2017; Tourmaline and Wortzel 2018.

24. On Rivera at the National Portrait Gallery see Neese 2015. On Cristina Hayworth see La Fountain-Stokes 1999a; Méndez-Méndez 2015, 258; *El Nuevo Día* 2011; *Primera Hora* 2013; Ríos Ávila 1993; Rodríguez Guerra 2003. On Luis Carle, see Naughton 2017.

25. See Norris 2014 for a discussion of Carrera's and Hillz's appearances in *RuPaul's Drag Race*.

26. Newton 1979 and Rupp and Taylor 2003 highlight the negotiations between drag and trans experience. For the history of transsexuality and transgenderism in the United States see Halberstam 2018; Meyerowitz 2002; Stryker 2008. Foerster 2012 discusses how French laws banning drag performance in the late 1940s and 1950s led many entertainers to have sex-change operations in Morocco and then return to Paris as women, leading to the apogee of transsexual cabaret in France.

27. "In her own show, as Marga [Gomez] cross-dresses into Irma's glamorous, alluring, seemingly heterosexual Latina nightclub performer, she becomes, in her own words, a 'female impersonator'" (Sandoval-Sánchez and Sternbach 2001, 123). Also see Sandoval-Sánchez and Sternbach 1996. On drag kings, see Halberstam 1998. On the drag king scene in Puerto Rico, see Chacón O'Farrill 2017; Jackson 2018a; Martínez 2017.

28. On queer migration/queer diaspora studies, see Cantú 2009; Luibhéid and Cantú

2005; Patton and Sánchez-Eppler 2000; Wesling 2008. For a discussion of Latinx queer migrations and culture see La Fountain-Stokes 2009; Rivera-Servera 2012; J. M. Rodríguez 2003, 2014.

29. On *Mariposas en el andamio*, also see Bejel 2001, 196–210; Foster 2010.

30. Wesling posed her initial question at the American Comparative Literature Association's conference held in San Juan, Puerto Rico, in 2002. Also see Wesling 2012.

31. I wish to thank Alexander Ramsey and Aaron J. Stone for bringing Berman's essay to my attention, and Kerry White for highlighting C. Riley Snorton's work. Also see Appiah 1991; Bond 2018; Chen 2012, 136–37.

32. See, for example, Rizki 2019; Valencia 2019.

33. See *TSQ: Transgender Studies Quarterly* 1, nos. 1–2 (2014). Also see the special issue on "Trans-" of *WSQ: Women's Studies Quarterly* 36, nos. 3–4 (Fall–Winter 2008).

34. See Decena 2011; Lozada 2006; Peña 2013; Perlongher 2019; Robles 2015; Sívori 2004.

35. See Fiet 2007, 128. Zaragoza 1990 also describes gay drag queens wearing makeup replacing the traditional male heterosexual blackface performers, crediting Ricardo E. Alegría as a source. See Alegría 1949, 1954, 1956; Bofill Calero 2014; Fiet 2006; Harris 2001, 2003; Jiménez 2004, 252; King 2004–5; Martínez Sosa 1984; Ungerleider Kepler 2000; Zaragoza 1995.

36. On Lozada, see Jiménez 2004, 109–11.

37. For a previous elaboration on translocas, see La Fountain-Stokes 2011b.

38. See Alvarez 2014, 18 n. 3.

39. For a broad overview of Puerto Rican migration to the United States see Duany 2002, 2017. Also see essays by Vargas-Ramos and Duany in Birkenmaier 2021.

40. On contemporary Puerto Rican migration see Duany 2017; López Maldonado 2018; Meléndez and Vargas-Ramos 2017; Mora, Dávila, and Rodríguez 2018. The high concentration of Puerto Ricans in Orlando explains the profound impact of the Pulse massacre of 2016 on this community; see La Fountain-Stokes 2016b, 2018c.

41. Also see Bonilla 2018b; Bonilla and LeBrón 2019; Klein 2018; Morales 2019; Rebollo-Gil 2018.

42. See Aranda 2007; Duany 2002, 2011, 2017; Flores 1993, 2000, 2009; Sánchez González 2001.

43. On Puerto Rican translocality, see Cruz-Malavé 2002; Duany 2002, 2017; Grosfoguel 2003; Lao-Montes 1997; Martínez-San Miguel 2014; Santos-Febres 1993.

44. See Aranda 2007; Ayala and Bernabe 2007; Duany 2002, 2011, 2017; Grosfoguel 2003; Lao-Montes 1997; Negrón-Muntaner 2004, 2007; Santos-Febres 1993. Also see Erman 2018.

45. For discussion of Dominican translocality, see García-Peña 2016; Stevens 2019.

46. On the links between migration and Puerto Rican theater and performance, also see Martínez Tabares 1997a; Sandoval-Sánchez 1999, 2005; Stevens 2004.

47. On the regulation of Puerto Rican sexualities see Briggs 2002; Cruz-Malavé 2007b; Findlay 2014; Guzmán 2006; La Fountain-Stokes 1999a, 2009, 2018; La Fountain-Stokes and Martínez-San Miguel 2018; Negrón-Muntaner 2004; Sandoval-Sánchez 1997; Vidal-Ortiz 2011.

48. On queer Puerto Rican vernacular language, see La Fountain-Stokes 2007a; R. Ramírez 1999.

49. I am using "transloca" and its plural "translocas" as a noun. In Spanish, these terms can also be verb forms, specifically the informal command and the second-person singular present-tense conjugation of the verb *translocar* (to translocate), a verb that circulates in technical and scientific discourse, including physiology, biochemistry, and genetics.

50. These longings for a different, potential world also appear, for example, in Lío Villahermosa's performances of *bomba*, a traditional vernacular Afro–Puerto Rican dance, which he dances while wearing a skirt usually reserved for female performers; see Lladó Ortega 2019; Valecce 2018.

51. On Moura, also see *OLD* 2013.

52. Ortiz 1995 uses the culinary metaphor of the Cuban *ajiaco*, or stew (comparable to the American metaphor of the "melting pot"), as a way to envision cultural transformation. See Arroyo 2003b for a nuanced discussion of Ortiz. Sandoval-Sánchez and Sternbach 2001 propose "transculturation to the second power" (16–33), tracing how Latin American intellectuals and artists such as Ángel Rama, Nancy Morejón, and Silvia Spitta reconceptualized and updated Ortiz's term.

53. On Sarduy, see Lopes 2002, 72–73; Lugo Bertrán 2018, 101–4; Montero 1988, 1998; Ortíz 2007; Sifuentes-Jáuregui 2002, 119–50.

54. Also see Butler 1993, 2004.

55. I performed as "Dr. Lola Lolamento Mentosán de San Germán" out of drag (but wearing butterfly wings) as early as 2004 in my solo piece *Abolición del pato*. See La Fountain-Stokes 2015. For a discussion of inner (psychic, linguistic, affective) transvestism that does not entail actual cross-dressing, see Lopes's essay "E eu não sou um travesti também?" (2002, 67–88).

56. See Moraga and Anzaldúa (1981) 1983, 23; also see Moya 2002, 45–57. I also embrace autoethnography and anecdotal theory in my essay on gay shame (La Fountain-Stokes 2011a) and on performing *Abolición del pato* (La Fountain-Stokes 2015).

57. Also see Pitts, Ortega, and Medina 2020.

Chapter 1

1. See the homophobic diatribe against *afeminados (locas)* in the San Juan carnival of 1927: "Era digno de verse el espectáculo que ofrecían las nutridas comparsas de hombres-mujeres, que están dando, por un momento, la triste sensación de que éste es un País de hombres invertebrados, maricones por temperamento y por idiosincracia" (*J'accuse* 1927, 6). I thank Javier Almeyda-Loucil for identifying this source. For an example of a controversy regarding the use of the term *locas* in a Puerto Rican gay liberationist publication see L. M. Rodríguez 1974, who responds to complaints about the use of the following text in a classified ad: "*Se necesitan: hombres, mujeres, locas, cachaperas, dispuestas a luchas por su derecho a ser Gay*" (3, emphasis in the original).

2. On Perlongher, Lemebel, and Arenas, see Arboleda Ríos 2011; Blanco 2020; Blanco and Poblete 2010; Contardo 2018; Olivares 2013; Ortíz 2007; Palmeiro 2011; Ríos Ávila 1998, 2009, 2013. On Ricky Martin, see La Fountain-Stokes 1999a, 2018d; Negrón-Muntaner 2004; Quiroga 2000, 181–90.

3. Also see Jones 2009.

4. Numerous sources, including specialized dictionaries, scholarly publications, and literary works, offer definitions of the standard and vernacular usages of *loca* in Spanish. See Arenas 1992, 103–4; Fernández-Alemany and Sciolla 1999, 159; García and Alonso 2001, 108–9; González 2014; Guasch 1991, 89–108; Paz Pérez 1998a, 141; 1998b, 53, 55, 65, 68, 73, 126; Ramírez 1993, 117–21; Real Academia Española 2001, 2018; Rodríguez González 2008, 255–56; Sancho Ordóñez 2011, 101; Sívori 2004, 15, 77–98; Vaquero and Morales 2005, 464.

5. "Yo soy esta marica que escribe, la marica que tenía siete años en la Transición, la marica fusilada, encarcelada por los fascistas en la dictadura" (Vidarte 2010, 41).

6. Christian states that the *ataques de nervios* "include episodes of shouting and screaming; incoherence; and the loss of muscular control that can often lead to falling, experienced by a Latina" (2019, 71).

7. The lyrics of the song are by Perucho Torcat and the arrangement by Willie Colón. See https://fania.com/record/de-ti-depende/

8. On Sánchez González 2001, also see La Fountain-Stokes 2007b.

9. The reference is to Deleuze and Guattari 1986a, 20.

10. Sánchez González inverts the order of Pérez's phrase *sitio y lengua*. See Galarte 2011 for a trans Chicanx reflection.

11. Also see Costa 2014.

12. Lionel Cantú Jr. is best known for *The Sexuality of Migration: Border Crossings and Mexican Immigrant Men* (2009), which was edited by Nancy A. Naples and Salvador Vidal-Ortiz. Cantú died in 2002 due to complications from surgery; he was an assistant professor of sociology at the University of California, Santa Cruz (UCSC). The UCSC Cantú Queer Center was named in his honor in 2004 (West n.d.). I first met Cantú at the Latin American Studies Association (LASA) meeting in Miami in 2000. See "Lionel Cantu Jr." 2002 and West n.d. Also see "Editors' Preface" and "Editors' Introduction" in Cantú 2009.

13. This omission led to a heated exchange between Alvarez and myself at the LASA Gender and Sexuality Pre-conference Meeting held at the Women's Building in San Francisco in May 2012.

14. For more analysis of the Venezuelan context see Ochoa 2014.

15. J. M. Rodríguez (2003, 5–36) also highlights the centrality of the term "diva" for queer Latinidad.

16. On Mario Montez, gay shame, and Latinx shamelessness, see Crimp 2002; Cruz-Malavé 2015a; R. González (with Frances Negrón-Muntaner) 2009; Halberstam 2005b; Muñoz 2014; Pérez 2005. In La Fountain-Stokes 2011a, I propose *sinvergüencería* and "gay shame, Latina- and Latino-style," as useful antidotes to the prevalence of unmodified "gay shame" in contemporary queer theory (Halperin and Traub 2009).

17. Also see Hurtado and Sinha 2016.

18. Koch died in 2009; I don't know if it was her personal choice to translate *loca* as "gay." For praise of her translation, see González Echevarría 1993. Koch's beautiful obituary of Arenas appeared in *Revista Iberoamericana* in 1991.

19. On the impact of the term "gay" in Latin America, see Meccia 2006; Vidal-Ortiz, Viteri, and Serrano Amaya 2014. On gay, queer, and earlier terms, see Figari 2016; Fiol-Matta 2016.

20. Schnabel's painting of Arenas, titled *Portrait of a Freedom Fighter* (1984), is part of the permanent collection of the Toledo Museum of Art in Ohio.

21. Also see Lewis 2010, 73–105; Quiroga 2000, 124–44.

22. See particularly Peña 2013, 157–76. Ortíz 2007 discusses the term *loca* in relation to Reinaldo Arenas and Severo Sarduy.

23. González 2014 structures her keyword essay "La Loca" around the work of Lemebel. Also see Fiol-Matta 2016.

24. See Falconí Trávez 2018; Falconí Trávez, Castellanos, and Viteri 2014; Ferguson 2003, 2019; Hames-García 2011; Johnson 2001; Muñoz 1999; J. M. Rodríguez 2003, 2014; Snorton and Haritaworn 2013.

Chapter 2

1. See dedication in Daniels (2009, 47): "Honramos a Jorge Steven López Mercado, quien fue decapitado, desmembrado y cuyo cuerpo fue parcialmente quemado en Puerto Rico en lo que parece ser un crimen de odio." Del Puente 1986 includes newspaper documentation of crimes against gay and trans subjects in Puerto Rico. Also see Laureano 2016; Toro-Alfonso 2007.

2. See Jiménez 2004, 109–11.

3. Nina Flowers described herself as "fierce," "fabulous," and "unique" in a *RuPaul's Drag Race* promotional video for Logo TV available on YouTube (Logo 2013). "Eleganza" and "extravaganza" are catchphrases used by RuPaul Charles in *RuPaul's Drag Race*. On Flowers, also see Ardín Pauneto 2002; Baines 2010; Chernoff 2014; Clavell Carrasquillo 2006; Daniels 2009; Davis 2016, 60–61; Edgar 2011; Flowers 2012; Goldmark 2015; Jenkins 2017; Kohlsdorf 2014; Pagnoni Berns 2014; WOWPresents 2013. Regarding *RuPaul's Drag Race*, see Brennan and Gudelunas 2017; Daems 2014; Davis 2016; De Villiers 2012; Edgar 2011; Fitzgerald and Marquez 2020; Goldmark 2015; Mèmeteau 2014. On RuPaul, see Balzer 2005; Schewe 2009.

4. See episode 9 ("Reunited!") of season 1 of *RuPaul's Drag Race* (2009).

5. On Flores and Purcell de Ogenio, see Barnhardt 2017.

6. See episodes 6 ("Absolut Drag Ball") and 7 ("Extra Special Edition") of season 1 of *RuPaul's Drag Race* (2009).

7. On the ambivalent phenomenon of Puerto Ricans on *RuPaul's Drag Race*, also see Anthony 2014; Goldmark 2015; Kohlsdorf 2014; Marcel 2014; Mayora 2014; Morrison 2014; Norris 2014. Many Puerto Rican contestants, particularly the ones from the island, have been stigmatized for their limited command of the English language, or rather, for speaking Hispanic English, as opposed to Standard American English, African American English, or other more accepted regional dialects, generating humor at their expense. See Anthony 2014; Goldmark 2015; Mayora 2014.

8. See episode 1 ("Drag on a Dime") of season 1 of *RuPaul's Drag Race* (2009).

9. According to *Merriam-Webster*, "extravaganza" refers to "a lavish or spectacular show or event"; "something extravagant"; "a literary or musical work marked by extreme freedom of style and structure and usually by elements of burlesque or parody." See https://www.merriam-webster.com/dictionary/extravaganza

10. For example, Flores attended a Catholic parochial school, the Colegio Santa Rosa de Bayamón (personal communication, Yolanda Arroyo Pizarro, July 2019).

11. See Mèmeteau 2014; Schewe 2009.

12. On La Lupe, see Quiroga 2000, 161–68. Zentella 2014 discusses African American ambivalence and at times hostility towards Latinxs and the Spanish language (624-25).

13. This outtake was first screened as part of the third episode of *Under the Hood* (2009).

14. The topic of HIV/AIDS moves center stage in the next episode of *Drag Race* (episode 4, "Mac Viva-Glam Challenge"), in which several contestants address their experiences with the pandemic.

15. As Sívori indicates, "Las locas 'se producen,' en un proceso análogo al que realizan las travestis, los transformistas y las *drag queens* sobre su cuerpo, 'se montan' en el habla y también 'montan' un contexto y una serie de objetos de referencia. La identidad de loca es puesta en acto asumiendo esa voz" (2004, 78).

16. See episode 8 ("Grand Finale").

17. Kiesling 2004 discusses the use of "dude" as a term of address among heterosexual young men. I thank Marcos Rohena-Madrazo for this comparison.

18. As recently as February of 2019, a journalist in *TV Guide* indicated: "You'll be hard-pressed to find Season 1 streaming anywhere online, though, which is why it's considered the 'lost' season" (Hatchett 2019).

19. Speculation on the website Reddit and on the *Feast of Fun* podcast about the unavailability of season 1 included rumors that the producers were unable to obtain music rights for songs by Britney Spears and Destiny's Child and that there were lawsuits. There were also comments over the low production values and the poor quality of the image. See https://redd.it/1dz82n and *Feast of Fun* number 2575 with drag queen Vivacious.

20. See La Fountain-Stokes 2007a; R. Ramírez 1993, 1999; Vidal-Ortiz 2011.

21. *Drama Drag* was created by Nina Flowers and was the precursor to Tracks Nightclub's *Drag Nation*, a monthly drag show held on the last Friday of the month (*Westworld* 2013).

22. On the centrality of dancing in a nightclub for queer Latino worldmaking see Kornhaber 2016; Lawrence 2016; Rivera-Servera 2012; J. M. Rodríguez 2014, 2016; Torres 2016.

23. I wish to thank Rachel ten Haaf for suggesting that Nina Flowers looked like the Statue of Liberty, in which Flowers's horns become a crown.

24. See Breasted 1977; Erman 2018; Vega 1984.

25. Regarding anti-LGBQ and antitrans violence, see Callier 2011; Halberstam 2005a, 22–75; Hanhardt 2013; Namaste 2000, 135–56; Spade 2015.

26. On Jorge Steven López Mercado, see Burgos Pérez 2012; Callier 2011; CNN 2009; Colón Ortiz 2010a, 2010b; Figueroa Rosa 2009; Figueroa Rosa, Rivera Quiñones, and Hernández 2009; Font 2009; Hannah 2010; Mirzoeff 2010a, 2010b; *El Nuevo Día* 2009a; Rice-González 2016b; Ríos Ávila 2010a, 2010b; Shokooh Valle 2009; Vera Rojas 2015. López Mercado's former boyfriend Luis Conti (2020) indicates that Steven was fond of speaking in the feminine and using terms such as "Loca, La Sis, Mi amiga, la perra, la mujer, la ponka, esa jerga de hace 10 años que se usa particularmente en la escena gay

pobre y diversa que se ve en espacios como El Cojo y Santurce." Regarding violence, queerness, and LGBTQ issues in Puerto Rico, also see Laureano 2016; Ríos Ávila 2007; Rodríguez-Madera 2009; Román 2012; Toro-Alfonso 2007.

27. See La Fountain-Stokes 2018d for a recent historical overview. Also see Laureano 2016.

28. Fiol-Matta 2016 (228) also discusses the highly publicized murder of Daniel Zamudio by neo-Nazis in Chile in 2012.

29. On Xtravaganza, see Nakiska 2013. On her murder and its representation in the documentary *Paris Is Burning* see Butler 1993, 81–98; Fusco 1995; Halberstam 2005a, 51–52; Hilderbrand 2013; hooks 1992; Hutchinson 1997, 573–75; Namaste 2000, 9–23; Prosser 1998, 21–60. See Halberstam 2005a and Bettcher 2014 for useful summaries of Prosser's and Namaste's trans critiques of Butler.

30. See Petersen 2011 for an analysis of the media coverage of Matthew Shepard's and James Byrd Jr.'s deaths. Halberstam (2005a, 22–75) and Snorton (2017, 177–98) analyze the coverage and representation of Brandon Teena's, Lisa Lambert's, and Phillip DeVine's deaths.

31. According to Ríos Ávila 2010a, "De los muchos testimonios que abundan en YouTube y en la prensa sobre Jorge Steven, la causa gay se ha centrado en los que lo presentan como un muchacho bueno, trabajador, obediente, lleno de alegría y de deseos de vivir. La madre destaca su bondad. Algunos amigos hasta lo dibujan como un angelito. Es como si la víctima, para que funcione verdaderamente, tuviese que ser la nena buena, una Barbie hogareña y dulce."

32. On Ríos Ávila's queer psychoanalytic critique, see Esteves-Wolff 2020, 45–51. On the queer politics of Spanglish, see La Fountain-Stokes 2006. April Carrión, Queen Bee Ho, and Zahara Montiere appeared in YouTube videos celebrating López Mercado's life; they also appear in the documentary *Mala Mala* (Santini and Sickles 2014).

33. Valencia 2019 highlights a different tactic of mourning, which is to place the body of the victim at the site of violence as a type of commemoration and denunciation of injustice.

34. An example of third-wave feminism's selective recuperation of the term "bitch" is Bitch Media. See https://www.bitchmedia.org/about-us

35. Also see Laureano 2016, 301–21, on Ángel Colón Maldonado, whom local media nicknamed "El Ángel de los Solteros." Colón Maldonado is believed to have killed twenty-seven men. Alice Flecha Cruz (n.d.) offers a digital archive of press clippings on this case. See http://www.observatoriomovil.com/el--ngel-de-los-solteros.html

36. On the murder of Kevin Fret, see Aviles 2019; BBC News 2019; Beaumont-Thomas 2019; Exposito 2019a; Garza 2019; Guy 2019; Merrett 2019; Montoya-Gálvez 2019; Remezcla Estaff 2019; Roiz 2019b; Zraick 2019.

37. On Ozuna, see Ayala Gordián 2019; Fernandez 2019; Runtagh 2019. On the homophobic slur made by Don Omar, see Donohue 2019. Don Omar's original tweet is available at https://twitter.com/DONOMAR/status/1087772084548395008

38. See Ayala Gordián 2019. A July 21, 2019, headline indicates that a suspect in the murder was killed (Rivera Puig 2019).

39. On Fret's pioneering status as an openly gay trap singer, see Jackson 2018b, 2019. On queer reggaeton singers, see Villegas 2019. For an advance of Fret's third song "Mala" see Cepeda 2019.

40. See Rapetón 2018a.

41. Also see Rapetón 2018b.

42. Also see interview with *El Calce* uploaded onto YouTube on January 10, 2019, the same day of the singer's death. On women singers, see Fiol-Matta 2017.

43. For a discussion of *mala mala* see La Fountain-Stokes 2018a. Fret uses the term *mala mala* in his song "Mala," which was released posthumously in May 2019. Fret uploaded a video titled "2 meses después de cirujía [*sic*] de lipo marcación" ("Two Months after Liposuction Surgery") on YouTube on June 9, 2017.

44. On Griselda Blanco, see Tikkanen 2019.

45. "Despacito" won Latin Grammy awards in 2017 for Record of the Year, Song of the Year, Best Urban Fusion/Performance, and Best Short Form Music Video, and was nominated but did not win any Grammys in 2018.

46. On Doryann Fret, see Roiz 2019a. Credits for the "Soy así" video on YouTube indicate "Soy Asi Prod. by Tercero & Gordo Gas" and "Olympus Klub Music & La Buena Vida Music Group."

47. According to Bonilla 2018a, "Throughout his videos Bad Bunny himself flaunts a traditionally queer aesthetic with painted nails, flamboyant glasses, pastel colors, short shorts, and other style choices that trouble traditional paradigms of masculinity. Although he has not identified as anything but heterosexual, many queer-identified youth find in his look a certain solidarity with their own transgressions of traditional gender scripts." Viera 2018 is more guarded. Also see Capó 2020; Daw 2019; Exposito 2020.

48. Villano Antillano's *Spotify* biography states, "I'm not a role model, I'm a role villain," also highlighting "his fearless persona and what his dissidence as an openly bisexual MC has meant to the LGBTTIQ community on the island." See https://open.spotify .com/artist/1pi7nGhOM7PTHR5YEgXVGq/about

Chapter 3

1. On Latin American *travestis* and poverty, see Campuzano 2009; Kulick 1998; Ochoa 2014; Pelúcio 2009; Rodríguez-Madera 2009; Wayar 2019.

2. According to Mora, Dávila, and Rodríguez 2018 (quoted in McPhaul 2018), 25 percent of Puerto Ricans in the mainland United States live in poverty. Also see Duany 2017. On Latinas/os and poverty, see Zavella 2017.

3. On Sylvia Rivera's trans activism, see Clendinen and Nagourney 1999; Cohen 2008; Galarte 2020; Gan 2007; Halberstam 2018; Marcus 1993; Phillips and Olugbala 2006; Retzloff 2007; Shepard 2002, 2004a, 2004b, 2013; Stryker and Bettcher 2016.

4. According to the *Tesoro lexicográfico del español de Puerto Rico, jaibería* means "habilidad, astucia" (ability, cunning) as well as "maña y artimaña" (skill and trick), noting these particularly as traits of rural folks ("especialmente del campesino boricua"). Scholars have proposed *jaiba* politics as an anticolonial strategy of resistance and negotiation; see Esteves-Wolff 2020; Grosfoguel, Negrón-Muntaner, and Georas 1997; Negrón-Muntaner 2004.

5. See "oxymoron," https://www.merriam-webster.com/dictionary/oxymoron

6. "Financial or other assistance to an individual or family from a city, state, or

national government" (Dictionary.com). See http://dictionary.reference.com/browse/welfare

7. On biopolitics, see Smith 2007.

8. On welfare queens, see Adair 2000; Briggs 2002; Cohen 1997; Hancock 2004; Levin 2019; Smith 2007; Zucchino 1997.

9. For a critique of Lewis, also see Cruz-Malavé 2007b, 100–3.

10. Also see Spears 2000.

11. On *The Queen* see Davenport 2017; Nyong'o 2018. The more recent *I Am the Queen* focuses on the lives of Jolizza Colon, Bianca Feliciano, Julissa Ortiz, and Ginger Valdez. On queer Puerto Ricans in Chicago, see La Fountain-Stokes, Torres, and Rivera-Servera 2011; Rivera-Servera 2012.

12. On LGBTQ poverty and antinormativity, also see Duggan 2003; Hanhardt 2013; Spade 2015; Sycamore 2004; Vaid 1995.

13. In a 1972 interview, Marsha P. Johnson explained STAR members' preference for the term "transvestite" over "drag queen" (1992, 119). Also see Duberman 1993, 125.

14. Woodlawn expressed ambivalent feelings and at time resisted the label of "drag queen," which she found demeaning (Woodlawn and Copeland 1992, 241, 253).

15. On drag and poverty, see Newton 1979. On drag and camp, see Garber 1992; Meyer 1994, 2010; Muñoz 1999.

16. On *Paris Is Burning*, see Bailey 2013; Butler 1993, 81–98; Collins 2019; Dockray 2015; Fusco 1995; Goldsby 1993; Halberstam 2018; Hilderbrand 2013; hooks 1992; Johnson 2003, 76–103; Mèmeteau 2014, 68–76; Meyer 2010, 105–39; Reddy 1998; Rivera Colón 2009, 222–64.

17. On the House of Xtravaganza see Cruz-Malavé 2007b, 178–82; Hilderbrand 2013; Lawrence 2011; Rivera Colón 2009.

18. Rivera Colón 2012 offers an analysis of the New York City House Ball community from a Christian perspective. Bailey 2013; Johnson (2003, 76–103); and Reddy 1998 focus on houses as alternative kin systems.

19. See *Kirkus Reviews* 2017; *Publishers Weekly* 2017. "Angel" is also the name of the HIV-positive drag queen character in the Broadway musical *Rent*, which featured the Puerto Rican gay actor Wilson Cruz in that role.

20. See Betancourt 2017; Fitzgerald and Marquez 2000, 171, 173; Kenny 2017.

21. On *Pose*, see Brennan 2019; Fitzgerald and Marquez 2000, 250–1; Galanes 2018; Kirkland 2019; Poniewozik 2018.

22. On Garçon, see Shapiro 2019.

23. On the representation of antitrans violence see Brennan 2019; Kirkland 2019.

24. Davenport (2017, 132) highlights the documentary *How Do I Look?* (Busch 2005) as a more positive representation of the New York City ballroom scene.

25. Muñoz (1999, 102) contextualizes the work of Italian Marxist Antonio Gramsci, reading performer Vaginal Davis as a Gramscian organic intellectual.

26. See Aikin 2013; Muñoz 1999.

27. Mateik's 2002 documentary is very valuable, albeit the filmmaker only interviewed non-Latinx white subjects regarding Sylvia Rivera. On *The Death and Life of Marsha P. Johnson*, see Abele 2017; Desta 2017b; Edelstein 2017; Jaworowski 2017; Lee 2017. On Tourmaline's accusations, see Anderson 2017; Mock 2017; Tourmaline 2017; Urquhart 2017; Weiss 2017. For a refutation of Tourmaline's claims, see Ennis 2018; Juzwiak 2017.

28. Also see the documentary by Viruet Álvarez 2011. For a discussion of *Mala Mala*, see La Fountain-Stokes 2018a.

29. On Erika Lopez, see Castillo 2017; La Fountain-Stokes 2009, 93–130; Laffrado 2002. Ganser 2011 offers a particularly interesting analysis of Lopez in relation to diverse contemporary feminist formations such as third-wave feminism, postfeminism, and "chick lit."

30. On Beauvoir's sentence, see Mann and Ferrari 2017.

31. On Basquiat as a Puerto Rican artist see Negrón-Muntaner 2004, 115–44.

32. According to *Broadway World* (BWW News Desk 2011) and to Milosheff 2011, Lopez "has performed at locations as varied as San Francisco (California), New York City, Edinburg (Scotland), London and Manchester (England), and Oslo (Norway)." BAAD! produced her final run at the Clemente Soto Velez Cultural Center in the Lower East Side of Manhattan in 2011 (see Milosheff 2011). I used video documentation from her 2009 show at BAAD! and a video on YouTube (MonsterGirlMovies 2011) in preparing my analysis. Full audio of her final performance is also available; see Lopez and Monster Girl Media 2011.

33. It first appeared online in 2002 as a personal chronicle (similar to the Latin American literary genre of the *crónica*) titled "Postcards from the Welfare Line: The Rise and Fall of Erika Lopez." Lopez self-published it in 2003 as part of an artisanal, hand-bound photocopied book with Masonite covers and sculptural details called *Grandma Lopez's Country-Mad Fried Chicken Book* and then as part of *The Girl Must Die* in 2010. See La Fountain-Stokes 2009, 128–30.

34. See Lopez 1997a, 1998, 2001.

35. California has the eighth-largest population of Puerto Ricans in the United States ("Puerto Ricans in California" 2016).

36. See Park 2019.

37. Lopez in fact did run a DIY microbusiness producing and selling T-shirts, artisanal books, and welfare beauty products such as "Crack Ho' Glow Smack n' Blow Root-Beer Flavored Lip Balm" and "Brother Can You Spare a Dime" soap, which were available for a limited time in the 2000s on the artist's website and at her presentations. An illustration for the lip balm appears in Lopez 2010, 93. The stigmatized epithet "crack ho" (crack-cocaine-using prostitute) serves an analogous function to that of "welfare queen."

38. On Süskind, see Popova 2003.

39. On Kovick, see Delgado 2001.

40. Latinx articulations of abjection and aesthetics include Alvarado 2018; Cruz-Malavé 1997; and Sandoval-Sánchez 2005.

41. Woodlawn and Copeland 1992, 7. On Holly Woodlawn, see Davies 2009; Flatley 1970; Grimes 2015; Modern Eccentrics 2016 (on the paintings of Woodlawn by Sadie Lee); Morris 2003; Negrón-Muntaner 2004, 87–114; 2015; Ortiz 2016; Trebay 2013, 2015; Woodlawn and Copeland 1992; Yacowar 1993; Young 2011.

42. Woodlawn and Copeland 1992, 102.

43. Also see Negrón-Muntaner 2015.

44. *Your Dictionary* defines "speed queen" as "(idiomatic, slang): The feminine form of speed freak; a drug addict, that abuses stimulants/uppers in particular." See https://www.yourdictionary.com/speed-queen

45. On *Trash*, see Davies 2009; Negrón-Muntaner 2004, 87–115; Yacowar 1993, 39–46.

46. Also see Vega 1984.

47. "When I was asked to commit sex acts with a bottle, it didn't dawn on me that I could possibly be embarrassed by this performance in the future . . . what made it even more embarrassing was that people actually thought my beer bottle charade was real!" (Woodlawn and Copeland 1992, 144).

48. On Monica Beverly Hillz, see Cuby 2018; Felion 2013; Ford 2014; Hillz 2018; Kacala 2013; Michelson 2013; Nichols 2014; Norris 2014; Oliver 2012; Peeples 2013; Reynolds 2018; Rodriguez 2018; Stransky 2013. For general information on season 5, see Logo Press 2012.

49. On *RuPaul's Drag Race* see Goldmark 2015 and the essays in Brennan and Gudelunas 2017 and in Daems 2014.

50. See Felion 2013. On Serena ChaCha, see Brusselaers 2017. On Lineysha Sparx's linguistic challenges, see Anthony 2014, 54–57.

51. On RuPaul, see Fitzgerald and Marquez 2020; Schewe 2009; Woo 2017.

52. See Nunn 2013; Stransky 2013. Neal 2013 offers a queer analysis of Jay-Z and discusses Lorde's *Zami: A New Spelling of My Name.*

53. On Carmen Carrera see Brennan and Gudelunas 2017; Daems 2014.

54. See Felion 2013; Hillz 2018.

55. See Oliver 2012.

56. See 50Faggots 2013; Peeples 2013. Also see Cuby 2018, where Hillz states, "I've talked before about having been a sex worker and escorting as a means for survival and to help pay for my transition."

57. See Cuby 2018; Hillz 2018; Levin 2018; Reynolds 2018; Rodriguez 2018.

58. According to Duberman, Rivera "did love drag . . . Ivan [Valentin] and Sylvia . . . tended to look like boys or butch dykes even when dressed in full drag . . . [but] neither Sylvia nor Ivan was interested in having cosmetic surgery to burnish the illusion. And that helps to explain why Sylvia never attempted to work as a performer, though by the mid-sixties there were many more such opportunities opening up in New York than had recently been the case" (1993, 125).

59. See Rivera 1973.

60. See Gan 2007; Retzloff 2007; Shepard 2004a, 2004b, 2013. On the Sylvia Rivera Law Project, see Mananzala and Spade 2008, 63–68.

61. See Finch 1999; Emmerich 2016; Tourmaline and Wortzel 2018. Rivera is fictionalized as La Miranda and interpreted by the Cuban American actor Guillermo Díaz in Finch 1999. The character of Ray/Ramona played by Puerto Rican actor Jonny Beauchamp in Emmerich 2016 shares Rivera's birth name (Ray); Beauchamp has stated that he based his performance on Rivera (see Brown 2015; Crummy 2015). According to the *Happy Birthday, Marsha!* website, the Cuban American trans actress Eve Lindley plays Rivera. Also see Tang 2017, 381–85; Walker 2016.

62. See Duberman 1993, 20–24; Marcus 1993.

63. Regarding Rivera's involvement with the Young Lords, see Cotter 2015; Cruz-Malavé 2017a; Feinberg 1998, 123; Morales 2016, 63–66; S. Rivera 1998, 108; Wanzer-Serrano 2015, 117–18.

64. See Cain 2004; Shepard 2004a; Stein 2019, 17.

65. Cruz-Malavé (2007b, 2017b) offers valuable insights regarding Menchú and truth-telling in *testimonio*.

66. See Marcus 1993; Rivera 1998, 2002, 2007.

67. See Rivera 2007. I recorded and subsequently transcribed, edited, and published Rivera's speech. It has since been reprinted without attribution in Untorelli Press 2013.

68. See Page for a discussion of Tourmaline's "years of work into making available online the history of Sylvia Rivera and Marsha P. Johnson" (2017, 137).

69. See Bell 1970.

70. Also reprinted in Stein 2019, 213.

71. See Bell 1971b; Cohen 2008; Johnson 1992; Lewis 2017.

72. Wicker's (1973) account was published in the leading gay periodical *The Advocate*. This article also appears in Stein 2019, 294–96.

73. A transcription of Rivera's 1973 speech appears under the title "Y'all Better Quiet Down" in Untorelli Press 2013, 30–31.

74. See Rivera 2007. I thank Lauren A. Darnell for her analysis of Rivera's LGMNY speech in our graduate seminar Trans Latinx American Drag at the University of Michigan, Ann Arbor, in 2015.

75. See Shepard 2002, 2004b.

Chapter 4

1. Cullen organized an even more ambitious exhibit titled *Arte ≠ Vida: Actions by Artists of the Americas, 1960–2000* at the Museo del Barrio in 2008; see Cullen 2008. The six artists included in the *Here and There* exhibit (which was also shown at the Blaffer Gallery of the Art Museum of the University of Houston and at the Museo de Arte de Ponce in Puerto Rico) were Nayda Collazo-Lloréns, Charles Juhász-Alvarado, Freddie Mercado, Ana Rosa Rivera Marrero, Carlos Rivera Villafañe, and Aarón Salabarrías Valle.

2. On queer Latin American (including Brazilian) neobaroque and *neobarroso*, see Bialostozky 2017; Lopes 1999; Lugo Bertrán 2018; Perlongher 2016; Ríos Ávila 2009, 2013; Sifuentes-Jáuregui 2002, 119–50; 2014, 173–94.

3. Also see Mosquera 1996.

4. Also see Alexander and Ulysse 2015; Queeley and Ulysse 2015; Ulysse 2015.

5. See Ulysse 2014. Glissant expanded upon the notion of *Creolité* first articulated by Patrick Chamoiseau, Jean Bernabé, and Raphaël Confiant in their volume *Eloge de la créolité* (*In Praise of Creoleness*) in 1989.

6. See Ríos Ávila 2013 for a discussion of José Antonio Maravall's and John Beverley's conceptualizations of the baroque.

7. On Freddie Mercado, see Álvarez Lezama 1995a, 1995b, 1995c; Barragán 1998; Barsy Janer 2018, 2019; Cotter 2001; Cullen 2001, 52–63; Cullen 2008, 16–83; Jiménez 2004; Ramos 1998; Reyes Franco 2007; Santiago 2017b; Smith 2008; Toro 2011; Venegas 1998; Weinstein 2007. Mercado does not appear in Fiet 2004.

8. See Fiet 1997b; 2004, 319–65; 2012; Martínez Tabares 1997a; C. Rivera 2014; Rosado 1997; Seda 2018. Also see Montgomery 2016 for a very useful overview of Fiet's "alternative theater practices" (452). Nelson Rivera is critical of the term "alternative" and frames the discussion in terms of "experimental theater" (2016, 21–25).

9. Mercado has participated in numerous collaborations with María De Azúa, including her *Hacer el amor a una mujer triste* (play by Roberto Ramos-Perea, 1998), and in Zora Moreno's staging of *Con machete en mano* (Producciones Flor de Cahillo, 2000). On Moreno, see C. Rivera 2014.

10. I collaborated (as Lola von Miramar) with Mercado twice in 2011 in San Juan: on January 20 at Asuntos Efímeros at El Cabaré, hosted by Mickey Negrón, and on February 14 at the Librería Mágica (*13 rosas y una Lola para el amor*), hosted by Mairym Cruz Bernal and the PEN Club of Puerto Rico.

11. "Mi obra es un performance constante" (Mercado, quoted in M. Ramírez 1999). A similar quotation appears in Weinstein 2007. On Roche Rabell, see Bleys 2000; Cruz-Malavé 1995. On Nahum B. Zenil, see Bleys 2000; Domínguez Ruvalcaba 2007; Viego 2011. Zenil frequently paints images in which he appears with Kahlo.

12. *Noches de Galería* (*Gallery Nights*) were a monthly cultural event during the 1980s and 1990s; they were held on the first Thursday of the month in San Juan.

13. Kugelmass 1993, 138–39, documents a different, militaristic, self-described "apolitical" drag performance based on Desert Storm inspired by Brazilian carnival *caricatas* at the Village Halloween Parade in New York City.

14. See Gelpí 1993 and C. Rivera 2014 for a critique of the paternalist nature of Pedreira's vision. There is an ample bibliography on the topic of the encyclopedia in Jorge Luis Borges's work.

15. See Javier Rivera 2007; Reyes Franco 2007.

16. For a discussion of Puerto Rican rewritings of "The Ugly Duckling" see La Fountain-Stokes 2007a.

17. Mercado had a solo show in the Dominican Republic in 2013 titled *Las Caras de Freddie*, which was held at the Colegio Dominicano de Artistas Plásticos (CODAP). For video documentation of this exhibit see Grullón 2014. For video documentation and analysis of the 2013 performance at MACPR, see Barsy Janer 2018, 137–42; 2019; Mercado 2013.

18. See Grupo Editorial EPRL 2014.

19. On Zika in Puerto Rico, see Rodríguez-Díaz et al. 2017.

20. See http://hemi.nyu.edu/hemi/en/enc02-penas/item/1905-enc02-ivette-roman

21. Barsy Janer offers an insightful analysis of Mercado's use of dolls (2018, 115–34; 2019).

22. Mercado appeared in El Manjar de los Dioses's video "Déjame vivir" in 2000.

23. Mercado appears in and was the artistic director for Circo's video "La sospecha," filmed in 2003 (Circo 2003; Soto 2003). Also see Fernández Barreto 2003; Pagán Sánchez 2003; Vélez 2006.

24. See Juliá 2000; Roche 2000. Mercado appeared with José Luis Abreu as part of Andanza's debut in Puerto Rico. On Andanza, see Villanúa and Villanúa 2007.

25. On Mercado's collaborations with Sterling, see Aponte Ramos 1997; De Cuba Romero n.d.; Reyes Angleró 2007; Rivera Sánchez 2011; *San Juan Star* 2007.

26. See Cullen 2001, 58.

27. See Mercado 2001, 2006; Pantojas 2005; Viguié 2003.

28. See Bliss 1991.

29. Mercado presented *Coco Barroco* as part of *Aproximación del Caribe* at CODAP in Santo Domingo in 1995 and as part of *Caribe: Exclusión, fragmentación y paraíso* at

the Museo Extremeño e Iberoamericano de Arte Contemporáneo in Badajoz, Spain, in 1998. He returned to Spain in 2000 with Andanza. In 2001, he participated in *Aquí y Allá: Six Artists from San Juan, PR* at the Museo del Barrio in New York. In 2002 he performed in Lima, Peru, at the Hemispheric Institute of Performance and Politics' *Encuentro* and attended the ARCO art fair in Madrid, sponsored by Galerías Botello. He also accompanied El manjar de los dioses in their shows in New York and worked with the rock band Circo. In 2008, he was included in *Arte ≠ Vida: Actions by Artists of the Americas, 1960–2000* at the Museo del Barrio. In 2013, he exhibited the solo show *Las caras de Freddie: Por que todos somos frutas y estamos sabrosas* at CODAP. In 2017, Mercado was one of the main draws at the MECA International Art Fair in San Juan (see Olivares 2017; Sargent 2017).

30. See Santiago 2017b.

31. See https://www.gofundme.com/freddie-mercado

32. Venegas (1998, 281) echoes this sentiment.

33. Barsy Janer 2018 also describes her initial reactions to seeing Mercado when she was a young child. On the *unheimlich*, see Ríos Ávila 2002, 191–93.

34. Also see Reyes Franco 2007; Santiago 2017b; Toro 2011.

35. See Cullen 2008, 58–83, for a detailed description of the performance work of Joaquín Mercado.

36. On *cuir* Latin/o American art and drag, see Bleys 2000; Domínguez Ruvalcaba 2007; López and Nogueira 2013; Prieto Stambaugh 2019.

37. See Casas 2000 for an image of the Yeguas's performance of *Las dos Fridas*.

38. On Aguilar, see Bleys 2000; Viego 2011; Yarbro-Bejarano 1998.

39. See Masiello 2001, 53–55; Richard 1994, 2018.

40. See Associated Press 2019; Gallardo 2019.

41. On Bowery, see Atlas 2001.

42. See Blanco 1942; Flores 1993; González 1989; Torres 1998; Zenón Cruz 1975.

43. See Yeager 1998.

44. Also see Balzer 2005.

45. See Jiménez 2004, 259.

46. On Ruddys Martínez ("La Pantoja de Puerto Rico") and Martínez's impersonator Carlos Latre, see Meca 2017; Serra 2014. On Alex Soto, see Tirado 2015. On Johnny Ray Rodríguez, see La Fountain-Stokes 2017a. On Víctor Alicea, see La Fountain-Stokes 2018b, 224–26. On Alberic Prados, see La Fountain-Stokes 2018a. On Dreuxilla Divine, see Brugueras 2015; Guzmán 2014; Qué Pasa Gay PR 2012.

47. On Walter Mercado, also see Barradas 2016; Colón-Zayas 2012; Costantini and Tabsch 2020; Hedrick 2013.

48. Several exceptions to this performative silence appear in documentary footage included in Forbes 2011. Mercado also read the lyrics of a song at Alegría Rampante's Teatro Tapia show (Alfredo 2016).

49. Barragán 1998, 17.

50. Mercado also appeared as a two-faced female subject at Charles Juhász-Alvarado's and Domingo Sánchez's *Text Mix Road Movie: Boxeo* (2000) held at the Museo de Arte de Puerto Rico; see Cullen 2001, 16. Photos appear in Cullen 2001, 18, as well as in Zaya and Marxuach 2000, 118–19. Mercado also used the doll/mannequin format at the *Cuerpo/Materia: Performance 2000–2014* exhibit (see Toro 2014).

51. See Garber 1992 for a discussion of the terms "transvestism," "cross-dressing," and "drag."

52. "Girl, don't speak so loudly, for the loveliest thing God has given women is their voices." Felisa Rincón de Gautier, quoted in Cruz 2002.

53. Miller and Taylor identify women who portray historical female figures as performing "*auto/biography*, as this kind of historical presentation represents a negotiation between the autobiographical self of the writer-performer and the biographical record of the historical personage" (Miller, Taylor, and Carver 2003, 7).

54. See Martorell 2000; Villanueva Collado 2000.

55. Also see my discussion of Jorge Merced's impersonation of Silva in chapter 6.

56. According to Alfredo 2016, in Alegría Rampante's Tapia Theater concert, Mercado appeared as "La Diva Tarde" (The Late Diva), "un claro homenaje a Felisa Rincón de Gautier" (a clear homage to Felisa Rincón de Gautier).

57. See Rodríguez Juliá 1981, (1983) 2004, on the social and historical importance of funerals in Puerto Rico. Also see Arroyo 2015; Roach 1996; Taylor 2003.

58. On Johnny Rodriguez and El Cotorrito, also see Fundación Nacional para la Cultura Popular 2014b; Laureano 2007; 2016, 81–85. Díaz-Zambrana 2013 discusses *Puerto Rico en carnaval*. A souvenir program of El Cotorrito ("The Little Parrot") is available at https://www.queermusicheritage.com/fem-littleparrot.html

59. My mother recounts seeing Johnny Rodríguez perform dressed as Myrta Silva in nightclubs in New York City in the early 1950s. Personal communication, Ramona Stokes.

60. See Gruber 1972; Norris 1969; Ramos 1988.

61. The musical was called *Fela*. See Cruz 2002; Maldonado and Torres 1984.

62. See Lázaro 2019; Ortiz Díaz 2015.

63. Also see Fiol-Matta 2008.

64. See Fiol-Matta 2008, 2010, 2017.

Chapter 5

1. For example, see the discussion of *locas* and *viejos* in Loíza as documented by Alegría 1954, 1956; Bofill Calero 2014; Fiet 2007, 2019; King 2004–5.

2. On race as a social category and system of oppression, see Bonilla-Silva 2018; Fanon 1967; Haney-López 1994; Maldonado-Torres 2008; Omi and Winant 1994.

3. On nationalism, see Anderson 1992; Kernerman 2005. On the performativity of gender and race, see Butler 1990, 1993; Lugones 2003, 2008, 2017.

4. Also see Garber 1992, 267–352; Johnson 2003, 2016. Sieg (2002, 2) discusses "ethnic drag," defined as "not only cross-racial casting on stage, but, more generally, the performance of 'race' as masquerade," particularly in West Germany.

5. On colonial subjectivity see Grosfoguel 2003; Negrón-Muntaner 2004. Open-access photo and video documentation of *You Don't Look Like* is available at the Hemispheric Institute of Performance and Politics' Digital Video Library (Cardona 2003); my analysis focuses on this recording and on the published script (Cardona 1997, 1998). On *You Don't Look Like*, see Arroyo 2002; Den Tandt 1999, 88; Fiet 2004, 339–42; Godreau 2015; Homar 2010; La Fountain-Stokes 2011b; Martínez Tabares 1997a, 1997b, 2004; Montgomery 2016; Rivero 2006.

6. On Blackness and Afrodiasporic culture in Puerto Rico, see Abadía-Rexach 2012; Alegría Ortega and Ríos González 2005; Dinzey-Flores 2013; Godreau 2015; González 1989, 1990; Jiménez-Muñoz 1995, 2002; Jiménez Román and Flores 2010; Rivero 2005; Rodríguez-Silva 2012; Zenón Cruz 1974–75.

7. On *Moonlight*, see Scott 2016. The film is based on Tarell Alvin McCraney's play *In Moonlight Black Boys Look Blue*.

8. See Abadía-Rexach 2016; García 2016; Peña López 2016. Abadía-Rexach is also part of the Colectivo Ilé that produces the radio program *Negras* (Fullana Acosta 2019).

9. Eduardo Alegría is a leading gay performer and the front man for the alternative rock band Alegría Rampante; see Blasini 2007; La Fountain-Stokes 1997b, 2011b, 2018b; Noel 2001. On *Ah mén*, see Arroyo 2007; Cardona 2016; Rivera-Velázquez and Torres Narváez 2016. On *Hasta el cuello*, see Arroyo 2018; Fiet 2016; Ríos Ávila 2018.

10. See the "Javier Cardona" artist profile available at the Hemispheric Institute of Performance and Politics website. On Rosa Luisa Márquez, see Gaspar Concepción 2005; La Fountain-Stokes 2018b, 190–93; Márquez 1992; Martínez Tabares 1997b.

11. For example, in Márquez's *Otra maldad de Pateco* (1987), based on a short story by Ana Lydia Vega, Cardona appears in the lead role of a Black man during the time of slavery who is in love with María la O. José Clemente's face is black while his body is white, as he discovers when he sees his reflection in the river. This leads him to cry so much that the river floods and the orisha Ogún speaks to him. The performance includes a cloth doll that has a hand mirror on the other side.

12. On Llompart and Vázquez, see Homar 2010; MACPR 2013.

13. See Cardona 2015; "Educational Theatre Faculty" n.d.; Rivero 2006.

14. Cardona, quoted in Hagerman 2018.

15. Vidal-Ortiz 2014 coined the phrase "white person of color" to acknowledge the complexity and privilege of light-skinned persons from historically marginalized groups who enjoy the benefits of hegemonic whiteness but are also challenged for their identity, ethnicity, and language. Also see La Fountain-Stokes 1999b, 2002, 2008, 2011a, 2015.

16. I am referring to the archival recording of a performance of *You Don't Look Like* that took place at the Julia de Burgos Theater at the University of Puerto Rico, Río Piedras (Cardona 2003).

17. See Díaz Cárdenas 2016.

18. On Dominicans in Puerto Rico, see Duany 2011, 187–207; Martínez-San Miguel 2003, 151–200. On Latin music see Aparicio 1998; Flores 2000.

19. "Chianita" is a Black character interpreted by white actress Angela Meyer. "Pirulo el Colorao" is a blackface character by Raymond Arrieta. "Ruperta la Caimana" is a drag character created by Víctor Alicea borrowing mannerisms and expressions from Myrta Silva (Ribera Chevremont 2017). "Cuco Pasurín" is a character created by Antonio Sánchez "El Gangster" on his TV program *No te duermas*. "Willy el Merenguero" was a character interpreted by Melwin Cedeño.

20. For a feminist critique of "Snow White," see Bacchilega 1997, 27–48.

21. Weems 2012, 63.

22. See La Fountain-Stokes 2007a and 2009, 131–68; Rivera-Servera 2012, 71–85.

23. The tale appears as number 53 in volume 1, titled "Little Snow White"; see Grimm 2015, 170–78. Zipes 2015 discusses how the Brothers Grimm collected and edited the folktales. Also see Saunders 2008.

24. Also see Hedrick 2008. I wish to thank Raúl Moarquech Ferrera-Balanquet for recommending Eze 1997.

25. See Friedrichsmeyer, Lennox, and Zantop 1998.

26. Cottrell et al. 1937. On Disney and race, see Willetts 2013.

27. Cardona will declare that the mirror is broken, but does not actually break a physical mirror on stage.

28. See Rodríguez-Silva 2012.

29. See Aranda 2007; Barreto 1998, 2001; Flores 1993, 2009.

30. *Bunga* is an onomatopoeic word that is not registered in Spanish; *agua* means water. See "Bunga bunga" in Wikipedia for a discussion of its purported Australian origins and more recent iterations in Italy.

31. See Díaz 2005; Ríos Ávila 2002, 195–210.

32. I wish to thank Ramón H. Rivera-Servera for pointing out this reference.

33. See Saunders 2008, 123–25.

34. Miguel Villafañe is a renowned photographer and filmmaker who is married to Rosa Luisa Márquez (see *El Nuevo Día* 2009b). His photos are available on the Hemispheric Institute of Performance and Politics Digital Video Library website (Cardona 2003).

35. For a fuller discussion of the history and importance of the three magi in Puerto Rico, see Quintero Rivera 1998.

36. See Cardona 1997, 49; Cardona 1998, 15. Scholars such as Arroyo 2002 and Rivero 2006 also refer to the ninth image as a Rastafarian.

37. While *madama* can reference prostitution, it can also be used "como fórmula de cortesía o título de honor, equivalente a señora" (as a courtesy formula or title of honor, equivalent to a lady) (RAE, https://dle.rae.es/).

38. See Bishop-Sanchez 2016, 167–204; Solberg 1995.

39. On Sarria, see Fitzgerald and Marquez 2020, 244–47; Retzloff 2007. On Joan Jett Blakk, see Bogad 2005; Jeffreys 1993; Jones 2019; Kai 2019; Meyer 2010, 33–37.

40. "Iron slippers were then heated over a fire. The queen had to put them on and dance in them, and her feet were miserably burned, but she had to keep dancing in them until she danced herself to death" (Grimm 2015, 178).

41. On Ortiz, see La Fountain-Stokes 2018b; Santiago 2013. Ortiz has done numerous drag theatrical performances, including in Leo Cabranes-Grant's *Por el medio . . . si no hay más remedio*, where he plays Jichi (He/She) Hernández, and in Raúl de Cárdenas's *La Ceci*. On Rice-González, see La Fountain-Stokes 2016a; Viñales 2018.

Chapter 6

1. The Latin American musical genre of the bolero is defined in the *Diccionario de la lengua española* as a "canción de ritmo lento, bailable, originaria de Cuba, muy popular en el Caribe, de compás de dos por cuatro y letras melancólicas" (Real Academia Española). This is intrinsically different from the definition of "bolero" as "a Spanish dance characterized by sharp turns, stamping of the feet, and sudden pauses in a position with one arm arched over the head" (Merriam-Webster). See Castillo Zapata 2009; Knights 2006a, 2006b; Morad 2014, 2015; Quintero Rivera 2005, 300–10; Quiroga 1994, 2000; Santiago Torres 2012; Strongman 2007; Suárez 2008; Vargas 2008, 2012; Zavala 2000.

2. Teo 2001 identifies several elements of *In the Mood for Love* beyond the plot (including the musical score, costume, and mise-en-scène) as agents of "aesthetic abstraction" that acquire equal if not greater importance with regards to the development of a dreamlike, nostalgic atmosphere.

3. On Veloso, also see Leu 2006. Chavela Vargas (1919–2012) was a Costa Rican performer who made her career in Mexico. She was renowned for her masculine self-presentation and deep voice. On Vargas, see Alvarado 2016; Gund and Kyi 2017; Strongman 2007; Yarbro-Bejarano 1997. On female masculinity see Halberstam 1998.

4. On Sánchez's novel, also see Horn 2006; Strongman 2007.

5. Foster 2000 also writes about Paquita that "indeed, one could even venture to say that there is something about her that recalls a drag-queen imitation of Loretta Holloway, Billie Holiday, or Sophie Tucker in bad times" (n.p.). Also see Alzate 2009; Vargas 2012, 103–5.

6. Three times I fooled you, three times I fooled you, three times I fooled you: the first, out of rage, the second, for whimsy, the third, for pleasure. The song is by R. Macedo.

7. Vargas 2012 describes and analyzes Paquita's drag impersonators (104–5).

8. See La Fountain-Stokes 2018b, 37–41.

9. On the original (1997–2002) and second (2005) productions of *El bolero fue mi ruina*, see Ferrer 1999; García Gámez 2019, 150–63; Glickman 1997; La Fountain-Stokes 1997a; 2018b, 115–17; Méndez 1997b; Moreno 1999. On a controversy in Mexico regarding the quality of this play, see de Ita 2001 and Prieto Stambaugh 2001. In the 2017 production, Merced appears in the starring role of Loca in addition to three new actors and characters: Chad Carstarphen in the role of Pasión/Passion, Cedric Leiba Jr. as Vida/Life, and Gabriel Hernández as Muerte/Death. See BronxNet 2017; La Fountain-Stokes 2017b; 2018b, 118–23; Rivera and Merced 2017.

10. On *bugarrones*, see R. Ramírez 1993, 1999. The term is similar to Sívori's (2004) *chongos* as used in Argentina, as I discuss in chapter 1, and to the Mexican term *mayates* (Prieur 1998).

11. On Ramos Otero, see Arroyo 1994, 2001; Díaz 2018; Gelpí 1993; La Fountain-Stokes 2009, 19–63; Martínez-San Miguel 2003; Ríos Ávila 1998; Rosa 2011. Scholarly discussions of "Loca la de la locura" include Barradas 2006; Cruz-Malavé 1993, 259; 1995, 158–59; 2002, 12–14; 2015b; Rangelova 2007; Vaquer Fernández 2019, 64–69.

12. See Ramos Otero 1990. I borrow Amy Prince's translation of Loca as "The Queen of Madness" and Nene Lindo as "Pretty Baby."

13. On Caribbean masculinity, see Cortés 2015; Jiménez 2004; R. Ramírez 1993, 1999. For a discussion of Lucecita's masculinity and Blackness, see Fiol-Matta 2017, 172–225; Rivero 2005, 72–86. On drag kings in Puerto Rico, see Jackson 2018a and Martínez 2017.

14. I use the word "machismo" with trepidation, well aware of its limitations (Hurtado and Sinha 2016; R. Ramírez 1993, 1999). On Puerto Rican masculinity also see Findlay 2014.

15. Ramos Otero left Puerto Rico shortly after he graduated from the University of Puerto Rico in Río Piedras with a BA in social sciences. See Costa 1991; Gelpí 1993, 2000; La Fountain-Stokes 2009; Ríos Ávila 1998.

16. See Cortés-Vélez 2018; Cruz-Malavé 1993; Gelpí 1993; Martínez-San Miguel 2003, 323–96.

17. *El bolero fue mi ruina* was performed at the University of Puerto Rico, Río Piedras. Pregones does not include references to "Un tabaco de la Colombiana, un pasesito de la Peruana y todo el oro blanco de los Incas" (possible references to marijuana and cocaine) or to "el inhalador de nitrato" (amyl nitrate or poppers), and also does not include the phrase "Hipodérmica como el verano" (hypodermic like the summer). It does maintain references to some sexual activity. See Ramos Otero 1992, 239.

18. On Benjamin's storyteller, see White 2017. Also see Ong 1982 on oral storytelling and the transmission of information through speech.

19. All translations of Ramos Otero in this chapter are mine. For a different translation of "Loca la de la locura" see Ramos Otero 1990.

20. Merced has affirmed that the play is intrinsically about the bolero (La Fountain-Stokes 2018e, 154).

21. On melodrama in Latin America see Sadlier 2009.

22. On Sara Montiel as a queer icon see Guilbert 2018; Prieto 2013.

23. Hormigueros was the site for a well-known scandal in 1944 regarding the intersexual Emelina/Emelino Troche, who wanted to marry a woman; see Baerga Santini 2002. The word *hormigueros* means "anthills"; Ramos Otero might have intended to take advantage of the name's potential metaphoricity.

24. Numerous artists have portrayed the historic tensions between the Latin American Left and queer subjects. See Gutiérrez Alea and Tabío 1993; Puig 1976; Rodríguez Martinó 1990.

25. Also see Ludmer's (2004) discussion of women who kill.

26. See La Fountain-Stokes 2018e.

27. Norzagaray Street is an important perimeter marker of the colonial city of Old San Juan, while Christopher Street—the site of the landmark Stonewall Inn—is a historic site of gay North American culture and resistance.

28. On Merced, see La Fountain-Stokes 2018e; A. López 2003; A. Rodríguez 1999; Vásquez 2003, 147–53.

29. See "Jorge B. Merced," *Pregones PRTT* website, https://pregonesprtt.org/pregon es_team/jorge-b-merced/

30. On Pregones, see Colón 1991; Kanellos 2008; Leonard 2006; Morón Espinosa 2015; Pregones Theater n.d.; Rizk 2017; Vásquez 2003.

31. The 2013 Pregones Theater / Puerto Rican Traveling Theater (PRTT) merger is documented on the company's website, https://pregonesprtt.org/

32. On *El abrazo / The Embrace* also see Vásquez 2003, 86–93.

33. On the Asunción Playwrights Project, also see García Gámez 2019, 175; La Fountain-Stokes 2004.

34. Merced discusses his participation in *El abrazo* and *Máscaras* in his interview with Vásquez 2003, 147–53.

35. See discussion of Barbara Kent (La Fountain-Stokes 2018e, 146).

36. I cite Silverman's translation of Ulrich's phrase (1992, 340).

37. On Pantojas, see Jiménez 2004; Laureano 2007; C. Rivera 2014; N. Rivera 2018.

38. Pantojas appears on the cover of the *En Rojo* supplement with the title "Pantojas: ¿Dónde está mi lugar en la Revolución?" The title of the interview is slightly different (Rodríguez Martinó 1990). As the interviewer states, "Pero más que el ataque de los

religiosos a Pantojas le ha dolido el rechazo de los que él, por afinidad propia y común ideología, ha identificado como suyos: los independentistas" (21).

39. On queer migration, see Cantú 2009; Guzmán 1997, 2006; La Fountain-Stokes 2009; Luibheid and Cantú 2005; Manalansan 2003; Martínez-San Miguel 2003, 2011, 2014.

40. On the Village Halloween Parade and the Christopher Street Promenade, see Kugelmass 1993, 1994.

41. See Guzmán 1997 for a detailed ethnographic account of La Escuelita. Aponte-Parés 2001 and Aponte-Parés and Merced 1998 offer a history and analysis of early Puerto Rican gay activism in New York and Boston.

42. La Fountain-Stokes 2018e, 151.

43. For a discussion of the Puerto Rican LGBTQ theater scene, see La Fountain-Stokes 2018b, 124–31. On Marat, see La Fountain-Stokes 2018b, 224–26; C. Rivera 2014; Soto-Crespo 1998; Vaquer Fernández 2019, 58–64.

44. I am mostly using the video documentation of the June 2001 performance of *El bolero fue mi ruina* in Monterrey, Mexico, available through the Hemispheric Institute Digital Video Library. See http://hidvl.nyu.edu/video/001012297.html. In the original short story, the braid was red (Ramos Otero 1992, 237).

45. The original set design was by Regina García in 1997. Yanko Bakulic updated García's design in 2005. (Information provided by Arnaldo J. López for Pregones Theater.)

46. "Dos Cruces" was composed by Carmelo Larrea in 1952. Los Tres Diamantes' version appears in the Mexican film *Se solicitan modelos* (1954), featuring the Spanish actress Sara Montiel. Ricardo Pons served as musical director of *El bolero fue mi ruina* from 1997 to 1999. Desmar Guevara took over from 2000 to 2002 and once again in 2005–6.

47. Costumes used from 1997 to 2002 were the collective creation of Pregones Theater. Harry Nadal designed the costumes for the 2005 production.

48. Ramírez refers to the work of Gilmore 1990, indicating: "To be a man is more than the mere fact of having been born male. The man has to demonstrate his manhood and have this manhood recognized" (R. Ramírez 1999, 33). Also see Barradas 2006; Findlay 2014; García Toro, Ramírez, and Solano Castillo 2007; Toro-Alfonso 2009.

49. On cockroaches and Latinidad, see La Fountain-Stokes 2014.

50. Aparicio (1998, 175–76) and Arce (2017, 225–72) discuss Toña la Negra's life and work. Toña la Negra sings "Oración Caribe" in the 1948 Mexican film *Revancha*, which features the Cuban vedette Ninón Sevilla.

51. Alvan Colón Lespier initially designed the lighting for *El bolero* (1997–99) and was later replaced by Esteban Lima (2000–2002, 2005–6).

52. On the Puerto Rican singer and composer Sylvia Rexach (1922–1961), see Rodríguez Santaliz 2008; Vázquez González 2016. Lío Villahermosa created the performance *Inédita*, starring the actress Isel Rodríguez as Rexach (Reyes Angleró 2018).

53. This reaction would coincide with the excitement of gay Cuban audiences when the character of Miguel (Francisco Gattorno) would appear in Gutiérrez Alea and Tabío's *Strawberry and Chocolate* (1993); Miguel is more traditionally masculine than the two male leads.

54. "Niebla del riachuelo" is a 1937 tango with music by the Argentine Juan Carlos Cobián and lyrics by the Argentine Enrique Cadícamo. It was composed for the film *La fuga* (dir. Luis Saslavsky).

55. "Si te cojo" appears in Ismael Rivera y sus cachimbo's album *De todas maneras rosas* (1977). See Abadía-Rexach 2014. Aparicio 1998 offers a feminist critique of salsa, while Colón-Montijo 2018 approaches Ismael Rivera from the perspective of "wounded masculinities" and homosociality. The artist Marta Pérez García has a 2018 installation on domestic violence titled *Si te cojo . . . cuerpo, mujer, rotura* (I'm Gonna Get You . . . Body, Woman, Rupture), which has been exhibited in Washington, DC, and at the MACPR.

56. Lucho Gatica was a Chilean bolero singer, film actor, and television host; see Russonello 2018.

57. This sentiment echoes the lyrics of songs interpreted by Paquita la del Barrio that I quoted earlier in this chapter.

58. The *Diccionario de la lengua española* of the Real Academia Española defines *beso negro* as "práctica de estimulación sexual que consiste en besar el ano."

59. See R. Ramírez 1993, 1999; Ramírez, García Toro, and Solano Castillo 2005, 2007; Vidal-Ortiz et al. 2010.

60. See Buesa 2018, 157–58. According to Pérez Firmat 2008, Buesa was greatly maligned by high-brow readers who considered his verses too popular.

Chapter 7

1. See Baudelaire 1995; Wayar, presentation at the University of Michigan, Ann Arbor, September 20, 2019. Also see Wayar 2019. Scholars have analyzed the experiences of transgender cabaret performers in Brazil (Trevisan 2000, 244–46), France (Foerster 2012), Montreal (Namaste 2005), and the United States (Newton 1979).

2. On the process of bodily modification see Kulick 1998; Prieur 1998; Namaste 2005, 71–98; Plemons 2017; Valentine 2007.

3. Fausto Fernós's turn to bodybuilding represents a rather different process of *transloca* body transformation.

4. Regarding La Escuelita, see Amico 2006; Díaz 2012a, 2012b; Germosén 2001; Guzmán 1997; Musto 2016; Raab 1994. Regarding Times Square and queer sociality, see Delany 1999.

5. On Lady Catiria, see Ayala 1999; Díaz 2012a, 2012b; Fleming 1995, 1996; Germosén 2001; Mistress Maddie 2009; Musto 2007; Ortiz-Fonseca 2019; Plaza 2008; *POZ* 1999; Raab 1994; Sheridan n.d.; Suggs 1999. I created the Wikipedia article on Lady Catiria in August 2009: https://en.wikipedia.org/wiki/Lady_Catiria

6. On Chacón, see Chacón 2016; Negrón-Muntaner 2004, 238–40; Rodríguez Juliá 1986, 103–49. On Suggs, see Masters 2012.

7. The Miss Continental Pageant is a major drag and transgender pageant held yearly in Chicago. See Baim and Keehnen 2011, 371–449. On Lady Catiria's participation, see Baim and Keehnen 2011, 384. Videos are available from JF Enterprises. See http://www.thebatonshowlounge.com/continentalpageantry.html

8. It is not clear if Lady Catiria died at the age of thirty-nine or forty. I have found two birth dates for Catiria Reyes: March 27, 1959 (IMDb) and October 2, 1959 (*Lady Catiria: The Best*, DVD). She passed away on May 2 or 3, 1999.

9. See Ayala 1999; Germosén 2001; Mistress Maddie 2009; Musto 2007; Plaza 2008; *POZ* 1999; Sheridan n.d.

10. On Coccinelle, see Foerster 2012, 77–98; Namaste 2005, 19. On Orlan, see Orlan 2002; Prosser 1998, 61–65. On Arsenault, see Rudakoff 2012. On Cassils, see the numerous pieces in *QED* 6, no. 1 (Spring 2019).

11. There are competing definitions for "outsider art." See Wojcik 2016, 6.

12. On kitsch, also see Varderi 1996.

13. Fernández 2011 documents Antonia San Juan's frustration at having her gender identity questioned after portraying the trans character La Agrado.

14. On trans memoir see Schewe 2009.

15. On lip-synching, see Farrier 2016; Fitzgerald and Marquez 2020, 189–214; Newton 1979.

16. Some artists' lip-synch performances have more widely been identified as artistry, for example the work of John Epperson, who appears as Lypsinka (Evans 2009; Jeffreys 2008; Román 1998, 95–101).

17. "Mechanical reproduction" has also been translated as "technological reproducibility" (Benjamin 2010). Also see Estavillo (Guzmán 1997, 222).

18. In this sense it is interesting to compare lip-synch with karaoke. See Zhou and Tarocco 2007.

19. On Dana International, see Ben-zvi 1998; Gross 2013; Solomon 2003.

20. Also see "Maganuna" article in Wikipedia, https://en.wikipedia.org/wiki/Maga nuna. Yael Ben-zvi indicates that Dana International is credited for the lyrics of "Cinque Milla" and Ofer Nissim for the music, and that "an Israeli news website published an article in 2012 (https://e.walla.co.il/item/2505343) saying that during one of Dana's visits to Berlin a drag queen shouted at her on the street 'cinquemilla, allora, allora,' inspiring her to write this song" (personal communication, October 27, 2019).

21. Savyon Zabar, better known as "Big Ben," owned and managed La Nueva Escuelita from 1996 until 2016, when the club closed after forty-nine years in operation; Zabar died in 2017 from accidental erotic asphyxiation while engaging in sex with a man in New York City (Alcorn and Rayman 2017).

22. According to *Your Dictionary*, one of the meanings of "pinkwashing" is "(LGBT) The practice of presenting something, particularly a state, as gay-friendly in order to soften or downplay aspects of its reputation considered negative." See https://www.your dictionary.com/pinkwashing

23. See Estavillo (Guzmán 1997) for more analysis of the drag show at La Escuelita. Estavillo does not identify any of the drag performers by name, but does offer a rich assessment of their symbolic importance for the minoritarian subjects in the audience. Regarding the centrality of nightclubs for queer Latinxs, see Aponte-Parés 2001; Aponte-Parés and Merced 1998; Rivera-Servera 2012; J. M. Rodríguez 2014; Torres 2016.

24. Sophy is not a lesbian icon in Puerto Rico the way Lucecita Benítez is.

25. Rosie Pérez mentions visiting La Escuelita with John Leguizamo to see Lady Catiria's show four times to prepare for her portrayal of Googie Gómez, a character formerly presented by Rita Moreno in *The Ritz* (Pérez quoted Musto 2007).

26. On erotic dancers, their subjectivities, and their complex relationships with patrons, see Hemmingson 2008; Maia 2012; Pilcher 2017.

27. See Berlatsky 2015; Pullen 2005.

28. Regarding the wedding of Greg de Silva and Arnaldo Cruz-Malavé in Massachusetts before the legalization of equal marriage in the United States, see *People en Español* 2008–9.

29. Jennifer López has inherited the physical identifications of Iris Chacón and Lady Catiria. See Beltrán 2002; Negrón-Muntaner 2004, 228–46. On Tongolele (Yolanda Montes) and Ninón Sevilla, see Gutiérrez 2010.

·30. Evans 2009 argues that *To Wong Foo?* is not a remake of the Australian film, as both were in production simultaneously. Lady Catiria comments on *To Wong Foo?* in Raab 1994. For a reading of drag queens as angels, see Hammond 1996. On Joey Arias, see Davenport 2017. On John Leguizamo's drag performances, see Lockhart 1998.

31. See entry on Candis Cayne in Fleisher (1996, 107–8) and in Germosén 2001.

32. Raab 1994 describes Lady Catiria being the host of the La Escuelita show; I never witnessed this.

33. The speech is currently available on YouTube (That's Entertainment 2018). Also see Fleming 1996; Suggs 1999.

34. See *POZ* website. Lady Catiria is also quoted in Raab 1994.

35. The Silence = Death collective was created in New York City in 1985 by Avram Finkelstein, Brian Howard, Oliver Johnston, Charles Kreloff, Chris Lione, and Jorge Socarrás (Kerr 2017). The poster was finalized in December 1986 and first wheat-pasted in February 1987 (Finkelstein 2013).

36. On Barbra Herr, see Baim and Keehnen 2011, 406–7; Fernós 2019; Gomez 2009; La Fountain-Stokes 2018b, 96–101; Qué Pasa Gay PR 2014; Shapiro 2016; Vargas Casiano 2018.

37. On *Los Nutcrackers* see BAADBronx 2017; Moustakas 2016.

38. Barbra Herr is the daughter of Ramona Rivera (1930–73) and Albert Hernández (Gómez 2009).

39. See Vargas Casiano 2018.

40. Herr's participation in the Miss Continental Elite pageant is documented in Baim and Keehnen 2011, 448; also see Fernós 2019 and Germosén 2011. On *I'm Still Herr* see Shapiro 2016; Simón 2016.

41. According to Gamson 1998 (258 n. 35), this episode was aired on December 12, 1995. See Gamson 1998, 138–69. Gamson quotes Barbra Herr on page 161.

42. Lantelme 2002 refers to Amazing Grace as "the 'Amazing, Electrifying Grace.'"

43. *I'm Still Herr* was written by Rob Bailey-Millado with musical direction by Rachel Kaufman. It was performed at the Duplex bar in Greenwich Village in 2014; at the Bronx Academy of Arts and Dance for BAAD! ASS Women (2016); and at the Julia de Burgos Latino Cultural Center during the FUERZAfest Latinx LGBT festival (2016).

44. Herr is extremely close to her father, as her frequent postings on Facebook in 2015–20 document; she lived in Puerto Rico in 2015 to take care of him.

45. *Trans-mission* played from May 5 to 14, 2017, at the Teatro Círculo, 64 East Fourth Street, New York City, with original music by Vir-Amicus and light design by Omayra Garriga. See Arroyo 2017; La Fountain-Stokes 2018b, 96–101.

46. On Lizza Fernanda (Luis Felipe Díaz), also see González-Laguer 2015; La Fountain-Stokes 2018b, 93–95. On Soraya, see La Fountain-Stokes 2018a; Santini and Sickles 2014.

Epilogue

1. On artists in Puerto Rico, see Alfaro Pérez 2020; Jackson 2016, 2018a, 2020a, 2020b; Laureano 2007, 2016.

Works Cited

50Faggots. 2013. "Monica Beverly Hillz Gets Personal in New SocialScope Interview." YouTube, April 17. https://youtu.be/_8g0kh43q7I

Abad-Santos, Anthony, and Joe Reid. 2014. "A Taxonomy of Drag Queens on 'RuPaul's Drag Race.'" *The Wire*, February 21. https://www.theatlantic.com/culture/archive/20 14/02/guide-all-different-kinds-drag-queens-rupauls-drag-race/358383/

Abadía-Rexach, Bárbara I. 2012. *Musicalizando la raza: La racialización en Puerto Rico a través de la música*. San Juan: Ediciones Puerto.

Abadía-Rexach, Bárbara I. 2014. "De aquí pa'llá y de allá pa'cá: Los 'toques' de la migración en la bomba puertorriqueña." *Relaciones Internacionales* 25: 123–41.

Abadía-Rexach, Bárbara I. 2016. "El duelo del racismo." *El Nuevo Día*, November 7. https://www.elnuevodia.com/opinion/buscapie/el-duelo-del-racismo/

Abele, Robert. 2017. "'The Death and Life of Marsha P. Johnson' a Poignant Portrait of a Transgender Activist." *Los Angeles Times*, October 5. http://www.latimes.com/ente rtainment/movies/la-et-mn-capsule-death-life-marsha-johnson-review-20171005 -story.html

Abreu, José Luis (Fofé). 2017. "Antonio Pantojas: La libertad del ser." *Univision*, October 3. https://www.univision.com/musica/ulab-music/antonio-pantojas-la-libertad-del -ser

Absurdo PR. 2019. "Documentary 'Cuirizando' | Turning Queer." YouTube, July 2. https://youtu.be/oB3OKS0OqAk

Acosta, Tino, dir. (1965) 2005. *Puerto Rico en Carnaval*. n.p.: Vanguard Latino. DVD.

Adair, Vivyan Campbell. 2000. *From Good Ma to Welfare Queen: A Genealogy of the Poor Woman in American Literature, Photography and Culture*. New York: Garland.

AFI. 2017. *Before Night Falls*. American Film Institute. https://catalog.afi.com/Catalog /moviedetails/53885

Aikin, Susana. 2013. *Digging Up the Salt Mines: A Film Memoir*. New York: Ishta Press.

Aikin, Susana, and Carlos Aparicio, dirs. 1990. *The Salt Mines*. San Francisco: Frameline. DVD.

Aikin, Susana, and Carlos Aparicio, dirs. 1995. *The Transformation*. San Francisco: Frameline. DVD.

Aizura, Aren Z. 2018. *Mobile Subjects: Transnational Imaginaries of Gender Reassignment*. Durham, NC: Duke University Press.

Alcorn, Chauncey, and Graham Rayman. 2017. "Former Owner of Midtown Gay Club

Found Strangled to Death in Upper West Side Apartment." *New York Daily News*, January 6. https://www.nydailynews.com/new-york/owner-midtown-gay-club-fou nd-strangled-death-nyc-article-1.2937166

Alegría, Ricardo E., dir. (1949) 2014. "La Fiesta de Santiago, Loíza Aldea, Julio 1949." Centro de Investigaciones Históricas, Universidad de Puerto Rico. Instituto de Cultura Puertorriqueña. YouTube. https://youtu.be/ooU43HobJaM

Alegría, Ricardo E. 1954. *La fiesta de Santiago Apóstol en Loíza Aldea*. Madrid: ARO, Artes Gráficas.

Alegría, Ricardo E. 1956. "The Fiesta of Santiago Apóstol (St. James the Apostle) in Loíza, Puerto Rico." *Journal of American Folklore* 69, no. 272 (April–June): 123–34.

Alegría Ortega, Idsa E., and Palmira N. Ríos González, eds. 2005. *Contrapunto de género y raza en Puerto Rico*. Río Piedras: Centro de Investigaciones Sociales, Universidad de Puerto Rico.

Alexander, M. Jacqui, and Gina Athena Ulysse. 2015. "Groundings on Rasanblaj with M. Jacqui Alexander." *emisférica* 12, no. 1. https://hemisphericinstitute.org/en/emi sferica-121-caribbean-rasanblaj/12-1-essays/e-121-essay-alexander-interview-with -gina.html

Alfaro Pérez, Luis D. 2020. "Drag shows virtuales, la nueva realidad ante el COVID-19." *Pulso estudiantil*, 26 de junio. https://pulsoestudiantil.com/drag-shows-virtuales-la -nueva-realidad-ante-el-covid-19/

Alfredo. 2016. "Alegría Rampante en el Tapia: Héroes del Reino Marciano." *Puerto Rico Indie*, November 23. https://puertoricoindie.com/2016/11/23/alegria-rampante-en -el-tapia/

Algarín, Miguel. 1975. "Introduction: Nuyorican Language." In *Nuyorican Poetry: An Anthology of Puerto Rican Words and Feelings*, edited by Miguel Algarín and Miguel Piñero, 9–20. New York: Morrow.

Allen, Jafari Sinclaire. 2009. "For 'the Children' Dancing the Beloved Community." *Souls* 11, no. 3: 311–26.

Almaguer, Tomás. 1994. *Racial Fault Lines: The Historical Origins of White Supremacy in California*. Berkeley: University of California Press.

Almodóvar, Pedro, dir. 1999. *All About My Mother*. Culver City: Columbia TriStar Home Video. DVD.

Alvarado, Leticia. 2018. *Abject Performances: Aesthetic Strategies in Latino Cultural Production*. Durham, NC: Duke University Press.

Alvarado, Lorena. 2016. "Never Late: Unwelcome Desires and Diasporas in Chavela Vargas' Last Works." *Women and Performance* 26, no. 1: 17–35.

Alvarez, Sonia E. 2009. "Construindo uma política feminista translocal da tradução." *Revista Estudos Feministas* 17, no. 3 (September–December): 743–53.

Alvarez, Sonia E. 2014. "Introduction to the Project and the Volume: Enacting a Translocal Feminist Practice of Translation." In Alvarez et al., 1–18.

Alvarez, Sonia E., Claudia de Lima Costa, Verónica Feliu, Rebecca J. Hester, Norma Klahn, and Millie Thayer, eds. 2014. *Translocalities/Translocalidades: Feminist Politics of Translation in the Latin/a Américas*. Durham, NC: Duke University Press.

Álvarez Lezama, Manuel. 1995a. "The Body in Masks and Metaphors." *San Juan Star*, October 8: 16–17.

Álvarez Lezama, Manuel. 1995b. "Expansion in the Art World." *San Juan Star*, February 2: 44.

Álvarez Lezama, Manuel. 1995c. "Los novísimos: Espacios de libertad en las artes visuales de Puerto Rico a fines del siglo XX." In *Polifonía salvaje: Ensayos de cultura y política en la postmodernidad*, edited by Irma Rivera Nieves and Carlos Gil, 245–57. San Juan: Editorial Postdata and Universidad de Puerto Rico.

Alzate, Gastón. 2009. "Paquita la del Barrio and Translocal Theatricality: Performing Counter(pos)modernity." In Bixler and Seda, 160–78.

Amico, Stephen. 2006. "*Su Casa Es Mi Casa*: Latin House, Sexuality, Place." In *Queering the Popular Pitch*, edited by Sheila Whiteley and Jennifer Rycenga, 131–54. New York: Routledge.

Anderson, Benedict. 1992. *Imagined Communities: Reflections on the Origin and Spread of Nationalism*. Rev. ed. London: Verso.

Anderson, Tre'vell. 2017. "Trans Filmmaker Reina Gossett Accuses 'The Death and Life of Marsha P. Johnson' Creator of Stealing Work." *Los Angeles Times*, October 9. http://www.latimes.com/entertainment/movies/la-et-mn-marsha-p-johnson-doc -reina-gossett-david-france-20171009-htmlstory.html

Anthony, Libby. 2014. "Dragging with an Accent: Linguistic Stereotypes, Language Barriers and Translingualism." In Daems, 49–66.

Anzaldúa, Gloria E. (1987) 1999. *Borderlands / La frontera: The New Mestiza*. 2nd ed. San Francisco: Aunt Lute Books.

Anzaldúa, Gloria E. (1991) 2009. "To(o) Queer the Writer—Loca, escritora y chicana." In *The Gloria Anzaldúa Reader*, edited by AnaLouise Keating, 163–75. Durham, NC: Duke University Press.

Anzaldúa, Gloria E. 2002. "Now Let Us Shift . . . the Path of Conocimiento . . . Inner Work, Public Acts." In *This Bridge We Call Home: Radical Visions for Transformation*, edited by Gloria E. Anzaldúa and AnaLouise Keating, 540–78. New York: Routledge.

Aparicio, Frances R. 1988. "La Vida Es un Spanglish Disparatero: Bilingualism in Nuyorican Poetry." In *European Perspectives on Hispanic Literature in the United States*, edited by Genevieve Fabre, 147–60. Houston: Arte Público Press.

Aparicio, Frances R. 1998. *Listening to Salsa: Gender, Latin Popular Music, and Puerto Rican Cultures*. Hanover, NH: Wesleyan University Press and University Press of New England.

Aparicio, Frances R. 2019. *Negotiating Latinidad: Intralatina/o Lives in Chicago*. Urbana: University of Illinois Press.

Aponte-Parés, Luis. 2001. "Outside/In: Crossing Queer and Latino Boundaries." In *Mambo Montage: The Latinization of New York*, edited by Agustín Lao-Montes and Arlene Dávila, 363–85. New York: Columbia University Press.

Aponte-Parés, Luis, and Jorge B. Merced. 1998. "*Páginas Omitidas*: The Gay and Lesbian Presence." In *The Puerto Rican Movement: Voices from the Diaspora*, edited by Andrés Torres and José E. Velázquez, 296–315. Philadelphia: Temple University Press.

Aponte Ramos, Lola. 1997. "Experimentación y canciones de amargue, o cuando una artista de cabaret se llama Awilda Sterling." *Claridad*, April 25–May 1: 26–27.

Appiah, Kwame Anthony. 1991. "Is the Post- in Post-modernism the Post- in Postcolonial?" *Critical Inquiry* 17 (Winter): 336–57.

Aranda, Elizabeth M. 2007. *Emotional Bridges to Puerto Rico: Migration, Return Migration, and the Struggles of Incorporation*. Lanham, MD: Rowman and Littlefield.

Aranda-Alvarado, Rocío. 2012. "The Body in Caribbean Art." In *Caribbean: Art at the*

Crossroads of the World, edited by Deborah Cullen and Elvis Fuentes, 305–25. New York: El Museo del Barrio and Yale University Press.

Arboleda Ríos, Paola. 2011. "¿Ser o estar 'queer' en Latinoamérica? El devenir emancipador en: Lemebel, Perlongher y Arenas." *Íconos* 39: 111–21.

Arce, B. Christine. 2017. *México's Nobodies: The Cultural Legacy of the Soldadera and Afro-Mexican Women*. Albany: State University of New York Press.

Ardín Pauneto, Aixa A., dir. 2002. *Elyíbiti: Historia del activismo LGBTT en Puerto Rico desde los 70 a mediados de los 90*. Oakdale, MN: Imation Enterprises Corp. DVD.

Arenas, Reinaldo. 1992. *Antes que anochezca: Fábula*. Barcelona: Tusquets Editores.

Arenas, Reinaldo. 1993. *Before Night Falls*. Translated by Dolores M. Koch. New York: Viking.

Armstrong, Elizabeth, and Víctor Zamudio-Taylor. 2000. *Ultrabaroque: Aspects of Post Latin American Art*. San Diego: Museum of Contemporary Art.

Arrizón, Alicia. 2006. *Queering Mestizaje: Transculturation and Performance*. Ann Arbor: University of Michigan Press.

Arroyo, Joselo. 2017. "Intensidad de Herr en 'Trans-mission.'" *Fundación Nacional para la Cultura Popular*, May 22. https://prpop.org/2017/05/intensidad-de-herr-en-trans-mission/

Arroyo, Jossianna. 1994. "Manuel Ramos Otero: Las narrativas del cuerpo más allá de *Insularismo*." *Revista de Estudios Hispánicos* (Río Piedras) 31: 303–24.

Arroyo, Jossianna. 2001. "Exilio y tránsitos entre la Norzagaray y Christopher Street: Acercamientos a una poética del deseo homosexual en Manuel Ramos Otero." *Revista Iberoamericana* 67, nos. 194–95: 31–54.

Arroyo, Jossianna. 2002. "*Mirror, Mirror on the Wall*: Performing Racial and Gender Identities in Javier Cardona's *You Don't Look Like*." In *The State of Latino Theater in the United States: Hybridity, Transculturation, and Identity*, edited by Luis A. Ramos-García, 152–71. New York: Routledge.

Arroyo, Jossianna. 2003a. "Sirena canta boleros: Travestismo y sujetos transcaribeños en *Sirena Selena vestida de pena*." *CENTRO Journal* 15, no. 2 (Fall): 39–51.

Arroyo, Jossianna. 2003b. *Travestismos culturales: Literatura y etnografía en Cuba y Brasil*. Pittsburgh: University of Pittsburgh, Instituto Internacional de Literatura Iberoamericana.

Arroyo, Jossianna. 2007. "*Ah-mén* de Javier Cardona: El teatro como provocación." *Ollantay* 15, nos. 29–30: 189–92.

Arroyo, Jossianna. 2015. "Cities of the Dead: Performing Life in the Caribbean." *LASA Forum* 46 (Spring): 35–40.

Arroyo, Jossianna. 2016. "Interview with Javier Cardona." Translated by Ramón H. Rivera-Servera. In Johnson and Rivera-Servera, 275–81.

Arroyo, Jossianna. 2018. "Indebted Citizens: Ruin and Mediation in Contemporary Puerto Rico." Paper presented at the Latin American Studies Association International Congress, Barcelona, Catalunya, May 26.

Asencio, Marysol. 2011. "'Locas,' Respect, and Masculinity: Gender Conformity in Migrant Puerto Rican Gay Masculinities." *Gender and Society* 25, no. 3: 335–54.

Associated Press. 2019. "In Mexico, Controversy over Effeminate Emiliano Zapata Painting." *NBC News*, December 11. https://www.nbcnews.com/feature/nbc-out/mexico-controversy-over-effeminate-emiliano-zapata-painting-n1099756

Atlas, Charles, dir. (2001) 2004. *The Legend of Leigh Bowery*. New York: Palm Pictures. DVD.

Aviles, Gwen. 2019. "Fans Mourn Fatal Shooting of Openly Gay Rapper Kevin Fret in Puerto Rico." *NBC News*, January 11. https://www.nbcnews.com/news/latino/fans -mourn-fatal-shooting-openly-gay-rapper-kevin-fret-puerto-n957671

Avilés-Santiago, Manuel. 2014. "No Puppet's Land: The Role of Social Media in Puerto Rico's Mainstream Television." *Journal of Latin American Communication Research* 4, no. 2: 52–70.

Ayala, César J., and Rafael Bernabe. 2007. *Puerto Rico in the American Century: A History since 1898*. Chapel Hill: University of North Carolina Press.

Ayala, Hermes. 2019. "Villano Antillano no confía en la hipocresía sexual: 'La gente ya despertó' (VIDEO)." *El Calce*, October 29. https://elcalce.com/jarana/villano-antilla no-no-confia-la-hipocresia-sexual-la-gente-ya-desperto-video/

Ayala, Miguel. 1999. "Lady Catiria: 1959–1999." *En La Vida* 36 (June): 10.

Ayala Gordián, José. 2019. "Kevin Fret Murder Probe Continues, Rocking Latin Music World as Fret's Mother Breaks Silence." *Billboard*, April 16. https://www.billboard .com/articles/business/8506963/ozuna-manager-respond-allegations-kevin-fret -mother-murder

BAADBronx. 2017. "Los Nutcrackers 2017." *BAADBronx.org*. http://www.baadbronx.org /los-nutcrackers-2017.html

Bacchilega, Cristina. 1997. *Postmodern Fairy Tales: Gender and Narrative Strategies*. Philadelphia: University of Pennsylvania Press.

Baerga Santini, María del Carmen. 2002. "Cuerpo subversivo, norma seductora: Un capítulo de la historia de la heterosexualidad en Puerto Rico." *Op. Cit.* 14: 49–95.

Bailey, Marlon M. 2013. *Butch Queens Up in Pumps: Gender, Performance, and Ballroom Culture in Detroit*. Ann Arbor: University of Michigan Press.

Baim, Tracy, and Owen Keehnen. 2011. *Jim Flint: The Boy from Peoria*. Chicago: Prairie Ave. Productions.

Baines, Jenettha J. 2010. "Nina Flowers." In *100 of the Most Influential Gay Entertainers*, 190–92. Kernersville, NC: A-Argus Better Book Publishers.

Baker, Roger. 1994. *Drag: A History of Female Impersonation in the Performing Arts*. New York: New York University Press.

Baker, Sean, dir. 2015. *Tangerine*. Los Angeles: Magnolia Home Entertainment. DVD.

Balderston, Daniel, and Donna J. Guy, eds. 1997. *Sex and Sexuality in Latin America*. New York: New York University Press.

Balzer, Carsten. 2005. "The Great Drag Queen Hype: Thoughts on Cultural Globalisation and Autochthony." *Paideuma* 51: 111–31. http://www.jstor.org/stable/40341889

Banes, Sally. 1994. *Writing Dancing in the Age of Postmodernism*. Hanover: Wesleyan University Press and University Press of New England.

Barnhardt, Adam. 2017. "One Nation, under Drag." *Met Media*, March 13. https://www .mymetmedia.com/metrosphere/one-nation-drag/

Barradas, Efraín. 2003. "Boris Izaguirre o vivir del glamour." *Claridad*, July 31–August 8: 22–24.

Barradas, Efraín. 2006. "El macho como travesti: Propuesta para una historia del machismo en Puerto Rico." *Revista Fuentes Humanísticas* (Mexico) 18, no. 33: 141–51.

Barradas, Efraín. 2016. "El Evangelio según San Walter o de las contradicciones de la Era de Acuario." *Revista Iberoamericana* 82, no. 257 (October–December): 743–55.

Barragán, Paco. 1998. "Caribe: Exclusión, fragmentación y paraíso." *Noticias de arte,* Summer: 16–17.

Barreto, Amílcar Antonio. 1998. *Language, Elites, and the State: Nationalism in Puerto Rico and Quebec.* Westport, CT: Praeger.

Barreto, Amílcar Antonio. 2001. *The Politics of Language in Puerto Rico.* Gainesville: University Press of Florida.

Barsy Janer, Marina. 2018. "Tricksters of the Spectatorial: The Decolonial Proposals of Performance Artivism through the Encounters with La Pocha Nostra and Freddie Mercado." PhD diss., University of Essex.

Barsy Janer, Marina. 2019. "Becoming Doll: Radical Objectification in the Performance of Freddie Mercado." *Performance Research* 24, no. 6: 95–102.

Baudelaire, Charles. 1995. *The Painter of Modern Life and Other Essays.* Translated by Jonathan Mayne. London: Phaidon Press.

Baudrillard, Jean. 1988. "Simulacra and Simulations." In *Selected Writings,* edited by Mark Poster, 166–84. Stanford, CA: Stanford University Press.

Baumann, Jason, ed. 2019. *The Stonewall Reader.* New York: Penguin Books.

BBC News. 2019. "Kevin Fret: Gay Rapper Shot Dead in Puerto Rico Aged 24." January 11. https://www.bbc.com/news/world-us-canada-46833286

Beaumont-Thomas, Ben. 2019. "Kevin Fret, Gay Latin Trap Rapper, Shot Dead in Puerto Rico." *The Guardian,* January 11. https://www.theguardian.com/music/2019/jan/11/kevin-fret-gay-latin-trap-rapper-shot-dead-puerto-rico

Beauvoir, Simone de. (1949) 1989. *The Second Sex.* Translated by H. M. Parshley. New York: Vintage Books.

Bejel, Emilio. 2001. *Gay Cuban Nation.* Chicago: University of Chicago Press.

Bell, Arthur. 1970. "Sylvia Goes to College: 'Gay Is Proud' at NYU." *Village Voice,* October 15: 61.

Bell, Arthur. 1971a. *Dancing the Gay Lib Blues: A Year in the Homosexual Liberation Movement.* New York: Simon and Schuster.

Bell, Arthur. 1971b. "STAR Trek: Transvestites in the Street." *Village Voice,* July 15: 1, 46. https://thespiritwas.tumblr.com/post/18264877034/star-trek-sylvia-star-house-leave-the-lower

Beltrán, Mary. 2002. "The Hollywood Latina Body as Site of Social Struggle: Media Constructions of Stardom and Jennifer Lopez's 'Cross-Over Butt.'" *Quarterly Review of Film and Video* 19, no. 1: 71–86.

Beltrán, Mary. 2017. "Television." In Vargas, Mirabal, and La Fountain-Stokes, 221–24.

Benjamin, Walter. 1968a. "The Storyteller: Reflections on the Work of Nicolai Leskof." In *Illuminations: Essays and Reflections,* edited by Hannah Arendt, translated by Harry Zohn, 83–110. New York: Schocken Books.

Benjamin, Walter. 1968b. "The Work of Art in the Age of Mechanical Reproduction." In *Illuminations: Essays and Reflections,* edited by Hannah Arendt, translated by Harry Zohn, 217–51. New York: Schocken Books.

Benjamin, Walter. 2010. "The Work of Art in the Age of Its Technological Reproducibility [First Version]." Translated by Michael W. Jennings. *Grey Room* 39 (Spring): 11–38.

Ben-zvi, Yael. 1998. "Zionist Lesbianism and Transsexual Transgression: Two Representations of Queer Israel." *Middle East Report* 206 (Spring): 26–28.

Bergmann, Emilie L., and Paul Julian Smith, eds. 1995. *¿Entiendes? Queer Readings, Hispanic Writings*. Durham, NC: Duke University Press.

Berlanga, Ángel. 2010. "La muerte del autor: Adiós a Roberto Cantoral." *Página 12*, August 18. https://www.pagina12.com.ar/diario/suplementos/radar/9-6386-2010 -08-18.html

Berlant, Lauren. 1997. *The Queen of America Goes to Washington City: Essays on Sex and Citizenship*. Durham, NC: Duke University Press.

Berlatsky, Noah. 2015. "Actresses and Sex Workers Aren't So Different After All." *Pacific Standard*, August 21. https://psmag.com/social-justice/actresses-and-sex-workers -arent-so-different

Berman, Jessica. 2017. "Is the Trans in Transnational the Trans in Transgender?" *Modernism/Modernity* 24, no. 2 (April): 217–44.

Betancourt, Manuel. 2016. "'RuPaul's Drag Race' Champions Diversity Except When It Comes to Its Puerto Rican Queens." *Remezcla*, March 28. http://remezcla.com/featu res/film/rupauls-drag-race-puerto-rican-queens/

Betancourt, Manuel. 2017. "Don't You Dare Compare 'Kiki' to 'Paris Is Burning.'" *Vice*, February 28. https://www.vice.com/en_us/article/jpnen7/dont-you-dare-compare -kiki-to-paris-is-burning

Bettcher, Talia. 2014. "Feminist Perspectives on Trans Issues." In *The Stanford Encyclopedia of Philosophy*, edited by Edward N. Zalta. Spring. https://plato.stanford.edu/arch ives/spr2014/entries/feminism-trans/

Bialostozky, Jacqueline. 2017. "Aesthetics of the Surface: Post-1960s Latin American Queer Rewritings of the Baroque." PhD diss., University of California, Berkeley.

Birkenmaier, Anke, ed. 2021. *Caribbean Migrations: The Legacies of Colonialism*. New Brunswick, NJ: Rutgers University Press.

Bishop-Sanchez, Kathryn. 2016. *Creating Carmen Miranda: Race, Camp, and Transnational Stardom*. Nashville: Vanderbilt University Press.

Bixler, Jacqueline E., and Laurietz Seda, eds. 2009. *Trans/acting: Latin American and Latino Performing Arts*. Lewisburg, PA: Bucknell University Press.

Blanco, Fernando A., ed. 2020. *La vida imitada: Narrativa, performance y visualidad en Pedro Lemebel*. Madrid: Iberoamericana Vervuert.

Blanco, Fernando A., and Juan Poblete, eds. 2010. *Desdén al infortunio: Sujeto, comunicación y público en la narrativa de Pedro Lemebel*. Santiago: Editorial Cuarto Propio.

Blanco, Tomás. (1942) 1948. *El prejuicio racial en Puerto Rico*. 2nd ed. San Juan: Biblioteca de Autores Puertorriqueños.

Blasini, Gilberto M. 2007. "¡Bien Gorgeous! The Cultural Work of Eduardo Alegría." *CENTRO Journal* 19, no. 1 (Spring): 250–73.

Blasini, Gilberto M. 2011. "Raro." *80grados*, May 6. http://www.80grados.net/raro/

Bleys, Rudi. 2000. *Images of Ambiente: Homotextuality and Latin American Art, 1810– Today*. London: Continuum.

Bliss, Peggy Ann. 1991. "Intellectual Climate Permeates Biennial's Opening." *San Juan Star*, February 26: 29.

Boal, Augusto. (1974) 1985. *Theatre of the Oppressed*. Translated by Charles A. and Maria-Odilia Leal McBride. New York: Theatre Communications Group.

Bofill Calero, Jaime O. 2014. "Bomba, danza, calipso y merengue: Creación del espacio social en las fiestas de Santiago Apóstol de Loíza." *Latin American Music Review* 35, no. 1 (Spring–Summer): 115–38.

Bogad, L. M. 2005. "Sturm un Drag: Thee Fabulous Camp-pains of Miss Joan JettBlakk." In *Electoral Guerrilla Theatre: Radical Ridicule and Social Movements*, 121–64. New York: Routledge.

Bond, Emma. 2018. "Trans-gender, Trans-national: Crossing Binary Lines." In *Writing Migration through the Body*, 71–109. Cham, Switzerland: Palgrave Macmillan.

Bonilla, Yarimar. 2018a. "Bad Bunny, Good Scapegoat: How 'El Conejo Malo' Is Stirring a 'Moral Panic' in Post-hurricane Puerto Rico." *Billboard*, November 13. https://www.billboa rd.com/articles/columns/latin/8484776/bad-bunny-scapegoat-guest-column

Bonilla, Yarimar. 2018b. "How Puerto Ricans Fit into an Increasingly Anti-immigrant U.S." *Washington Post*, January 19. https://www.washingtonpost.com/news/posteverything/wp/2018/01/19/how-the-u-s-will-replace-immigrant-workers-with-puerto-ricans/

Bonilla, Yarimar, and Marisol LeBrón, eds. 2019. *Aftershocks of Disaster: Puerto Rico before and after the Storm*. Chicago: Haymarket Books.

Bonilla-Silva, Eduardo. 2018. *Racism without Racists: Color-Blind Racism and the Persistence of Racial Inequality in America*. Lanham, MD: Rowman and Littlefield.

Borràs, Maria Lluïsa, and Antonio Zaya, eds. 1998. *Caribe insular: Exclusión, fragmentación y paraíso*. Badajoz: Museo Extremeño e Iberoamericano de Arte Contemporáneo (MEIAC) and Casa de América Madrid.

Bourdieu, Pierre. 1984. *Distinction: A Social Critique of the Judgement of Taste*. Translated by Richard Nice. Cambridge, MA: Harvard University Press.

Bourgois, Philippe. 1995. *In Search of Respect: Selling Crack in El Barrio*. Cambridge: Cambridge University Press.

Braga-Pinto, César. 2002. "Supermen and Chiquita Bacana's Daughters: Transgendered Voices in Brazilian Popular Music." In *Lusosex: Gender and Sexuality in the Portuguese-Speaking Word*, edited by Susan Canty Quinlan and Fernando Arenas, 187–207. Minneapolis: University of Minnesota Press.

Brantley, Ben. 2013. "Review/Theater: Exploring Sexes and Identities." *New York Times*, August 30. https://www.nytimes.com/1993/08/30/theater/review-theater-exploring-sexes-and-identities.html

Braziel, Jana Evans. 2008. *Artists, Performers, and Black Masculinity in the Haitian Diaspora*. Bloomington: Indiana University Press.

Breasted, Mary. 1977. "30 in Puerto Rican Group Held in Liberty I. Protest." *New York Times*, October 26: 30.

Breathnach, Paddy, dir. 2016. *Viva*. Dublin: Element Pictures Distribution. DVD.

Brennan, Matt. 2019. "'This Can't Happen on "Pose"': How TV's Queerest Show Made Its Most Emotional Episode Yet." *Los Angeles Times*, July 9. https://www.latimes.com/entertainment/tv/la-et-st-pose-ryan-murphy-janet-mock-trans-woman-violence-20190709-story.html

Brennan, Niall, and David Gudelunas, eds. 2017. *RuPaul's Drag Race: Shifting the Visibility of Drag Culture and the Boundaries of Reality TV*. New York: Palgrave Macmillan.

Briggs, Laura. 2002. "*La Vida*, Moynihan, and Other Libels: Migration, Social Science, and the Making of the Puerto Rican Welfare Queen." *CENTRO Journal* 14, no. 1: 75–101.

Bronski, Michael. 2002. "Sylvia Rivera: 1951–2002. No Longer on the Back of the Bumper." *Z Magazine*, April 1. https://zcomm.org/zmagazine/sylvia-rivera-1951-2002-by-michael-bronski/

BronxNet. 2017. *The Bolero Was My Downfall.* July 20. https://www.bronxnet.org/watch/videos/531/

Brown, Emma. 2015. "Discovery: Jonny Beauchamp." *Interview*, September 25. https://www.interviewmagazine.com/film/discovery-jonny-beauchamp

Brown, Jayna. 2013. "Hip Hop, Pleasure, and Its Fulfillment." *Palimpsest* 2, no. 2: 147–50.

Brown, Wendy. 2015. *Undoing the Demos: Neoliberalism's Stealth Revolution.* Brooklyn, NY: Zone Books.

Bruckman Blondet, Vivian, dir. 2013. *Desmaquilladas.* NEO-DIVEDCO. San Juan: Imperfecto Cine. https://vimeo.com/344047356

Brugueras, Melba. 2015. "Tal cual: Se quitará el maquillaje." *Primera Hora*, June 3. https://www.pressreader.com/puerto-rico/primera-hora/20150603/282514362142099

Brusselaers, Dieter. 2017. "'Pick Up a Good Book and Go Read': Art and Legitimacy in *RuPaul's Drag Race.*" In Brennan and Gudelunas, 45–59.

Buesa, José Ángel. 2018. *Yo, poeta: Poesía completa.* Madrid: Editorial Verbum.

"Bunga bunga." *Wikipedia.* https://en.wikipedia.org/wiki/Bunga_bunga

Burgos, Julia de. (1938) 1997. "Ay ay ay de la grifa negra." In *Poema en veinte surcos*, 52–53. 3rd ed. Río Piedras: Ediciones Huracán.

Burgos Pérez, Osvaldo. 2012. "Comunidades LGTTB: Con sus derechos en el clóset." In *Puerto Rico y los derechos humanos: Una intersección plural*, ed. José Javier Colón Morera and Idsa E. Alegría Ortega, 245–75. San Juan: Ediciones Callejón.

Busch, Wolfgang, dir. 2005. *How Do I Look?* Astoria, NY: Art from the Heart. DVD.

Butler, Judith. 1990. *Gender Trouble: Feminism and the Subversion of Identity.* New York: Routledge.

Butler, Judith. 1993. *Bodies That Matter: On the Discursive Limits of "Sex".* New York: Routledge.

Butler, Judith. 2004. *Undoing Gender.* Boca Raton, FL: Routledge.

BWW News Desk. 2011. "Monster Girl Productions and BAAD Present THE WELFARE QUEEN, Opens 9/15." *Broadway World*, September 15. https://www.broadwayworld.com/article/Monster-Girl-Productions-BAAD-Present-THE-WELFARE-QUEEN-Opens-915-20110906-page7

bxboi161. 2009. "The Legendary Lady Catiria Miss Continental Plus / Miss Continental R.I.P." YouTube, June 1. https://youtu.be/POd5VrSIc64

Cain, Paul D. 2004. "David Carter: Historian of the Stonewall Riots." *Gay Today*, July 1. http://gaytoday.com/interview/070104in.asp

Calderón, Yecid (Pinina Flandes). 2016. *Deviniendo loca: Textualidades de una marica sureada.* Santiago: Los libros de la mujer rota.

Calle 13. (2007) 2009. *Tango del pecado.* Directed by Israel Lugo and Gabriel Coss. YouTube, October 25. http://youtu.be/7pRE2ATdWaU

Callier, Durell M. 2011. "A Call to Love: In Remembrance of Our Quare Saints." *Qualitative Research Journal* 11, no. 2 (November): 85–94.

Caminero-Santangelo, Marta. 1998. *The Madwoman Can't Speak, or, Why Insanity Is Not Subversive.* Ithaca, NY: Cornell University Press.

Campbell, Andy. 2015. "Realism against #Realness: Wu Tsang, #Realness, and *RuPaul's*

Drag Race." In *Hashtag Publics: The Power and Politics of Discursive Networks*, edited by Nathan Rambukkana, 155–68. New York: Peter Lang.

Campuzano, Giuseppe. 2008. *Museo Travesti del Perú*. Peru: Institute of Development Studies.

Campuzano, Giuseppe. 2009. "Contemporary *Travesti* Encounters with Gender and Sexuality in Latin America." *Development* 52, no. 1: 75–83.

Campuzano, Giuseppe. 2013. *Saturday Night Thriller y otros escritos, 1998–2013*. Edited by Miguel A. López. Lima: Estruendomudo.

Cantú, Lionel, Jr. 2009. *The Sexuality of Migration: Border Crossings and Mexican Immigrant Men*. Edited by Nancy A. Naples and Salvador Vidal-Ortiz. New York: New York University Press.

Capó, Julio, Jr. 2020. "Counter-editorial: Bad Bunny Is Queer to Me." *Abusable Past*, May 27. https://www.radicalhistoryreview.org/abusablepast/counter-editorial-bad-bunny-is-queer-to-me/

Cardona, Javier. 1997. *You don't look like. Conjunto* 106 (May–August): 47–49.

Cardona, Javier. 1998. *You don't look like . . .* Translated by Annette Guevárez and Lowell Fiet. In *Segundo simposio de Caribe 2000: Hablar, nombrar, pertenecer*, edited by Lowell Fiet and Janette Becerra, 13–17. San Juan: Caribe 2000 / Universidad de Puerto Rico.

Cardona, Javier. 2003. *You don't look like . . .* Hemispheric Institute Digital Video Library. http://hidvl.nyu.edu/video/000512616.html

Cardona, Javier. 2015. "Activando la esperanza: Artes para la edu-acción (dentro y fuera de la prisión)." *Conjunto* 174 (January–March): 76–77.

Cardona, Javier. 2016. *Ah mén*. Translated by Andreea Micu and Ramón H. Rivera-Servera. In Johnson and Rivera-Servera, 243–63.

Carter, David. 2004. *Stonewall: The Riots That Sparked the Gay Revolution*. New York: St. Martin's Press.

Casas, Francisco. 2000. "The Equine Lips of Exile." In Fusco, 220–22.

Case, Sue-Ellen. 1988–89. "Towards a Butch-Femme Aesthetic." *Discourse* 11, no. 1 (Fall–Winter): 55–73.

Cassara, Joseph. 2018. *The House of Impossible Beauties*. New York: Ecco.

Castillo, Debra A. 2017. "Perineum: Erika Lopez." *Studies in 20th and 21st Century Literature* 42, no. 1, article 7. https://doi.org/10.4148/2334-4415.1970

Castillo Zapata, Rafael. 2009. *Fenomenología del bolero*. Caracas: Fundación Celarg.

Castro Vega, Bryan Karhu. (Ana Macho). 2019. "Las 'drag queens' de la revolución queer en Puerto Rico." *Merodea*, March 1. https://merodea.com/trabajo/women-we-heart/las-drag-queens-de-la-revolucion-queer-en-puerto-rico/

Cepeda, Eduardo. 2018. "Latin Trap Rapper Bad Bunny Is Redefining Masculinity in a Genre Steeped in Machismo." *WBUR*, August 8. https://www.wbur.org/artery/2018/08/08/latin-trap-bad-bunny-masculinity

Cepeda, Eduardo. 2019. "Watch a Clip from 'Mala,' Kevin Fret's Posthumously Released Video." *Remezcla*, May 14. https://remezcla.com/music/kevin-fret-new-video/

Chacón, Iris. 2016. *Yo soy Iris Chacón*. Florida: IBEL Group Publishing.

Chacón O'Farrill, Zorian. 2017. "El mundo de las drag kings." *Índice*, February 10. http://www.indicepr.com/noticias/2017/02/10/house/68160/el-mundo-de-las-drag-kings/

Chauncey, George. 1994. *Gay New York: Gender, Urban Culture, and the Makings of the Gay Male World, 1890–1940*. New York: Basic Books.

Chen, Mel Y. 2012. *Animacies: Biopolitics, Racial Mattering, and Queer Affect*. Durham, NC: Duke University Press.

Chernoff, Carolyn. 2014. "Of Women and Queens: Gendered Realities and Re-education in RuPaul's Drag Empire." In Daems, 148–67.

Christian, Christopher. 2019. "The Analyst as Interpreter: Ataque de Nervios, Puerto Rican Syndrome, and the Inexact Interpretation." In *Psychoanalysis in the Barrios: Race, Class, and the Unconscious*, edited by Patricia Gherovici and Christopher Christian, 71–86. New York: Routledge.

Circo. 2003. "La sospecha." Art direction by Freddie Mercado Velázquez. YouTube. http://youtu.be/0WPrLeajUc0

Cirne-Lima, Henrique, and Josué Pellot, dirs. (2010) 2015. *I Am the Queen*. Burbank: Cinema Libre Studio. DVD.

Cirne-Lima, Henrique, and Josué Pellot, dirs. 2012. *The Other Side of the Queen*. Film.

Cixous, Hélène. 1976. "The Laugh of the Medusa." *Signs* 1, no. 4 (Summer): 875–93.

Clavell Carrasquillo, Manuel. 2006. "Identidades en reconstrucción: Las transforma-ciones de Nina Flowers y Eros The Club." *ZONAi*, February 11. http://www.carnadas.org/blog/?p=411

Clavell Carrasquillo, Manuel. 2013. "Te Cuento 013- 'Zal Zi Puedes' a las noches de fan-tasía" (Radio Universidad de Puerto Rico). *Mixcloud*. https://www.mixcloud.com/te cuento/te-cuento-013-zal-zi-puedes-a-las-noches-de-fantas%C3%ADa/. Podcast.

Clendinen, Dudley, and Adam Nagourney. 1999. *Out for Good: The Struggle to Build a Gay Rights Movement in America*. New York: Simon and Schuster.

CNN. 2009. "Suspect Charged with Murder in Slaying of Gay Teen in Puerto Rico." November 18. http://www.cnn.com/2009/CRIME/11/18/puerto.rico.gay.teen.slain /index.html

Cobas, José A., Jorge Duany, and Joe R. Feagin, eds. 2016. *How the United States Racial-izes Latinos: White Hegemony and Its Consequences*. New York: Routledge.

Cohen, Cathy. 1997. "Punks, Bulldaggers, and Welfare Queens: The Radical Potential of Queer Politics?" *GLQ* 3, no. 4: 437–65.

Cohen, Stephan L. 2008. *The Gay Liberation Youth Movement in New York: An Army of Lovers Cannot Fail*. New York: Routledge.

Collado, Morgan Robyn. 2012. "On Actually Keeping Queer Queer: A Critical Response." *NU Writing* 1. https://openjournals.neu.edu/nuwriting/home/article/view/58/44

Collado, Morgan Robyn. 2014. *Make Love to Rage*. Toronto: biyuti publishing.

Collazo, Valeria. 2011. "Taller de Otra Cosa anuncia su nueva producción." *8ogrados*, April 29. http://www.80grados.net/taller-de-otra-cosa-anuncia-su-nueva-produccion/

Collins, K. Austin. 2019. "*Paris Is Burning* Is Back—and So Is Its Baggage." *Vanity Fair*, June 18. https://www.vanityfair.com/hollywood/2019/06/paris-is-burning-docume ntary-drag-jennie-livingston-interview

Colón, Alvan. 1991. "El teatro boricua de Pregones en los Estados Unidos." *Conjunto* 88 (July–September): 47–49.

Colón-Montijo, César. 2018. "Specters of Maelo: An Ethnographic Biography of Ismael 'Maelo' Rivera." PhD diss., Columbia University.

Colón Ortiz, Jorge A. 2010a. "The Consequences of Hate in Puerto Rico." *The New Every-day*, June 11. http://mediacommons.org/tne/pieces/consequences-hate-puerto-rico

Colón Ortiz, Jorge A. 2010b. "Jorge Steven Lopez and Matthew Shepard: Two Crimes, One Motive." *The New Everyday*, June 11. http://mediacommons.org/tne/pieces/jor ge-steven-lopez-and-matthew-shepard-two-crimes-one-motive-0

Colón Pizarro, Mariam. 2011. "Poetic Pragmatism: The Puerto Rican Division of Community Education (DIVEDCO) and the Politics of Cultural Production, 1949–1968." PhD diss., University of Michigan, Ann Arbor.

Colón-Zayas, Eliseo. 2012. "Amanecer en la Era de Acuario: Walter Mercado, estrella del *performance camp* y *queer*." *DeSignis* 19: 67–78.

Contardo, Óscar. 2018. "El corazón rabioso del hombre loca." *Gatopardo*, November 20. https://gatopardo.com/reportajes/escritor-pedro-lemebel/

Conti, Luis. 2020. Email communication, January 27.

Cornejo, Giancarlo. 2019. "*Travesti* Dreams Outside in the Ethnographic Machine." *GLQ* 25, no. 2: 457–82.

Cortés, Jason. 2015. *Macho Ethics: Masculinity and Self-Representation in Latino-Caribbean Narrative.* Lanham, MD: Bucknell University Press.

Cortés-Vélez, Dinorah. 2018. "Clara Gardenia Otero, Palmira Parés y el feminismo queer de Manuel Ramos Otero." *CENTRO Journal* 30, no. 2 (Summer): 68–87.

Costa, Claudia de Lima. 2014. "Introduction to Debates about Translation: Lost (and Found?) in Translation: Feminisms in Hemispheric Dialogue." In Alvarez et al., 19–36.

Costa, Marithelma. 1991. "Entrevista: Manuel Ramos Otero." *Hispamérica* 20, no. 59: 59–67.

Costantini, Cristina, and Kareem Tabsch, dirs. 2020. *Mucho Mucho Amor: The Legend of Walter Mercado.* Netflix. Film.

Cotera, María Eugenia. 2017. "Feminisms." In Vargas, Mirabal, and La Fountain-Stokes, 64–68.

Cotter, Holland. 2001. "Tourists, Jungle Sprites and the Logic of Dreams on Fantasy Island." *New York Times*, March 9: 37. https://www.nytimes.com/2001/03/09/arts/art-review-tourists-jungle-sprites-and-the-logic-of-dreams-on-fantasy-island.html

Cotter, Holland. 2015. "When the Young Lords Were Outlaws in New York." *New York Times*, July 23. https://www.nytimes.com/2015/07/24/arts/design/when-the-young-lords-strove-to-change-new-york.html

Cottrell, William, et al., dirs. (1937) 2001. *Snow White and the Seven Dwarfs.* Walt Disney Enterprises. Burbank, CA: Buena Vista Home Entertainment. DVD.

Cousineau-Levine, Penny. 2017. "Cher's 'Half-Breed' and the Hybrid Masquerades of Kent Monkman's Miss Chief Testickle." *Americana* 13, no. 1. http://americanaejournal.hu/vol13no1mixed/cousineau-levine

Crichlow, Wesley E. A. 2004. *Buller Men and Batty Bwoys: Hidden Men in Toronto and Halifax Black Communities.* Toronto: University of Toronto Press.

Crimp, Douglas. 2002. "Mario Montez, for Shame." In *Regarding Sedgwick: Essays on Queer Culture and Critical Theory*, edited by Stephen M. Barber and David L. Clark, 57–70. New York: Routledge.

Croft, Clare, ed. 2017. *Queer Dance: Meaning and Makings.* New York: Oxford University Press.

Crummy, Colin. 2015. "Stonewall's Jonny Beauchamp Is 'a Trans and Queer Ally.'" *i-D*, November 6. https://i-d.vice.com/en_us/article/vbexzm/stonewalls-jonny-beauchamp-is-a-trans-and-queer-ally

Cruz, Noel, dir. 2002. *Doña Fela: Documental biográfico inspirado en la vida de Felisa Rincón Vda. de Gautier.* San Juan: Producciones Noel Cruz.

Cruz-Malavé, Arnaldo. 1993. "Para virar al macho: La autobiografía como subversión en la cuentística de Manuel Ramos Otero." *Revista Iberoamericana* 59, nos. 162–63: 239–63.

Cruz-Malavé, Arnaldo. 1994. *El primitivo implorante: El "sistema poético del mundo" de José Lezama Lima.* Amsterdam: Rodopi.

Cruz-Malavé, Arnaldo. 1995. "Towards an Art of Transvestism: Colonialism and Homosexuality in Puerto Rican Literature." In Bergmann and Smith, 137–67.

Cruz-Malavé, Arnaldo. 1997. "'What a Tangled Web!': Masculinity, Abjection, and the Foundations of Puerto Rican Literature in the United States." In Balderston and Guy, 234–49.

Cruz-Malavé, Arnaldo. 2002. "Colonial Figures in Motion: Globalization and Translocality in Contemporary Puerto Rican Literature in the United States." *CENTRO Journal* 14, no. 2 (Fall): 5–25.

Cruz-Malavé, Arnaldo. 2007a. "The Oxymoron of Sexual Sovereignty: Some Puerto Rican Literary Reflections." *CENTRO Journal* 19, no. 1 (Spring): 51–73.

Cruz-Malavé, Arnaldo. 2007b. *Queer Latino Testimonio, Keith Haring, and Juanito Xtravaganza: Hard Tails.* New York: Palgrave Macmillan.

Cruz-Malavé, Arnaldo. 2015a. "Between Irony and Belief: The Queer Diasporic Underground Aesthetics of José Rodríguez-Soltero and Mario Montez." *GLQ* 21, no. 4: 585–615.

Cruz-Malavé, Arnaldo 2015b. "Transnationalism and Manuel Ramos Otero's 'Traveling Theater' of Return." *emisférica* 12, no. 1. https://hemisphericinstitute.org/en/emisferi ca-121-caribbean-rasanblaj/12-1-dossier/e-121-dossier-cruz-malave-transnationali sm-and-manuel-ramos.html

Cruz-Malavé, Arnaldo. 2017a. "Memorialization and Presence: Capturing the Legacies of the Young Lords in New York." *ARTMargins* 6, no. 2 (June): 72–90.

Cruz-Malavé, Arnaldo. 2017b. "Testimonio." In Vargas, Mirabal, and La Fountain-Stokes, 228–31.

Cruz-Malavé, Arnaldo, and Martin F. Manalansan IV, eds. 2002. *Queer Globalizations: Citizenship and the Afterlife of Colonialism.* New York: New York University Press.

Cuadra, Ivonne. 2003. "¿Quién canta? Bolero y ambigüedad genérica en *Sirena Selena vestida de pena* de Mayra Santos Febres." *Revista de Estudios Hispánicos* (Río Piedras) 30, no. 1: 153–63.

Cuby, Michael. 2018. "These Trans and Cis Female Drag Queens Have Some Words for RuPaul." *Them*, March 6. https://www.them.us/story/these-queens-have-some-wor ds-for-rupaul

Cuchí Coll, Isabel. 1969. *Historia de la esclavitud en Puerto Rico.* San Juan: Sociedad de Puerto Rico, Sociedad de Autores Puertorriqueños.

Cullen, Deborah, ed. 2001. *Here and There / Aquí y Allá: Six Artists from San Juan.* New York: El Museo del Barrio.

Cullen, Deborah, ed. 2008. *Arte ≠ Vida: Actions by Artists of the Americas, 1960–2000.* New York: El Museo del Barrio.

Cullen, Deborah. 2011. "*Arte ≠ Vida:* A History and Reflection on the Project." *emisférica* 8, no. 1 (Summer). https://hemisphericinstitute.org/en/emisferica-81/8-1-essays/ar te-vida-a-history-and-reflection-on-the-project.html

Currah, Paisley, Richard M. Juang, and Shannon Price Minter, eds. 2006. *Transgender Rights.* Minneapolis: University of Minnesota Press.

Cvetkovich, Ann. 2003. *An Archive of Feelings: Trauma, Sexuality, and Lesbian Public Cultures*. Durham, NC: Duke University Press.

Daems, Jim, ed. 2014. *The Makeup of* RuPaul's Drag Race: *Essays on the Queen of Reality Shows*. Jefferson, NC: McFarland.

Daniels, Michael. 2009. "¡LOCA!" *Outlook: Columbus* 14, no. 7 (December): 47.

Davenport, Jeremiah. 2017. "From the Love Ball to RuPaul: The Mainstreaming of Drag in the 1990s." PhD diss., Case Western Reserve University, Cleveland, OH.

Davies, Jon. 2009. *Trash: A Queer Film Classic*. Vancouver: Arsenal Pulp Press.

Dávila, Verónica, and Marisol LeBrón. 2019. "How Music Took Down Puerto Rico's Governor." *Washington Post*, August 1. https://www.washingtonpost.com/outlook /2019/08/01/how-music-took-down-puerto-ricos-governor/

Davis, Fernando, and Miguel A. López. 2010. "Micropolíticas cuir: Transmariconizando el Sur." *Ramona* 99: 8–9.

Davis, John. 2016. *The Essential RuPaul: Herstory, Philosophy and Her Fiercest Queens*. Melbourne: Smith Street Books.

Daw, Stephen. 2019. "Bad Bunny on Representing Gender Fluidity in His Art: 'I Think It's My Responsibility.'" *Billboard*, March 20. https://www.billboard.com/articles/ne ws/pride/8503370/bad-bunny-gender-fluidity-gq-interview

DeCaro, Frank. 2019. *Drag: Combing through the Big Wigs of Showbusiness*. New York: Rizzoli.

de Certeau, Michel. 1985. "Practices of Space." In *On Signs*, edited by Marshall Blonsky, 122–45. Baltimore: Johns Hopkins University Press.

Decena, Carlos Ulises. 2011. *Tacit Subjects: Belonging and Same-Sex Desire among Dominican Immigrant Men*. Durham, NC: Duke University Press.

De Cuba Romero, Natalia. n.d. "Come to the Cabaret." *San Juan Star*. Photocopy.

DeFrantz, Thomas F., and Anita González, eds. 2014. *Black Performance Theory*. Durham, NC: Duke University Press.

de Ita, Fernando. 2001. "Encuentro Monterrey 2001: Memoria, atrocidad y resistencia." *Revista Cultural El Ángel, Periódico Reforma* (Mexico), June 24: n.p.

de Jesús, Dyanis. 2001. "El arte que se pone." Photos by Rosario Fernández. *Vidacool*. Photocopy.

Delany, Samuel R. 1999. *Times Square Red, Times Square Blue*. New York: New York University Press.

Del Castillo, Nelson. 2000. "Ivette Román al rescate del cabaret." *Primera Hora*, November 29: 3B.

Deleuze, Gilles, and Félix Guattari. 1986a. *Kafka: Toward a Minor Literature*. Translated by Dana Polan. Minneapolis: University of Minnesota Press.

Deleuze, Gilles, and Félix Guattari. 1986b. *Nomadology: The War Machine*. Translated by Brian Massumi. New York: Semiotext(e).

Delgado, Ray. 2001. "Kris Kovick, 50, Author, Cartoonist, Activist." *San Francisco Chronicle*, November 8. http://www.sfgate.com/news/article/Kris-Kovick-50-author-carto onist-activist-2859581.php

del Puente, José Ramón. 1986. *El homosexualismo en Puerto Rico: ¿crimen, pecado, o enfermedad?* Río Piedras: n.p.

Del Valle, Sara. 1995. "Adiós a un gran artista . . ." *Claridad*, October 6–12: 16–17.

Den Tandt, Catherine. 1999. "All That Is Black Melts into Air: *Negritud* and Nation in

Puerto Rico." In *Caribbean Romances: The Politics of Regional Representation*, edited by Belinda J. Edmonson, 76–91. Charlottesville: University Press of Virginia.

Desta, Yohana. 2017a. "Catching Up with BeBe Zahara Benet, the Very First Winner of *RuPaul's Drag Race*." *Vanity Fair*, March 23. https://www.vanityfair.com/hollywood /2017/03/bebe-zahara-benet-rupauls-drag-race

Desta, Yohana. 2017b. "Meet the Transgender Activist Fighting to Keep Marsha P. Johnson's Legacy Alive." *Vanity Fair*, October 3. https://www.vanityfair.com/hollywood /2017/10/the-death-and-life-of-marsha-p-johnson-victoria-cruz

De Villiers, Nicholas. 2012. "*RuPaul's Drag Race* as Meta-reality Television." *Jump Cut* 54 (Fall): n.p. https://www.ejumpcut.org/archive/jc54.2012/deVilRuPaul/index.html

Diamond, Elin, ed. 1996. *Performance and Cultural Politics*. London: Routledge.

Díaz, Carmen Graciela. 2018. "The Travelling Theater of Manuel Ramos Otero." *CEN-TRO Journal* 30, no. 2 (Summer): 114–39.

Díaz, Luis Felipe. 2005. "Una lectura sicoanalítica de 'En el fondo del caño hay un negrito' de José Luis González." In *Modernidad literaria puertorriqueña*, 139–66. San Juan: Isla Negra and Editorial Cultural.

Díaz, Luis Felipe. 2012a. "Datos de Luis Felipe y Lizza Fernanda. De 1976 a 2012." *(Post) modernidad puertorriqueña*, April 14. http://postmodernidadpuertorriquena.blogsp ot.com/2012/04/datos-de-luis-felipe-y-lizza-fernanada.html

Díaz, Luis Felipe. 2012b. "Memorias: Puertorriqueñidad y transculturación mariconil." *(Post)modernidad puertorriqueña*, May 7. http://postmodernidadpuertorriquena.bl ogspot.com/2012/05/blog-post.html

Díaz Cárdenas, Jonathan. 2016. "'¿Mama, qué será lo que quiere el negro?': La curiosa historia detrás de la canción." *Al día*, February 22. www.aldia.co/historias/mama -que-sera-lo-que-quiere-el-negro-la-curiosa-historia-detras-de-la-cancion

Díaz-Zambrana, Rosana. 2013. "La jaula de las locas se abrió: Nuevas estrategias y aperturas de identidades sexuales en el cine contemporáneo puertorriqueño." In *Actas del 4to Coloquio ¿Del otro la'o? Perspectivas sobre sexualidades queer*, edited by Beatriz Llenín Figueroa, 65–77. Cabo Rojo: Editora Educación Emergente.

Di Iorio Sandín, Lyn. 2004. *Killing Spanish: Literary Essays on Ambivalent U.S. Latino/a Identity*. New York: Palgrave Macmillan.

Dinzey-Flores, Zaire Zenit. 2013. *Locked In, Locked Out: Gated Communities in a Puerto Rican City*. Philadelphia: University of Pennsylvania Press.

Dockray, Heather. 2015. "Why Celebrate Brooklyn's 'Paris Is Burning' Screening Sparked a Fire on Facebook." *BrooklynBased.com*, May 13. http://brooklynbased.com/blog/20 15/05/13/celebrate-brooklyns-paris-burning-screening-sparked-fire-facebook/

Dolan, Jill. 2005. *Utopia in Performance: Finding Hope at the Theater*. Ann Arbor: University of Michigan Press.

Domínguez Ruvalcaba, Héctor. 2007. "The Perturbing Dress: Transvestism in Visual Arts." In *Modernity and the Nation in Mexican Representations of Masculinity: From Sensuality to Bloodshed*, 33–53. New York: Palgrave Macmillan.

Domínguez Ruvalcaba, Héctor. 2016. *Translating the Queer: Body Politics and Transnational Conversations*. London: Zed.

Dong, Arthur E., dir. 1995. *The Question of Equality*. Part 1: *Out Rage '69*. San Francisco: KQED Video. VHS.

Donohue, Caitlin. 2019. "Don Omar Sparks Controversy Surrounding Homophobic

Social Media Posts about Ozuna." *Remezcla*, January 23. https://remezcla.com/mu
sic/bad-bunny-ozuna-don-omar-homophobic-comments/

Doonan, Simon. 2019. *Drag: The Complete Story.* London: Laurence King.

Dry, Jude. 2020. "'Mucho Mucho Amor' Trailer: Netflix Documentary on Gay Latinx
Icon Walter Mercado." *IndieWire*, June 29. https://www.indiewire.com/2020/06/mu
cho-mucho-amor-trailer-netflix-gay-latin-walter-mercado-1234570457/

Duany, Jorge. 2002. *The Puerto Rican Nation on the Move: Identities on the Island and in
the United States.* Chapel Hill: University of North Carolina Press.

Duany, Jorge. 2005. "The Rough Edges of Puerto Rican Identities: Race, Gender, and
Transnationalism." *Latin American Research Review* 40, no. 3 (2005): 177–90.

Duany, Jorge. 2011. *Blurred Borders: Transnational Migration between the Hispanic
Caribbean and the United States.* Chapel Hill: University of North Carolina Press.

Duany, Jorge. 2017. *Puerto Rico: What Everyone Needs to Know.* New York: Oxford University Press.

Duberman, Martin. 1993. *Stonewall.* New York: Dutton.

Duggan, Lisa. 2003. *The Twilight of Equality? Neoliberalism, Cultural Politics, and the
Attack on Democracy.* Boston: Beacon Press.

Dunlap, David W. 2002. "Sylvia Rivera, 50, Figure in Birth of the Gay Liberation Movement." *New York Times*, February 20. https://www.nytimes.com/2002/02/20/nyregi
on/sylvia-rivera-50-figure-in-birth-of-the-gay-liberation-movement.html

Dussel, Enrique. 2012. "Transmodernity and Interculturality: An Interpretation from
the Perspective of Philosophy of Liberation." *Transmodernity* 1, no. 3 (Spring): 29–59.

Edelstein, David. 2017. "The Death and Life of Marsha P. Johnson Is a Shattering Documentary." *Vulture.com*, October 5. http://www.vulture.com/2017/10/the-death-and
-life-of-marsha-p-johnson-is-shattering.html

Edgar, Eir-Anne. 2011. "Xtravaganza! Drag Representation and Articulation in *RuPaul's
Drag Race*." *Studies in Popular Culture* 34, no. 1 (Fall): 133–46.

"Educational Theatre Faculty: Javier Cardona." n.d. *Department of Music and Performing
Arts Professions,* NYU Steinhardt. http://steinhardt.nyu.edu/music/edtheatre/peop
le/faculty/cardona (no longer online).

Emmerich, Roland, dir. (2015) 2016. *Stonewall.* Santa Monica, CA: Lionsgate. DVD.

Ennis, Dawn. 2018. "Inside the Fight for Marsha P. Johnson's Legacy." *Advocate*, January 23. https://www.advocate.com/arts-entertainment/2018/1/23/inside-fight-mars
ha-p-johnsons-legacy

Erman, Sam. 2018. *Almost Citizens: Puerto Rico, the U.S. Constitution, and Empire.* New
York: Cambridge University Press.

Escuelita. 2000. *The Best of Lady Catiria.* New York. Videocassette (VHS).

Esterrich, Carmelo. 2018. *Concrete and Countryside: The Urban and the Rural in 1950s
Puerto Rican Culture.* Pittsburgh: University of Pittsburgh Press.

Esteves-Wolff, Cristina. 2020. "Disrupting Colonial Identity: Puerto Rican Subjectivities
in Cultural Essays." *CENTRO Journal* 32, no. 1 (Spring): 33–63.

Evans, Alex. 2009. "How Homo Can Hollywood Be? Remaking Queer Authenticity
from *To Wong Foo* to *Brokeback Mountain*." *Journal of Film and Video* 61, no. 4
(Winter): 41–54.

Exposito, Suzy. 2019a. "Death of Gay Trap Star Kevin Fret Highlights Crisis in Puerto

Rico." *Rolling Stone*, January 11. https://www.rollingstone.com/music/music-latin/ke vin-fret-gay-trap-star-murdered-puerto-rico-777229/

Exposito, Suzy. 2019b. "Inside Residente and Bad Bunny's Meeting with Puerto Rico Governor Rosselló." *Rolling Stone*, January 16. https://www.rollingstone.com/music /music-latin/residente-bad-bunny-meet-governor-rossello-puerto-rico-778809/

Exposito, Suzy. 2020. "Bad Bunny in Captivity." *Rolling Stone*, May 14. https://www.roll ingstone.com/music/music-features/bad-bunny-cover-story-lockdown-puerto-rico -new-albums-996871/

Eze, Emmanuel Chukwudi. 1997. "The Color of Reason: The Idea of 'Race' in Kant's Anthropology." In *Postcolonial African Philosophy: A Critical Reader*, edited by Emmanuel Chukwudi Eze, 103–31. Oxford: Blackwell.

Falconí Trávez, Diego, ed. 2018. *Inflexión marica: Escrituras del descalabro gay en América Latina*. Barcelona: Editorial Egales.

Falconí Trávez, Diego, Santiago Castellanos, and María Amelia Viteri, eds. 2014. *Resentir lo queer en América Latina: Diálogos desde/con el Sur*. Barcelona: Editorial Egales.

Fanon, Frantz. 1967. *Black Skin, White Masks*. Translated by Charles Lam Markmann. New York: Grove Press.

Farrier, Stephen. 2016. "That Lip-Synching Feeling: Drag Performance as Digging the Past." In *Queer Dramaturgies: International Perspectives on Where Performance Leads Queer*, edited by Alyson Campbell and Stephen Farrier, 192–209. Houndmills: Palgrave Macmillan.

"Fausto Fernós." 2018. Wikipedia. https://en.wikipedia.org/wiki/Fausto_Fern%C3%B3s

Feast of Fun. 2018a. "About Us." *Feast of Fun*. https://feastoffun.com/about/

"Feast of Fun." 2018b. Wikipedia. https://en.wikipedia.org/wiki/Feast_of_Fun

Feast of Fun. 2019. "Jade Sotomayor & Monica Beverly Hillz—Beef Empanadas— Cooking with Drag Queens." YouTube, October 10. https://youtu.be/jZSNApAAzL0

Feinberg, Leslie. 1998. *Trans Liberation: Beyond Pink or Blue*. Boston: Beacon.

Feliciano Díaz, Enrique. 2014. "Gilda Navarra." *Fundación Nacional para la Cultura Popular*, June 26. http://prpop.org/biografias/gilda-navarra/

Felion, Marc. 2013. "FOF #1771—Monica Beverly Hillz Spillz the Tea." *Feast of Fun*, April 8. https://feastoffun.com/podcast/2013/04/08/fof-1771-monica-beverly-hillz-spillz -the-tea/

Ferguson, Roderick A. 2003. *Aberrations in Black: Toward a Queer of Color Critique*. Minneapolis: University of Minnesota Press.

Ferguson, Roderick A. 2019. *One-Dimensional Queer*. Medford, MA: Polity Press.

Fernandez, Alexia. 2019. "Latin Singer Ozuna Reveals He Was the Victim of an Extor- tion Attempt over an 'Intimate Video.'" *People*, January 23. https://people.com/mus ic/latin-singer-ozuna-admits-victim-extortion-attempt/

Fernández, Imma. 2011. "Antonia San Juan: 'Estoy harta de que nieguen mi feminidad.'" *El periódico*, September 14. https://www.elperiodico.com/es/ocio-y-cultura/201109 14/antonia-san-juan-estoy-harta-de-que-nieguen-mi-feminidad-1149284

Fernández-Alemany, Manuel, and Andrés Sciolla. 1999. *Mariquitas y marimachos: Guía completa de la homosexualidad*. Madrid: Nuer Ediciones.

Fernández Barreto, Cristina. 2003. "Sin pausa la agenda del Circo." *El Nuevo Día*, July 22: n.p.

Fernández Retamar, Roberto. 1989. *Caliban and Other Essays*. Translated by Edward Baker. Minneapolis: University of Minnesota Press.

Fernós, Fausto. 2019. "FOF #2780—the Puerto Rican Bombshell, Barbra Herr." *Feast of Fun*, September 17. https://feastoffun.com/podcast/2019/09/17/fof-2780-the-puerto-rican-bombshell-barbra-herr/

Ferrer, Melba. 1999. "Mapping Life through a Bolero." *San Juan Star*, May 4: n.p.

Ferreras, Alberto, dir. 2014. *Habla Men*. New York: HBO Latino.

Ferreras, Alberto, dir. 2017. *Lesson #6*. Written by Alberto Ferreras. New York: New Yorkian.

Fetta, Stephanie. 2018. *Shaming into Brown: Somatic Transactions of Race in Latina/o Literature*. Columbus: Ohio State University Press.

Fiet, Lowell. 1995. "Comedia del taller de Pantojas: ¡Ay, Bendito! y otras pocas vergüenzas." *Claridad*, September 8–14: 26.

Fiet, Lowell. 1997a. "El teatro puertorriqueño: Puente aéreo entre ambas orillas." *Conjunto* 106 (May-August): 55–59.

Fiet, Lowell. 1997b. "Encuentro de Teatro Alternativo: ¿Por qué 'Alternativo'?" In *Caribe 2000: Definiciones, identidades y culturas regionales y/o nacionales*, edited by Lowell Fiet and Janette Becerra, 141–46. San Juan: Caribe 2000 / Universidad de Puerto Rico.

Fiet, Lowell. 1998. "Hablar, nombrar, pertenecer: El juego entre el idioma y la identidad en la(s) cultura(s) caribeña(s)." In *Segundo simposio de Caribe 2000: Hablar, nombrar, pertenecer*, edited by Lowell Fiet and Janette Becerra, 5–11. San Juan: Caribe 2000 / Universidad de Puerto Rico.

Fiet, Lowell. 1999. "Re-imágenes de un teatro popular." In *A Gathering of Players and Poets / Un convite de poetas y teatreros: Proceedings of the Caribbean 2000 Symposium III (1998)*, edited by Lowell Fiet and Janette Becerra, 159–67. San Juan: Caribe 2000 / Universidad de Puerto Rico.

Fiet, Lowell. 2004. *El teatro puertorriqueño reimaginado: Notas críticas sobre la creación dramática y el performance*. San Juan: Ediciones Callejón.

Fiet, Lowell. 2006. "Las Fiestas (imparables) de Santiago Apóstol." *Claridad*, August 17–24: 16, 29.

Fiet, Lowell. 2007. *Caballeros, vejigantes, locas y viejos: Santiago Apóstol y los performeros afropuertorriqueños*. San Juan: Terranova Editores.

Fiet, Lowell. 2012. "Una breve historia crítica del teatro puertorriqueño." In *Historia de Puerto Rico*, edited by Luis E. González Vales and María Dolores Luque, 545–80. Vol. 4, *Historia de las antillas*, edited by Consuelo Naranjo Orovio. Madrid: Ediciones Doce Calles.

Fiet, Lowell. 2016. "'Hasta el cuello' (y más allá) de Javier Cardona." *Claridad*, December 7: n.p.

Fiet, Lowell. 2019. *An Archipelago of Caribbean Masks*. Kingston: Ian Randle Publishers; San Juan: Isla Negra Editores.

Figari, Carlos. 2016. "Queer Articulations." In Martínez-San Miguel, Sifuentes-Jáuregui, and Belausteguigoitia, 231–38.

Figueroa Rosa, Bárbara J. 2009. "Espeluznante crimen de odio contra joven homosexual." *Primera Hora*, November 16. https://www.primerahora.com/noticias/policia-tribunales/notas/espeluznante-crimen-de-odio-contra-joven-homosexual/

Figueroa Rosa, Bárbara J., Ivelisse Rivera Quiñones, and Maribel Hernández. 2009.

"Arrestan sospechoso de aparente crimen de odio por homofobia." *Primera Hora*, November 17. https://www.primerahora.com/noticias/policia-tribunales/notas/arre stan-sospechoso-de-aparente-crimen-de-odio-por-homofobia/

Finch, Nigel, dir. (1995) 1999. *Stonewall*. New York: Fox Lorber Home Video. DVD.

Findlay, Eileen J. Suárez. 2014. *We Are Left without a Father Here: Masculinity, Domesticity, and Migration in Postwar Puerto Rico*. Durham, NC: Duke University Press.

Finkelstein, Avram. 2013. "LGBTQ at NYPL: The Silence = Death Poster." *New York Public Library*, November 22. https://www.nypl.org/blog/2013/11/22/silence-equals-dea th-poster

Fiol-Matta, Licia. 2008. "Chencha's Gait." *Women and Performance* 18, no. 3 (November): 287–301.

Fiol-Matta, Licia. 2010. "Camina como Chencha: La ética cínica de Myrta Silva." *Papel Máquina* (Santiago de Chile) 2, no. 4 (August): 121–41.

Fiol-Matta, Licia. 2016. "Queer/Sexualities." In Martínez-San Miguel, Sifuentes-Jáuregui, and Belausteguigoitia, 217–30.

Fiol-Matta, Licia. 2017. *The Great Woman Singer: Gender and Voice in Puerto Rican Music*. Durham, NC: Duke University Press.

Fior. 2016. "Fior—Backstabber (Official Video) ft. Nina Flowers." YouTube, September 25. https://youtu.be/Rq9zxgHLhk4

Fitzgerald, Tom, and Lorenzo Marquez. 2020. *Legendary Children: The First Decade of RuPaul's Drag Race and the Last Century of Queer Life*. New York: Penguin Books.

Fitzsimons, Tim. 2019. "Drag Troupe 'The Sisters of Perpetual Indulgence' Mark 40 Years of 'Dragtivism.'" *NBC News*, April 20. https://www.nbcnews.com/feature/nbc-out/drag-troupe-sisters-perpetual-indulgence-mark-40-years-dragtivism-n996701

Fitzsimons, Tim, and Alexander Kacala. 2019. "Drag Queen Sashays into Trump Impeachment Hearings." *NBC News*, November 13. https://www.nbcnews.com/feat ure/nbc-out/drag-queen-sashays-trump-impeachment-hearings-n1081261

Flatley, Guy. 1970. "He Enjoys Being a Girl." *New York Times*, November 15: D15.

Flecha Cruz, Alice. n.d. "Artículos de prensa sobre 'El Ángel de los Solteros.'" *Observatorio Móvil*. http://www.observatoriomovil.com/el--ngel-de-los-solteros.html

Fleisher, Julian. 1996. *The Drag Queens of New York: An Illustrated Field Guide*. New York: Riverhead.

Fleming, Bill. 1995. "Bill F. Does Labor Day Weekend: Chicago's Miss Continental Pageant." *Newsletter of the Lesbian, Gay, Bisexual and Transgendered Health Science Librarians Special Interest Group (SIG) of the Medical Library Association* 2, no. 1 (October).

Fleming, Bill. 1996. "Paris Takes Chicago: A Trip to the Miss Continental U.S.A. 1996–97 Pageant." *Newsletter of the Lesbian, Gay, Bisexual and Transgendered Health Science Librarians Special Interest Group (SIG) of the Medical Library Association* 3, no. 1 (October).

Flores, Juan. 1980. *The Insular Vision: Pedreira's Interpretation of Puerto Rican Culture*. New York: Centro de Estudios Puertorriqueños, Hunter College, CUNY.

Flores, Juan. 1993. *Divided Borders: Essays on Puerto Rican Identity*. Houston: Arte Público Press.

Flores, Juan. 2000. *From Bomba to Hip-Hop: Puerto Rican Culture and Latino Identity*. New York: Columbia University Press.

Flores, Juan. 2009. *The Diaspora Strikes Back: Caribeño Tales of Learning and Turning.* New York: Routledge.

Flores, Juan, and George Yúdice. 1990. "Living Borders / Buscando America: Languages of Latino Self-Formation." *Social Text* 24: 57–84.

Flores Charneco, Santiago. (1996) 1998. "Freddie Mercado: Puerto Rico." In Borràs and Zaya, 177.

Flores Charneco, Santiago. 2002. "*Coco barroco.*" Concept and performance by Freddie Mercado. Drawings by Freddie Mercado. Chronicle by Santiago Flores Charneco. In Lugo Bertrán, n.p.

Flores Charneco, Santiago. 2003. "Freddy Mercado viste su cuerpo." Photographs by Raúl Ramírez. *Orificio* 3: 42–45.

Flowers, Nina. 2009. "Loca" (with DJ Ranny). In *Loca (feat. Nina Flowers).* Apple Music. https://music.apple.com/us/album/loca-feat-nina-flowers/341471922

Flowers, Nina. 2010. "Locas in Da House" (with William Umana). In *Start Your Engines EP (Remixes).* Apple Music. https://music.apple.com/us/album/start-your-engines -ep-remixes/399281636

Flowers, Nina. 2012. "About Me." *NinaFlowers.com.* http://ninaflowers.com/about-me/

Foerster, Maxime. 2012. *Elle ou lui? Une histoire des transsexuels en France.* Paris: Musardine.

Font, Susana. 2009. "El brutal asesinato de Jorge Steven Lopez Mercado." *AmbienteG. com*, November 23. http://www.ambienteg.com/glbt-en-el-mundo/el-brutal-asesin ato-de-jorge-steven-lopez-mercado

Forbes, Ozzie. 2011. "Freddie Mercado por Ozzie Forbes." YouTube, January 15. https:// youtu.be/blAJffKiFHU

Ford, Zack. 2014. "The Quiet Clash between Transgender Women and Drag Queens." *Think Progress*, June 25. https://thinkprogress.org/the-quiet-clash-between-transge nder-women-and-drag-queens-297a9da4c5f6/

Foster, David William. 2000. "Paquita la del Barrio: Singing Feminine Rage." *Ciber- Letras* 2. http://www.lehman.cuny.edu/ciberletras/v01n02/Foster.htm

Foster, David William. 2010. "Documenting Queer, Queer Documentary." *Revista Can- adiense de Estudios Hispánicos* 35, no. 1: 105–19.

Foucault, Michel. 1995. *Discipline and Punish: The Birth of the Prison.* Translated by Alan Sheridan. New York: Vintage.

Foucault, Michel. 2001. *Fearless Speech.* Edited by Joseph Pearson. Los Angeles, CA: Semiotext(e).

Foucault, Michel. 2006. *History of Madness.* Translated by Jonathan Murphy and Jean Khal. New York: Routledge.

France, David, dir. 2017. *The Death and Life of Marsha P. Johnson.* Netflix. Film.

Franco, Jean. 1999. "The Mares of the Apocalypse (1996)." In *Critical Passions: Selected Essays*, edited by Mary Louise Pratt and Kathleen Newman, 109–22. Durham, NC: Duke University Press.

Fret Family. 2018. "Kevin Fret—Soy Asi." YouTube, April 8. https://youtu.be/H7-gSwvoo8M

Freud, Sigmund. (1919) 2003. *The Uncanny.* Translated by David McLintock. New York: Penguin Putnam.

Freud, Sigmund. 1975. *Three Essays on the Theory of Sexuality.* Translated by James Strachey. New York: Basic Books.

Friedrichsmeyer, Sara, Sara Lennox, and Susanne Zantop, eds. 1998. *The Imperialist Imagination: German Colonialism and Its Legacy.* Ann Arbor: University of Michigan Press.

Fullana Acosta, Mariela. 2019. "'Negras' hace historia en radio." *El Nuevo Día*, July 14. https://www.elnuevodia.com/entretenimiento/farandula/notas/negras-hace-historia-en-radio/

Fundación Nacional para la Cultura Popular. 2014a. "Antonio Pantojas." April 14. https://prpop.org/biografias/antonio-pantojas/

Fundación Nacional para la Cultura Popular. 2014b. "Johnny Rodríguez." June 26. https://prpop.org/biografias/johnny-rodriguez/

Fusco, Coco. 1995. "Who's Doing the Twist? Notes toward a Politics of Appropriation." In *English Is Broken Here: Notes on Cultural Fusion in the Americas*, 65–77. New York: New Press.

Fusco, Coco. 2000. *Corpus Delecti: Performance Art of the Americas.* New York: Routledge.

Galanes, Philip. 2018. "Ryan Murphy and Janet Mock on 'Pose,' Diversity and Netflix." *New York Times*, May 23. https://www.nytimes.com/2018/05/23/arts/television/pose-ryan-murphy-janet-mock.html

Galarte, Francisco J. 2011. "Notes from a Trans* Chicana/o Survivor." *Mujeres Talk*, October 24. https://mujerestalk.org/2011/10/24/notes-from-a-trans-chicanao-survivor/

Galarte, Francisco J. 2020. "Transgender Studies and Latina/o/x Studies." *Oxford Research Encyclopedia of Literature*, March. https://doi.org/10.1093/acrefore/9780190201098.013.349

Gallardo, Gabriel. 2019. "The Mexican Artist Who Challenges Sexist Culture through His Paintings." *Cultura Colectiva*, December 11. https://culturacolectiva.com/art/fabian-chairez-erotic-paintings

Gamson, Joshua. 1998. *Freaks Talk Back: Tabloid Talk Shows and Sexual Nonconformity.* Chicago: University of Chicago Press.

Gan, Jessi. 2007. "'Still at the Back of the Bus': Sylvia Rivera's Struggle." *CENTRO Journal* 19, no. 1 (Spring): 124–39.

Ganser, Alexandra. 2011. "*Lap Dancing for Mommy*: Queer Intermediality, Chick Lit, and Trans-generational Feminist Mediation in Erika Lopez's Illustrated Narratives." *Amerikastudien / American Studies* 56, no. 2: 219–40.

Garber, Marjorie. 1992. *Vested Interests: Cross-Dressing and Cultural Anxiety.* New York: Routledge.

García, Marlene, and José Ramón Alonso. 2001. *Diccionario ilustrado de voces eróticas cubanas.* Madrid: Celeste Ediciones.

García, William. 2016. "The Burial of Chianita La Negra: White Fragility and Blackface in Puerto Rico." *Latino Rebels*, November 8. http://www.latinorebels.com/2016/11/08/the-burial-of-chianita-la-negra-white-fragility-and-blackface-in-puerto-rico/

García Canclini, Néstor. (1990) 1995. *Hybrid Cultures: Strategies for Entering and Leaving Modernity.* Minneapolis: University of Minnesota Press.

García Gámez, Pablo. 2019. "Desde el margen: Teatro alterno y comunidades hispanas de Nueva York 1997–2017." PhD diss., City University of New York.

García Lorca, Federico. 1955. "Ode to Walt Whitman." Translated by Ben Belitt. *Poetry* 85, no. 4 (January): 187–92.

García Lorca, Federico. 1987. *Poeta en Nueva York*. Barcelona: Cátedra.

García-Peña, Lorgia. 2016. *The Borders of Dominicanidad: Race, Nation, and Archives of Contradiction*. Durham, NC: Duke University Press.

García Toro, Víctor I., Rafael L. Ramírez, and Luis Solano Castillo, eds. 2007. *Los hombres no lloran: Ensayos sobre las masculinidades*. Río Piedras: Ediciones Huracán.

Garza, Frida. 2019. "Kevin Fret, Latin Trap's First Openly Gay Artist, Murdered in Puerto Rico." *Jezebel*, January 11. https://jezebel.com/kevin-fret-latin-traps-first-op enly-gay-artist-murder-1831670272

Gaspar Concepción, Jessica Aymee. 2005. "Resistance and Transformation in the 'Other' Puerto Rican Theater: Performances of Rosa Luisa Márquez, 1986–1998." PhD diss., University of Wisconsin, Madison.

Gates, Henry Louis, Jr. 1988. *The Signifying Monkey*. New York: Oxford University Press.

Gay, Roxane. 2017. *Hunger: A Memoir of (My) Body*. New York: HarperCollins.

Géliga Quiñones, Jaime Andrés. 2016. "'Estar perra es la onda': Arte, escena y miradas drag en la Ciudad de México." MA thesis, Colegio de México.

Gelpí, Juan G. 1993. *Literatura y paternalismo en Puerto Rico*. San Juan: Editorial de la Universidad de Puerto Rico.

Gelpí, Juan G. 2000. "Conversación con Manuel Ramos Otero: Nueva York, 3 de mayo de 1980." *Revista de Estudios Hispánicos* (Río Piedras) 27, no. 2: 401–10.

Genet, Jean. (1943) 1963. *Our Lady of the Flowers*. Translated by Bernard Frechtman. New York: Grove Press.

Germosén, José. 2001. "Survival of the Fiercest: Five New York Girls Strive for Drag Divinity at the Miss Continental Pageant." *Village Voice*, August 28: 58–59.

Gherovici, Patricia. 2003. *The Puerto Rican Syndrome*. New York: Other Press.

Gilbert, Sandra M., and Susan Gubar. 1979. *The Madwoman in the Attic: The Woman Writer and the Nineteenth-Century Literary Imagination*. New Haven: Yale University Press.

Gilmore, David D. 1990. *Manhood in the Making: Cultural Concepts of Masculinity*. New Haven: Yale University Press.

Gilpin, Margaret, and Luis Felipe Bernaza, dirs. 1996. *Mariposas en el andamio*. New York: Latin American Video Archives. Videocassette (VHS).

Glanz, James, and Frances Robles. 2018. "How Storms, Missteps and an Ailing Grid Left Puerto Rico in the Dark." *New York Times*, May 6. https://www.nytimes.com/intera ctive/2018/05/06/us/puerto-rico-power-grid-hurricanes.html

Glasser, Ruth. 1995. *My Music Is My Flag: Puerto Rican Musicians and Their New York Communities, 1917–1940*. Berkeley: University of California Press.

Glazer, Nathan, and Daniel P. Moynihan. 1970. *Beyond the Melting Pot: The Negroes, Puerto Ricans, Jews, Italians, and Irish of New York City*. 2nd ed. Cambridge, MA: MIT Press.

Glickman, Nora. 1997. "Manuel Ramos Otero: El bolero fue mi ruina." *Latin American Theatre Review* 31, no. 1 (Fall): 170–73.

Godreau, Isar P. 2015. *Scripts of Blackness: Race, Cultural Nationalism, and U.S. Colonialism in Puerto Rico*. Champaign: University of Illinois Press.

Goldmark, Matthew. 2015. "National Drag: The Language of Inclusion in *RuPaul's Drag Race*." *GLQ* 21, no. 4: 501–20.

Goldsby, Jackie. 1993. "Queens of Language: *Paris Is Burning.*" In *Queer Looks: Perspectives on Lesbian and Gay Film and Video*, edited by Martha Gever, Pratibha Parmar, and John Greyson, 108–15. New York: Routledge.

Gomez, Julio, dir. 2009. "Portrait of a Lady: Story of Barbra Herr." YouTube. https://yo utu.be/Ohm4ahY6jDc

Gómez-Peña, Guillermo. 1996. *The New World Border: Prophecies, Poems, and Loqueras for the End of the Century.* San Francisco: City Lights.

Gómez-Peña, Guillermo. 2012–16. "Notes from Technotopia 3.0: On the 'Creative City' Gone Wrong (An Anti-gentrification Philosophical Tantrum)." *Arts in a Changing America.* https://artsinachangingamerica.org/notes-technotopia-3-0-guillermo-go mez-pena/

González, José Luis. 1959. "En el fondo del caño hay un negrito." In *Cuentos puertorriqueños de hoy*, edited by René Marqués, 83–88. San Juan: Club del libro.

González, José Luis. (1980) 1989. *El país de cuatro pisos y otros ensayos.* Rev. ed. Río Piedras: Ediciones Huracán.

González, José Luis. 1993. *Puerto Rico: The Four-Storeyed Country and Other Essays.* Translated by Gerald Guinness. Maplewood, NJ: Waterfront Press.

González, Melissa M. 2014. "*La Loca.*" *TSQ* 1, nos. 1–2 (May): 123–25.

González, Rita. 2009. "*Boricua* Gazing: An Interview with Frances Negrón-Muntaner." In Halperin and Traub, 88–100.

González Echevarría, Roberto. 1993. "An Outcast of the Island: *Before Night Falls* by Reinaldo Arenas. Translated by Dolores M. Koch." *New York Times*, October 24. https://www.nytimes.com/1993/10/24/books/an-outcast-of-the-island.html

González-Laguer, Joelle, dir. 2015. *Luis/Lizza.* San Juan: Loka Productions. Video.

Gossett, Reina. 2012a. "Sylvia Rivera 10 Year Memorial." *The Spirit Was . . .*, February 18. https://thespiritwas.tumblr.com/post/17831883099/sylvia-rivera-10-year-memo rial/

Gossett, Reina. 2012b. "Ten Posts for Sylvia Rivera's Ten Year Memorial." *The Spirit Was . . .*, July 31. https://thespiritwas.tumblr.com/post/28415757544/ten-posts-for-sylvia -riveras-ten-year-memorial

Gossett, Reina, Eric A. Stanley, and Johanna Burton, eds. 2017. *Trap Door: Trans Cultural Production and the Politics of Visibility.* Cambridge, MA: MIT Press.

Gramling, David, and Aniruddha Dutta. 2016. "Introduction." *TSQ* 3, nos. 3–4 (November): 333–56.

Green, Rashaad Ernesto, dir. (2011) 2013. *Gun Hill Road.* Burbank, CA: Virgil Films. DVD.

Gregg, Ron. 2013. "Fashion, Thrift Stores and the Space of Pleasure in the 1960s Queer Underground Film." In *Birds of Paradise: Costume as a Cinematic Spectacle*, edited by Marketa Uhlirova, 293–304. London: Koenig Books.

Grimes, William. 2015. "Holly Woodlawn, Transgender Star of 1970s Underground Films, Dies at 69." *New York Times*, December 7. https://www.nytimes.com/2015/12 /07/movies/holly-woodlawn-transgender-star-of-1970s-underground-films-dies-at -69.html

Grimm, Jacob. 1921. *Grimm's Fairy Tales.* Adapted by Edwin Gile Rich. Boston: Small, Maynard.

Grimm, Jacob, and Wilhelm Grimm. 2015. *The Original Folk and Fairy Tales of the Broth-*

ers Grimm: The Complete First Edition. Edited by Jack Zipes. Princeton, NJ: Princeton University Press.

Grosfoguel, Ramón. 2003. *Colonial Subjects: Puerto Ricans in a Global Perspective.* Berkeley: University of California Press.

Grosfoguel, Ramón, Frances Negrón-Muntaner, and Chloé S. Georas. 1997. "Beyond Nationalist and Colonialist Discourses: The *Jaiba* Politics of the Puerto Rican Ethno-Nation." In Negrón-Muntaner and Grosfoguel, 1–38.

Gross, Aeyal. 2013. "Post/Colonial Queer Globalisation and International Human Rights: Images of LGBT Rights." *Jindal Global Law Review* 4, no. 2 (November): 98–130.

Gruber, Ruth. 1972. *Felisa Rincón de Gautier: The Mayor of San Juan.* New York: Crowell.

Grullón, Oscar, dir. 2014. "Espejo: Las caras de Freddie." Santo Domingo: Jornada Extra, Fundación Prensa Civil Quisqueyana. YouTube. http://youtu.be/Mrmgk7RCF2k

Grupo Editorial EPRL. 2014. "Rafael M. Labra High School / Museum of Contemporary Art." *Enciclopedia de Puerto Rico.* https://enciclopediapr.org/en/encyclopedia/rafael-m-labra-high-school-museum-of-contemporary-art/

Guasch, Oscar. 1991. *La sociedad rosa.* Barcelona: Anagrama.

Guilbert, Georges-Claude. 2018. "Sara Montiel." In *Gay Icons: The (Mostly) Female Entertainers Gay Men Love*, 131–32. Jefferson, NC: McFarland.

Gund, Catherine, and Daresha Kyi, dirs. 2017. *Chavela.* New York: Aubin Pictures.

Gutiérrez, Laura G. 2010. *Performing Mexicanidad: Vendidas y Cabareteras on the Transnational Stage.* Austin: University of Texas Press.

Gutiérrez, Laura G. 2017. "Rasquachismo." In Vargas, Mirabal, and La Fountain-Stokes, 184–87.

Gutiérrez Alea, Tomás, and Juan Carlos Tabío, dirs. (1993) 2003. *Strawberry and Chocolate.* Burbank, CA: Miramax Home Entertainment. DVD.

Guy, Jack. 2019. "Kevin Fret: Rapper Shot to Death in Puerto Rico at 24." *CNN*, January 11. https://www.cnn.com/2019/01/11/americas/kevin-fret-gay-rapper-dead-scli-intl/index.html

Guzmán, Manolo. 1997. "Pa la Escuelita con mucho cuidao y por la orillita: A Journey through the Contested Terrains of the Nation and Sexual Orientation." In Negrón-Muntaner and Grosfoguel, 209–28.

Guzmán, Manolo. 2006. *Gay Hegemony / Latino Homosexualities.* New York: Routledge.

Guzmán, Marcos Billy. 2014. "Cuando los hombres se maquillan: Una mirada al transformismo en la cultura social y del entretenimiento en Puerto Rico." *El Nuevo Día*, May 13. http://larrylafountain.blogspot.com/2014/05/

Haase, Donald. 2004. "Feminist Fairy-Tale Scholarship." In *Fairy Tales and Feminism: New Approaches*, edited by Donald Haase, 1–36. Detroit: Wayne State University Press.

Hagerman, Catherine. 2018. "Doctoral Student Receives Grant for Performance Theater Project." *Indiana University Bloomington School of Education*, February 1. https://education.indiana.edu/news-events/_news/2018/jan-jun/2018-02-01-otero.html

Haggerty, George E., ed. 2000. *Gay Histories and Cultures: An Encyclopedia.* New York: Garland.

Halberstam, J. Jack. 1998. *Female Masculinity.* Durham, NC: Duke University Press.

Halberstam, J. Jack. 2005a. *In a Queer Time and Place: Transgender Bodies, Subcultural Lives.* New York: New York University Press.

Halberstam, J. Jack. 2005b. "Shame and White Gay Masculinity." *Social Text* 23, nos. 3–4 (Fall–Winter): 219–33.

Halberstam, J. Jack. 2011. *The Queer Art of Failure*. Durham, NC: Duke University Press.

Halberstam, J. Jack. 2012. *Gaga Feminism: Sex, Gender, and the End of Normal*. Boston: Beacon Press.

Halberstam, J. Jack. 2018. *Trans*: A Quick and Quirky Account of Gender Variability*. Berkeley: University of California Press.

Halperin, David M., and Valerie Traub, eds. 2009. *Gay Shame*. Chicago: University of Chicago Press.

Hames-García, Michael. 2011. "Queer Theory Revisited." In Hames-García and Martínez, 19–45.

Hames-García, Michael, and Ernesto Javier Martínez, eds. 2011. *Gay Latino Studies: A Critical Reader*. Durham, NC: Duke University Press.

Hammond, Joyce. 1996. "Drag Queen as Angel: Transformation and Transcendence in *To Wong Foo, Thanks for Everything, Julie Newmar*." *Journal of Popular Film and Television* 24, no. 3 (Fall): 106–14.

Hancock, Ange-Marie. 2004. *The Politics of Disgust: The Public Identity of the Welfare Queen*. New York: New York University Press.

Haney-López, Ian. 1994. "The Social Construction of Race: Some Observations on Illusion, Fabrication, and Choice." *Harvard Civil Rights–Civil Liberties Review* 29: 1–62.

Hanhardt, Christina B. 2013. *Safe Space: Gay Neighborhood History and the Politics of Violence*. Durham, NC: Duke University Press.

Hankins, Sarah. 2015. "'I'm a Cross between a Clown, a Stripper, and a Streetwalker': Drag Tipping, Sex Work, and a Queer Sociosexual Economy." *Signs* 40, no. 2 (Winter): 441–66.

Hanna, Alex. 2013. "Lipsyncing for Your Life: A Highly Detailed Survival Analysis of *RuPaul's Drag Race*." *Jezebel*, March 11. http://jezebel.com/5989981/lipsyncing-for-your-life-a-highly-detailed-survival-analysis-of-rupauls-drag-race

Hannah, Daryl. 2010. "Suspect in Murder of Gay Puerto Rican Teen Pleads Guilty." *GLAAD*, May 13. https://www.glaad.org/2010/05/13/suspect-in-murder-of-gay-puerto-rican-teen-pleads-guilty

Haritaworn, Jin, Adi Kuntsman, and Silvia Posocco, eds. 2014. *Queer Necropolitics*. New York: Routledge.

Harries, Elizabeth Wanning. 2004. "The Mirror Broken: Women's Autobiography and Fairy Tales." In *Fairy Tales and Feminism: New Approaches*, edited by Donald Haase, 99–111. Detroit: Wayne State University Press.

Harris, Max. 2001. "Masking the Site: The Fiestas de Santiago Apostol in Loíza, Puerto Rico." *Journal of American Folklore* 114, no. 453: 358–69.

Harris, Max. 2003. "El Mas Chiquito de To' Los Santos (Puerto Rico)." In *Carnival and Other Christian Festivals: Folk Theology and Folk Performance*, 33–47. Austin: University of Texas Press.

Hatchett, Keisha. 2019. "Where Are Your Favorite Queens from *RuPaul's Drag Race* Season 1?" *TV Guide*, February 2. https://www.tvguide.com/news/rupauls-drag-race-season-1-where-are-they-now/

Hedrick, Tace. 2013. "Neoliberalism and Orientalism in Puerto Rico: Walter Mercado's Queer Spiritual Capital." *CENTRO Journal* 25, no. 1 (Spring): 2–30.

Hedrick, Todd. 2008. "Race, Difference, and Anthropology in Kant's Cosmopolitanism." *Journal of the History of Philosophy* 46, no. 2: 24–68.

Hemmingson, Michael. 2008. *Zona Norte: The Post-structural Body of Erotic Dancers and Sex Workers in Tijuana, San Diego and Los Angeles: An Auto/ethnography of Desire and Addiction*. Newcastle upon Tyne: Cambridge Scholars.

Hernández, Jaime. 2004. *Locas: The Maggie and Hopey Stories. A Love and Rockets Book*. Seattle: Fantagraphics Books.

Hernández, Tanya Katerí. 2017. "Afro-Latinas/os." In Vargas, Mirabal, and La Fountain-Stokes, 7–9.

Herr, Barbra. 2016. "Remembering My Trans Mom and Sister Lady Catiria." Facebook, November 20. https://www.facebook.com/photo.php?fbid=10154347141234143

Herrera, Patricia. 2020. *Nuyorican Feminist Performance: From the Café to Hip Hop Theater*. Ann Arbor: University of Michigan Press.

Highleyman, Liz. 2009. "Sylvia Rivera: A Woman before Her Time." In *Smash the Church, Smash the State! The Early Years of Gay Liberation*, edited by Tommi Avicolli Mecca, 172–75. San Francisco: City Lights.

Hilderbrand, Lucas. 2013. *Paris Is Burning: A Queer Film Classic*. Vancouver: Arsenal Pulp Press.

Hillz, Monica Beverly. 2018. "I'm a Trans Woman and a Drag Queen. Despite What RuPaul Says, You Can Be Both." *Washington Post*, March 9. https://www.washingtonpost.com/news/post-nation/wp/2018/03/09/im-a-trans-woman-and-a-drag-queen-despite-what-rupaul-says-you-can-be-both/

Hinderer Cruz, Max Jorge. 2011. "TROPICAMP: Some Notes on Hélio Oiticica's 1971 Text." *Afterall* 28 (Autumn–Winter): n.p. https://www.afterall.org/journal/issue.28/tropicamp-pre-and-post-tropic-lia-at-once-some-contextual-notes-onh-lio-oiticica-s-1971-te

Homar, Susan. 2010. "Contemporary Dance in Puerto Rico, or How to Speak of These Times." In *Making Caribbean Dance: Continuity and Creativity in Island Cultures*, edited by Susanna Sloat, 211–24. Gainesville: University Press of Florida.

hooks, bell. 1992. "Is Paris Burning?" In *Black Looks: Race and Representation*, 145–56. Boston: South End.

Horn, Maja. 2006. "Bolero Bad Boys: Luis Rafael Sánchez's 'La importancia de llamarse Daniel Santos.'" *Latin American Literary Review* 34, no. 67 (January–June): 148–60.

Hughes, Holly, and David Román, eds. 1998. *O Solo Homo: The New Queer Performance*. New York: Grove Press.

Huppke, Rex W. 2010. "Gay Couple Take Podcast Medium, Go Large." *Chicago Tribune*, April 25. https://www.chicagotribune.com/news/ct-xpm-2010-04-24-ct-met-gay-podcast-20100424-story.html

Hurtado, Aída, and Mrinal Sinha. 2016. *Beyond Machismo: Intersectional Latino Masculinities*. Austin: University of Texas Press.

Hutchinson, Darren Lenard. 1997. "Out Yet Unseen: A Racial Critique of Gay and Lesbian Legal Theory and Political Discourse." *Connecticut Law Review* 29, no. 2 (Winter): 561–645.

Irizarry, Yoryie. 2019. "Paro nacional, perreo y Antonio Pantojas." *Yoryie Irizarry punto net*, August 15. https://yoryieirizarry.net/paro-nacional-perreo-y-antonio-pantojas/

J'accuse. 1927. "El Carnaval de San Juan, juego de AFEMINADOS." February 12: 6. La Colección Puertorriqueña. https://issuu.com/coleccionpuertorriquena/docs/jaccuse_02-12-1927

Jackson, Jhoni, 2016. "7 Queens Pushing Puerto Rico's Drag Scene Pa'Lante." *Remezcla*, May 18. http://remezcla.com/lists/culture/7-queens-pushing-puerto-ricos-drag-scene-pa-la nte/

Jackson, Jhoni. 2018a. "Drag Kings Get Their Due in Puerto Rico's Burgeoning Queer Movement." *Paper*, February 19. http://www.papermag.com/drag-kings-queer-puer to-rico-2536820698.html

Jackson, Jhoni. 2018b. "Kevin Fret Is Latin Trap's First Openly Gay Pioneer." *Paper*, April 25. http://www.papermag.com/kevin-fret-gay-latin-trap-pioneer-2563261994.html

Jackson, Jhoni. 2019. "'I'm Here to Change People's Minds': Remembering Kevin Fret, Gay Trapero." *Rolling Stone*, March 7. https://www.rollingstone.com/music/music-la tin/remembering-kevin-fret-gay-latin-trap-singer-804256/

Jackson, Jhoni. 2020a. "Meet Puerto Rico's Queer and Trans Change-Makers." *Paper*, July 2. https://www.papermag.com/puerto-rico-queer-trans-pride-2646310968.html

Jackson, Jhoni. 2020b. "This Puerto Rican Drag House Dedicated a Full Virtual Show to Buscabulla's 'Regresa.'" *Remezcla*, June 22. https://remezcla.com/music/puerto-rico -drag-house-haus-of-vanguardia-show-buscabulla-regresa/

Jana, Reena. 2001. "'Six Artists from San Juan': El Museo del Barrio." *Art News* 100, no. 5 (May): 190.

"Javier Cardona." n.d. *HIDVL Artist Profiles*. Hemispheric Institute of Performance and Politics. https://hemisphericinstitute.org/en/hidvl-collections/itemlist/category/324 -jcardona.html

Javier Rivera, María de Lourdes. 2007. "acerca circa." *La no-aptitud para la humani- dad* (blog), April. http://laverdaddelasmentiras.blogspot.com/2007/04/acerca-circa .html

Jaworowski, Ken. 2017. "Review: 'The Death and Life of Marsha P. Johnson' Explores a Mystery." *New York Times*, October 5. https://www.nytimes.com/2017/10/05/movies /the-death-and-life-of-marsha-p-johnson-review.html

Jeffreys, Joe E. 1993. "Joan Jett Blakk for President: Cross-Dressing at the Democratic National Convention." *TDR* 37, no. 3 (Autumn): 186–95.

Jeffreys, Joe E. 2008. "The Soundplay's the Thing: A Formal Analysis of John (aka Lypsinka) Epperson's Queer Performance Texts." In *"We Will Be Citizens": New Essays on Gay and Lesbian Theatre*, edited by James Fisher, 177–84. Jefferson, NC: McFarland.

Jenkins, Sarah Tucker. 2013. "Hegemonic 'Realness'? An Intersectional Feminist Analy- sis of *RuPaul's Drag Race*." MA thesis, Florida Atlantic University.

Jenkins, Sarah Tucker. 2017. "Spicy. Exotic. Creature. Representations of Racial and Eth- nic Minorities on *RuPaul's Drag Race*." In Brennan and Gudelunas, 77–90.

Jiménez, Félix. 2004. *Las prácticas de la carne: Construcción y representación de las mas- culinidades puertorriqueñas*. San Juan: Ediciones Vértigo.

Jiménez, Félix. 2007. "[a. k. a.: The Sex/Salsa/Identity Show]." In Negrón-Muntaner, 241–54.

Jiménez-Muñoz, Gladys M. 1995. "¡Xiomara mi hejmana! Diplo y el travestismo racial en el Puerto Rico de los años cincuenta." *Bordes* 2: 15–27.

Jiménez-Muñoz, Gladys M. 2002. "The Black-Face of Puerto Rican Whites: Race and Representation in Postwar Puerto Rico." *Latino Review of Books* (2002): 99–117.

Jiménez Román, Miriam, and Juan Flores, eds. 2010. *The Afro-Latin@ Reader: History and Culture in the United States*. Durham, NC: Duke University Press.

Johnson, E. Patrick. 1998. "Feeling the Spirit in the Dark: Expanding Notions of the Sacred in the African-American Gay Community." *Callaloo* 21, no. 1 (Spring): 399–416.

Johnson, E. Patrick. 2001. "'Quare' Studies, or (Almost) Everything I Know about Queer Studies I Learned from My Grandmother." *Text and Performance Quarterly* 21, no. 1: 1–25.

Johnson, E. Patrick. 2003. *Appropriating Blackness: Performance and the Politics of Authenticity*. Durham, NC: Duke University Press.

Johnson, E. Patrick, ed. 2016. *No Tea, No Shade: New Writings in Black Queer Studies*. Durham, NC: Duke University Press.

Johnson, E. Patrick, and Ramón H. Rivera-Servera, eds. 2016. *Blacktino Queer Performance*. Durham, NC: Duke University Press.

Johnson, Marsha P. 1992. "Rapping with a Street Transvestite Revolutionary: An Interview with Marcia Johnson." In *Out of the Closets: Voices of Gay Liberation*, edited by Karla Jay and Allen Young, 112–20. New York: New York University Press.

Johnson, Sylvester. 2015. "Monstrosity, Colonialism, and the Racial State." *J19* 3, no. 1 (Spring): 173–81.

Jones, Chris. 2019. "Before Mayor Pete, There Was Joan Jett Blakk for President!" *Chicago Tribune*, May 22. https://www.chicagotribune.com/entertainment/theater/ct -ott-blakk-president-steppenwolf-jones-0524-story.html

Jones, Jessica E. 2009. "Spatializing Sexuality in Jaime Hernandez's *Locas*." *Aztlán* 34, no. 1 (Spring): 35–64.

Jordenö, Sara, dir. (2016) 2017. *Kiki*. Written by Sara Jordenö and Twiggy Pucci Garçon. Orland Park, IL: MPI Media Group. DVD.

Juliá, Luis Enrique. 2000. "Andanza en la península ibérica." *El Nuevo Día*, July 19: 116.

Juzwiak, Rich. 2017. "Who Owns Marsha P. Johnson's Story?" *Jezebel*, October 13. https:// jezebel.com/who-owns-marsha-p-johnsons-story-1819347978

Kacala, Alexander. 2013. "Hunty Games: Monica Reveals She's Trans and Jinkx Spoofs Mimi Imfurst." *Philly Magazine*, February 5. https://www.phillymag.com/news/2013 /02/05/hunty-games-monica-reveals-trans-jinkx-spoofs-mimi-imfurst/

Kai, Maiysha. 2019. "'I Can't Stop': With *Ms. Blakk for President, Moonlight* Writer Tarell Alvin McCraney Campaigns as an Unlikely Candidate." *The Root*, June 7. https://www .theroot.com/i-can-t-stop-with-ms-blakk-for-president-moonlight-1835287680

Kanellos, Nicolás. 2008. "Pregones Theater." *The Greenwood Encyclopedia of Latino Literature*, edited by Nicolas Kanellos, 2: 907. Westport, CT: Greenwood Press.

Kenny, Glenn. 2017. "Review: 'Kiki': The Vogueing Scene, Still a Refuge for Gay and Transgender Youth." *New York Times*, February 28. https://www.nytimes.com/2017 /02/28/movies/kiki-review.html

Kernerman, Gerald. 2005. *Multicultural Nationalism: Civilizing Difference, Constituting Community*. Vancouver: UBC Press.

Kerr, Theodore. 2017. "How Six NYC Activists Changed History with 'Silence = Death.'" *Village Voice*, June 20. https://www.villagevoice.com/2017/06/20/how-six-nyc-activ ists-changed-history-with-silence-death/

Khubchandani, Kareem. 2015. "Lessons in Drag: An Interview with LaWhore Vagistan." *Theatre Topics* 25, no. 3 (September): 285–94.

Kidron, Beeban, dir. (1996) 2002. *To Wong Foo, Thanks for Everything! Julie Newmar.* Universal City, CA: Universal. DVD.

Kiesling, Scott F. 2004. "Dude." *American Speech* 79, no. 3 (Fall): 281–305.

King, Rosamond S. 2004–5. "Dressing Down: Male Transvestism in Two Caribbean Carnivals." *Sargasso* Special Issue (2004–5): 25–36.

King, Rosamond S. 2014. *Island Bodies: Transgressive Sexualities in the Caribbean Imagination.* Gainesville: University Press of Florida.

Kirkland, Justin. 2019. "*Pose* Made TV History with a Brave Conversation about Transgender Violence." *Esquire*, July 10. https://www.esquire.com/entertainment/tv/a283 43224/pose-candy-death-season-2-episode-4-tv-history/

Kirkus Reviews. 2017. "*The House of Impossible Beauties* by Joseph Cassara." October 11. https://www.kirkusreviews.com/book-reviews/joseph-cassara/the-house-of-impos sible-beauties/

Klein, Naomi. 2018. *The Battle for Paradise: Puerto Rico Takes on the Disaster Capitalists.* Chicago: Haymarket Books.

Kleinhans, Chuck. 1991. "*Ethnic Notions. Tongues Untied:* Mainstreams and Margins." *Jump Cut* 36 (May): 108–11.

Kleinhans, Chuck, and Julia Lesage. 1991. "Interview with Marlon Riggs: Listening to the Heartbeat." *Jump Cut* 36 (May): 119–26.

Knights, Vanessa. 2006a. "Queer Pleasures: The Bolero, Camp, and Almodóvar." In *Changing Tunes: The Use of Pre-existing Music in Film,* edited by Phil Powrie and Robynn Stilwell, 91–104. Aldershot, Hants, England: Ashgate.

Knights, Vanessa. 2006b. "Tears and Screams: Performances of Pleasure and Pain in the Bolero." In *Queering the Popular Pitch,* edited by Sheila Whiteley and Jennifer Rycenga, 83–99. New York: Routledge.

Koch, Dolores M. 1991. "Reinaldo Arenas, con los ojos cerrados (julio 16, 1943–diciembre 7, 1990)." *Revista Iberoamericana* 57, nos. 155–56 (April–September): 685–88.

Kohlsdorf, Kai. 2014. "Policing the Proper Queer Subject: *RuPaul's Drag Race* in the Neoliberal 'Post' Moment." In Daems, 67–87.

Kornhaber, Spencer. 2016. "The Singular Experience of the Queer Latin Nightclub." *The Atlantic,* June 17. http://www.theatlantic.com/entertainment/archive/2016/06/orlan do-shooting-pulse-latin-queer-gay-nightclub-ramon-rivera-servera-intrerview/48 7442/

Kourias, Gia. 1997. "Emotional Rescue." *Time Out New York*, May 8–15. Photocopy.

Kramer, Larry. 1978. *Faggots.* New York: Random House.

Kristeva, Julia. 1982. *Powers of Horror: An Essay on Abjection.* Translated by Leon S. Roudiez. New York: Columbia University Press.

Kugelmass, Jack. 1993. "'The Fun Is in Dressing Up': The Greenwich Village Halloween Parade and the Reimagining of Urban Space." *Social Text* 36 (Autumn): 138–52.

Kugelmass, Jack. 1994. *Masked Culture: The Greenwich Village Halloween Parade.* Photography by Mariette Pathy Allen. New York: Columbia University Press.

Kulick, Don. 1998. *Travesti: Sex, Gender, and Culture among Brazilian Transgendered Prostitutes.* Chicago: University of Chicago Press.

Kulick, Don, and Charles Klein. 2009. "Scandalous Acts: The Politics of Shame among Brazilian *Travesti* Prostitutes." In Halperin and Traub, 312–38.

Lacan, Jacques. 2002. "The Mirror Stage as Formative of the Function of the I as Revealed in Psychoanalytic Experience." In *Écrits: A Selection*. Translated by Bruce Fink, 3–9. New York: W.W. Norton.

Laffrado, Laura. 2002. "Postings from Hoochie Mama: Erika Lopez, Graphic Art, and Female Subjectivity." In *Interfaces: Women, Autobiography, Image, Performance*, edited by Sidonie Smith and Julia Watson, 406–29. Ann Arbor: University of Michigan Press.

La Fountain-Stokes, Lawrence. 1997a. "Bolero, memoria y violencia." *Conjunto* 106 (May–August): 68–69.

La Fountain-Stokes, Lawrence. 1997b. "*Spookiricans* de Eduardo Alegría." *Claridad*, June 6–12: 29.

La Fountain-Stokes, Lawrence. 1998. "Queer Puerto Ricans on Parade, T-Shirts with the Flag, and the Performance of the National." *Dirty Goat* (Austin, TX) 9: 1–9.

La Fountain-Stokes, Lawrence. 1999a. "1898 and the History of a Queer Puerto Rican Century: Gay Lives, Island Debates, and Diasporic Experience." *CENTRO Journal* 11, no. 1 (Fall): 91–109.

La Fountain-Stokes, Lawrence. 1999b. "Los nenes con los nenes y las nenas con las nenas." In *Sissies and Tomboys: Gender Nonconformity and Homosexual Childhood*, edited by Matthew Rottnek, 236–44. New York: New York University Press.

La Fountain-Stokes, Lawrence. 2002. "*De un pájaro, las dos alas*: Travel Notes of a Queer Puerto Rican in Havana." *GLQ* 8, nos. 1–2: 7–33.

La Fountain-Stokes, Lawrence. 2004. "Pregones Theater's 2003 Asunción Playwrights Project." *Latin American Theatre Review* 37, no. 2 (Spring): 141–46.

La Fountain-Stokes, Lawrence. 2006. "La política queer del espanglish." *Debate feminista* 17, no. 33 (April): 141–53.

La Fountain-Stokes, Lawrence. 2007a. "Queer Ducks, Puerto Rican *Patos*, and Jewish American *Feygelekh*: Birds and the Cultural Representation of Homosexuality." *CENTRO Journal* 19, no. 1 (Spring): 192–229.

La Fountain-Stokes, Lawrence. 2007b. Review of *Boricua Literature: A Literary History of the Puerto Rican Diaspora* by Lisa Sánchez González. *Arizona Journal of Hispanic Cultural Studies* 11: 232–34.

La Fountain-Stokes, Lawrence. 2008. "Queer Diasporas, Boricua Lives: A Meditation on Sexile." *Review: Literature and Arts of the Americas* 41, no. 2 (Fall): 294–301.

La Fountain-Stokes, Lawrence. 2009. *Queer Ricans: Cultures and Sexualities in the Diaspora*. Minneapolis: University of Minnesota Press.

La Fountain-Stokes, Lawrence. 2011a. "Gay Shame, Latina- and Latino-Style: A Critique of White Queer Performativity." In Hames-García and Martínez, 55–80.

La Fountain-Stokes, Lawrence. 2011b. "Translocas: Migration, Homosexuality, and Transvestism in Recent Puerto Rican Performance." *emisférica* 8, no. 1 (Summer). https://hemisphericinstitute.org/en/emisferica-81/8-1-essays/translocas.html

La Fountain-Stokes, Lawrence. 2014. "Martina, Catalina, Elián, and the Old Man: Queer Tales of a Transnational Cuban Cockroach." In *Animal Acts: Performing Species Today*, edited by Una Chaudhuri and Holly Hughes, 84–91. Ann Arbor: University of Michigan Press.

La Fountain-Stokes, Lawrence. 2015. "*Abolición del pato*: Discourses of Puerto Rican Queer Modernity and Performance." In *Queering Paradigms V: Queering Narratives of Modernity / Queerizando narrativas de la modernidad*, edited by María Amelia Viteri and Manuela Picq with Ana María Garzón and Marcelo Aguirre, 271–95. Quito: FLACSO Ecuador; Frankfurt am Main: Peter Lang.

La Fountain-Stokes, Lawrence. 2016a. "Learning to Unlove Andy Gibb: Race, Beauty, and the Erotics of Puerto Rican Black Male Queer Pedagogy." In Johnson and Rivera-Servera, 542–54.

La Fountain-Stokes, Lawrence. 2016b. "Queer Puerto Ricans and the Burden of Violence." *QED* 3, no. 3 (Fall): 99–102.

La Fountain-Stokes, Lawrence. 2017a. "Johnny Ray es Ya Ustedes Saben Quien." *80grados*, August 4. http://www.80grados.net/johnny-ray-es-ya-ustedes-saben-quien/

La Fountain-Stokes, Lawrence. 2017b. "Regreso triunfal de *El bolero fue mi ruina*." *Claridad*, July 6–12: 18–19.

La Fountain-Stokes, Lawrence. 2018a. "Being *Mala Mala*: Documentary Film and the Cultural Politics of Puerto Rican Drag and Trans Identities." *Caribbean Studies* 46, no. 2 (July–December): 3–30.

La Fountain-Stokes, Lawrence. 2018b. *Escenas transcaribeñas: Ensayos sobre teatro, performance y cultura*. San Juan: Isla Negra Editores.

La Fountain-Stokes, Lawrence. 2018c. "Nunca Olvidar / To Never Forget: Pulse Orlando." *GLQ* 24, no. 1 (January): 17–26.

La Fountain-Stokes, Lawrence. 2018d. "Reflexions / Reflexiones: Recent Developments in Queer Puerto Rican History, Politics, and Culture." *CENTRO Journal* 30, no. 2 (Summer): 502–40.

La Fountain-Stokes, Lawrence. 2018e. "Translocalizando a la draga: Una entrevista inédita de 2002 con el actor y director Jorge B. Merced." *CENTRO Journal* 30, no. 2 (Summer): 140–61.

La Fountain-Stokes, Lawrence, and Yolanda Martínez-San Miguel. 2018. "Revisiting Queer Puerto Rican Sexualities: Queer Futures, Reinventions, and Un-disciplined Archives—Introduction." *CENTRO Journal* 30, no. 2 (Summer): 6–41.

La Fountain-Stokes, Lawrence, Lourdes Torres, and Ramón H. Rivera-Servera. 2011. "Towards an Archive of Latina/o Queer Chicago: Art, Politics, and Social Performance." In *Out in Chicago: LGBT History at the Crossroads*, edited by Jill Austin and Jennifer Brier, 127–53. Chicago: Chicago History Museum.

Lantelme, Brian. 2002. "Sally's Hideaway: A History." *Sally's Hideaway*. http://www.sallys-hideaway.com/A_History.html

Lao-Montes, Agustín. 1997. "Islands at the Crossroads: Puerto Ricanness Traveling between the Translocal Nation and the Global City." In Negrón-Muntaner and Grosfoguel, 169–88.

Lara, Irene. 2007. "Beyond Caliban's Curses: The Decolonial Feminist Literacy of Sycorax." *Journal of International Women's Studies* 9, no. 1: 80–98.

Laureano, Javier E. 2007. "Antonio Pantojas se abre el traje para que escuchemos el mar: Una historia de vida transformista." *CENTRO Journal* 19, no. 1 (Spring): 330–49.

Laureano, Javier E. 2016. *San Juan Gay: Conquista de un espacio urbano de 1948 a 1991*. San Juan: Editorial del Instituto de Cultura Puertorriqueña.

Lawrence, Tim. 2011. "'Listen, and You Will Hear All the Houses That Walked There

Before': A History of Drag Balls, Houses and the Culture of Voguing." In Chantal Regnault, *Voguing and the Gay Ballroom Scene of New York City, 1989–92*, edited by Stuart Baker, 3–10. London: Soul Jazz.

Lawrence, Tim. 2016. "Life and Death on the Pulse Dance Floor: Transglocal Politics and the Erasure of the Latinx in the History of Queer Dance Culture." *Dancecult* 8, no. 1: 1–25.

Lázaro, P. 2019. "Puerto Rico's First Female Mayor Doña Fela Is Celebrated as a 'Fashion Icon' in New Exhibit." *De Bulevar*, October 12. https://debulevar.com/2019/10/12/pu erto-ricos-first-female-mayor-dona-fela-is-celebrated-as-a-fashion-icon/

Lee, Benjamin. 2017. "The Death and Life of Marsha P Johnson Review: Trans Icon Inspires Stirring Documentary." *The Guardian*, October 5. https://www.theguardian .com/film/2017/oct/05/death-life-marsha-p-johnson-review-documentary

Lefebvre, Henri. 1991. *The Production of Social Space*. London: Blackwell.

Legarreta, Elizabeth. 2018. "Villano Antillano, el rapero bisexual que le respondió a Anuel." *El Calce*, September 26. https://elcalce.com/featured/entrevista-exclusiva-vi llano-antillano-el-rapero-bisexual-que-le-respondio-a-anuel/

Lemebel, Pedro. 2001. *Tengo miedo torero*. Santiago: Editorial Planeta Chilena.

Lemebel, Pedro. 2003. *My Tender Matador*. Translated by Katherine Silver. New York: Grove Press.

Leonard, Robert H. 2006. "Teatro Pregones: The Twin Rigors of Art and Community, or Not the People Who Said Green." In *Performing Communities: Grassroots Ensemble Theaters Deeply Rooted in Eight U.S. Communities* by Robert H. Leonard and Ann Kilkelly, 147–56. Oakland, CA: New Village Press.

Lepore, Amanda, and Thomas Flannery Jr. 2017. *Doll Parts: A Memoir*. New York: Regan Arts.

Le Talec, Jean-Yves. 2008. *Folles de France: Repenser l'homosexualité masculine*. Paris: La Découverte.

Le Talec, Jean-Yves. 2009. "Genre et militantisme homosexuel: l'importance des folles et du camp." In *Le sexe du militantisme*, edited by Olivier Fillieule and Patricia Roux, 205–22. Paris: Les Presses de Sciences Po.

Leu, Lorraine. 2006. *Brazilian Popular Music: Caetano Veloso and the Regeneration of Tradition*. Burlington, VT: Ashgate.

Levin, Josh. 2019. *The Queen: The Forgotten Life behind an American Myth*. New York: Little, Brown.

Levin, Sam. 2018. "Who Can Be a Drag Queen? RuPaul's Trans Comments Fuel Calls for Inclusion." *The Guardian*, March 8. https://www.theguardian.com/tv-and-radio/20 18/mar/08/rupaul-drag-race-transgender-performers-diversity

Levitt, Lauren. 2013. "Reality Realness: *Paris is Burning* and *RuPaul's Drag Race*." *Inter-ventions* 3, no. 1. https://interventionsjournal.wordpress.com/2013/11/07/reality-rea lness-paris-is-burning-and-rupauls-drag-race/

Lewin, Elisabeth. 2009. "Feast of Fools' 'Obamafication' Yields Feast of Fun." *Podcasting News*, March 17. Archived April 20, 2009, at the Wayback Machine.

Lewis, Abram J. 2017. "Trans History in a Moment of Danger: Organizing within and beyond 'Visibility' in the 1970s." In Gossett, Stanley, and Burton, 57–89.

Lewis, Oscar. 1966. *La Vida: A Puerto Rican Family in the Culture of Poverty—San Juan and New York*. New York: Random House.

Lewis, Vek. 2010. *Crossing Sex and Gender in Latin America*. New York: Palgrave Macmillan.

Lima, Lázaro. 2005. "Locas al Rescate: The Transnational Hauntings of Queer *Cubanidad.*" In *Cuba Transnational*, edited by Damián J. Fernández, 79–103. Gainesville: University Press of Florida.

"Lionel Cantu Jr." 2002. *SFGate*, June 1. http://www.sfgate.com/bayarea/article/Lionel-Cantu-Jr-2831690.php

"The Little Parrot." n.d. *Queer Music Heritage*. Edited by J. D. Doyle. http://queermusicheritage.com/fem-littleparrot.html

Livingston, Jennie, dir. (1990) 2005. *Paris Is Burning*. Burbank, CA: Miramax Home Entertainment. DVD.

Lladó Ortega, Mónica. 2019. "*Queering bomba*: Rupturas con lo heteronormativo en la bomba puertorriqueña." *CENTRO Journal* 31, no. 2 (Summer): 110–36.

Lockhart, Melissa Fitch. 1998. "Queer Representations in Latino Theatre." *Latin American Theatre Review* 31, no. 2 (Spring): 67–78.

Logo. 2013. "*RuPaul's Drag Race*: The Lost Season Ru-Vealed. Meet Nina Flowers!—LogoTV." YouTube, September 23. https://youtu.be/EDWvByTF20I

Logo Press. 2012. "The Queens of 'RuPaul's Drag Race' Season Five Begin Their Battle for the Crown on Monday, January 28 on Logo." *Logo Press*, December 10. https://press.logotv.com/press-releases/2012/12/10/the-queens-of-rupaul-s-drag-race-season-five-begin-their-battle-for-the-crown-on-monday-january-28-on-logo

Lopes, Denilson. 1999. *Nós os mortos: melancolia e neo-barroco*. Rio de Janeiro: Sette Letras.

Lopes, Denilson. 2002. *O homem que amava rapazes e outros ensaios*. Rio de Janeiro: Aeroplano.

López, Arnaldo J. 2003. "Teatro Pregones: Interview with Jorge Merced, Associate Director." *Performing Communities: The Grassroots Ensemble Theater Research Project*. Community Arts Network. http://web.archive.org/web/20030129155524/http://www.communityarts.net/readingroom/archive/perfcomm/pregones/interviews/pregones-merced.php

Lopez, Erika. 1997a. *Flaming Iguanas: An Illustrated All-Girl Road Novel Thing*. New York: Simon and Schuster.

Lopez, Erika. 1997b. *Lap Dancing for Mommy: Tender Stories of Disgust, Blame and Inspiration*. Seattle: Seal Press.

Lopez, Erika. 1998. *They Call Me Mad Dog! A Story for Bitter, Lonely People*. New York: Simon and Schuster.

Lopez, Erika. 2001. *Hoochie Mama: The Other White Meat*. New York: Simon and Schuster.

Lopez, Erika. 2002. "Postcards from the Welfare Line: The Rise and Fall of Erika Lopez." *Junction-City / Progressive America*, March 24. http://www.junction-city.com/content/lopez.asp (no longer online)

Lopez, Erika. 2003. *Grandma López's Country-Mad Fried Chicken Book. Nothing Left but the Smell: A Republican on Welfare*. San Francisco: Tiny-Fisted Book Publishers.

Lopez, Erika. 2006. *Nothing Left but the Smell: A Republican on Welfare*. ErikaLopez.com, July 11. http://www.erikalopez.com

Lopez, Erika. 2010. *The Girl Must Die: A Monster Girl Memoir*. San Francisco: Monster Girl Media.

Lopez, Erika. 2018. "Revenge of the White Girls." *ErikaLopez.com*. http://www.erikalopez.com/

Lopez, Erika, and Monster Girl Media. 2011. "Erika Lopez as Kitten Lopez in the Final Show of 'The Welfare Queen.'" *Archive.org*, October 10. https://archive.org/details/ErikaLopezAsKittenLopezInTheFinalShowOftheWelfareQueen

López, Miguel A. 2014. "Museum, Musex, Mutext, Mutant: Giuseppe Campuzano's Transvestite Machine." *Guggenheim.* http://blogs.guggenheim.org/map/museum-musex-mutext-mutant-giuseppe-campuzanos-transvestite-machine/

López, Miguel A., with Giuseppe Campuzano. 2013. *The Museo Travesti del Perú and the Histories We Deserve. Visible.* Workbook 2. https://www.visibleproject.org/blog/the-museo-travesti-del-peru-and-the-histories-we-deserve-by-giuseppe-campuzano-and-miguel-lopez/

López, Miguel A., and Fernanda Nogueira. 2013. "The *Cuir* Machine." *Review: Literature and Arts of the Americas* 46, no. 1: 117–25.

López Maldonado, Cesiach. 2018. "Boricuas viven su retiro en República Dominicana." *Primera Hora*, August 30. https://www.primerahora.com/noticias/puerto-rico/notas/boricuas-viven-su-retiro-en-republica-dominicana/

Loss, Jacqueline. 2013. "Crossed Destinies." In *Dreaming in Russian: The Cuban Soviet Imaginary*, 50–77. Austin: University of Texas Press.

Lozada, Ángel. 2006. *No quiero quedarme sola y vacía.* San Juan: Editorial Isla Negra.

lpatwct. 2009. "Shannel and Nina Flowers at Drama Drag LOCA." YouTube. http://you tu.be/umqHVLl9lNI

Ludmer, Josefina. 1985. "Tretas del débil." In *La sartén por el mango*, edited by Patricia Elena González and Eliana Ortega, 47–54. Río Piedras: Ediciones Huracán.

Ludmer, Josefina. 1991. "Tricks of the Weak." In *Feminist Perspectives on Sor Juana Inés de la Cruz*, edited by Stephanie Merrim, 86–93. Detroit: Wayne State University Press.

Ludmer, Josefina. 2004. *The Corpus Delicti: A Manual of Argentine Fictions.* Translated by Glen S. Close. Pittsburgh: University of Pittsburgh Press.

Lugo Bertrán, Dorian. 1998. "Noventa y ochos." In *100 años después . . . Cien artistas contemporáneos.* Exhibition catalog. Arsenal de la Puntilla, San Juan, Puerto Rico.

Lugo Bertrán, Dorian. 2002. *Saqueos: Antología de producción cultural.* San Juan: Editorial Noexiste.

Lugo Bertrán, Dorian. 2018. "Hypertelic Genders in the Neobaroque Cosmos: Queer Theory and Latin American Cinema in the Glocal Context (Regarding *From Afar* [Desde allá, 2015] by Lorenzo Vigas)." Translated by Rebecca Sumner Burgos. *L'Atalante* 26 (July-December): 95–110.

Lugo Bertrán, Dorian. n.d. "Crónicas de la vida nocturna gay y lésbica de Puerto Rico." Manuscript.

Lugones, María. 2003. *Pilgrimages/Peregrinajes: Theorizing Coalition against Multiple Oppressions.* Lanham, MD: Rowman and Littlefield.

Lugones, María. 2008. "The Coloniality of Gender." *Worlds and Knowledges Otherwise* (Spring): 1–17.

Lugones, María. 2017. "Decolonial." In Vargas, Mirabal, and La Fountain-Stokes, 43–47.

Luibhéid, Eithne, and Lionel Cantú Jr., eds. 2005. *Queer Migrations: Sexuality, U.S. Citizenship, and Border Crossings.* Minneapolis: University of Minnesota Press.

Luish. 2018. "Queer ALIENation." *Bloomington Latino*, March 20. http://bloomingtonlatino.org/enterteainment/queer-alienation/

MACPR. 2013. *Coreografía del error: CONDUCTA de Viveca Vázquez.* San Juan: Museo de Arte Contemporáneo de Puerto Rico.

Maguire, Gregory. 1995. *Wicked: The Life and Times of the Wicked Witch of the West*. New York: ReganBooks.

Maia, Suzana. 2012. *Transnational Desires: Brazilian Erotic Dancers in New York*. Nashville: Vanderbilt University Press.

Maissonet, Luis A., dir. (1959) 2014. *Juan sin seso*. Script by René Marqués. División de Educación de la Comunidad (DIVEDCO). Instituto de Cultura Puertorriqueña. YouTube, September 12. https://youtu.be/bmOXLW4JkG8

Maldonado, Premier, and Wilson Torres. 1984. *Fela (remembranza musical inspirada en la vida de Doña Felisa Rincón de Gautier)*. Hialeah Gardens, FL: F.A.M.E. Sound recording.

Maldonado-Torres, Nelson. 2008. "La descolonización y el giro des-colonial." *Tabula Rasa* 9 (July–December): 61–72.

MalongoMiusiTv. 2018. "Diferente—Mike Duran ft Kevin Fret (Video Oficial)." YouTube, July 18. https://youtu.be/K_CQrjLvDeA

Manalansan IV, Martin F. 2003. *Global Divas: Filipino Gay Men in the Diaspora*. Durham, NC: Duke University Press.

Mananzala, Rickke, and Dean Spade. 2008. "The Nonprofit Industrial Complex and Trans Resistance." *Sexuality Research and Social Policy* 5, no. 1 (March): 53–71.

Mann, Bonnie, and Martina Ferrari, eds. 2017. *"On ne naît pas femme: on le devient": The Life of a Sentence*. New York: Oxford University Press.

Marat, Abniel. 1986. *dios en el* Playgirl *de noviembre*. Río Piedras: Editorial Edil.

Marcel, Mary. 2014. "Representing Gender, Race and Realness: The Television World of America's Next Drag Superstars." In Daems, 13–30.

Marcus, Eric. 1993. "The Drag Queen: Rey 'Sylvia Lee' Rivera." In *Making History: The Struggle for Gay and Lesbian Equal Rights, 1945–1990 (an Oral History)*, 187–96. Interview. New York: Harper Perennial.

Marez, Curtis. 2017. "Popular Culture." In Vargas, Mirabal, and La Fountain-Stokes, 167–71.

Marqués, René. (1953) 1969. *The Oxcart / La carreta*. Translated by Charles Pilditch. New York: Scribner.

Márquez, Rosa Luisa. 1992. *Brincos y saltos: El juego como disciplina teatral*. Puerto Rico: Ediciones Cuicaloca and Colegio Universitario de Cayey.

Marrero Rodríguez, Rosalina. 2014. "La otra cara de 'Francheska.'" *El Nuevo Día*, February 27: n.p.

Marsh Kennerly, Catherine. 2009. *Negociaciones culturales: Los intelectuales y el proyecto pedagógico del estado muñocista*. San Juan: Ediciones Callejón.

Martin, Douglas. 2013. "Mario Montez, a Warhol Glamour Avatar, Dies at 78." *New York Times*, October 3. http://www.nytimes.com/2013/10/04/arts/mario-montez-a-warhol-glamour-avatar-dies-at-78.html

Martínez, Gabriela. 2017. "'Dark Kings,' 'Meta Queens': Puerto Rico's Drag Scene Gets a Makeover." *NBC News*, August 11. https://www.nbcnews.com/feature/nbc-out/dark-kings-meta-queens-puerto-rico-s-drag-scene-gets-n790861

Martínez, Rubén. 1994. "Carmen, a.k.a. Marcus Kuiland-Nazario." *High Performance* 17: 36–37.

Martínez-San Miguel, Yolanda. 2003. *Caribe Two Ways: Cultura de la migración en el Caribe insular hispánico*. San Juan: Ediciones Callejón.

Martínez-San Miguel, Yolanda. 2011. "Female Sexiles? Toward an Archeology of Displacement of Sexual Minorities in the Caribbean." *Signs* 36, no. 4 (Summer): 813–36.

Martínez-San Miguel, Yolanda. 2014. *Coloniality of Diasporas: Rethinking Intra-colonial Migrations in a Pan-Caribbean Context.* New York: Palgrave Macmillan.

Martínez-San Miguel, Yolanda, Ben. Sifuentes-Jáuregui, and Marisa Belausteguigoitia, eds. 2016. *Critical Terms in Caribbean and Latin American Thought: Historical and Institutional Trajectories.* New York: Palgrave Macmillan.

Martínez-San Miguel, Yolanda, and Sarah Tobias. 2016. "Introduction: Thinking beyond Hetero/Homo Normativities." In *Trans Studies: The Challenge to Hetero/Homo Normativities*, edited by Yolanda Martínez-San Miguel and Sarah Tobias, 1–17. New Brunswick, NJ: Rutgers University Press.

Martínez Sosa, Luis, dir. 1984. *Las fiestas de Santiago Apóstol en Loíza.* Producciones Vegigante and Fundación Puertorriqueña de las Humanidades. YouTube. https://yo utu.be/ztt7PLBD560

Martínez Tabares, Vivian. 1997a. "La escena puertorriqueña vista desde fuera/dentro." *Conjunto* 106 (May–August): 3–12.

Martínez Tabares, Vivian. 1997b. "Rosa Luisa Márquez: De *Jardín de pulpos* a *Godot*." *Conjunto* 106 (May–August): 38–46.

Martínez Tabares, Vivian. 2004. "Caribbean Bodies, Migrations, and Spaces of Resistance." *TDR* 48 (Summer): 24–32.

Martorell, Antonio. 2000. "White Christmas." Translated by Andrew Hurley. In *Contemporary Puerto Rican Installation Art: The Guagua Aérea, the Trojan Horse and the Termite*, by Laura Roulet, 101–8. Río Piedras: Editorial de la Universidad de Puerto Rico.

Masiello, Francine. 2001. *The Art of Transition: Latin American Culture and Neoliberal Crisis.* Durham, NC: Duke University Press.

Masters, Troy. 2012. "Donald Suggs Is Dead at 51." *Gay City News*, October 10. https://www.gaycitynews.com/donald-suggs-is-dead-at-51/

Mateik, Tara, dir. 2002. *Sylvia.* Chicago: Video Data Bank. DVD. https://youtu.be/ybn H0HB0lqc

Mayora, R. Gabriel. 2014. "Cover, Girl: Branding Puerto Rican Drag in 21st-Century U.S. Popular Culture." In Daems, 106–23.

Mayora, R. Gabriel. 2018. "Her Stonewall Legend: The Fictionalization of Sylvia Rivera in Nigel Finch's *Stonewall*." *CENTRO Journal* 30, no. 2 (Summer): 452–77.

Mbembe, Achile. 2003. "Necropolitics." Translated by Libby Meintjes. *Public Culture* 15, no. 1 (Winter): 11–40.

McIntyre, Joanna, and Damien W. Riggs. 2017. "North American Universalism in *RuPaul's Drag Race*: Stereotypes, Linguicism, and the Construction of 'Puerto Rican Queens.'" In Brennan and Gudelunas, 81–76.

McPhaul, John. 2018. "Study: One in 4 Puerto Ricans in Mainland US Is Poor." *San Juan Star*, May 24: 3.

Meca, Gemma. 2017. "*Crónicas Marcianas*: ¿Qué fue de los colaboradores del imbatible fenómeno televisivo?" *Cotilleo.es*, July 20. https://www.cotilleo.es/fue-los-personaj es-cronicas-marcianas/

Meccia, Ernesto. 2006. *La cuestión gay: Un enfoque sociológico.* Buenos Aires: Gran Aldea Editores.

Meléndez, Edwin, and Carlos Vargas-Ramos, eds. 2017. *State of Puerto Ricans 2017.* New York: Centro Press.

Melo, Juan Carlos. 2013. "Difícil vivir del transformismo en Puerto Rico." *Metro*, March 22. https://www.metro.pr/pr/entretener/2013/03/22/dificil-vivir-transformismo-puerto-rico.html

Mèmeteau, Richard. 2014. *Pop culture: Réflexions sur les industries du rêve et l'invention des identités.* Paris: Zones.

Memmi, Albert. 1965. *The Colonizer and the Colonized.* Translated by Howard Greenfeld. Boston: Beacon Press.

Méndez, Juan M. 1997a. "¿Cómo se traduce 'performance'?" *El Diario / La Prensa*, May 8: 21.

Méndez, Juan M. 1997b. "Dressed for the Bolero." *El Diario / La Prensa*, February 13.

Méndez-Méndez, Serafín. 2015. "Lesbian, Gay, Bisexual, Transgender, and Transsexual (LGBTT) Movement." In Serafín Méndez-Méndez with Ronald Fernández, *Puerto Rico Past and Present: An Encyclopedia*, 2nd ed., 257–64. Santa Barbara, CA: Greenwood.

Menstrual, Naty. 2012. *Batido de trolo.* Buenos Aires: Milena Caserola.

Mercado, Freddie. 2001. Interview with author. San Juan, Puerto Rico, January.

Mercado, Freddie. 2006. Interview. *Frente sónico.* http://www.frentesonico.com/ (no longer online)

Mercado, Freddie. (2013) 2014. *Viaje . . . Sé.* In *Mind the Gap: Panel Discussion at the Museo de Arte Contemporáneo in Puerto Rico*, ESCALA (Essex Collection of Art from Latin America). Vimeo, February 24. https://vimeo.com/87479881

Merced, Jorge. 1994a. "Teatro y Sida." *Ollantay Theater Magazine* 2, no. 2 (Summer–Fall): 20–26.

Merced, Jorge. 1994b. "Teatro y Sida." *CENTRO Journal* 6, nos. 1–2 (Spring): 174–76.

Merced, Jorge. 2003. "Interview with Jorge Merced, Artistic Director of Teatro Pregones." In Vásquez, 147–53.

Merced, Jorge. 2007. "Pregones Theater: Asunción Playwrights Project." *Ollantay Theater Magazine* 15, nos. 29–30: 181–85.

Merewether, Charles. 2000. "From Inscription to Dissolution: An Essay on Expenditure in the Work of Ana Mendieta." In Fusco, 134–51.

Merrett, Robyn. 2019. "Gay Latin Music Star Kevin Fret, 24, Shot and Killed in Puerto Rico." *People*, January 10. https://people.com/music/latin-singer-kevin-fret-dead-shot-peurto-rico/

Meruane, Lina. 2014. *Viral Voyages: Tracing AIDS in Latin America.* Translated by Andrea Rosenberg. New York: Palgrave Macmillan.

Meyer, Moe, ed. 1994. *The Politics and Poetics of Camp.* London: Routledge.

Meyer, Moe. 2010. *An Archaeology of Posing: Essays on Camp, Drag, and Sexuality.* Madison, WI: Macater Press.

Meyerowitz, Joanne. 2002. *How Sex Changed: A History of Transsexuality in the United States.* Cambridge, MA: Harvard University Press.

Michelson, Noah. 2013. "Monica Beverly Hillz, 'RuPaul's Drag Race' Contestant, Discusses Coming Out as Transgender." *Huffpost Gay Voices*, February 5. https://www.huffpost.com/entry/monica-beverly-hillz-transgender_n_2617975

Millán Ferrer, Alida. 1994. "Las penas saben nadar." *Claridad*, September 2–8: 24.

Miller, Lynn C., Jacqueline Taylor, and M. Heather Carver, eds. 2003. *Voices Made Flesh: Performing Women's Autobiography.* Madison: University of Wisconsin Press.

Milosheff, Peter. 2011. "BAAD! Presents the Welfare Queen." *Bronx Times*, August 29. https://bronx.com/baad-presents-the-welfare-queen/

Mirzoeff, Nicholas. 2010a. "Introduction: The Murder of Jorge Steven López Mercado." *The New Everyday*, September 16. http://mediacommons.org/tne/pieces/introducti on-murder-jorge-steven-l-pez-mercado

Mirzoeff, Nicholas. 2010b. "Slaughter Everyday: Sovereignty, the Animal and Homophobia." *The New Everyday*, June 11. http://mediacommons.org/tne/pieces/slaughter-eve ryday-sovereignty-animal-and-homophobia

Mistress Maddie. 2009. "Grande Dame of the Week: The Late Great Lady Catiria Reyes!" *A Day with the Mistress Borghese*, May 5. http://mistressmaddie.blogspot.com/2009 /05/grande-dame-of-week.html

Mitchell, Larry. (1977) 2019. *The Faggots and Their Friends between Revolutions*. Brooklyn, NY: Nightboat Books.

Mock, Janet. 2017. "Janet Mock: Why I Celebrate and Stand by Tourmaline." *Allure*, October 13. https://www.allure.com/story/janet-mock-why-i-stand-by-reina-gosse tt-marsha-p-johnson

Modern Eccentrics. 2016. "And Then He Was a She—Paintings of Holly Woodlawn by Sadie Lee." *Modern Eccentrics*, May 16. https://moderneccentrics.wordpress.com/20 16/05/16/and-then-he-was-a-she-paintings-of-holly-woodlawn-by-sadie-lee/

Molloy, Sylvia, and Robert McKee Irwin, eds. 1998. *Hispanisms and Homosexualities*. Durham, NC: Duke University Press.

Monserrate, Rafael, and Carlos Maldonado, dirs. 2014. *Las Muchachas*. Quepasagaypr. com, Munglopr Munglo. YouTube. https://youtu.be/VMbca01HseQ

Monsiváis, Carlos. 2010. *Que se abra esa puerta: Crónicas y ensayos sobre la diversidad sexual*. Mexico City: Editorial Paidós Mexicana.

MonsterGirlMovies. 2011. "Erika Lopez's 'The Welfare Queen.'" YouTube, October 10. https://youtu.be/b9-bYaE9tsQ

Montero, Oscar. 1988. *The Name Game: Writing/Fading Writer in* De donde son los cantantes. Chapel Hill: University of North Carolina Department of Romance Languages.

Montero, Oscar. 1998. "The Signifying Queen: Critical Notes from a Latino Queer." In Molloy and Irwin, 161–74.

Montgomery, David T. 2016. "Applied Theater and Citizenship in the Puerto Rican Community: Artistic Citizenship in Practice." In *Artistic Citizenship: Artistry, Social Responsibility, and Ethical Praxis*, edited by David J. Elliott, Marissa Silverman, and Wayne D. Bowman, 447–68. New York: Oxford University Press.

Montoya-Gálvez, Camilo. 2019. "Openly Gay Rapper Murdered in Puerto Rico amid Wave of Violence." *CBS News*, January 10. https://www.cbsnews.com/news/kevin-fr et-dead-openly-gay-rapper-murdered-in-puerto-rico-amid-wave-of-violence/

Mora, Marie T., Alberto Dávila, and Havidán Rodríguez. 2018. *Population, Migration, and Socioeconomic Outcomes among Island and Mainland Puerto Ricans: La Crisis Boricua*. Lanham, MD: Lexington Books.

Morad, Moshe. 2014. *Fiesta de diez pesos: Music and Gay Identity in Special Period Cuba*. Farnham: Ashgate.

Morad, Moshe. 2015. "Queer Bolero: Bolero Music as an Emotional and Psychological Space for Gay Men in Cuba." *Psychology Research* 5, no. 10 (October): 565–84.

Moraga, Cherríe L. 2011. "Still Loving in the (Still) War Years: On Keeping Queer Queer."

In *A Xicana Codex of Changing Consciousness: Writings, 2000–2010*, 175–92. Durham, NC: Duke University Press.

Moraga, Cherríe L., and Gloria E. Anzaldúa, eds. (1981) 1983. *This Bridge Called My Back: Writings by Radical Women of Color.* 2nd ed. New York: Kitchen Table / Women of Color Press.

Morales, Ed. 2019. *Fantasy Island: Colonialism, Exploitation, and the Betrayal of Puerto Rico.* New York: Bold Type Books.

Morales, Iris. 2016. "Women Organizing Women." In *Through the Eyes of Rebel Women: The Young Lords 1969–1976*, edited by Iris Morales, 43–85. New York: Red Sugarcane Press.

Moreno, Iani del Rosario. 1999. "Denver: El Centro Su Teatro presenta al Teatro Pregones de Nueva York y su obra 'El bolero fue mi ruina.'" *Gestos* 14, no. 27: 177–78.

Morón Espinosa, Antonio César. 2015. "El teatro escrito en español en la Ciudad de Nueva York: Búsqueda y generación de identidad(es) desde la dramaturgia." *Latin American Theatre Review* 48, no. 2 (Spring): 87–105.

Morris, Gary. 2003. "'Fabulous Gowns but No Pussy!': An Interview with Holly Woodlawn." *Bright Lights Film Journal* 40 (May). https://brightlightsfilm.com/fabulous-go wns-but-no-pussy-an-interview-with-holly-woodlawn/

Morrison, Josh. 2014. "'Draguating' to Normal: Camp and Homonormative Politics." In Daems, 124–47.

Morrissey, Paul, dir. (1970) 1998. *Trash.* Producer Andy Warhol. Chatsworth, CA: Image Entertainment. DVD.

Mosquera, Gerardo, ed. 1996. *Beyond the Fantastic: Contemporary Art Criticism from Latin America.* Cambridge, MA: MIT Press.

Moura, Evna. 2013. *Translocas.* http://cargocollective.com/evnamoura/Translocas

Moustakas, Tiffany. 2016. "LGBTQ-inclusive Christmas Play." *The Riverdale Press*, December 8. https://riverdalepress.com/stories/LGBTQ-inclusive-Christmas-play ,61350

Moya, Paula M. L. 2002. *Learning from Experience: Minority Identities, Multicultural Struggles.* Berkeley: University of California Press.

Mulvey, Laura. 2009. "Visual Pleasure and Narrative Cinema" (1989). In *Visual and Other Pleasures*, 14–30. New York: Palgrave Macmillan.

Muñoz, José Esteban. 1999. *Disidentifications: Queers of Color and the Performance of Politics.* Minneapolis: University of Minnesota Press.

Muñoz, José Esteban. 2009. *Cruising Utopia: The Then and There of Queer Futurity.* New York: New York University Press.

Muñoz, José Esteban. 2014. "Wise Latinas." *Criticism* 56, no. 2: 249–65.

Muñoz, José Esteban. 2020. *The Sense of Brown.* Edited by Joshua Chambers-Letson and Tavia Nyong'o. Durham, NC: Duke University Press.

Musto, Michael. 1995. "Lost in Yonkers: Sylvia Rivera May Be the Rosa Parks of Gay Rights, but on the Streets, She's Just Another Homeless Queen." *Village Voice*, May 30: 25.

Musto, Michael. 2007. "A Rosie by Any Other Name . . ." Interview with Rosie Pérez. *Out* 16, no. 5 (November): 46–48.

Musto, Michael. 2016. "RIP Latin LGBT Dance Club Escuelita." *Paper*, March 2. https:// www.papermag.com/rip-lgbt-dance-club-escuelita-1637308305.html

Nakiska, Tempe. 2013. "The Legacy of Venus Xtravaganza." *Dazed*, November 20. http:// www.dazeddigital.com/fashion/article/17921/1/the-legacy-of-venus-xtravaganza

Namaste, Viviane K. 2000. *Invisible Lives: The Erasure of Transsexual and Transgendered People*. Chicago: University of Chicago Press.

Namaste, Viviane K. 2005. *C'était du spectacle! L'histoire des artistes transsexuelles à Montréal, 1955–1985*. Montreal: McGill-Queen's University Press.

Namaste, Viviane K. 2011. *Sex Change, Social Change: Reflections on Identity, Institutions, and Imperialism*. Toronto: Women's Press.

Naughton, Jake. 2017. "Gay Life in New York, between Oppression and Freedom." *New York Times*, June 22. https://lens.blogs.nytimes.com/2017/06/22/gay-life-in-new-yo rk-between-oppression-and-freedom/

NBC Miami. 2018. "Hispanic Rapper Kevin Fret Arrested for Battery in Miami." June 21. https://www.nbcmiami.com/news/local/hispanic-rapper-kevin-fret-arrested-for-ba ttery-in-miami/2044541/

Neal, Mark Anthony. 2013. "Trafficking in Monikers: Jay-Z's 'Queer' Flow." *Palimpsest* 2, no. 2: 156–61.

Neese, Joseph. 2015. "Sylvia Rivera Becomes First Trans American to Have Portrait in the Smithsonian." *MSNBC*, October 27. http://www.msnbc.com/msnbc/sylvia-rive ra-becomes-first-trans-american-have-portrait-the-smithsonian

Negrón-Muntaner, Frances. 2004. *Boricua Pop: Puerto Ricans and the Latinization of American Culture*. New York: New York University Press.

Negrón-Muntaner, Frances, ed. 2007. *None of the Above: Puerto Ricans in the Global Era*. New York: Palgrave Macmillan.

Negrón-Muntaner, Frances. 2015. "'I Just Wanted People to Hear My Voice': An Interview with Holly Woodlawn." *Public Books*, December 11. http://www.publicbooks .org/i-just-wanted-people-to-hear-my-voicean-interview-with-holly-woodlawn/

Negrón-Muntaner, Frances. 2018. "The Emptying Island: Puerto Rican Expulsion in Post-Maria Time." *emisférica* 14, no. 1. https://hemisphericinstitute.org/en/emisfer ica-14-1-expulsion/14-1-essays/the-emptying-island-puerto-rican-expulsion-in-po st-maria-time.html

Negrón-Muntaner, Frances, and Ramón Grosfoguel, eds. *1997. Puerto Rican Jam: Essays on Culture and Politics*. Minneapolis: University of Minnesota Press.

Newton, Esther. (1972) 1979. *Mother Camp: Female Impersonators in America*. Phoenix ed. Chicago: University of Chicago Press.

Nichols, James. 2014. "Carmen Carrera and Monica Beverly Hillz Address 'Drag Race' Transphobia Allegations." *Huffpost Queer Voices*, April 1. https://www.huffpost.com /entry/drag-race-transphobia_n_5072399

Noel, Urayoán. 2001. "Los grises felices: El evangelio pop según Súperaquello y El manjar de los dioses." *El cuarto del quenepón*. Biblioteca virtual: música. February 1. http://cuarto.quenepon.org/ (no longer online).

Noel, Urayoán. 2014. *In Visible Movement: Nuyorican Poetry from the Sixties to Slam*. Iowa City: University of Iowa Press.

Normal, Abby. 2012. "Nina Flowers Is a Star." *Yahoo! Voices*, April 11. https://theabbynor mal.wordpress.com/2014/08/06/nina-flowers-is-a-star/

Norris, Laurie. 2014. "Of Fish and Feminists: Homonormative Misogyny and the Trans*Queen." In Daems, 31–48.

Norris, Marianna. 1969. *Doña Felisa, a Biography of the Mayor of San Juan*. New York: Dodd, Mead.

El Nuevo Día. 2009a. "Adiós a Jorge Steven entre reclamos de justicia y respeto." November 23. https://www.elnuevodia.com/noticias/locales/notas/adios-a-jorge-steven-en tre-reclamos-de-justicia-y-respeto/

El Nuevo Día. 2009b. "El poder de narrar con la mirada." June 25. https://www.elnuevod ia.com/entretenimiento/cultura/notas/el-poder-de-narrar-con-la-mirada/

El Nuevo Día. 2011. "Transexual busca convertirse en senador de la Palma." April 25. https://www.elnuevodia.com/noticias/politica/notas/transexual-busca-convertirse -en-senador-de-la-palma/

El Nuevo Día. 2013. "Recuerdan la era dorada de la discoteca Bachelor." August 16. https://www.elnuevodia.com/entretenimiento/musica/notas/recuerdan-la-era-dora da-de-la-discoteca-bachelor/

Nunn, Jerry. 2013. "Monica Beverly Hillz Puts on Her Best Face for RuPaul." *Windy City Times,* February 6. http://www.windycitymediagroup.com/lgbt/Monica-Beverly-Hi llz-puts-on-her-best-face-for-RuPaul/41434.html

Nyong'o, Tavia. 2018. *Afro-Fabulations: The Queer Drama of Black Life.* New York: New York University Press.

Obejas, Achy. 2000. "'Feast of Fools,' a Celebration of Diversity: Colorful Fausto Fernós, an Appropriate Host for Radical Faeries." *Chicago Tribune,* March 31: 28.

Ochoa, Marcia. 2004. "Ciudadanía perversa: Divas, marginación y participación en la 'loca-lización.'" In *Políticas de ciudadanía y sociedad civil en tiempos de globalización,* edited by Daniel Mato, 239–56. Caracas: FACES, Universidad Central de Venezuela.

Ochoa, Marcia. 2008. "Perverse Citizenship: Divas, Marginality, and Participation in 'Loca-Lization.'" *WSQ* 36, nos. 3–4 (Fall–Winter): 146–69.

Ochoa, Marcia. 2014. *Queen for a Day: Transformistas, Beauty Queens, and the Performance of Femininity in Venezuela.* Durham, NC: Duke University Press.

Oiticica, Hélio. 2011. "Mario Montez, Tropicamp." *Afterall* 28: 16–21. https://www.afterall .org/publications/journal/issue.28/mario-montez-tropicamp

Oiticica, Hélio, and Mario Montez. 2014. "Héliotape with Mario Montez (1971)." *Criticism* 56, no. 2: 379–404.

Olalquiaga, Celeste. 1992. *Megalopolis: Contemporary Cultural Sensibilities.* Minneapolis: University of Minnesota Press.

OLD. 2013. "Evna Moura: Translocas." Interview. *Revista OLD* 23 (July): 14–25. https://is suu.com/felipeabreu/docs/old_23_low

Olivares, Enrique. 2017. "No todo tiene que ser neoliberalismo: La ruta al MECA." *La Marginal,* June 7. http://lamarginalpr.com/no-todo-tiene-que-ser-neoliberalismo-la -ruta-al-meca/

Olivares, Jorge. 2013. *Becoming Reinaldo Arenas: Family, Sexuality, and the Cuban Revolution.* Durham, NC: Duke University Press.

Oliver, Angela. 2012. "Owensboro Man to Compete on TV Drag Show." *Messenger Inquirer* (Owensboro, KY), December 31: C1. ProQuest.

Omi, Michael, and Howard Winant. 1994. *Racial Formation in the United States: From the 1960s to the 1990s.* New York: Routledge.

Ong, Walter. 1982. *Orality and Literacy: The Technologizing of the Word.* London: Methuen.

Oquendo-Villar, Carmen, and José Correa Vigier, dirs. 2012. *La Aguja / The Needle.* Puerto Rico: The Needle Productions, LLC. DVD.

Orlan. 2002. *Orlan, 1964–2001*. Vitoria-Gasteiz: Artium; Salamanca: Ediciones Universidad de Salamanca.

Ortiz, Fernando. (1947) 1995. *Cuban Counterpoint: Tobacco and Sugar*. Translated by Harriet de Onís. Durham, NC: Duke University Press.

Ortiz, Reyna. 2017. *T, Stands for Truth: In Search of the Queen*. Chicago: Trans Fusion.

Ortíz, Ricardo L. 2007. *Cultural Erotics in Cuban America*. Minneapolis: University of Minnesota Press.

Ortiz, Roberto. 2016. "An Underground Survivor at the Oscars: Holly Woodlawn, Puerto Rican Actor." *Mediático*, April 4. http://reframe.sussex.ac.uk/mediatico/2016/04/04/an-underground-survivor-at-the-oscars-holly-woodlawn-puerto-rican-actor/

Ortiz Díaz, Gabriela. 2015. "Fela en mosaico frente al mar." *Fundación Nacional para la Cultura Popular*, March 29. https://prpop.org/2015/03/fela-en-mosaico-frente-al-mar/

Ortiz-Fonseca, Louie. 2019. "Remembering NYCs Queen of Nightlife: Lady Catiria, HIV-Positive Transgender Performer." *The Body*, December 5. https://www.thebody.com/article/lady-catiria-reyes-legendary-hiv-positive-trans-performer

Osorio, Ruth. 2017. "Embodying Truth: Sylvia Rivera's Delivery of *Parrhesia* at the 1973 Christopher Street Liberation Day Rally." *Rhetoric Review* 36, no. 2: 151–63.

O'Toole, Emer. 2017. "Guerrilla Glamour: The Queer Tactics of Dr. Panti Bliss." *Éire-Ireland* 52, nos. 3-4 (Fall/Winter): 104–21.

Pabón-Colón, Jessica Nydia. 2016. "'Daring to Be 'Mujeres Libres, Lindas, Locas': An Interview with the Ladies Destroying Crew of Nicaragua and Costa Rica." In *La Verdad: An International Dialogue on Hip Hop Latinidades*, edited by Jason Nichols and Melissa Castillo-Garsow, 203–13. Columbus: Ohio State University Press.

Pabón-Colón, Jessica Nydia. 2018. *Graffiti Grrlz: Performing Feminism in the Hip Hop Diaspora*. New York: New York University Press.

Pabón-Colón, Jessica Nydia. 2019. "Yo Soy Boricua *Feminista*, Pa'que Tu Lo Sepas! Notes from a DiaspoRican on Performing Outsider Identity." In *Latina Outsiders: Remaking Latina Identity*, edited by Grisel Y. Acosta and Roberta Hurtado, 169–74. London: Routledge.

Pagán Sánchez, José R. 2003. "Circo le da vida y color a La Sospecha." *El Nuevo Día*, June 12: n.p.

Page, Morgan M. 2017. "*One from the Vaults*: Gossip, Access, and Trans History-Telling." In Gossett, Stanley, and Burton, 135–46.

Pagnoni Berns, Fernando Gabriel. 2014. "'For Your Next Drag Challenge,' You Must Do Something: Playfulness without Rules." In Daems, 88–105.

Palmeiro, Cecilia. 2011. *Desbunde y felicidad: De la Cartonera a Perlongher*. Buenos Aires: Título.

Pantojas, Antonio. 2005. *Estoy Aquí*. Episode 3. September 16. Television program, Channel 6, Puerto Rico TV.

Paquita la del Barrio. 1993. *Tres veces te engañé*. Discos Musart, CDP-1052.

Park Jin-hai. 2019. "Body Odor Class Gap Guided Bong Joon-ho's 'Parasite.'" *Korea Times*, May 29. https://www.koreatimes.co.kr/www/art/2019/06/689_269700.html

Patton, Cindy, and Benigno Sánchez-Eppler, eds. 2000. *Queer Diasporas*. Durham, NC: Duke University Press.

Paz Pérez, Carlos. 1998a. *Diccionario cubano de habla popular y vulgar*. Madrid: Agualarga Editores.

Paz Pérez, Carlos. 1998b. *La sexualidad en el habla cubana*. Madrid: Agualarga Editores.

Pedreira, Antonio S. (1934) 1973. *Insularismo*. Río Piedras: Edil.

Peeples, Jase. 2013. "Monica Beverly Hillz Talks Life before *Drag Race*." *The Advocate*, April 13. https://www.advocate.com/politics/transgender/2013/04/18/monica-bever ly-hillz-talks-life-drag-race

Pelaez Lopez, Alan. 2018. "The X in Latinx Is a Wound, Not a Trend." *Color Bloq*, September 13. https://www.colorbloq.org/the-x-in-latinx-is-a-wound-not-a-trend

Pelúcio, Larissa. 2009. "'Sin papeles' pero con glamur. Migración de travestis brasileñas a España (Reflexiones iniciales)." *VIBRANT—Vibrant Virtual Brazilian Anthropology* 6, no. 1: 170–97.

Peña, Susana. 2011. "Gender and Sexuality in Latina/o Miami: Documenting Latina Transsexual Activists." In *Historicising Gender and Sexuality*, edited by Kevin P. Murphy and Jennifer M. Spear, 229–46. Malden, MA: Wiley-Blackwell.

Peña, Susana. 2013. *¡Oye Loca! From the Mariel Boatlift to Gay Cuban Miami*. Minneapolis: University of Minnesota Press.

Peña López, Brenda I. 2016. "Sepultan a 'Chianita' por considerarla racista." *El Nuevo Día*, November 2. https://www.elnuevodia.com/entretenimiento/television/notas /sepultan-a-chianita-por-considerarla-racista/

People en Español. 2008–9. "Contra viento y marea." December 2008–January 2009: 140.

Pérez, Emma. 1991. "Sexuality and Discourse: Notes from a Chicana Survivor." In *Chicana Lesbians: The Girls Our Mothers Warned Us About*, edited by Carla Trujillo, 159–84. Berkeley: Third Woman Press.

Pérez, Hiram. 2005. "You Can Have My Brown Body and Eat It, Too!" *Social Text* 23, nos. 3–4 (Fall-Winter): 171–91.

Pérez Firmat, Gustavo. 1994. *Life on the Hyphen: The Cuban-American Way*. Austin: University of Texas Press.

Pérez Firmat, Gustavo. 2008. "Leyendo a Buesa." *Encuentro de la cultura cubana* 50: 5–13.

Pérez Rosario, Vanessa. 2014. *Becoming Julia de Burgos: The Making of a Puerto Rican Icon*. Urbana: University of Illinois Press.

Perkins, Alexandra Gonzenbach. 2017. *Representing Queer and Transgender Identity: Fluid Bodies in the Hispanic Caribbean and Beyond*. Lanham, MD: Bucknell University Press.

Perlongher, Néstor. 1987. *O negócio do michê: Prostituição viril em São Paulo*. São Paulo: Editora Brasiliense.

Perlongher, Néstor. 2016. "Neobarroco y neobarroso." In *Medusario: Muestra de poesía latinoamericana*, edited by Roberto Echavarren, José Kozer, and Jacobo Sefamí, 21–33. Santiago: Ril Editores.

Perlongher, Néstor. 2019. *Plebeian Prose*. Translated by Frances Riddle. Cambridge: Polity.

Perugorría, Jorge, dir. 2015. *Fátima o el Parque de la Fraternidad*. Madrid: Premium Cine. DVD.

Petersen, Jennifer. 2011. *Murder, the Media, and the Politics of Public Feelings: Remembering Matthew Shepard and James Byrd Jr*. Bloomington: Indiana University Press.

Phillips, Layli, and Shomari Olugbala. 2006. "Sylvia Rivera: Fighting in Her Heels: Stonewall, Civil Rights, and Liberation." In *The Human Tradition in the Civil Rights Movement*, edited by Susan M. Glisson, 309–34. Lanham, MD: Rowman and Littlefield.

Pierce, Joseph M. 2020. "I Monster: Embodying Trans and Travesti Resistance in Latin America." *Latin American Research Review* 55, no. 2: 305–21. https://doi.org/10.252 22/larr.563

Pietri, Pedro. 2015. *Pedro Pietri: Selected Poetry.* Edited by Juan Flores and Pedro López Adorno. San Francisco: City Lights.

Pilcher, Katy. 2017. *Erotic Performance and Spectatorship: New Frontiers in Erotic Dance.* London: Routledge.

Pina Girona, Gloriva. 2013. "Análisis e implicaciones psicológicas y sociales del 'chisme' dirigido a figuras públicas puertorriqueñas." PhD diss., Universidad del Turabo, Puerto Rico.

Pitts, Andrea J. 2016. "Gloria E. Anzaldúa's *Autohistoria-teoría* as an Epistemology of Self-Knowledge/Ignorance." *Hypatia* 31, no. 2 (Spring): 352–69.

Pitts, Andrea J., Mariana Ortega, and José Medina, eds. 2020. *Theories of the Flesh: Latinx and Latin American Feminisms, Transformation, and Resistance.* New York: Oxford University Press.

Platón, Lydia. 1997. "Otras experiencias de identidad: El lenguaje corporal en el teatro y la danza contemporánea en el Puerto Rico de los 90." Paper presented at the Caribbean Studies Association Conference, Barranquilla, Colombia, May 27–30. *El cuarto del quenepón.* Biblioteca virtual: movimiento corporal. August 1. http://cuarto.quen epon.org/ (no longer online).

Plaza, Damian Omar. 2008. "Catiria (Lady Catiria) Reyes (1959–1999)." *Find a Grave Memorial.* https://www.findagrave.com/memorial/25885382/catiria-reyes

Plemons, Eric. 2017. *The Look of a Woman: Facial Feminization Surgery and the Aims of Trans-medicine.* Durham, NC: Duke University Press.

Poniewozik, James. 2018. "Review: 'Pose' Demands to Be Seen." *New York Times,* June 1. https://www.nytimes.com/2018/06/01/arts/television/pose-review-fx-ryan-murp hy.html

Popova, Yanna B. 2003. "'The Fool Sees with His Nose': Metaphoric Mappings in the Sense of Smell in Patrick Süskind's *Perfume.*" *Language and Literature* 12, no. 2: 135–51.

Pose. 2018–19. Seasons 1–2. FX. https://www.fxnetworks.com/shows/pose

Power-Sotomayor, Jade. 2019. "Putting Puerto Rico's Best (Black) Face Forward: Ramón Rivero's 'Diplo' and Racialized Performances of Liberation." *Latino Studies* 17, no. 2: 142–63.

POZ. 1999. "Obits: Lady Catiria." August. http://www.poz.com/articles/217_11313 .shtml

Preciado, Paul B. 2011. "The Ocaña We Deserve: Campceptualism, Subordination and Performative Practices." In José Pérez Ocaña, *Ocaña,* 412–38. Barcelona: Ajuntament de Barcelona, Institut de Cultura: Polígrafa.

Preciado, Paul B. 2013. *Testo Junkie: Sex, Drugs, and Biopolitics in the Pharmacoporno-graphic Era.* Translated by Bruce Benderson. New York: The Feminist Press.

Pregones Theater. n.d. "Pregones History." *Hemispheric Institute Digital Video Library.* https://hemisphericinstitute.org/en/hidvl-collections/itemlist/category/519-pregon es.html

Prieto, Carlos. 2013. "Sara Montiel, el extraño caso de un ícono sexual, feminista y gay en pleno franquismo." *El Confidencial,* April 14. https://www.elconfidencial.com/cu

ltura/2013-04-14/sara-montiel-el-extrano-caso-de-un-icono-sexual-feminista-y-g
ay-en-pleno-franquismo_495223/

Prieto Stambaugh, Antonio. 2000. "Camp, *Carpa* and Cross-Dressing in the Theater of Tito Vasconcelos." In Fusco, 83–96.

Prieto Stambaugh, Antonio. 2001. "Las ex-centricidades del performance: Un encuentro en las fronteras del hemisferio." *Conjunto* 122: 108–10.

Prieto Stambaugh, Antonio. 2014. "'RepresentaXión' de un muxe: La identidad performática de Lukas Avendaño." *Latin American Theatre Review* 48, no. 1 (Fall): 31–53.

Prieto Stambaugh, Antonio. 2019. "Performance Artists in Latin America." In *Global Encyclopedia of Lesbian, Gay, Bisexual, Transgender, and Queer (LGBTQ) History*, edited by Howard Chiang, 1223–28. Farmington Hills, MI: Gale.

Prieur, Annick. 1998. *Mema's House, Mexico City: On Transvestites, Queens, and Machos.* Chicago: University of Chicago Press.

Primera Hora. 2013. "Transexual Christina Hayworth vive en condiciones infrahumanas." January 23. https://www.primerahora.com/noticias/puerto-rico/notas/transex ual-christina-hayworth-vive-en-condiciones-infrahumanas/

Prosser, Jay. 1998. *Second Skins: The Body Narratives of Transsexuality.* New York: Columbia University Press.

Proyecto Matria, and Kilómetro Cero. 2019. *La persistencia de la indolencia: Feminicidios en Puerto Rico. 2014–2018. Kilómetro Cero.* https://www.kilometro0.org/informes

Puar, Jasbir K. 2007. *Terrorist Assemblages: Homonationalism in Queer Times.* Durham, NC: Duke University Press.

Puar, Jasbir K. 2017. *The Right to Maim: Debility, Capacity, Disability.* Durham, NC: Duke University Press.

Publishers Weekly. 2017. "*The House of Impossible Beauties.*" December 4. https://www.pu blishersweekly.com/978-0-06-267697-9

"Puerto Ricans in California, the United States, and Puerto Rico, 2014." 2016. Centro/ Center for Puerto Rican Studies, Hunter College, CUNY. https://centropr.hunter.cu ny.edu/sites/default/files/data_sheets/PuertoRicans-CA_v6.pdf

Puig, Manuel. (1976) 1979. *The Kiss of the Spider Woman.* Translated by Thomas Colchie. New York: Knopf.

Pullen, Kirsten. 2005. *Actresses and Whores: On Stage and in Society.* Cambridge: Cambridge University Press.

Queeley, Andrea, and Gina Athena Ulysse. 2015. "Rasanblaj Continua: A Conversation with Gina Athena Ulysse." *Anthropology Now*, November 14. http://anthronow.com /online-articles/rasanblaj-continua

"Queens by Category: Latino Queens." n.d. *RuPaul's Drag Race Wiki.* http://logosrupaul sdragrace.wikia.com/wiki/Queens_By_Category

Qué Pasa Gay PR (Carlos Alberto Maldonado-Virella and Rafael Maldonado). 2012. "Exclusiva: Dreuxilla Divine, una mujer camaleónica." September. http://pruebaqp g1.blogspot.com/2012/09/exclusiva-dreuxilla-divine-una-mujer.html

Qué Pasa Gay PR. 2014. "Barbra Herr: De New York a Morovis y directo a Circo Bar (Oct 11)." October. http://quepasagaypr.blogspot.com/2014/10/barbra-herr-de-new -york-morovis-y.html

Quinn, Rachel Afi. 2016. "El rostro negro dominicano y la Quisqueya *Queer* de Rita Indiana Hernández." In *Nuestro Caribe: Poder, raza y postnacionalismos desde los límites del mapa LGBTQ*, edited by Mabel Cuesta, 254–69. San Juan: Isla Negra Editores.

Quintero Rivera, Ángel G., ed. 1998. *Vírgenes, magos y escapularios: Imaginería, etnicidad y religiosidad popular en Puerto Rico*. San Juan: Fundación Puertorriqueña de las Humanidades.

Quintero Rivera, Ángel G. 2005. *¡Salsa, sabor y control! Sociología de la música "tropical."* Mexico City: Siglo XXI Editores.

Quiroga, José. 1994. "(Queer) Boleros of a Tropical Night." *Travesía* 3, nos. 1–2: 199–214.

Quiroga, José. 2000. *Tropics of Desire: Interventions from Queer Latin/o America*. New York: New York University Press.

Raab, Vicky. 1994. "NYC Mambo Queens at La Escuelita, Every Weekend Is a Halloween of Sorts." *Newsday* (Long Island, NY), October 31: B04. ProQuest.

Ramírez, Catherine S. 2017. "Assimilation." In Vargas, Mirabal, and La Fountain-Stokes, 14–18.

Ramírez, Mercedes T. H. 1999. "España mira a nuestros artistas." *El Nuevo Día*, January 10: 12–17.

Ramírez, Rafael L. 1993. *Dime capitán: Reflexiones sobre la masculinidad*. Río Piedras: Ediciones Huracán.

Ramírez, Rafael L. 1999. *What It Means to Be a Man: Reflections on Puerto Rican Masculinity*. Translated by Rosa E. Casper. New Brunswick, NJ: Rutgers University Press.

Ramírez, Rafael L., Víctor I. García Toro, and Luis Solano Castillo. 2005. "Dando y cogiendo: Los puertorriqueños y el deseo homoerótico." *CENTRO Journal* 17, no. 1: 107–21.

Ramírez, Rafael L., Víctor I. García Toro, and Luis Solano Castillo. 2007. "El deseo homoerótico." In García Toro, Ramírez, and Solano Castillo, 173–208.

Ramos, Francisco José. 1998. "La insumisión de la experiencia artística (Una conflagración de pensamientos)." In *100 años después . . . Cien artistas contemporáneos.* Exhibition catalog. Arsenal de la Puntilla, San Juan, Puerto Rico. November 25. http://www.dmz-pr.com/cien/paco.html (no longer online).

Ramos, Josean. 1988. *Palabras de mujer: Una época reflejada en la vida de Felisa Rincón.* San Juan: Editorial Universidad de América.

Ramos Otero, Manuel. 1979. "El cuento de la Mujer del Mar." In *El cuento de la Mujer del Mar*, 87–116. Río Piedras: Ediciones Huracán.

Ramos Otero, Manuel. 1990. "The Queen of Madness." Translated by Amy Prince. *Portable Lower East Side* 7, no. 1: 113–23.

Ramos Otero, Manuel. 1992. "Loca la de la locura." In *Cuentos de buena tinta*, 233–40. San Juan: Instituto de Cultura Puertorriqueña.

Rangelova, Radost. 2007. "Nationalism, States of Exception, and Caribbean Identities in *Sirena Selena vestida de pena* and 'Loca la de la locura.'" *CENTRO Journal* 19, no. 1 (March): 75–88.

Rapetón. 2018a. "Entrevista a Kevin Fret, el primer trapero abiertamente gay." YouTube, April 10. https://youtu.be/RND9FzG-AJI

Rapetón. 2018b. "Golpean a Kevin Fret por solo ser gay." YouTube, June 20. https://youtu.be/x3L6cwCo6bE

Real Academia Española (RAE). 2001. "Loco, ca." *Diccionario de la lengua española*. 22nd ed. http://lema.rae.es/drae/

Real Academia Española (RAE). 2018. "Loco, ca." *Diccionario de la lengua española*. Tricentenary ed. https://dle.rae.es/

Rebollo-Gil, Guillermo. 2018. *Writing Puerto Rico: Our Decolonial Moment*. New York: Palgrave Macmillan.

Reddy, Chandan. 1998. "Home, Houses, Non-identity: *Paris Is Burning.*" In *Burning Down the House: Recycling Domesticity*, edited by Rosemary Marangoly George, 355–79. Boulder, CO: Westview Press.

Reed, Lou. 1972. "Walk on the Wild Side." *Transformer*. LP.

Remezcla Estaff. 2019. "Kevin Fret, Who Billed Himself as First Openly Gay Latin Trap Artist, Murdered in Puerto Rico." *Remezcla*, January 10. http://remezcla.com/music/kevin-fret-latin-trap-murder/

Retzloff, Tim. 2007. "Eliding Trans Latino/a Queer Experience in U.S. LGBT History: José Sarria and Sylvia Rivera Reexamined." *CENTRO Journal* 19, no. 1 (Spring): 140–61.

Reyes, Raúl A. 2015. "A Forgotten Latina Trailblazer: LGBT Activist Sylvia Rivera." *NBC News*, October 6. https://www.nbcnews.com/news/latino/forgotten-latina-trailblazer-lgbt-activist-sylvia-rivera-n438586

Reyes Angleró, Mariana. 2007. "Hija de una diosa feliz." *El Nuevo Día*, April 29. Gale General OneFile.

Reyes Angleró, Mariana. 2018. "*Inédita*, una pieza de Lío Villahermosa." *8ogrados*, June 27. https://www.80grados.net/inedita-una-pieza-de-lio-villahermosa/

Reyes Franco, Marina. 2007. "Freddie Mercado: Una vida de performance." *Primera Hora*, May 3: 79. https://marinareyesfranco.tumblr.com/post/173672838247/freddie-mercado-una-vida-de-performance-peri%C3%B3dico

Reyes Franco, Marina. 2019. "Freddie Mercado en ¡Se va armar la Gorda!" YouTube, July 26. https://youtu.be/O7IF5DUq6X4

Reynolds, Daniel. 2018. "The Meaning of RuPaul's Apology: What Changed from 2014 to 2018?" *The Advocate*, March 10. https://www.advocate.com/transgender/2018/3/10/meaning-rupauls-apology-what-changed-2014-2018

Ribera Chevremont, Helda. 2017. "Víctor Alicea crea personaje en defensa de los artistas." *HeldaHoy.com*, August 1. http://www.heldahoy.com/2017/08/01/victor-alicea-crea-personaje-en-defensa-de-los-artistas/

Rice-González, Charles. 2016a. *I Just Love Andy Gibb: A Play in One Act*. In Johnson and Rivera-Servera, 509–41.

Rice-González, Charles. 2016b. "Latino/a Visibility and a Legacy of Power and Love." *QED* 3, no. 3 (Fall): 157–59.

Richard, Nelly, ed. 1994. "El caso 'Simón Bolívar.'" *Revista de Crítica Cultural* no. 9 (November): 5–36.

Richard, Nelly. 2004a. *Cultural Residues: Chile in Transition*. Translated by Alan West-Durán and Theodore Quester. Minneapolis: University of Minnesota Press.

Richard, Nelly. 2004b. "Gender Contortions and Sexual Doubling: Transvestite Parody." In *Masculine/Feminine: Practices of Difference(s)*, translated by Silvia R. Tandeciarz and Alice A. Nelson, 43–53. Durham, NC: Duke University Press.

Richard, Nelly. 2018. *Abismos temporales: Feminismo, estéticas travestis y teoría queer*. Santiago: Ediciones Metales Pesados.

Ricourt, Milagros, and Ruby Danta. 2002. *Hispanas de Queens: Latino Panethnicity in a New York City Neighborhood*. Ithaca, NY: Cornell University Press.

Riggs, Marlon, dir. 1987. *Ethnic Notions*. San Francisco: California Newsreel. Videocassette (VHS).

Riggs, Marlon, dir. (1989) 2008. *Tongues Untied*. San Francisco: Frameline. DVD.

Ríos Ávila, Rubén. 1993. "El show de Cristina." Interview with Cristina Hayworth. *Piso 13* (Edición Gay) (San Juan, PR) 2, no. 3: 13.

Ríos Ávila, Rubén. 1995. "Gaiety Burlesque: Homosexual Desire in Puerto Rican Literature." In *Polifonía salvaje: Ensayos de cultura y política en la postmodernidad*, edited by Irma Rivera Nieves and Carlos Gil, 138–46. San Juan: Editorial Postdata.

Ríos Ávila, Rubén. 1998. "Caribbean Dislocations: Arenas and Ramos Otero in New York." In Molloy and Irwin, 101–19.

Ríos Ávila, Rubén. 2002. *La raza cómica: Del sujeto en Puerto Rico*. San Juan: Ediciones Callejón.

Ríos Ávila, Rubén. 2007. "Queer Nation." In *Los otros cuerpos: Antología de temática gay, lésbica y queer desde Puerto Rico y su diáspora*, edited by David Caleb Acevedo, Moisés Agosto Rosario, and Luis Negrón, 293–307. San Juan: Editorial Tiempo Nuevo.

Ríos Ávila, Rubén. 2009. "Locas barrocas: Néstor Perlonger y Pedro Lemebel." *Hotel Abismo* 4: 94–103.

Ríos Ávila, Rubén. 2010a. "Homo Freak." *PedroJulioSerrano.com*, January 29. https://pedrojulioserrano.com/2010/01/29/homo-freak/

Ríos Ávila, Rubén. 2010b. "Homo Freak." Translated by Erik Carrión Orlandi. *The New Everyday*, June 11. http://mediacommons.org/tne/pieces/homo-freak

Ríos Ávila, Rubén. 2013. "Perlongher pasea por el parque Lezama." In *Lezama Lima: Orígenes, revolución y después*, edited by Teresa Basile and Nancy Calomarde, 177–86. Buenos Aires: Corregidor.

Ríos Ávila, Rubén. 2018. "Atmósferas de la crisis: Arte y performance en Puerto Rico." Paper presented at the Latin American Studies Association International Congress, Barcelona, Catalunya, May 26.

Ritchie, Jason. 2010. "How Do You Say 'Come Out of the Closet' in Arabic? Queer Activism and the Politics of Visibility in Israel-Palestine." *GLQ* 16, no. 4: 557–76.

Rivera, Carlos Manuel. 2014. *Para que no se nos olvide: Ensayos de interpretación sobre un teatro puertorriqueño marginal*. San Juan: Instituto de Cultura Puertorriqueña.

Rivera, Nelson. 1997. *Visual Artists and the Puerto Rican Performing Arts, 1950–1990: The Works of Jack and Irene Delano, Antonio Martorell, Jaime Suárez, and Oscar Mestey-Villamil*. New York: Peter Lang.

Rivera, Nelson. 2016. *Hinca por ahí: Escritos sobre las artes y asuntos limítrofes*. San Juan: Ediciones Callejón.

Rivera, Nelson. 2018. "Antonio Pantojas, in memoriam." *80grados*, February 2. http://www.80grados.net/antonio-pantojas-in-memoriam/

Rivera, Soldanela, and Jorge B. Merced. 2017. "Jorge Merced: Actor, Activist, Associate Artistic Director Pregones/PRTT." *Notes from a Native Daughter*, May 21. Podcast. https://www.notesfromanativedaughter.com/episodes/2017/5/21/jorge-merced-actor-activist-associate-artistic-director-pregonesprtt

Rivera, Sylvia. 1972. "Transvestites: Your Half Sisters and Half Brothers of the Revolution." *Come Out* 2, no. 8 (Winter): 10.

Rivera, Sylvia. (1973) 2019. "L020A Sylvia Rivera, 'Y'all Better Quiet Down' Original

Authorized Video, 1973 Gay Pride Rally NYC." LoveTapesCollective. YouTube, May 23. https://youtu.be/Jb-JIOWUw1o

Rivera, Sylvia. 1998. "I'm Glad I Was in the Stonewall Riot." In Leslie Feinberg, *Trans Liberation: Beyond Pink or Blue*, 106–9. Boston: Beacon.

Rivera, Sylvia. 2002. "Queens in Exile, the Forgotten Ones." In *GenderQueer: Voices from beyond the Sexual Binary*, edited by Joan Nestle, Clare Howell, and Riki Wilchins, 67–85. Los Angeles: Alyson Publications.

Rivera, Sylvia. 2007. "Sylvia Rivera's Talk at LGMNY, June 2001, Lesbian and Gay Community Services Center, New York City." Transcribed and edited by Lauren Galarza and Lawrence La Fountain-Stokes. *CENTRO Journal* 19, no. 1 (Spring): 116–23.

Rivera Colón, Edgar. 2009. "Getting Life in Two Worlds: Power and Prevention in the New York City House Ball Community." PhD diss., Rutgers University, New Brunswick.

Rivera Colón, Edgar. 2012. "Between the Runway and the Empty Tomb: Bodily Transformation and Christian Praxis in New York City's House Ball Community." In *Christianity and Culture in the City: A Postcolonial Approach*, edited by Samuel Cruz, 49–67. Lanham, MD: Lexington Books.

Rivera Puig, Miguel. 2019. "Matan a sospechoso de muerte de Kevin Fret." *El Vocero*, July 21. https://www.elvocero.com/ley-y-orden/matan-a-sospechoso-de-muerte-de-kevin-fret/article_e70be962-ac06-11e9-8af5-af6de4c56113.html

Rivera Sánchez, Roberto G. 2011. "'El Rito' de Awilda Sterling-Duprey." Vimeo, September 21. https://vimeo.com/29357060

Rivera-Servera, Ramón H. 2012. *Performing Queer Latinidad: Dance, Sexuality, Politics*. Ann Arbor: University of Michigan Press.

Rivera-Servera, Ramón H. 2017. "History in Drag: Latina/o Queer Affective Circuits in Chicago." In *The Latina/o Midwest Reader*, edited by Omar Valerio-Jiménez, Santiago Vaquera-Vásquez, and Claire F. Fox, 185–96. Champaign: University of Illinois Press.

Rivera-Velázquez, Celiany, and Beliza Torres Narváez. 2016. "Homosociality and Its Discontents: Puerto Rican Masculinities in Javier Cardona's *Ah mén*." In Johnson and Rivera-Servera, 264–74.

Rivero, Yeidy M. 2005. *Tuning Out Blackness: Race and Nation in the History of Puerto Rican Television*. Durham, NC: Duke University Press.

Rivero, Yeidy M. 2006. "Channeling Blackness, Challenging Racism: A Theatrical Response." *Global Media and Communication* 2, no. 3: 335–54.

Riviere, Joan. 1929. "Womanliness as Masquerade." *International Journal of Psychoanalysis* 10: 303–13.

Rizk, Beatriz J. 2017. "American Theatre on a Latin Beat: Interviewing Pregones after 38 Years on the Stages of New York." *Latin American Theatre Review* 50, no. 2: 201–15.

Rizki, Cole. 2019. "Latin/x American Trans Studies: Toward a *Travesti*-Trans Analytic." *TSQ* 6, no. 2 (May): 145–55.

Roach, Joseph. 1996. *Cities of the Dead: Circum-Atlantic Performance*. New York: Columbia University Press.

Robinson, Walter. 2002. "Report from ARCO." *Artnet*, February 14. http://www.artnet.com/Magazine/reviews/robinson/robinson2-14-02.asp

Robles, Víctor Hugo. 2015. *El diario del Che gay en Chile*. Santiago: Siempreviva.

Roche, Mario Edgardo. 2000. "Pisa firme en España." *Primera Hora*, May 22. Photocopy.

Rodríguez, Arnaldo. 1999. "Multipremiado actor amante de la comida hindú." *Impacto*, March 23: 16. ProQuest.

Rodríguez, Jorge. 2017. "Fallece Antonio Pantojas." *El Vocero*, October 3. http://www.el vocero.com/escenario/fallece-antonio-pantojas/article_c5e97096-a7bd-11e7-93e4 -2bc7bac40975.html

Rodríguez, Juana María. 2003. *Queer Latinidad: Identity Practices, Discursive Spaces.* New York: New York University Press.

Rodríguez, Juana María. 2011. "Queer Sociality and Other Sexual Fantasies." *GLQ* 17, nos. 2–3: 331–48. https://doi.org/10.1215/10642684-1163427

Rodríguez, Juana María. 2014. *Sexual Futures, Queer Gestures, and Other Latina Longings.* New York: New York University Press.

Rodríguez, Juana María. 2016. "Voices: LGBT Clubs Let Us Embrace Queer Latinidad, Let's Affirm This." *NBC News*, June 16. http://www.nbcnews.com/storyline/orlando -nightclub-massacre/voices-lgbt-clubs-let-us-embrace-queer-latinidad-let-s-n59 3191

Rodríguez, Luis M. 1974. "Enfoques: Palabras." *Pa'fuera!* 1, no. 3 (November): 3, 15.

Rodriguez, Mathew. 2018. "'Drag Race' Contestant Monica Beverly Hillz Responds to RuPaul's Transitioning Comments: 'Our Bodies Do Not Equate Our Identity.'" *Into*, March 4. https://www.intomore.com/culture/drag-race-contestant-monica-bever ly-hillz-responds-to-rupauls-transitioning-comments-our-bodies-do-not-equate -our-identity

Rodríguez, Maya. 2019. "Detrás de las dragas de Río Piedras: Entrevista a Misandra Bolac y Ana Macho." *Melange PR*, May 9. https://melangepr.wixsite.com/melange /post/detr%C3%A1s-de-las-dragas-de-r%C3%ADo-piedras-entrevista-a-misandra -bolac-y-ana-macho

Rodríguez, Richard T. 2017. "X Marks the Spot." *Cultural Dynamics* 29, no. 3: 202–13.

Rodríguez de Ruiz, Alexandra, and Marcia Ochoa. 2016. "Translatina Is about the Journey: A Dialogue on Social Justice for Transgender Latinas in San Francisco." In *Trans Studies: The Challenge to Hetero/Homo Normativities*, edited by Yolanda Martínez-San Miguel and Sarah Tobias, 154–71. New Brunswick, NJ: Rutgers University Press.

Rodríguez-Díaz, Carlos E., Adriana Garriga-López, Souhail M. Malavé-Rivera, and Ricardo Vargas-Molina. 2017. "Zika Virus Epidemic in Puerto Rico: Health Justice Too Long Delayed." *International Journal of Infectious Diseases* 65 (December): 144–47. http://dx.doi.org/10.1016/j.ijid.2017.07.017

Rodríguez González, Félix. 2008. *Diccionario gay-lésbico: Vocabulario general y argot de la homosexualidad.* Madrid: Editorial Gredos.

Rodríguez Guerra, Mario. 2003. "Perfil Comunitario: Christina Hayworth." *Nuevos Tiempos*, Fall. www.stonewallvets.org/CristinaHayworth.htm

Rodríguez Guerra, Mario. 2006. "De travesti a sacerdote." *OrgulloBoricua.net.* https:// web.archive.org/web/20071017000516/http://www.orgulloboricua.net/comunidad /noticias/locales/2006_antonio_pantojas_030106.html

Rodríguez Juliá, Edgardo. 1981. *Las tribulaciones de Jonás.* Río Piedras: Ediciones Huracán.

Rodríguez Juliá, Edgardo. (1983) 2004. *Cortijo's Wake / El entierro de Cortijo.* Translated by Juan Flores. Durham, NC: Duke University Press.

Rodríguez Juliá, Edgardo. 1986. *Una noche con Iris Chacón.* Río Piedras: Editorial Antillana.

Rodríguez-Madera, Sheilla. 2009. *Género trans: Transitando por las zonas grises.* San Juan: Terranova Editores.

Rodríguez Martinó, Graciela. 1990. "Pantojas: ¿Cuál es mi lugar en la Revolución?" *Claridad*, November 29–December 5: 20–21.

Rodríguez Santaliz, Virianai. 2008. *Sylvia Rexach . . . : Pasión adentro*. San Juan: Ediciones Callejón.

Rodríguez-Silva, Ileana. 2012. *Silencing Race: Disentangling Blackness, Colonialism, and National Identities in Puerto Rico*. New York: Palgrave Macmillan.

Rodríguez Vega, Myrna E. 2007. *Yo también . . . pinturas, instalaciones y performance*. Freddie Mercado, La Pintadera Gallery. Exhibition catalog. San Juan: La Pintadera.

Rodriguez y Gibson, Eliza. 2014. "Drag Racing the Neoliberal Circuit: Latina/o Camp and the Contingencies of Resistance." In *The Un/Making of Latina/o Citizenship*, edited by Ellie D. Hernández and Eliza Rodriguez y Gibson, 39–62. New York: Palgrave Macmillan.

Roiz, Jessica. 2019a. "5 Things to Know about Kevin Fret, the Gay Latin Trap Artist Killed in Puerto Rico." *Billboard*, January 11. https://www.billboard.com/articles/col umns/latin/8493138/who-was-kevin-fret-death-gay-trap-artist

Roiz, Jessica. 2019b. "Openly Gay Latin Trap Artist Kevin Fret Shot and Killed at 24." *Billboard*, January 10. https://www.billboard.com/amp/articles/columns/latin/8493 026/kevin-fret-dead-latin-trap-artist-dies/

Rojas, Orlando, dir. 2002. *Las noches de Constantinopla*. Havana: El Paso Producciones. DVD.

Rolón, Rosalba, and Alvan Colón. 1997. "Pregones: Grupo, organización, empresa." Interview by Vivian Martínez Tabares. *Conjunto* 106 (May–August): 60–67.

Román, David. 1998. *Acts of Intervention: Performance, Gay Culture, and AIDS*. Bloomington: Indiana University Press.

Román, David. 2005. *Performance in America: Contemporary U.S. Culture and the Performing Arts*. Durham, NC: Duke University Press.

Román, David, Kalle Westerling, and Dan Venning. 2017. "Subjective Histories of Taylor Mac's 'Radical Faerie Realness Ritual' History." Review. *Theatre Journal* 69, no. 3: 403–15.

Román, Madeline. 2012. "Sobre el derecho y sobre lo humano: Inventario de violencias." In *Puerto Rico y los derechos humanos: Una intersección plural*, edited by José Javier Colón Morera and Idsa E. Alegría Ortega, 175–92. San Juan: Ediciones Callejón.

Romero, Ivette. 2017. "Freddie Mercado Performs at Amsterdam Art Week." *Repeating Islands*, November 23. https://repeatingislands.com/2017/11/23/freddie-mercado -performs-at-amsterdam-art-weekend/

Roque Ramírez, Horacio N. 2005. "A Living Archive of Desire: Teresita la Campesina and the Embodiment of Queer Latino Community Histories." In *Archive Stories: Facts, Fictions, and the Writing of History*, edited by Antoinette Burton, 111–35. Durham, NC: Duke University Press.

Roque Ramírez, Horacio N. 2008. "Memory and Mourning: Living Oral History with Queer Latinos and Latinas in San Francisco." In *Oral History and Public Memories*, edited by Paula Hamilton and Linda Shopes, 165–86. Philadelphia: Temple University Press.

Rosa, Alejandra, and Frances Robles. 2020. "Pandemic Plunges Puerto Rico Into Yet Another Dire Emergency." *New York Times*, July 8. https://www.nytimes.com/2020 /07/08/us/coronavirus-puerto-rico-economy-unemployment.html

Rosa, Jonathan. 2019. *Looking like a Language, Sounding like a Race: Raciolinguistic Ideologies and the Learning of Latinidad*. New York: Oxford University Press.

Rosa, Luis Othoniel. 2011. "Grave Melodies: Literature and Afterlife in Manuel Ramos Otero." *Revista Hispánica Moderna* 64, no. 2 (December): 167–79.

Rosado, José O. 1995. "Antonio Pantojas: Solo llegó, acompañado se va." *Claridad*, October 20–26: 26.

Rosado, José O. 1997. "Seis piezas 'liminales' de la 'nueva' nueva dramaturgia puertorriqueña." *Conjunto* 106 (May–August): 50–54.

Rosario, Frances, and Javier Colón. 2009. "Confiesa asesinato de joven homosexual." *El Nuevo Día*, November 17. https://www.elnuevodia.com/noticias/locales/notas/confi esa-asesinato-de-joven-homosexual/

Rosario, Gabino. 2013. "Freddie Mercado: Persistencia de propósitos trascendentales." Catalog, *Exposición Las Caras de Freddie: Por que todos somos frutas y estamos sabrosas*. Santo Domingo: Colegio Dominicano de Artistas Plásticos (CODAP).

Roure, Jodie G. 2011. "Gender Justice in Puerto Rico: Domestic Violence, Legal Reform, and the Use of International Human Rights Principles." *Human Rights Quarterly* 33, no. 3 (August): 790–825.

Roure, Jodie G. 2019. "Immigrant Women, Domestic Violence, and Hurricanes Irma and Maria in Puerto Rico: Compounding the Violence for the Most Vulnerable." *Georgetown Journal of Gender and the Law* 20, no. 3: 631–97.

Rubin, Gayle. 1984. "Thinking Sex: Notes for a Radical Theory of the Politics of Sexuality." In *Pleasure and Danger: Exploring Female Sexuality*, edited by Carole S. Vance, 267–319. Boston: Routledge and Kegan Paul.

Rudakoff, Judith, ed. 2012. *TRANS(per)FORMING Nina Arsenault: An Unreasonable Body of Work*. Bristol, UK: Intellect.

Ruiz, Sandra. 2019. *Ricanness: Enduring Time in Anticolonial Performance*. New York: New York University Press.

Runtagh, Jordan. 2019. "Ozuna's Lawyer Denies Singer Had Any Role in the Death of Artist Allegedly Extorting Him." *People*, January 25. https://people.com/music/ozu na-lawyer-denies-singer-had-role-kevin-fret-murder-extortion/

RuPaul's Drag Race All Stars. 2012. Season 1. Logo TV. http://www.logotv.com/

RuPaul's Drag Race All Stars. 2018–20. Seasons 4–5. VH1. http://www.vh1.com/

RuPaul's Drag Race. 2009–16. Seasons 1–8. Logo TV. http://www.logotv.com/

RuPaul's Drag Race. 2017–20. Seasons 9–12. VH1. http://www.vh1.com/

RuPaul's Drag U. 2010. Season 1. Logo TV. http://www.logotv.com/

Rupp, Leila J., and Verta Taylor. 2003. *Drag Queens at the 801 Cabaret*. Chicago: University of Chicago Press.

Russonello, Giovanni. 2018. "Lucho Gatica, 'the King of Bolero,' Is Dead at 90." *New York Times*, November 23. https://www.nytimes.com/2018/11/23/obituaries/lucho-gatica -dead.html

Sadlier, Darlene J., ed. 2009. *Latin American Melodrama: Passion, Pathos, and Entertainment*. Urbana: University of Illinois Press.

Said, Edward W. 1979. *Orientalism*. New York: Vintage.

Salas Rivera, Raquel. 2018. *Lo terciario / The Tertiary*. Oakland, CA: Timeless, Infinite Light.

Sánchez, Luis Rafael. 1988. *La importancia de llamarse Daniel Santos*. Hanover, NH: Ediciones del Norte.

Sánchez González, Lisa. 2001. *Boricua Literature: A Literary History of the Puerto Rican Diaspora*. New York: New York University Press.

Sancho Ordóñez, Fernando. 2011. "'Locas' y 'fuertes': Cuerpos precarios en el Guayaquil del siglo XXI." *Íconos* 39: 97–110.

Sandeen, Autumn. 2014. "In Revolution, the Trans Terms Sylvia Rivera Used." *The TransAdvocate*, April 30. http://www.transadvocate.com/in-revolution-the-trans-te rms-sylvia-rivera-used_n_13623.htm

Sandoval, Chela. 2000. *Methodology of the Oppressed*. Minneapolis: University of Minnesota Press.

Sandoval-Sánchez, Alberto. 1997. "Puerto Rican Identity Up in the Air: Air Migration, Its Cultural Representations, and Me 'Cruzando el Charco.'" In Negrón-Muntaner and Grosfoguel, 189–208.

Sandoval-Sánchez, Alberto. 1999. *José Can You See? Latinos On and Off Broadway*. Madison: University of Wisconsin Press.

Sandoval-Sánchez, Alberto. 2005. "Politicizing Abjection: Towards the Articulation of a Latino AIDS Queer Identity." In *Passing Lines*, edited by Brad Epps, Keja Valens, and Bill Johnson González, 311–19. Cambridge, MA: David Rockefeller Center for Latin American Studies and Harvard University Press.

Sandoval-Sánchez, Alberto, and Nancy Saporta Sternbach. 1996. "Rehearsing in Front of the Mirror: Marga Gomez's Lesbian Subjectivity as a Work-in-progress." *Women and Performance* 8, no. 2: 205–23. https://doi.org/10.1080/07407709608571240

Sandoval-Sánchez, Alberto, and Nancy Saporta Sternbach. 2001. *Stages of Life: Transcultural Performance and Identity in U.S. Latina Theater*. Tucson: University of Arizona Press.

San Juan Star. 2007. "Sterling Duprey Takes Center Stage." May 3: 6.

Santana, Analola. 2018. *Freak Performances: Dissidence in Latin American Theater*. Ann Arbor: University of Michigan Press.

Santiago, Esmeralda. 1993. *When I Was Puerto Rican*. Reading, MA: Addison-Wesley.

Santiago, Javier. 2013. "*Luberza golpea en el Corralón.*" *Fundación Nacional para la Cultura Popular*, February 23. https://prpop.org/2013/02/luberza-golpea-en-el-corra lon/

Santiago, Liz Sandra. 2017a. "Fallece el actor, bailarín y productor Antonio Pantojas." *Primera Hora*, October 2. https://www.primerahora.com/entretenimiento/farandu la/notas/fallece-el-actor-bailarin-y-productor-antonio-pantojas/

Santiago, Liz Sandra. 2017b. "Performero boricua lleva a Amsterdam la vida tras María." *El Nuevo Día*, November 21. https://www.elnuevodia.com/entretenimiento/cultura /notas/performero-boricua-lleva-a-amsterdam-la-vida-tras-maria/#

Santiago-Ortiz, Vilma. 2001. *Medicalizing Ethnicity: The Construction of Latino Identity in a Psychiatric Setting*. Ithaca, NY: Cornell University Press.

Santiago Torres, Alinaluz. 2012. *La poética del bolero en Cuba y Puerto Rico*. 2nd ed. San Juan: Editorial Isla Negra.

Santiago Túa, Lynet. 2015. "Con larga historia en PR el transformismo." *Metro*, July 17. http://www.pressreader.com/puerto-rico/metro-puerto-rico/20150717/281487865 033984

Santini, Antonio, and Dan Sickles, dirs. (2014) 2015. *Mala Mala*. New York: Strand. DVD.

Santos-Febres, Mayra. 1993. "The Translocal Papers: Gender and Nation in Contemporary Puerto Rican Literature." PhD diss., Cornell University.

Santos-Febres, Mayra. 2000a. *Sirena Selena*. Translated by Stephen A. Lytle. New York: Picador USA.

Santos-Febres, Mayra. 2000b. *Sirena Selena vestida de pena*. Barcelona: Mondadori.

Santos-Febres, Mayra. 2003. "La identidad es una ficción." *Orificio* no. 3: 38–40.

Santos-Febres, Mayra. 2005. "Caribe y travestismo." In *Sobre piel y papel*, 128–39. San Juan: Ediciones Callejón.

Santos-Febres, Mayra. 2013. "The Caribbean and Transvestism." Translated by Roberto del Valle Alcalá. In *The Cross-Dressed Caribbean: Writing, Politics, Sexualities*, edited by Maria Cristina Fumagalli, Bénédicte Ledent, and Roberto del Valle Alcalá, 159–66. Charlottesville: University of Virginia Press.

Sarduy, Severo. 1982. *La simulación*. Caracas: Monte Ávila Editores.

Sargent, Antwaun. 2017. "Caribbean Artists Shine at a New Art Fair in Puerto Rico." *Creators*, June 2. https://www.vice.com/en_us/article/43yvvd/meca-caribbean-artists-shine-at-a-new-art-fair-in-puerto-rico

Sartre, Jean-Paul. 1964. *Being and Nothingness: An Essay in Phenomenological Ontology*. Translated by Hazel E. Barnes. New York: Citadel Press.

Saunders, John Hanson. 2008. "The Evolution of Snow White: A Close Textual Analysis of Three Versions of the Snow White Fairy Tale." PhD diss., Pennsylvania State University.

Schewe, Elizabeth. 2009. "Serious Play: Drag, Transgender, and the Relationship between Performance and Identity in the Life Writing of RuPaul and Kate Bornstein." *Biography* 32, no. 4 (Fall): 670–95.

Schnabel, Julian, dir. 2000. *Before Night Falls*. Fineline Features. Los Angeles: New Line Home Entertainment. DVD.

Schulman, Michael. 2018. "Lady Bunny Is Still the Shadiest Queen Around." *New York Times*, September 29. https://www.nytimes.com/2018/09/29/style/lady-bunny-drag-queen.html

Scott, A. O. 2016. "'Moonlight': Is This the Year's Best Movie?" *New York Times*, October 20. https://www.nytimes.com/2016/10/21/movies/moonlight-review.html

Scott, Darieck B. 2010. *Extravagant Abjection: Blackness, Power, and Sexuality in the African American Literary Imagination*. New York: New York University Press.

Seda, Laurietz. 2009. "Trans/Acting: The Art of Living 'In-Between.'" In Bixler and Seda, 13–23.

Seda, Laurietz. 2018. *La Nueva Dramaturgia Puertorriqueña: trans/acciones de la identidad*. San Juan: Nuevos Cuadernos del Ateneo Puertorriqueño.

Selenick, Laurence. 2000. *The Changing Room: Sex, Drag and Theatre*. London: Routledge.

Serra, Oriol. 2014. "Las Pantojas de nuestra televisión: De La Panto de Puerto Rico a Yolanda Ramos." *Fórmula TV*, November 23. http://www.formulatv.com/noticias/42036/pantojas-ficticias-television-panto-puerto-rico-yolanda-ramos/

Shapiro, Ari. 2019. "'Pose' Choreographer Creates a Safe Space—On the Runway." *NPR*, July 11. https://www.npr.org/2019/07/11/740704882/pose-choreographer-creates-a-safe-space-on-the-runway

Shapiro, Eileen. 2016. "Barbra Herr." *Get Out!*, March 6. http://getoutmag.com/barbra-herr/

Shapiro, Gregg. 2006. "Feast of Fools Takes Gay Podcasting to New Heights." *AfterElton.com*, August 22. https://web.archive.org/web/20071017115042/http://www.afterelton.com/archive/elton/people/2006/8/fausto.html

Shay, Kray. 2012. "She Cunt." *Urban Dictionary*, February 25. https://www.urbandictionary.com/define.php?term=She%20Cunt

Shepard, Benjamin. 2002. "Amanda Milan and the Rebirth of Street Trans Activist Revolutionaries." In *From ACT UP to the WTO: Urban Protest and Community Building in the Era of Globalization*, edited by Benjamin Shepard and Ronald Hayduk, 156–63. London: Verso.

Shepard, Benjamin. 2004a. "History or Myth? Writing Stonewall." *Lambda Book Report* 13, no. 1/2 (August–September): 12–14.

Shepard, Benjamin. 2004b. "Sylvia and Sylvia's Children: A Battle for a Queer Public Space." In Sycamore, 97–112.

Shepard, Benjamin. 2013. "From Community Organization to Direct Services: The Street Trans Action Revolutionaries to Sylvia Rivera Law Project." *Journal of Social Service Research* 39, no. 1: 95–114.

Sheridan, Angel. n.d. "Lady Catiria." *Escuelita.com*. http://escuelita.com/escuelita_new /pages/dates/saturday_may_5th.htm (link no longer active).

Shokooh Valle, Firuzeh. 2009. "Puerto Rico: Hate Crime against Gay Teenager Causes Outrage." *Global Voices*, November 20. https://globalvoices.org/2009/11/20/puerto -rico-hate-crime-against-gay-teenager-causes-outrage/#

Sieg, Katrin. 2002. *Ethnic Drag: Performing Race, Nation, Sexuality in West Germany*. Ann Arbor: University of Michigan Press.

Sifuentes-Jáuregui, Ben. 2002. *Transvestism, Masculinity, and Latin American Literature: Genders Share Flesh*. New York: Palgrave Macmillan.

Sifuentes-Jáuregui, Ben. 2014. *The Avowal of Difference: Queer Latino American Narratives*. Albany: State University of New York Press.

Signorile, Michelangelo. 2014. "Sister Roma, Drag Performer, Talks about Leading Fight against Facebook Name Policy." *HuffPost*, September 20. https://www.huffpost.com /entry/sister-roma-facebook_n_5854116

Silverman, Kaja. 1992. *Male Subjectivity at the Margins*. New York: Routledge.

Simon, Frank, dir. (1968) 1990. *The Queen*. New York: First Run Features Home Video. DVD.

Simón, Yara. 2016. "NYC's First-Ever Latino LGBTQ Festival Kicks Off Today." *Remezcla*, May 11. http://remezcla.com/lists/culture/nyc-first-lgbtq-festival-fuerza-fest/

Sívori, Horacio Federico. 2004. *Locas, chongos y gays: Sociabilidad homosexual masculina durante la década de 1990*. Buenos Aires: Editorial Antropofagia.

Smith, Anna Marie. 2007. *Welfare Reform and Sexual Regulation*. New York: Cambridge University Press.

Smith, Roberta. 2008. "When the Conceptual Was Political." Art Review, "Arte No Es Vida": Actions by Artists of the Americas, 1960–2000. *New York Times*, February 1: 33. https://www.nytimes.com/2008/02/01/arts/design/01vida.html

Snorton, C. Riley. 2017. *Black on Both Sides: A Racial History of Trans Identity*. Minneapolis: University of Minnesota Press.

Snorton, C. Riley, and Jin Haritaworn. 2013. "Trans Necropolitics: A Transnational Reflection on Violence, Death, and the Trans of Color Afterlife." In Stryker and Aizura, 66–76.

Soberón Torchía, Édgar. 1999. *Hijos de Ochún*. San Juan: Isla Negra Editores.

Solberg, Helena, dir. (1995) 1998. *Carmen Miranda: Bananas Is My Business*. New York: Fox Lorber Home Video. DVD.

Solomon, Alisa. 2003. "Viva la Diva Citizenship: Post-Zionism and Gay Rights." In *Queer Theory and the Jewish Question*, edited by Daniel Boyarin, Daniel Itzkovitz, and Ann Pellegrini, 149–65. New York: Columbia University Press.

Sommer, Doris. 1991. *Foundational Fictions: The National Romances of Latin America.* Berkeley: University of California Press.

Sontag, Susan. (1964) 1966. "Notes on Camp." In *Against Interpretation*, 275–92. New York: Farrar, Straus and Giroux.

Soraya (Bárbara Santiago Solla). 2014. *Hecha a mano: Disforia de género.* San Juan: Lúdika Proyecto.

Soto, Edgardo. 2003. "Circo: Filmación del video 'La Sospecha.'" *Pulso Rock*, June. http://www.pulsorock.com/fotos/circo_lasospecha.php (link no longer active).

Soto-Crespo, Ramón. 1998. "Infiernos imaginarios: Puerto Rican Marginality in Abniel Marat's *dios en el Playgirl de noviembre* and Eugenio María de Hostos's *La peregrinación de Bayoán.*" *Modern Fiction Studies* 44, no. 1: 215–39.

Souza, Caridad. 2001. "Esta risa no es de loca." In Latina Feminist Group, *Telling to Live: Latina Feminist Testimonios*, 114–22. Durham, NC: Duke University Press.

Spade, Dean. 2015. *Normal Life: Administrative Violence, Critical Trans Politics, and the Limits of Law.* Durham, NC: Duke University Press.

Spears, Scott. 2000. "Queen." In Haggerty, 723.

SPIT! (Sodomites, Perverts, Inverts Together!) (Carlos Motta, John Arthur Peetz, Carlos María Romero). 2017. *The SPIT! Manifesto Reader.* London: Frieze Projects.

Stainton, Leslie. 1999. *Lorca: A Dream of Life.* New York: Farrar, Straus and Giroux.

Stein, Marc. 2019. *The Stonewall Riots: A Documentary History.* New York: New York University Press.

Stephens, Michelle Ann. 2014. *Skin Acts: Race, Psychoanalysis, and the Black Male Performer.* Durham, NC: Duke University Press.

Stevens, Camilla. 2004. *Family and Identity in Contemporary Cuban and Puerto Rican Drama.* Gainesville: University Press of Florida.

Stevens, Camilla. 2019. *Aquí and Allá: Transnational Dominican Theater and Performance.* Pittsburgh: University of Pittsburgh Press.

Stransky, Tanner. 2013. "'RuPaul's Drag Race' React: Monica Beverly Hillz Talks to EW about Her Shocking Runway Revelation." *Entertainment Weekly*, February 5. https://ew.com/article/2013/02/05/rupauls-drag-race-monica-beverly-hillz/

Strings, Sabrina, and Long T. Bui. 2014. "'She Is Not Acting, She Is': The Conflict between Gender and Racial Realness on *RuPaul's Drag Race.*" *Feminist Media Studies* 14, no. 5: 822–36.

Strongman, Roberto. 2007. "The Latin American Queer Aesthetics of *El Bolereo.*" *Canadian Journal of Latin American and Caribbean Studies* 32, no. 64: 39–78.

Stryker, Susan. 1994. "My Words to Victor Frankenstein above the Village of Chamounix: Performing Transgender Rage." *GLQ* 1, no. 3: 237–54.

Stryker, Susan. 2006. "(De)Subjugated Knowledges: An Introduction to Transgender Studies." In Stryker and Whittle, 1–17.

Stryker, Susan. 2008. *Transgender History.* Berkeley, CA: Seal Press.

Stryker, Susan, and Aren Z. Aizura, eds. 2013. *The Transgender Studies Reader 2.* New York: Routledge.

Stryker, Susan, and Talia M. Bettcher. 2016. "Introduction: Trans/Feminisms." *TSQ* 3, nos. 1–2 (May): 5–14.

Stryker, Susan, and Paisley Currah. 2016. "General Editor's Introduction." *TSQ* 3, nos. 3–4 (November): 331–32.

Stryker, Susan, and Jim Van Buskirk. 1996. *Gay by the Bay: A History of Queer Culture in the San Francisco Bay Area*. San Francisco: Chronicle Books.

Stryker, Susan, and Stephen Whittle, eds. 2006. *The Transgender Studies Reader*. New York: Routledge.

Suárez, Juan A. 2008. "The Puerto Rican Lower East Side and the Queer Underground." *Grey Room* 32 (Summer): 6–37.

Suárez, Juan A. 2014. "Jack Smith, Hélio Oiticica, Tropicalism." *Criticism* 56, no. 2: 295–328.

Suggs, Donald. 1999. "Queen of Hearts." *POZ* 48 (June): 81. http://www.poz.com/articl es/215_10189.shtml

Süskind, Patrick. (1985) 1986. *Perfume: The Story of a Murderer*. Translated by John E. Woods. New York: Alfred A. Knopf.

Sutherland, Juan Pablo. 2009. *Nación marica: Prácticas culturales y crítica activista*. Santiago: Ripio Ediciones.

Sycamore, Mattilda Bernstein, ed. 2004. *That's Revolting! Queer Strategies for Resisting Assimilation*. Brooklyn: Soft Skull Press.

Sycamore, Mattilda Bernstein, ed. 2012. *Why Are Faggots So Afraid of Faggots? Flaming Challenges to Masculinity, Objectification, and the Desire to Conform*. Oakland, CA: AK Press.

Sycamore, Mattilda Bernstein. 2013. *The End of San Francisco*. San Francisco: City Lights Books.

Talbot, Joe, dir. 2019. *The Last Black Man in San Francisco*. Santa Monica, CA: Lionsgate. Blu-ray.

Tang, Jeannine. 2017. "Contemporary Art and Critical Transgender Infrastructures." In Gossett, Stanley, and Burton, 363–92.

Taylor, Diana. 2003. *The Archive and the Repertoire: Performing Cultural Memory in the Americas*. Durham, NC: Duke University Press.

Taylor, Diana, and Roselyn Costantino, eds. 2003. *Holy Terrors: Latin American Women Perform*. Durham, NC: Duke University Press.

Teo, Stephen. 2001. "Wong Kar-wai's *In the Mood for Love*: Like a Ritual in Transfigured Time." *Senses of Cinema*. http://sensesofcinema.com/2001/wong-kar-wai/mood/

That's Entertainment. 2018. "Lady Catiria / Paris Frantz / Continental 1996." YouTube, March 2. https://youtu.be/oDI8IABz1pI

Thomas, Piri. 1967. *Down These Mean Streets*. New York: Knopf.

Tikkanen, Amy. 2019. "Griselda Blanco." *Encyclopaedia Britannica*. https://www.britann ica.com/biography/Griselda-Blanco

Tirado, Frances. 2015. "Dreuxilla Divine: 'Alex fue una institución.'" *Primera Hora*, April 11. https://www.primerahora.com/entretenimiento/farandula/notas/dreuxilla-divi ne-alex-fue-una-institucion/

Toro, Ana Teresa. 2011. "La muñeca soy yo." Photos by Ramón "Tonito" Zayas. *El Nuevo Día*, July 3: 10–13.

Toro, Ana Teresa. 2014. "Una muestra para repasar y repensar." *El Nuevo Día*, June 19: 68–69.

Toro-Alfonso, José. 1999. "Domestic Violence among Same Sex Partners in Puerto Rico." *Journal of Gay and Lesbian Social Services* 9, no. 1: 69–78.

Toro-Alfonso, José. 2007. *Por vía de la exclusión: Homofobia y ciudadanía en Puerto Rico*. San Juan: Estado Libre Asociado de Puerto Rico, Comisión de Derechos Civiles.

Toro-Alfonso, José, ed. 2009. *Lo masculino en evidencia: Investigaciones sobre la masculinidad*. Hato Rey, PR: Publicaciones Puertorriqueñas.

Toro-Alfonso, José, and Sheilla Rodríguez-Madera. 2004. "Domestic Violence in Puerto Rican Gay Male Couples: Perceived Prevalence, Intergenerational Violence, Addictive Behaviors, and Conflict Resolution Skills." *Journal of Interpersonal Violence* 19, no. 6 (June): 639–54.

Torrecilla, Arturo. 2004. *La ansiedad de ser puertorriqueño: Etnoespectáculo e hiperviolencia en la modernidad líquida.* San Juan: Ediciones Vértigo.

Torres, Arlene. 1998. "La Gran Familia Puertorriqueña 'Ej Prieta de Beldá' (The Great Puerto Rican Family Is Really Black)." In *Blackness in Latin America and the Caribbean,* vol. 2, edited by Arlene Torres and Norman E. Withen Jr., 285–307. Bloomington: Indiana University Press.

Torres, Justin. 2016. "In Praise of Latin Night at the Queer Club." *Washington Post,* June 13. https://www.washingtonpost.com/opinions/in-praise-of-latin-night-at-the-queer-club/2016/06/13/e841867e-317b-11e6-95c0-2a6873031302_story.html

Tourmaline. 2017. "Tourmaline on Transgender Storytelling, David France, and the Netflix Marsha P. Johnson Documentary." *Teen Vogue,* October 11. https://www.teenvogue.com/story/reina-gossett-marsha-p-johnson-op-ed

Tourmaline, and Sasha Wortzel, dirs. 2018. *Happy Birthday, Marsha!* San Francisco: Frameline. DVD.

TransLatin@ Coalition, Bamby Salcedo, and Karla Padrón. 2013. *TransVisible: Transgender Latina Immigrants in U.S. Society.* TransLatin@ Coalition. https://www.translatinacoalition.org/

Trebay, Guy. 2013. "Memories from the Wild Side." *New York Times,* November 3: ST8.

Trebay, Guy. 2015. "Remembering Holly Woodlawn, a Transgender Star of the Warhol Era." *New York Times,* December 7. https://www.nytimes.com/2015/12/10/fashion/remembering-holly-woodlawn-a-transgender-star-of-the-warhol-era.html

Trevisan, João Silvério. 2000. *Devassos no paraíso.* Rio de Janeiro: Editora Record.

Ulysse, Gina Athena. 2014. "Call for Submissions: Caribbean Rasanblaj." *Repeating Islands,* January 22. https://repeatingislands.com/2014/01/22/call-for-submissions-caribbean-rasanblaj/

Ulysse, Gina Athena. 2015. "Introduction: Caribbean Rasanblaj." *emisférica* 12, no. 1. https://hemisphericinstitute.org/en/emisferica-121-caribbean-rasanblaj/121-introduction

Under the Hood. 2009. Season 1. Logo TV. http://www.logotv.com/

Ungerleider Kepler, David. 2000. *Las fiestas de Santiago Apóstol en Loíza: La cultura afro-puertorriqueña ante los procesos de hibridación y globalización.* San Juan: Isla Negra Editores.

Untorelli Press. 2013. *Street Transvestite Action Revolutionaries: Survival, Revolt, and Queer Antagonist Struggle.* n.p.: Untorelli Press. https://untorellipress.noblogs.org/files/2011/12/STAR.pdf

Urquhart, Evan. 2017. "What Would Trans Art Look Like If It Was Only Made by Trans People?" *Slate,* October 13. http://www.slate.com/blogs/outward/2017/10/13/marsha_p_johnson_netflix_doc_raises_questions_over_what_trans_led_storytelling.html

Vaid, Urvashi. 1995. *Virtual Equality: The Mainstreaming of Gay and Lesbian Liberation.* New York: Anchor Books.

Valdivia, Angharad N. 2010. *Latino/as in the Media.* Cambridge: Polity Press.

Valecce, Anastasia. 2018. "*El hijo de Ruby:* Memorias de un futuro queer." *CENTRO Journal* 30, no. 2 (Summer): 182–98.

Valencia, Sayak. 2014. "Interferencias transfeministas y pospornográficas a la colonialidad del ver." *emisférica* 11, no. 1. https://hemisphericinstitute.org/en/emisferica-11 -1-decolonial-gesture/11-1-essays/interferencias-transfeministas-y-pospornografic as-a-la-colonialidad-del-ver.html

Valencia, Sayak. 2018. *Gore Capitalism.* Translated by John Pluecker. South Pasadena, CA: Semiotext(e).

Valencia, Sayak. 2019. "Necropolitics, Postmortem/Transmortem Politics, and Transfeminisms in the Sexual Economies of Death." *TSQ* 6, no. 2 (May): 180–93.

Valentine, David. 2007. *Imagining Transgender: An Ethnography of a Category.* Durham, NC: Duke University Press.

Valentín-Escobar, Wilson. 2011. "Bodega Surrealism: The Emergence of Latina/o Artivists in New York City, 1976–Present." PhD diss., University of Michigan, Ann Arbor.

Valis, Noël. 2002. *The Culture of Cursilería: Bad Taste, Kitsch, and Class in Modern Spain.* Durham, NC: Duke University Press.

Vaquer Fernández, Kadiri J. 2019. "Atrévete te-te, salte del clóset: Provocaciones sexuales y políticas en la producción cultural puertorriqueña." PhD diss., Vanderbilt University.

Vaquero, María, and Amparo Morales. 2005. *Tesoro lexicográfico del español de Puerto Rico.* Academia Puertorriqueña de la Lengua Española. San Juan: Editorial Plaza Mayor.

Varderi, Alejandro. 1996. *Severo Sarduy y Pedro Almodóvar: Del barroco al kitsch en la narrativa y el cine postmodernos.* Madrid: Pliegos.

Vargas, Deborah R. 2008. "Borderland Bolerista: The Licentious Lyricism of Chelo Silva." *Feminist Studies* 34, nos. 1–2 (Spring–Summer): 173–97.

Vargas, Deborah R. 2012. *Dissonant Divas in Chicana Music: The Limits of La Onda.* Minneapolis: University of Minnesota Press.

Vargas, Deborah R. 2014. "Ruminations on Lo Sucio as a Latino Queer Analytic." *American Quarterly* 66, no. 3 (September): 715–26.

Vargas, Deborah R., Nancy Raquel Mirabal, and Lawrence La Fountain-Stokes, eds. 2017. *Keywords for Latina/o Studies.* New York: New York University Press.

Vargas Casiano, Patricia. 2018. "Revive El Cotorrito." *Primera Hora,* April 2. https://www .primerahora.com/entretenimiento/cultura-teatro/notas/revive-el-cotorrito/

Vásquez, Eva C. 2003. *Pregones Theatre: A Theatre for Social Change in the South Bronx.* New York: Routledge.

Vázquez González, Elaine Enid. 2016. "Procesos de modernización, intimidad y lenguaje figurado en los boleros de Rafael Hernández y Sylvia Rexach." PhD diss., University of Puerto Rico, Río Piedras.

Vega, Bernardo. 1984. *Memoirs of Bernardo Vega: A Contribution to the History of the Puerto Rican Community in New York.* Edited by César Andréu Iglesias. Translated by Juan Flores. New York: Monthly Review Press.

Vega, Tanzina. 2012. "Commenting on a Death Gets a Puppet in Trouble." *New York Times,* December 16. https://www.nytimes.com/2012/12/17/business/media/la-com ay-of-superxclusivo-stirs-anger-over-comments-on-mans-death.html

Vélez, Pedro. 2002. "Puerto Rican Sun." *Artnet Magazine,* November 25. http://www.artnet.com/Magazine/reviews/velez/velez11-25-02.asp

Vélez, Pedro. 2006. "The New Scenesters." *Artnet Magazine,* February 8. http://www.artnet.com/magazineus/features/velez/velez2-8-06.asp

Vélez, Rubén. 2019a. "Meet the Local Queens: Ana Macho." *Her Campus at UPRM*, February 28. https://www.hercampus.com/school/uprm/meet-local-queens-ana -macho

Vélez, Rubén. 2019b. "Meet the Local Queens: Misandra Bolac." Her Campus at UPRM, March 7. https://www.hercampus.com/school/uprm/meet-local-queens-misandra -bolac

Venegas, Haydee. 1998. "Arte puertorriqueño de cara al milenio: Identidad, alteridad, y travestismo." In Borràs and Zaya, 271–81. Translated as "Puerto Rican Art at the Millennium: From the Search for an Identity to Transvestism," 337–43.

Vera Rojas, María Teresa. 2015. "Perturbaciones subversivas o sobre los márgenes de la 'buena vida' en *Mundo Cruel* de Luis Negrón." *Mitologías Hoy* 12 (Winter): 193–203.

Verguilla Torres, Lynnette. 1999. "La no sexualidad de Freddie Mercado." Photos by Fernando Paes and Jova Camacho. *Reacción*, March: 6.

Vidal, Teodoro. 1982. *Las caretas de cartón del Carnaval de Ponce.* San Juan: Ediciones Alba.

Vidal, Teodoro. 2003. *El vejigante ponceño.* San Juan: Ediciones Alba.

Vidal-Ortiz, Salvador. 2004. "On Being a White Person of Color: Using Autoethnography to Understand Puerto Ricans' Racialization." *Qualitative Sociology* 27, no. 2: 179–203.

Vidal-Ortiz, Salvador. 2011. "'Maricón,' 'Pájaro,' and 'Loca': Cuban and Puerto Rican Linguistic Practices, and Sexual Minority Participation, in U.S. Santería." *Journal of Homosexuality* 58, nos. 6–7: 901–18.

Vidal-Ortiz, Salvador, Carlos Decena, Héctor Carrillo, and Tomás Almaguer. 2010. "Revisiting *Activos* and *Pasivos:* Toward New Cartographies of Latino/Latin American Male Same-Sex Desire." In *Latino Sexualities: Probing Powers, Passions, Practices and Policies*, edited by Marysol Asencio, 253–73. New Brunswick, NJ: Rutgers University Press.

Vidal-Ortiz, Salvador, María Amelia Viteri, and José Fernando Serrano Amaya. 2014. "Resignificaciones, prácticas y políticas queer en América Latina: Otra agenda de cambio social." *Nómadas* 41: 185–201.

Vidarte, Paco. (2007) 2010. *Ética marica: Proclamas libertarias para una militancia LGBTQ.* 2nd ed. Barcelona: Editorial Egales.

Viego, Antonio. 2011. "The Place of Gay Male Chicano Literature in Queer Chicana/o Cultural Work." In Hames-García and Martínez, 86–104.

Viera, Mariana. 2018. "Bad Bunny's Embrace of Femininity Comes with a Caveat." *Vice*, October 4. https://www.vice.com/en_au/article/vbky9x/bad-bunnys-embrace-of-fe mininity-comes-with-a-caveat

Viguié, John E., prod. (2003) 2009. *Boricuas: Freddy M., Santurce.* Video. In DVD accompanying *Representación y fronteras: El performance en los límites del género*, edited by Stephany Slaughter and Hortensia Moreno. Mexico City: Programa Universitario de Estudios de Género, Universidad Autónoma Nacional de México.

Villa, Lucas. 2019. "How Bad Bunny Bridges LGBTQ and Latinx Identities with His Inclusive 'Caro' Video." *MTV*, February 6. http://www.mtv.com/news/3111819/bad -bunny-caro-video-lgbtq-inclusive/

Villanúa, Lolita, and Robert Villanúa. 2007. *Andanza: Imágenes y trayectoria.* San Juan: Andanza.

Villanueva Collado, Alfredo. 2000. "The Day We Went to See the Snow." In *Noche*

Buena: Hispanic American Christmas Stories, edited by Nicolás Kanellos, 182–86. Oxford: Oxford University Press.

Villegas, Richard. 2019. "11 Queer and Trans Artists Making Reggaeton and Dembow More Inclusive." *Remezcla*, January 23. https://remezcla.com/lists/music/queer-tra ns-reggaeton-dembow-artists/

Viñales, Andrew. 2018. "Varones in the Archive: A Queer Oral History Analysis with Two Black Puerto Rican Gay Men." *CENTRO Journal* 30, no. 2 (Summer): 162–81.

Viruet Álvarez, Cherilyn, dir. 2011. *La realidad detrás del maquillaje*. Arecibo, PR: Universidad de Puerto Rico, Arecibo. https://vimeo.com/29914704

Viteri, María Amelia. 2014. *Desbordes: Translating Racial, Ethnic, Sexual, and Gender Identities across the Americas*. Albany: State University of New York Press.

Viteri, María Amelia. 2017. "*Intensiones*: Tensions in Queer Agency and Activism in Latino América." *Feminist Studies* 43, no. 2: 405–17.

Vizcarrondo, Fortunato. (1942) 1976. *Dinga y mandinga*. San Juan: Instituto de Cultura Puertorriqueña.

Voynovskaya, Nastia. 2019. "DragTivism Teaches LGBTQ+ History and Empowerment with Rhinestones and False Lashes." *KQED*, June 12. https://www.kqed.org/arts/138 59216/dragtivism-teaches-lgbtq-history-and-empowerment-with-rhinestones-and -false-lashes

Walcott, Rinaldo. 2013. "Boyfriends with Clits and Girlfriends with Dicks: Hip Hop's Queer Future." *Palimpsest* 2, no. 2: 168–73.

Walker, John. 2016. "Eve Lindley Tells Us What It's Like to Play Her Trans Revolutionary Icon Onscreen." *Splinter*, November 7. https://splinternews.com/eve-lindley-tells-us -what-its-like-to-play-her-trans-re-1793863527

Walsh, John K. 1995. "A Logic in Lorca's *Ode to Walt Whitman*." In Bergmann and Smith, 257–78.

Wanzer-Serrano, Darrel. 2015. *The New York Young Lords and the Struggle for Liberation*. Philadelphia: Temple University Press.

Warhol, Andy, and Ronald Tavel, dirs. 1965. *Screen Test #2*. Film.

Wayar, Marlene. 2019. *Travesti: Una teoría lo suficientemente buena*. Buenos Aires: Editorial Muchas Nueces.

Weems, Carrie Mae. 2012. *Carrie Mae Weems: Three Decades of Photography and Video*. Edited by Kathryn E. Delmez. Nashville: Frist Center for the Visual Arts.

Weinstein, Joel. 2007. "Re: The Hash." *Rotund World* 43. http://rworld.thenextfewhours .com/43rd_Edition/index.html

Weiss, Suzannah. 2017. "'The Death and Life of Marsha P. Johnson' Creator Accused of Stealing Work from Filmmaker Tourmaline." *Teen Vogue*, October 8. https://www .teenvogue.com/story/marsha-p-johnson-documentary-david-france-reina-gossett -stealing-accusations

"The Welfare Queen." 2011. *NYDailyNews.com*, September 14. https://www.nydailynews .com/latino/latino-happenings-nueva-york-sept-14-20-article-1.952718

Wesling, Meg. 2002. "Is the 'Trans' in Transsexual the 'Trans' in Transnational?" Paper presented at the American Comparative Literature Association Conference, San Juan, Puerto Rico, April.

Wesling, Meg. 2008. "Why Queer Diaspora?" *Feminist Review* 90: 30–47.

Wesling, Meg. 2012. "Queer Value." *GLQ* 18, no. 1: 107–25.

West, Candace. n.d. "About Lionel Cantú Jr." *Cantú Queer Center*, University of California, Santa Cruz. https://queer.ucsc.edu/about-us/centers-namesake.html

Westworld. 2013. "Drag Nation: Best Ongoing Drag Event." Best of Denver, Arts and Entertainment, 2013. http://www.westword.com/best-of/2013/arts-and-entertainment/best-ongoing-drag-event-5159178

White, Richard. 2017. "Walter Benjamin: 'The Storyteller' and the Possibility of Wisdom." *Journal of Aesthetic Education* 51, no. 1 (Spring): 1–14.

Whitesel, Jason. 2014. *Fat Gay Men: Girth, Mirth, and the Politics of Stigma*. New York: New York University Press.

Wicker, Randy. 1973. "Gays Pour through New York." *The Advocate*, July 18: 3–5.

Wilchins, Riki. 2002. "A Woman for Her Time: In Memory of Stonewall Warrior Sylvia Rivera." *Village Voice*, February 27.

Willard, Avery. 1971. *Female Impersonation*. New York: Regiment.

Willetts, Kheli R. 2013. "Cannibals and Coons: Blackness in the Early Days of Walt Disney." In *Diversity in Disney Films: Critical Essays on Race, Ethnicity, Gender, Sexuality and Disability*, edited by Johnson Cheu, 9–22. Jefferson, NC: McFarland.

Willis, Deborah. 2012. "Photographing between the Lines: Beauty, Politics, and the Poetic Vision of Carrie Mae Weems." In *Carrie Mae Weems: Three Decades of Photography and Video*, edited by Kathryn E. Delmez, 33–41. Nashville: Frist Center for the Visual Arts.

Wojcik, Daniel. 2016. *Outsider Art: Visionary Worlds and Trauma*. Jackson: University Press of Mississippi.

Wolf, Stacy. 2008. "'Defying Gravity': Queer Conventions in the Musical 'Wicked.'" *Theatre Journal* 60, no. 1 (March): 1–21.

Woo, Jaime. 2017. "RuPaul Is Everything." *Jaime Woo* (blog), April 20. https://jaimewoo.com/blogs/news/rupaul-is-everything

Woodlawn, Holly, and Jeffrey Copeland. (1991) 1992. *A Low Life in High Heels: The Holly Woodlawn Story*. New York: Perennial.

WOWPresents. 2013. "Nina Flowers—RuPaul's Drag Race Casting Audition Tape." YouTube, November 19. https://youtu.be/znS58vr0dF4

Wynter, Sylvia. 1992. "Beyond Miranda's Meanings: Un/silencing the 'Demonic Ground' of Caliban's 'Woman.'" In *Out of the Kumbla: Caribbean Women and Literature*, edited by Carole Boyce Davies and Elaine Savory Fido, 355–72. Trenton, NJ: Africa World Press.

Yacowar, Maurice. 1993. *The Films of Paul Morrissey*. Cambridge: Cambridge University Press.

Yarbro-Bejarano, Yvonne. 1997. "Crossing the Border with Chabela Vargas: A Chicana Femme's Tribute." In Balderston and Guy, 33–43.

Yarbro-Bejarano, Yvonne. 1998. "Laying It Bare: The Queer/Colored Body in Photography by Laura Aguilar." In *Living Chicana Theory*, edited by Carla Trujillo, 277–305. Berkeley, CA: Third Woman Press.

Yeager, Steve, dir. 1998. *Divine Trash*. Petite Trasho Pictures. DVD.

Young, Tatiana Kalaniopua. 2011. "Transsituated Publics: From Christine Jorgensen to Holly Woodlawn." MA thesis, University of Texas, Austin.

Zaragoza, Edward C. 1990. "The Santiago Apóstol of Loíza, Puerto Rico." *Caribbean Studies* 23, nos. 1–2: 125–39.

Zaragoza, Edward C. 1995. *St. James in the Streets: The Religious Processions of Loíza Aldea, Puerto Rico.* Lanham, MD: Scarecrow Press.

Zavala, Iris M. 2000. *El bolero: Historia de un amor.* Madrid: Celeste.

Zavella, Patricia. 2017. "Poverty." In Vargas, Mirabal, and La Fountain-Stokes, 171–75.

Zaya, Antonio, and Michelle Marxuach. 2000. *Puerto Rico '00 [Paréntesis en la "ciudad"].* San Juan: M & M Proyectos.

Zayas, Ramón Tonito. 2011. "Las caras de Freddie Mercado." *El Nuevo Día,* July 3: n.p.

Zenón Cruz, Isabelo. 1974–75. *Narciso descubre su trasero: El negro en la cultura puertorriqueña.* 2 vols. Humacao, PR: Furidi.

Zentella, Ana Celia. 1997. *Growing Up Bilingual: Puerto Rican Children in New York.* Malden, MA: Blackwell.

Zentella, Ana Celia. 2014. "TWB (Talking while Bilingual): Linguistic Profiling of Latina/os, and Other Linguistic Torquemadas." *Latino Studies* 12, no. 4: 620–35. doi:10.1057/lst.2014.63

Zhou, Xun, and Francesca Tarocco. 2007. *Karaoke: The Global Phenomenon.* London: Reaktion.

Zipes, Jack. 2015. "Introduction: Rediscovering the Original Tales of the Brothers Grimm." In *Grimm and Grimm,* xix–xliii.

Zraick, Karen. 2019. "Kevin Fret, Openly Gay Latin Trap Artist, Is Shot and Killed in Puerto Rico." *New York Times,* January 10. https://www.nytimes.com/2019/01/10/us/kevin-fret-dead-puerto-rico.html

Zucchino, David. 1997. *Myth of the Welfare Queen: A Pulitzer Prize–Winning Journalist's Portrait of Women on the Line.* New York: Scribner.

Index

NOTE: Page numbers in *italics* indicate a figure.